ROME AND THE INVENTION OF THE PAPACY

The remarkable, and permanently influential, papal history known as the *Liber pontificalis* shaped perceptions and the memory of Rome, the popes, and the many-layered past of both city and papacy within western Europe. Rosamond McKitterick offers a new analysis of this extraordinary combination of historical reconstruction, deliberate selection, and political use of fiction, to illuminate the history of the early popes and their relationship with Rome. She examines the content, context, and transmission of the text, and the complex relationships between the reality, representation, and reception of authority that it reflects. The *Liber pontificalis* presented Rome as a holy city of Christian saints and martyrs, as the bishops of Rome established their visible power in buildings, and it articulated the popes' spiritual and ministerial role, accommodated within their Roman imperial inheritance. Drawing on wide-ranging and interdisciplinary international research, *Rome and the Invention of the Papacy* offers pioneering insights into the evolution of this extraordinary source, and its significance for the history of early medieval Europe.

Rosamond McKitterick is Professor Emerita of Medieval History at the University of Cambridge, a Fellow of Sidney Sussex College, and Chair of the Faculty of Archaeology, History and Letters of the British School at Rome. She was awarded the Dr A.H. Heineken International Prize in History in 2010. Her previous publications include *History and Memory in the Carolingian World* (2004), *Perceptions of the Past in the Early Middle Ages* (2006), *Charlemagne: The Formation of a European Identity* (2008), and two co-edited volumes on medieval Rome, *Rome Across Time and Space: Cultural Transmission and the Exchange of Ideas* (2011), and *Old Saint Peter's, Rome* (2013).

THE JAMES LYDON LECTURES IN MEDIEVAL HISTORY AND CULTURE

In the millennium between the fall of Rome and the Reformation – commonly known as the 'middle ages' – Europe emerged as something more than an idea, and many of the institutions, cultural forces and political ideas we associate with the 'modern' world were born. What is the continuing relevance of this era for contemporary society? And how are we to understand medieval history and culture on its own terms, rather than through the distorting prism of presentist concerns? These are among the most urgent and problematic questions facing medieval scholarship today.

The James Lydon Lectures in Medieval History and Culture, delivered at Trinity College Dublin and named for James Francis Lydon FTCD, Lecky Professor of History at Trinity College Dublin (1928 – 2013), is a biennial series providing a unique platform to reflect on these issues.

Series Editors:
Peter Crooks, David Ditchburn, Seán Duffy, Ruth Mazo Karras, Immo Warntjes

A full list of titles in the series can be found at:
www.cambridge.org/lydonlectures

ROME AND THE INVENTION OF THE PAPACY

The *Liber pontificalis*

Rosamond McKitterick

University of Cambridge

CAMBRIDGE
UNIVERSITY PRESS

Shaftesbury Road, Cambridge CB2 8EA, United Kingdom

One Liberty Plaza, 20th Floor, New York, NY 10006, USA

477 Williamstown Road, Port Melbourne, VIC 3207, Australia

314–321, 3rd Floor, Plot 3, Splendor Forum, Jasola District Centre, New Delhi – 110025, India

103 Penang Road, #05–06/07, Visioncrest Commercial, Singapore 238467

Cambridge University Press is part of Cambridge University Press & Assessment, a department of the University of Cambridge.

We share the University's mission to contribute to society through the pursuit of education, learning and research at the highest international levels of excellence.

www.cambridge.org
Information on this title: www.cambridge.org/9781108819237

DOI: 10.1017/9781108872584

First published 2020
First paperback edition 2022

A catalogue record for this publication is available from the British Library

ISBN   978-1-108-83682-1   Hardback
ISBN   978-1-108-81923-7   Paperback

*To my students in Part II of the Historical Tripos, Special Subject 'B',
University of Cambridge, 2011–15*

Contents

CONTENTS

CONTENTS

Maps

Preface

This book is a study of Rome and the popes in late antiquity and the early middle ages through the prism of the narrative known as the *Liber pontificalis*. A chronologically ordered serial biography of the bishops of Rome from St Peter to Pope Stephen V (†891), the *Liber pontificalis* was composed within the papal administration in Rome in the early sixth century, with continuations added in the seventh, eighth, and ninth centuries. It was the act of writing the *Liber pontificalis* that was the invention of the papacy, with a construction of the papal and apostolic past in early Christian Rome that was of seminal importance in the history of Latin Christendom. The *Liber pontificalis* articulates papal ideology and the Petrine succession. This book, therefore, is about the power of a text that shaped perceptions and the memory of Rome, the popes, and the many-layered past of both city and papacy within western Europe in the early middle ages. I offer a new analysis of the content, context, and transmission of this text, its remarkable combination of historical reconstruction, deliberate selection and political use of fiction, and of the complex relationship between the reality, representation, and reception of authority. I examine the text's construction of the Christian past of Rome as a holy city of Christian saints and martyrs, its representation of the way the bishops of Rome established their visible power within the city with the construction and embellishment of many churches and holy places, endeavoured in many respects to emulate the Roman emperors as rulers of the city, and defined their spiritual and ministerial role.

The book is based on the James C. Lydon Lectures in Medieval History and Culture delivered in Trinity College, Dublin in October

2018. It is a pleasure to record my thanks to TCD for the invitation and generous hospitality during a memorable week in Dublin, and especially to Seán Duffy and Immo Warntjes of TCD, and my audiences there, not least my invited 'respondents' Claudia Bolgia, Marios Costambeys, and Mayke de Jong, and all the members of the postgraduate seminar, for their comments, suggestions, and questions. The Dublin lectures, as the culmination of the past decade's work on this book, also emerged from the final-year undergraduate Special Subject 'B' on 'Rome and its Rulers, 476–769' that I taught in Cambridge to a succession of cohorts of wonderfully engaged, critically alert, and enthusiastic students. They accompanied me on unforgettable field trips to Rome and my gratitude to them is expressed in the dedication of this book. I should also like to thank Mike Styles and Keith Sykes for making these field trips possible, the former and current Directors of the British School at Rome, Christopher Smith and Stephen Milner, as well as the other members of staff, especially Stefania Peterlini for arranging special visits to sites, and Valerie Scott and Christine Martin for all their help. In the years working on Rome, the early popes, and the *Liber pontificalis*, I have benefitted from the collegiality and hospitality of a number of other institutions in addition to the BSR. My thanks therefore are due first of all to the American Academy in Rome, where I was the Lester K. Little Visiting Fellow in 2011, and to the successive Directors of the AAR, Carmela Vircillo Franklin, Christopher Celenza and Kimberly Bowes; to Rolf Große and the German Historical Institute in Paris, where I was a visiting scholar in 2016, as well as the Institut de recherche et d'histoire des textes in Paris, François Bougard, Michel Sot, Geneviève Bührer-Thierry and Regine Le Jan; and to Marco Stoffella and the University of Verona, where I was guest professor in 2019.

My understanding of the early medieval architecture, frescoes, and sculpture of Ravenna and Rome, and my examination across much of Western Europe of the extant early medieval manuscripts of the *Liber pontificalis*, were greatly facilitated by the award of a Leverhulme Emeritus Fellowship for 2018–19 and I should like to thank the Leverhulme Trust most warmly for this generous award and their support.

I should also like to thank the staff of the following libraries for their welcome, and for enabling me to examine the manuscripts of the *Liber pontificalis* and of related texts in their collections: Berlin, Staatsbibliothek; Bern, Burgerbibliothek; Brussels, Bibliothèque royale; Cambridge, University Library; Cologne, Dombibliothek; The Hague, Museum Meermanno-Westreenianum; Florence, Biblioteca Laurenziana; Laon, Bibliothèque municipale Suzanne Martinet; Leiden, Universiteitsbibliotheek; Lucca, Biblioteca Capitolare Feliniana; Milan, Biblioteca Ambrosiana; Modena, Biblioteca Capitolare; Munich, Bayerische Staatsbibliothek; Naples, Biblioteca Nazionale; Paris, Bibliothèque nationale de France; Rome, Biblioteca Apostolica Vaticana; Stuttgart, Württembergische Landesbibliothek; Verona, Biblioteca Capitolare; Vienna, Österreichische Nationalbibliothek; Wolfenbüttel, Herzog August Bibliothek.

The Dublin lectures were accompanied by many images. Because websites are notoriously volatile and URLs no less so, readers are invited to go to the relevant official websites of the places mentioned in the text, and especially of the libraries (whose full names will be found in the Index of Manuscripts) to find colour pictures of the buildings, frescoes, inscriptions, mosaics, and codices discussed. In quoting from the *Liber pontificalis,* I have used the Latin edition by Louis Duchesne and the excellent English translation made by Raymond Davis, to which only very minor alterations have been made where appropriate.

I am especially grateful to the two anonymous assessors for Cambridge University Press for extremely constructive and helpful criticism, and to my many friends and colleagues who have assisted me, sometimes inadvertently, in the course of writing this book by listening, answering questions, sending me copies of articles, and generally cheering me on, namely, Massimiliano Bassetti, Ralf Behrwald, Christine Carpenter, Donncdha Carroll, Carlo Cedro, Robert Coates-Stephens, Charlotte Denoël, Anna Dorofeeva, Robert Evans, Roy Flechner, Elizabeth Fowden, Federico Gallo, Clemens Gantner, Patrick Geary, the late Herman Geertman, András Handl, Olivier Hekster, Yitzhak Hen, Klaus Herbers, Matthew Hoskins, Caroline Humfress, Ketty Iannantuono, Carola Jäggi, Dennis Jussen, Ira Katznelson, Ann Kelders, Bea Leal, Carlos Machado, Lucy McKitterick, John Mitchell, John Morrill, Rory Naismith, Tom Noble, John Osborne, Sam Ottewill-Soulsby, Renato Pasta, Charles Pierce, Walter Pohl, Richard Pollard, Alastair Reid, Helmut Reimitz,

Magnus Ryan, Christian Sahner, Michele Salzman, Matthias Simperl, Rick Sowerby, Jonathan Steinberg, Marco Stoffella, Jo Story, Michel Summer, Gaia Elizabeta Unfer-Verre, the late Steven Uran, Andrea Verardi, Andrew Wallace-Hadrill, Immo Warntjes, Chris Wickham, Rowan Williams, and Philipp Winterhager. My special thanks to Mayke de Jong, who has been a wonderful and constant (sometimes daily) sounding board throughout the years over which I have been working on this book and has also read draft versions of chapters and offered excellent advice as well as much appreciated encouragement. Extra thanks are due to the members of various seminar groups and participants in workshops where I presented aspects of this book, especially in Amsterdam, Cambridge (CLANS, GEMS, and the Confraternitas Historica in Sidney Sussex College), Frankfurt, Helsinki, Princeton, Rome, and Utrecht for lively discussion. I remain very grateful for the congenial working environment I enjoy among all my colleagues in Sidney Sussex College, Cambridge.

I should also like to thank Erik Goosman of Mappa Mundi Cartography for drawing the map of the manuscript transmission of the *Liber pontificalis* and Lacey Wallace for permission to use her map of Rome, first published in *Old Saint Peter's Rome* (Cambridge, 2013), and Genevra Kornbluth for her permission to use her photograph of the Lateran Baptistery chapel of San Venanzio mosaic of Pope John IV on this book's jacket. It has been a great pleasure to work with Cambridge University Press, and I am particularly indebted to Liz Friend-Smith, the Senior Commissioning Editor, and to the production team at the Press, especially Jane Burkowski, Amy Lee, and Natasha Whelan, for all their hard work in seeing this book though the press.

I cannot imagine how I could have completed this book without my husband David's never-failing critical interest and encouragement; my final and most heartfelt thanks, as always, are for him.

Abbreviations

BEFAR	Bibliothèque des Écoles françaises d'Athènes et de Rome
Bischoff, *Katalog*	B. Bischoff, *Katalog der festlandischen Handschriften des neunten Jahrhunderts (mit Ausnahme der wisigotischen)*, 3 vols I: *Aachen–Lambach;* II: *Laon–Paderborn;* III: *Padua–Zwickau* (Wiesbaden, 1998–2014)
BAV	Biblioteca Apostolica Vaticana
BAV pal. lat.	Biblioteca Apostolica Vaticana, palatinus latinus
BAV reg. lat.	Biblioteca Apostolica Vaticana, codices reginenses latini
BAV Vat. lat.	Biblioteca Apostolica Vaticana, Vaticanus latinus
BM	Bibliothèque municipale
BnF lat.	Bibliothèque nationale de France manuscrit latin
BnF n.a.lat.	Bibliothèque nationale de France nouvelles acquisitions latines
CC	*Codex epistolaris Carolinus,* in the numbering sequence of the manuscript ÖNB 449, ed. W. Gundlach (with different numbering), *Codex epistolaris Carolinus,* MGH Epp 3, Epistolae merovingici et karolini aevi 1 (Berlin, 1892), pp. 269–653
CCCM	Corpus Christianorum, Continuatio Medievalis
CCSL	Corpus Christianorum, Series Latina
CLA	E. A. Lowe, *Codices Latini antiquiores,* 11 vols + Supplement (Oxford, 1935–71)

Clm	Munich, Bayerische Staatsbibliothek, Codices latini monacenses
Corpus	R. Krautheimer, S. Corbett, and V. Frankl, *Corpus basilicarum christianarum Romae: le basiliche cristiane antiche di Roma (sec. IV–IX) = The early Christian basilicas of Rome (IV–IX cent.)*, 5 vols (Vatican City, 1937–77)
CSEL	Corpus scriptorum ecclesiasticorum latinorum
csg	St Gallen Stiftsbibliothek, codices sangallenses
Davis, *Pontiffs*	R. Davis, *The Book of Pontiffs (Liber pontificalis): the Ancient Biographies of the First Ninety Roman Bishops to AD 715*, 3rd ed. (Liverpool, 2010)
Davis, *Eighth-Century Popes*	R. Davis, *The Lives of the Eighth-Century Popes (Liber pontificalis)*, 2nd ed. (Liverpool, 2007)
Davis, *Ninth-Century Popes*	R. Davis, *The Lives of the Ninth-Century Popes (Liber pontificalis): the Ancient Biographies of Ten Popes from AD 817–891* (Liverpool, 1995)
EME	*Early Medieval Europe*
JTS	*Journal of Theological Studies*
LP I, II	*Liber pontificalis,* ed. L. Duchesne, *Le* Liber pontificalis: *texte, introduction et commentaire*, 2 vols (Paris, 1886–92, repr. 1955)
MEFRA	*Mélanges de l'École française de Rome – Antiquité*
MEFRM	*Mélanges de l'École française de Rome – Moyen Âge*
MGH	Monumenta germaniae historica
AA	Auctores Antiquissimi
Conc.	Concilia
Epp	Epistolae
SRG	Scriptores rerum germanicarum in usum scholarum separatim editi
SRL	Scriptores rerum langobardicarum et italicarum
SRM	Scriptores rerum merovingicarum
SS	Scriptores in folio

LIST OF ABBREVIATIONS

Mommsen, *LP*   *Liber pontificalis,* ed. T. Mommsen, *Liber pontificalis*
                 (pars prior), MGH Gesta Pontificum Romanorum 1.1
                 (Berlin, 1898)
MS   manuscript, manuscrit, manoscritto
ÖNB   Österreichische Nationalbibliothek
PBSR   *Papers of the British School at Rome*
PL   *Patrologiae Cursus Completus, Series Latina,* ed.
                 J.-P. Migne
Settimane   *Settimane di studio del Centro Italiano di studi sull'alto*
                 medioevo
VLQ   Leiden, Universiteitsbibliotheek, Vossiani latini
                 quarto

The *Liber pontificalis*

Text and Context

Introduction

THE TITLE OF THIS BOOK, *ROME AND THE INVENTION OF THE PAPACY*, uses the word 'invention' in the original Latin sense of *inventio* (discovery), as well as the more recent one of an original creation with a function. I intend it to be a more evocative, or even provocative, word than 'formation' or 'development'. Indeed, I shall not be offering a straightforward history of the early medieval papacy in this book. Instead, my theme is the power of a text, with an extended case study of a particular text that charts the history of the early medieval papacy, namely, the *Liber pontificalis* or 'book of the pontiffs'.

The *Liber pontificalis* is the set of biographies of the popes starting with St Peter, first written by members of the papal administration in Rome in the sixth century and subsequently extended at various stages until the pontificate of Pope Stephen V at the end of the ninth century.[1] Quite apart from the importance of this text's evidence concerning the history of early medieval Rome, the *Liber pontificalis* is also a remarkable example of the self-representation of a particular institution in the form of an historical narrative. My concern in this book, therefore, is the way the *Liber pontificalis* constructed the popes and disseminated a particular representation of their history, their role, and of the city of Rome itself, within western Europe in the early middle ages. The *Liber pontificalis*, after all, is the only extant early medieval narrative history actually

---

[1] The definitive modern edition of the *Liber pontificalis* is L. Duchesne (ed.), *Le Liber pontificalis: texte, introduction et commentaire*, 2 vols (Paris, 1886–92, repr. 1955), hereafter *LP* I and II.

written in Rome. It is also the text in which most people in early medieval Spain, Gaul, North Africa, the British Isles, and even in Italy itself, would, or at least could, have read about Christian and contemporary Rome without ever having seen it. Set against the background of the wealth of sophisticated theological, pastoral, and exegetical treatises, letters, and sermons produced by the popes who form the subject of the *Liber pontificalis,* the text is remarkably selective in its representation of Rome and its bishops. For that reason, as well as the particular agenda of its contents, the text potentially had a key role to play within early medieval Europe in forming perceptions and shaping the memory of the city of Rome and of its bishops.[2]

The *Liber pontificalis,* in contrast to all the other texts emanating from Rome and the popes, is oddly laconic and formulaic and leaves out an extraordinary amount, known from other categories of evidence, relating to both general historical context and specific papal careers. The text's very oddities and omissions, however, need recognition, attention, and explication, not least because it was so widely disseminated within Italy as well as north of the Alps. I shall explore, therefore, the problematic relationship between reality, representation and reception, and the papacy itself as orchestrator of a new understanding of the Bishop of Rome both within and beyond the city.[3] Certainly, papal primacy, the apostolic succession, and doctrinal orthodoxy are major themes of this period. The churches, mosaics, frescoes, and inscriptions of Rome, as well as less conventional historical evidence in the form of liturgy and canon law, augment and complement the representation of the popes in the *Liber pontificalis;* all have generated specialist discussion. Consequently, I aim to offer a cross-disciplinary study of the sacred and the secular, and to invoke a range of different categories of historical evidence: textual, visual, and material. All this evidence needs to be set against the background of the ideological agenda developed in the *Liber pontificalis.*

---

[2] I offered preliminary comments about Frankish perceptions of Rome in McKitterick 2006.

[3] On the question of personal involvement of the popes see below, pp. 8–9 and 36.

Before I introduce the text and an outline of the historical context in which it was produced, it may be helpful to present a brief account of the principal themes that have emerged from the modern scholarship on late antique and early medieval Rome and the popes.

Rome and the *Liber pontificalis* in Modern Scholarship

The *Liber pontificalis* has been a constant resource for historians, art and architectural historians, and archaeologists since the nineteenth century, so I can only offer a brief and highly selective indication here of the wealth of scholarship that it has precipitated. My own understanding of the *Liber pontificalis* and its significance has benefitted enormously from the pioneering work of Giovanni Battista de Rossi, Louis Duchesne, and Theodor Mommsen in the nineteenth century.[4] More recently, studies focussed on specific aspects of the *Liber pontificalis* itself, such as those of Herman Geertman, Lidia Capo, Clemens Gantner, and Andrea Verardi, have helped to expose some of the problems of the text.[5] From the second half of the twentieth century, many excellent studies of the 'transformation of Rome in late antiquity' and the physical, topographical, and ideological impact of Christianity have appeared, in which Charles Pietri and his successors at the École française de Rome have been prominent.[6] A number of German scholars have greatly enhanced our understanding of the political and ecclesiological roles of the popes of the late eighth and the ninth century in particular, alongside many important contributions to the documentation of the institutional development of the papacy in the comprehensive scholarly biographies of the Italian *Enciclopedia dei papi*, and anglophone scholarship made since the 1970s, by Peter Llewellyn, Jeffrey Richards, and Tom Noble, among others.[7] Over the past two decades of this century in particular, John Curran's study of late antique Rome as *Pagan City and Christian Capital*

---

[4] Rossi 1864–77; Duchesne 1877 and *LP* I, pp. i–cclxii; Mommsen 1898.

[5] Geertman 1975, Geertman 2004, Geertman (ed.) 2003, Capo 2009, Gantner 2014, Verardi 2016.

[6] Pietri 1976, Blaudeau 2012b; Inglebert 1996.

[7] Borgolte 1995, Scholz 2006, Herbers 1996, Hartmann 2006, Hack 2006–7, Bray and Lanza (eds.) 2000, Richards 1976, Llewellyn 1974b (2nd ed. 1996), Noble 1984.

and William Harris's edited volume on the 'transformations' of late antique Rome were followed by the collaborative volumes on Rome and Constantinople edited by Lucy Grig and Gavin Kelly, on *Rome the Cosmopolis* led by Catherine Edwards and Greg Woolf, further volumes of collected papers on late antique Rome and its bishops, a set of incisive studies on the urban fabric by Robert Coates-Stephens, and Hendrik Dey on the Aurelian Walls.[8] All have presented new perspectives and new interpretations of both the material and documentary evidence. Nevertheless, the greater proportion of the scholarly literature on Rome as a city is concerned with the imperial city and late antiquity. Edwards and Woolf stress, for example, that

> Rome remained the cosmopolis because the power invested in it was still of use, because its claims to epitomize the empire were well worth defending to groups with the power to do so ... Rome the City was so deeply inscribed on the master texts of empire that it could never safely be erased; New Rome on the Hellespont indicates the power of empires, but the survival of Old Rome on the Tiber shows the limits of that power.[9]

Certainly art historians have charted the transformation of the city after that, in the wake of Richard Krautheimer's monumental *Corpus basilicarum Romae* and *Rome: Profile of a City,* though even Krautheimer was more concerned with the fourth, fifth, and twelfth centuries than with the period in between.[10] In the more recent work of such art historians and archaeologists as Herman Geertman, Sible de Blaauw, or Franz Alto Bauer, however, the transformations of the early middle ages have at last been given prominence.[11] Here the *Liber pontificalis* has been drawn on more critically as a source about particular buildings in Christian Rome, though the principal emphasis of all three scholars has been on the reigns of Popes Hadrian I and Leo III between 772 and 816.

---

[8] Curran 2000, Harris (ed.) 1999, Edwards and Woolf (eds.) 2003; Grig and Kelly (eds.) 2012; Cooper and Hillner (eds.) 2007, Behrwald and Witschel (eds.) 2012, Rapp and Drake (eds.) 2014, especially Ward Perkins 2014, Salzman 2014; Dunn (ed.) 2015; Coates-Stephens 1997, 1998, 1999, 2003b, 2006, 2012, 2017; Dey 2011.

[9] Edwards and Woolf 2003, p. 19.   [10] *Corpus;* Krautheimer 1980/2000.

[11] Geertman 1975, 2004, Blaauw 1994a, and Bauer 2004.

Early medieval Rome has also been the object of attention from other perspectives, such as doctrinal disputes, the cult of saints and martyrs, the diversity of the city's monasteries, the social and political role of the aristocracy, economic life, ceremonial, and the evolution of the liturgy.[12] Many of these developments have been associated with the history of particular buildings, notably San Clemente, Old St Peter's, the Lateran, Santa Maria Antiqua, Santa Maria Aracoeli and the Capitol, the Pantheon (Santa Maria ad martyres), Santa Prassede, and San Paolo fuori le mura, all of which have attracted concentrated and expert appraisal.[13] The physical city as well as the idea of Rome and its immense cultural capital, therefore, have prompted imaginative scholarly studies.[14] The second millennial celebrations of the city of Rome, furthermore, precipitated a host of studies, drawing in particular on new archaeological evidence and recent excavations, some of which are still in progress, especially the work of Roberto Meneghini and Riccardo Santangeli Valenzani, the outstanding collaborative volumes edited by Federico Guidobaldi and Alessandra Guiglia Guidobaldi, and the current archaeological project on the Lateran led by Ian Haynes and Paolo Liverani.[15]

Despite these excellent studies, the *Liber pontificalis* has still all too often been treated as a straightforward repository of a series of brief portraits of particular popes that offer a wealth of information about the church buildings and monuments they patronized in the city, with details simply extracted as corroborative evidence and considered in isolation

---

[12] I cite here only the more recent: Chazelle and Cubitt (eds.) 2007, Maskarinec 2018, Sotinel 2010, Salzman, Sághy, and Lizzi Testa (eds.) 2015, Leal 2016, Hansen 2003, Machado 2019, Delogu and Paroli (eds.) 1993, Marazzi 1998, Costambeys 2000, Ferrari 1957, Sansterre 1983, Baldovin 1987, Ó Carragáin and Neuman de Vegvar (eds.) 2007, Page 2010. See also Chapters 4 and 5 below.

[13] Guidobaldi 1992; McKitterick, Osborne, Richardson, and Story (eds.) 2013; Bosman, Haynes, and Liverani (eds.) 2020; Andaloro, Bordi, and Morgantin (eds.) 2016; Bordi, Osborne, and Rubery (eds.) 2020; Bolgia 2017; Moralee 2018; Camerlenghi 2018; Marder and Wilson-Jones (eds.) 2015.

[14] Bolgia, McKitterick, and Osborne (eds.) 2011.

[15] *Roma nell'alto medioevo* 2001; *Roma fra oriente a occidente* 2002; Meneghini and Santangeli Valenzani 2004; Guidobaldi and Guiglia Guidobaldi (eds.) 2002; Bosman, Haynes, and Liverani (eds.) 2020.

from their textual context. But no narrative history from the early middle ages can be regarded as an unproblematic source of facts, even if it might occasionally yield useful information. The *Liber pontificalis* needs to be considered in its entirety and all its complexity of purpose, as well as in its detail and in the historical context of its production, diffusion, and reception.

In past studies of the early medieval papacy the focus has tended to be on the period up to the beginning of the sixth century, and embracing the careers of Pope Leo I (440–61) and Pope Gelasius I (492–6) and all the excitement generated by the Laurentian schism and election of Pope Symmachus (498–514);[16] a few make the leap to Pope Gregory I (†604).[17] Papal letters, some of which have been labelled 'decretals',[18] sermons, theological works produced by these popes and their contemporaries, and the records of their debates in surviving conciliar material from the great church councils of the fifth and sixth centuries,[19] all delineate an apparently powerful institution with eloquent protagonists and a wide network of correspondents. New studies of particular popes such as Leo I, Gelasius I, and Gregory I have emphasized these writings and what they reflect of the pastoral and administrative roles of the Bishop of Rome.[20] Despite the markedly unenthusiastic and short entry about Pope Gregory I in the *Liber pontificalis* itself, which records little else besides a short list of his writings and his mission to the English, too many studies have assumed Gregory's own career and attitudes can be generalized as representative of all the early medieval popes.[21] An obvious factor is the sheer volume and quality of Gregory's own writings, widely disseminated in medieval Europe.[22] A seductive influence on

---

[16] Wirbelauer 1993.   [17] Markus 1997; Neil and Dal Santo (eds.) 2013.

[18] On the problem of the transformation of papal letters into papal decretals and decretal collections in the context of canon law see Dunn 2015b and Zechiel-Eckes 2013. More generally on papal letter collections see Jasper and Fuhrmann 2001, Allen and Neil (eds.) 2015, Dunn (ed.) 2015, D'Avray 2019, and below, pp. 151–7.

[19] See, for example, the translations by Price 2005; Price (ed.) 2009; Price, Booth, and Cubitt 2014.

[20] Salzman 2013; Neil and Allen 2014; Sessa 2012; Allen and Neil (eds.) 2013.

[21] A notable exception was Peter Llewellyn, who discussed the negative implications of the *Liber pontificalis* biography of Gregory I in Llewellyn 1974a.

[22] Usefully surveyed in Straw 1996, and see also Thacker 1998.

modern readers has been exerted by Gregory's role in the conversion of the English to Christianity, augmented by the Anglo-Saxon Bede's presentation thereof in his *Historia ecclesiastica gentis Anglorum* (*Ecclesiastical History of the English People*). This has led to undue emphasis on Gregory at the expense of his predecessors and successors.[23] The period from the sixth century onwards, moreover, cannot be comfortably rendered as a straightforward and stately progress of papal ideology, the achievement of 'freedom from Byzantium' and the embracing of the protection of the Franks by the second half of the eighth century.[24] In his comprehensive discussion of earlier historiography on the early medieval papacy, Tom Noble wrote the 'obituary' of this kind of linear approach, criticizing the failure to consider particular papal statements in their precise historical context, and the tendency to focus too exclusively on the jurisdictional, political, and diplomatic aspects of papal history. He made a plea for consideration of the historical and institutional contexts in which papal documents were produced, with particular reference to the letters emanating from the papal writing office.[25] Such an emphasis on context is no less important for the *Liber pontificalis,* as we shall now see.

The Text of the *Liber pontificalis*

The title *Liber pontificalis* is an eighteenth-century one, used by Giovanni Vignoli and made standard by Louis Duchesne; manuscripts from the early ninth century refer to it as *Liber episcopalis* or *acta/gesta pontificum urbis Romae.*[26] The distinctive narrative structure of the *Liber pontificalis* takes the form of serial biographies, from St Peter in the first century to Pope Stephen V at the end of the ninth century, 112 Lives in all,

---

[23] See for example Leyser 2016 and his references.

[24] See further below, pp. 16–24. Moorhead 2015 is essentially a summary of the *Liber pontificalis* up to the middle of the eighth century. The interpretations of the evidence offered in Ekonomou 2007 should be treated with caution. For an alternative view see McKitterick 2016a, 2018c.

[25] Noble 1995.

[26] Paris, BnF lat. 13729; see below, pp. 216–18, and Vignoli 1724–55; compare the rival edition by Bianchini (1662–1729, reprinted in *PL* 127 and 128 (Paris, 1852). A full account of the editions is Leclercq 1930, and see also Franklin 2017, with particular attention to Bianchini's work.

numbered in sequence in most of the earliest manuscripts. Despite this impression of being a single work, it was in fact produced in instalments, the first in the sixth century and covering the period from St Peter up to the author's or authors' own day, and then subsequently extended in continuations. Some of these continuations were constructed retrospectively, as I shall explain shortly, but most of them are contemporary with their subjects.

The original author as well as subsequent authors of the *Liber pontificalis* appear to have been officials within the papal administration, acting on their own initiative or else with papal involvement. Either they worked in the *scrinium,* that is, the archive and office in which the papal letters were written, or in the *vestiarium,* that is, essentially the office responsible for papal finances and assumed to have records of the papal endowments, properties, estates, and expenditure.[27] For access to the documentation on which the narrative rests it is generally thought that there would have needed to be considerable interchange between the two groups, if indeed their personnel were separate in this early period.[28] Analysis of the style of writing and use of the *cursus* or rhythmical prose, which involves a stylized way of ending phrases and sentences with a particular number and length of syllables, has begun to shed some light on the diversity of writers responsible for the various types of document within the papal administration. Pope Gregory I, for example, wrote very few of the letters sent out in his name.[29] Richard Pollard has demonstrated, furthermore, that up to the end of the seventh century almost all papal letters are characterized by the use of *cursus,* while the authors of the papal biographies in the *Liber pontificalis* for the same period do not use it. In the eighth century, however, there is little sign of a familiarity with the rules of *cursus* on the part of the writers of either the letters or the papal biographies, except for the author of the Life of Pope Gregory III and to a lesser extent those of Popes John VII (705–7), Constantine I (708–15), and Gregory II (715–31). A diversity of authorship and of educational background seems clear, though these differences might

[27] See Neil and Allen (eds.) 2014, pp. 11–14 and 127–39, and Noble 1990.
[28] Bougard 2009 at pp. 128–31. See Noble 1985 and McKitterick 2016a.
[29] Pollard 2013.

also reflect varying attitudes towards the appropriateness of a different stylistic register dictated by the genre.[30] Systematic analysis of the Latin of the text may well yield more precise knowledge.

In two prefatory letters at the beginning of the text, the *Liber pontificalis* is improbably credited to the late fourth-century Pope Damasus (366–84), writing at the prompting of Jerome (*c.*345–420), the patristic scholar. The letters are present in the earliest complete manuscripts,[31] though the oldest of these, now in Naples, is only from the later seventh century.[32] As I explain in more detail below, I am inclined to affirm these spurious letters as part of the original sixth-century composition, perhaps functioning as an inspiring claim about the illustrious initiators of a project subsequently carried out by others.[33] The letters may also be the way the authors signalled papal patronage of the enterprise. The crediting of the text by editors in the early modern period to the ninth-century papal *bibliothecarius* Anastasius has long since been discarded, apart from Anastasius's authorship of the ninth-century Lives of Popes Nicholas I and Hadrian II.[34]

The format of the *Liber pontificalis* is a deliberate recasting of the genre of imperial serial biography to write about the popes, with all the ideological implications such an historiographical choice implies. The structure of the biographies in the *Liber pontificalis* is directly comparable with such assemblies of biographies of Roman emperors as that from Julius Caesar to the Emperor Domitian in Suetonius, *De vita caesarum XII* (*Lives of the Twelve Caesars*), written in AD 119, or the later emperors in the *Historia Augusta* written in the fourth century AD.[35]

---

[30] On the criteria deployed for the presence or absence of *cursus* as an analytical identifier see Pollard 2009 and Pollard in press.

[31] Schelstrate 1692, I, pp. 369–75 was apparently the first to refute the validity of the Damasan and Hieronymian connection.

[32] Naples, Biblioteca Nazionale IV.A.8; see below, Chapter 6, pp. 185–6.

[33] See below, Chapter 3, pp. 69–70. On the two letters, compare Cuppo 2008, p. 67.

[34] The attribution of the text to Anastasius Bibliothecarius took rather longer to be rejected: but see Herbers 2009, Bougard 2008 and Bougard 2009, and Bauer 2006. See also the comments on the eighteenth-century editions in Franklin 2017 and the forthcoming work on the *Liber pontificalis* at St Denis in the twelfth century by Elizabeth A. R. Brown.

[35] McKitterick 2009. See also Vout 2009.

Despite the considerable variation in the length accorded each topic, there are consistent structural parallels between the contents of the late antique imperial biographical narratives and the *Liber pontificalis* in the formulaic presentation of information about the subject's name, origin, parentage, and career before and after elevation to the imperial or papal throne. These parallels extend to the details about disputed elections and rival candidates, challenges to his authority, public works, patronage, buildings, and religious observance, his length of reign, death, and burial.[36] The parallels can be set out schematically as follows:

SERIAL BIOGRAPHY: STRUCTURAL MODELS

Imperial Lives in Suetonius, *Lives of XII Caesars*; *Historia Augusta*; Eutropius, *Breviarium*; *Kaisergeschichte*; Aurelius Victor, *De Caesaribus*	Papal Lives in *Liber pontificalis*
Emperor's name and origin	Pope's name and origin
Life before he became emperor	Career before he became pope
Process of becoming emperor, including disputes and rivals	Election as pope, including disputes and rivals
Career as emperor, including rebellions	Career as pope, including challenges to authority
legislation	legislation
public works	public works
buildings	buildings
patronage	patronage
religious observance	religious observance
Death and burial	Death and burial
Length of reign	Length of reign

The *Liber pontificalis* is nevertheless a remarkably novel type of work in its emphases as well as its chief protagonists. It presented a new mode of argument; it created a new genre for subsequent historians of religious institutions to emulate; its adaptation of imperial serial biography implied that the popes were the successors to the emperors as the rulers of Rome; and it offered an alternative and Christian history of Rome.[37] The concentration on the city of Rome, moreover, is in complete accord with the obsession of so many ancient authors with Rome.[38] Just as

---

[36] For more extended arguments concerning the model provided by Roman imperial biographies see McKitterick 2011 and 2018c.

[37] Sot 1981.   [38] See below, Chapter 2, pp. 38, 60–1.

Cicero's conception of Rome in the *De republica,* for example, was of a city built up generation after generation, with a gradual accumulation of temples and monuments enshrining the memory of the people in stone, so too the *Liber pontificalis* represents a gradual accumulation, pope after pope, basilica after basilica, of the institutional and physical structures of the city.

A further structural model for the papal history was the *De viris illustribus* (*On Illustrious Men*) of Suetonius, emulated by Jerome in the fourth century with his *De viris illustribus,* a bio-bibliography of Christian writers in chronological order devised primarily as a reference tool for use in debates, though it also presented a case for Christian literature in relation to pagan authors.[39] As we shall see, later scribes and compilers of volumes containing the *Liber pontificalis* sometimes juxtaposed it with the *De viris illustribus,* and made it seem as if it were complementary to Jerome's text.[40] The two letters credited to Damasus and Jerome prefacing the *Liber pontificalis* may have helped to create this impression.[41] The author or authors of the *Liber pontificalis* appear to have had access, not only to the papal registers and the documents relating to church estates and property in the *vestiarium* noted above, but also to a range of existing chronographical lists and historical narratives, such as the Chronograph of 354,[42] the Eusebius–Jerome *Chronicon,* the *Historia ecclesiastica* of Eusebius–Rufinus, and other material relating to individual bishops of Rome. The early Roman martyr stories in circulation may well have been used in some instances, though the relationship of some of these to the *Liber pontificalis* and the dating of the written versions are notoriously problematic, exacerbated by the lack of any manuscript witnesses (except for one seventh-century palimpsested fragment) before the eighth century.[43] None of these models and sources can simply be understood as a series of texts that furnished information passively for the *Liber pontificalis.* The context and motive of each text

---

[39] Whiting 2015, and compare McClure 1979.   [40] See below, Chapter 3, pp. 73–4.

[41] Jerome, *De viris illustribus,* ed. Richardson, and see below, pp. 69–70.

[42] Burgess 2012 and Salzman 1990.

[43] On Roman martyr narratives see Pilsworth 2000, Costambeys 2000, Sághy 2015, Lanéry 2010, and Gioanni 2010. For English translations of the passions, mostly as printed in the early modern editions, see Lapidge 2018.

also needs to be taken into account in relation to their treatment on the part of the *Liber pontificalis* authors.[44]

The first stage of composition of the papal biographies can be dated soon after 536, as I explain in the final section of this chapter, and contains the Lives of the fifty-nine popes from Peter to Agapitus (535–6).[45] The editor of the definitive text in the late nineteenth century, Louis Duchesne, posited a first and revised edition several years apart in the sixth century. He surmised an earlier first edition of *c.*530 from the existence of two epitomes, labelled the Felician and the Cononian, both extant in late eighth-century Frankish manuscripts. As Geertman and others have argued, however, neither of these epitomes should be regarded as a primitive precursor of the *Liber pontificalis,* even though they yield important information about the dissemination of the full text.[46] I shall return to these epitomes and the questions the manuscripts raise in Chapter 6 below.

The subsequent sections of the *Liber pontificalis* were added in the seventh and early eighth centuries. From the presentation of the text in all the extant manuscripts, a decision seems to have been made to resume the composition of these serial biographies in the form of a seamless continuation of the existing text in which the same formulaic structure was retained. The authors of the continuations thereby neatly emphasized the underlying continuities of both the narrative and the institution, even if the content gradually becomes more obviously engaged with contemporary doctrinal and political concerns. Unfortunately, there are no obvious indications of when the decision to resume the story might have been taken. On the basis of the retrospective character and different prose style of the Lives of Silverius and Vigilius onwards, with only a hint of contemporary knowledge returning in the second and third decades of the seventh century, the resumption of work on the *Liber pontificalis* seems to have been no earlier than the pontificate of Pope Honorius (625–38); thereafter, in terms of composition at least,

---

[44] See further below, Chapter 2, pp. 61–5.   [45] Geertman 2009, and below, pp. 25–35.
[46] On Epitomes F and K see *LP* I, pp. xlix–lvii, but this element of the *Liber pontificalis's* redaction is open to challenge: see Geertman 2009, Verardi 2013, 2016, Simperl 2016, and McKitterick 2019. See also below, Chapter 6, pp. 195–201, for further discussion.

the biographies were produced one by one, or occasionally perhaps in small groups. Breaks were discerned by Duchesne between Lives 77 and 78 of Popes Eugenius I (654–7) and Vitalian (657–72) and Lives 79 and 80 of Popes Adeodatus II (672–6) and Donus (676–8),[47] but there are other plausible reconstructions. There may have been two attempts at the Life of Pope John VII (705–7).[48] These continuations may even correspond to specific phases of compilation, but their identification rests primarily on the internal evidence of the biographies themselves.

In the Life of Julius (337–52), the responsibilities for papal record-keeping and the preservation of historical memory were spelt out by the sixth-century authors: '[He] issued a decree . . . that the drawing up of all documents in the church should be carried out by the *primicerius notariorum,* whether they be bonds, deeds, donations, exchanges, transfers, wills, declarations or manumissions, the clerics in the church should carry them out in the church office.'[49] There are many references to the papal archive subsequently, both in the *Liber pontificalis* itself and by other early medieval visitors to Rome in search of particular material. The Anglo-Saxon Bede, for example, reports how Nothelm, a priest from London who went to Rome, was given permission by Pope Gregory II (715–31) to search through the archives of the holy Roman church.[50] Under Pope Hadrian I (772–95), moreover, an enormous effort of preservation was achieved with an assembly of a vast selection of the letters of Pope Gregory I.[51] Yet the *Liber pontificalis* is an entirely different kind of historical enterprise, being nothing less than the transformation of an archive into a distinctive historical narrative.[52] Whether in phases or Life by Life, the consistency of purpose and format is remarkable.

---

[47] *LP* I, pp. ccxxxi–xxxiii, and see also Duchesne 1877, pp. 205–6.

[48] On the seventh-century sections see my comments in McKitterick 2016a.

[49] *LP* I, Life 36, c. 3, p. 205: *Hic constitutum fecit . . . et notitia, quae omnibus pro fide ecclesiastica est, per notarios colligeretur, et omnia monumenta in ecclesia per primicerium notariorum confectio celebraretur, sive cautiones vel instrumenta aut donationes vel commutationes vel traditiones aut testamenta vel allegationes aut manomissiones clerici in ecclesia per scrinium sanctum celebrarentur;* trans. Davis, *Pontiffs,* p. 27.

[50] Bede, *Historia ecclesiastica gentis Anglorum,* ed. Colgrave and Mynors, p. 4.

[51] Pitz 1990; Straw 1996, pp. 47–8; Markus 1997, pp. 206–9.

[52] For a useful summary of the new ways of interpreting and writing about the past that emerged in late antiquity see Croke 2007. See also below, pp. 25–35.

The unifying theme for these seventh- and early eighth-century sections of the *Liber pontificalis* is the papal challenge to Byzantium and the patriarch of Constantinople in matters of doctrine within an historical framework. The text itself both represents and symbolizes the continuities in the institution while at the same time recording change and the gradual emergence of new themes. I therefore regard the Lives 60–90 as the second major part of the *Liber pontificalis*. There is some manuscript evidence that the portion of the text up to 715 was distributed in the early eighth century as a single entity, but it was thereafter itself augmented on a Life-by-Life basis in the eighth and ninth centuries.[53] These eighth-century sections of the *Liber pontificalis* offer further examples of variant versions;[54] an earlier and a later version of the Life of Pope Gregory II is extant,[55] and there are three versions of the Life of Pope Stephen II, that is, Life 94, including the famous 'Lombard' version.[56] Further, the beginning of a Life of Pope Constantine II was subsequently subsumed into the Life of Stephen III.[57] Life 94 of Stephen II, moreover, as we shall see in the final chapter of this book, has proved particularly interesting for what it suggests about the processes of dissemination outside Rome and local emendation of the text thereafter.

The three tentative subdivisions in the scheme below (**LP IIA–C**), therefore, simply correspond to particular climactic points in the narrative.[58] There is a consistent emphasis in the seventh-century Lives on the definition and upholding of orthodox Christian doctrine in the face of heretical ideas emanating from the emperor and patriarch in Constantinople. This might indicate, for instance, that the *Liber pontificalis* was intended to serve as a dossier of material prepared for particular moments of crisis for the papacy.[59] The Lateran Synod of 649, Pope Agatho's presentation at the Synod of Trullo in 680–1 and the rejection of Monothelitism, and the triumph of orthodoxy in which the Byzantine emperor is portrayed as abasing himself before Pope Constantine I in

---

[53] On the manuscripts see further below, Chapter 6, pp. 171–223.
[54] See below, pp. 180–1, 207–8.   [55] *LP* I, pp. 396–410 prints them in parallel columns.
[56] See Gantner 2013a.   [57] McKitterick 2018b.
[58] I make a case for the seventh-century continuations in McKitterick 2016a, pp. 246–62, though some of the details there have been adjusted here.
[59] For the doctrinal issues see Price 2014.

Constantinople in 715, are such moments. There is some clever sleight of hand on occasion: Pope Honorius, for example, was actually condemned by the sixth ecumenical council of Trullo 680–1 for error in relation to the Chalcedonian definition of the Trinity. Two extant letters by Honorius, however, came to be read as Honorius's defence of the orthodox position of Christ's single person but two natures, human and divine.[60] The *Liber pontificalis,* however, omits all mention of Honorius's intervention and maintains its representation of the popes as the unfaltering champions of orthodoxy.

In the schematic summary below, therefore, the divisions **IIA, IIB**, and **IIC** as well as **I, II**, and **IV** are simply an acknowledgement of the narrative rhythm; I offer them as a working hypothesis about possible phases of compilation.

LIBER PONTIFICALIS: PHASES OF PRODUCTION

LP I (= Duchesne's 2nd redaction) *c.*536, Lives 1–59/?60: Peter to Agapitus (†536)

LP IIA Lives 60–71: Silverius (†537) to Boniface V (†625)

LP IIB Lives 72–81: Honorius (†638) to Agatho (†681) but possible breaks before 672 and 676–8

LP IIC Lives 82–90: Leo II (†683) to Constantine I (†715)

LP III Eighth-century Lives 91 (two versions), 92, 93, 94 (three versions), 95, 96, 97 cc. 1–44, 97 cc. 45 to end: Gregory II (†731) to Hadrian I (†795)

LP IV Ninth century Lives 98–112: Leo III (†816) to Stephen V (†891)[61]

As I have indicated already, the manuscript transmission of the *Liber pontificalis* is a crucial consideration for any interpretation of the text, the hypothetical phases of production, and possible impact, and I shall be exploring this fully in the final chapter of this book. One of the peculiarities of the manuscript survival is that most of the earliest copies of the text are Frankish and produced in the Carolingian period.[62] Another is that most early medieval copies of the *Liber pontificalis* only go as far as Life 94 of Pope Stephen II (752–7); very few extant manuscripts from the late eighth or the ninth century go further than Life

---

[60] See Cubitt 2014, p. 46.

[61] Reproduced with modifications from McKitterick 2016a, p. 248.

[62] *LP* I, pp. clxiv–ccvi.

97 of Pope Hadrian I, a biography peculiar in any case in that the actual historical narrative really only covers the first three years of his pontificate to 774 (cc. 1–44); thereafter (cc. 44–94), the text is primarily concerned with Hadrian's embellishment of the churches of Rome. The later lives from Pope Leo III to Pope Stephen V (Lives 98–112) appear to have been much less widely circulated in the Carolingian period.[63] The first section, comprising Lives 1–59 (Peter to Agapitus), however, was the most widely circulated of all, and it is to this, and its sixth-century context of production, that I now turn.

The *Liber pontificalis*: Historical Context of Production

A brief sketch of political events may be helpful. The wider context for the *Liber pontificalis* is to be found in the profound political changes in Italy after 476. The Western Roman Empire had ceased to exist as a political entity with the deposition of Romulus Augustulus, or Romulus the 'Little Emperor' in 476 and the assumption of power by the Roman military commander Odovacer, who was proclaimed *rex* (king) by the army and established himself in the imperial capital of Ravenna.[64] Thereafter, the political balance within Italy and Italy's relationship with both the former Western provinces of the Empire and with the Eastern Empire were transformed. Britain, Gaul, Spain, and North Africa were now ruled by various 'barbarian' leaders,[65] and after Odovacer himself had been assassinated in 493, his place was taken by his murderer, Theodoric the Ostrogoth.[66] Like Odovacer, King Theodoric ruled from Ravenna, though he also established a palace in Verona and strengthened the city walls there. Like Odovacer, Theodoric maintained a Roman style of government until his death in 526, and there was

---

[63] Duchesne 1877; McKitterick 2016a; on the later sections see Bougard 2009, Herbers 2009 and below, Chapter 6, pp. 206–20.

[64] MacGeorge 2002, pp. 282–93.

[65] See Halsall 2005, and the relevant chapters in Fouracre (ed.) 2005. On Italy and the Exarchate of Ravenna see Brown 1979, 1984, Deliyannis 2010 and West-Harling (ed.) 2015.

[66] Amory 1997 and Arnold, Bjornlie, and Sessa (eds.) 2016.

considerable continuity in personnel and offices between the two regimes.

The political and legal position of the Eastern emperor in relation to Theodoric's Ostrogothic regime remains a matter of dispute, for the political relations between a king in Italy, bishop and senate in Rome, and the emperor in Constantinople were unprecedented.[67] Rome itself had rarely been the residence of the Western emperor for much of the fourth and fifth centuries, and both Odovacer and Theodoric had for the most part left Rome to its own devices. There are indications, nevertheless, of reverence for St Peter and an acknowledgement of the pope's authority within the church, even though the Goths were *homoion* Christians, sometimes labelled, not strictly accurately, 'Arians', who emphasized the humanity of Christ in their understanding of the Trinity.[68] The decades since 476 had afforded an opportunity, whether by default or design, for the staunchly catholic and orthodox Bishop of Rome to assert his leadership and claim some degree of autonomy, despite the diversity and wide spectrum of doctrinal opinion among the people of the city.[69] Rome had its own secular administration and the senatorial aristocracy were prominent in the city's affairs throughout the fifth and sixth centuries, though individual families maintained links with friends, colleagues, and family in both Ravenna and Constantinople.[70] As in many other cities in the West, moreover, the bishop and the clergy played an increasingly important role in the political, administrative, and social as well as religious life of the city.[71]

The renewal of Byzantine interest in the former Western province of Italy at least was allegedly precipitated by the murder of Theodoric's daughter Queen Amalasuintha early in 535. She had acted effectively as regent for her young son Athalaric, who had succeeded Theodoric as king, and conducted her own diplomatic relations with the Emperor Justinian. But Athalaric's early death made Amalasuintha accept as

---

[67] On the variable but still influential role of the senate see Clemente 2017.

[68] See Lizzi Testa 2013, Amory 1997, Sessa 2016; and on *homoion* Christians, Whelan 2018, especially pp. 85–108.

[69] Arnold 2017.   [70] Salzman 2017.

[71] On the late antique papacy see Behrwald and Witschel (eds.) 2012, Dunn (ed.) 2015, and Sessa 2012. On the 'republic' see Noble 1984, especially pp. 57–60.

co-ruler her cousin Theodohat, who was implicated in her murder.[72] The narrative of the 'Gothic wars' that ensued is largely dependent on the history of all the Emperor Justinian's wars written in the guise of memoirs in a classical Greek literary style by the Byzantine Greek author Procopius at the end of his own career.[73] Rather too much confidence has been placed in his reliability and accuracy, but he was undoubtedly one voice in a 'polyphony of opinions' in Constantinople about the Italian wars after 540.[74] With hindsight the wars in both Vandal Africa and Ostrogothic Italy have been characterized as Justinian's wars of *renovatio* or 'renewal of the Roman Empire', but in Italy they had limited success. The Byzantine armies, led first by Belisarius and then by Narses, met with considerable and protracted resistance within Italy from forces under the leadership of the Gothic rulers Witigis and subsequently Totila. Although the first stage of the war ended with a peace concluded in Ravenna in 540 and King Witigis and his family moved to Constantinople, Totila then emerged as leader of the resistance to the Byzantines. He even occupied Rome in the winter of 546–7 and again at the beginning of the year 550, but was killed in battle in 552.

The Byzantines' ultimate military success is symbolized by the document known as the Pragmatic Sanction. According to the preface, it was issued by the Emperor Justinian at the request of Pope Vigilius in the immediate aftermath of the defeat of the last Gothic army in 554. It was primarily designed to reassure the citizens of Rome that their claims of ownership to property would not be endangered by the recent conflict, and that all legal transactions concluded under the Ostrogothic regime, with the exception of any made during the reign of Totila, would be valid. By 584, the Byzantine government had established a foothold in Italy at Ravenna, ruled by a Byzantine official known as the Exarch, but it is not clear how this may have related to any regime in Rome, nor why this was so long after the end of the Gothic wars.[75] The Exarchate of Ravenna became an interesting colony of expatriates from the East

---

[72] For the contradictions of the Gothic regime see Amory 1997 and Wolfram 1988.

[73] Cameron 1985. An alternative interpretation is offered by Kaldellis 2004.

[74] See Boy 2014 and Cameron 2009. The phrase 'polyphony of opinions' is that of Van Hoof and Van Nuffelen 2017.

[75] Justinian, Pragmatic Sanction; Pelagius II, *Epistolae* 1, *PL* 72, cols 703–5.

together with 'Romans', 'Italians', and 'Goths', in which the archbishops of Ravenna played an increasingly important role.[76]

The establishment of the Exarchate may have been prompted by the third major factor in Italian politics in the later sixth century, namely, the arrival of the Lombards. After 568 they established themselves in the Po Valley, Trentino, Friuli, and Tuscia in the northern part of Italy, as well as Spoleto and Benevento;[77] their principal city was Pavia. They took over Veneto and Liguria in the seventh century and conquered the Byzantine Exarchate itself in 751. The Lombard kings had apparently been *homoion* Christians at first, though King Agilulf's wife Theodolinda was a catholic and corresponded with Pope Gregory I. From the later seventh century onwards the Lombard kings were catholic. Despite this, papal letters as well as the biographies of the popes in the *Liber pontificalis* are often perplexingly hostile towards the Lombards, portraying the kings, or more often the dukes of Spoleto and Benevento, as constantly seeking to encroach on 'papal territory'. Certainly, for much of the period between the later sixth and later eighth centuries, there were contested lands between the Exarchate, Lombard kingdom and the popes. These may have been disputes about ecclesiastical jurisdiction, rights to revenues and rents, or actual political control.[78] Papal appeals for military assistance against the Lombards, especially from the Franks and the new Carolingian rulers after 754, eventually led to Frankish support and protection and ultimately the conquest of the Lombard kingdom by Charlemagne in 773–4.[79] Byzantine intervention in Italy thereafter appears to be related to new Frankish offensives in Italy, competing interests in the Adriatic, and in response to local alliances in Naples and Benevento.[80]

---

[76] Brown 1984, Deliyannis 2010.   [77] Delogu 1995. See also La Rocca (ed.) 2002.

[78] See Marazzi 1998, Azzara 1997, and Costambeys 2000.

[79] See McKitterick 2008, pp. 107–18 and Costambeys, Innes, and MacLean 2011, pp. 56–67.

[80] This is surmised from the references to ambassadors in many narrative sources and the evidence of many manuscript sources and artefacts: see Granier 2002, Buckton 1988, Kaczynski 1988, and McCormick 2011.

Rome and Byzantium

Rome's relations with Byzantium in the aftermath of the Gothic wars need to be considered first of all at the practical level of whether any direct rule within the city was established. Secondly, there is the broader question of cultural influence and exchange.

It remains uncertain whether the Byzantine emperors actually installed their own official representatives in Rome, whether and when the de facto rule of the bishop and his secular and clerical administration took over, and under whose command there was military presence in Rome. The Byzantine general Narses fought off raids in Italy and was based in Rome, though the *Liber pontificalis* relates how he retreated to Naples and claims that he only returned to Rome at the request of Pope John III (561–74).[81] An added source of uncertainty indeed is that it is primarily the *Liber pontificalis* which is the principal, if occasional source. It is only in the late seventh-century sections of the narrative, for example, that there is reference to the army (*exercitus*), and in the eighth century to a *dux* (duke), a military title, and a 'duchy of Rome'. An undated inscription in Terracina, on the coast about fifty miles south-east of Rome, refers to a *consul* and *dux* Georgius, albeit without any indication of what he was the *dux*.[82] The style of the letter forms suggests a seventh- or eighth-century date. The ambiguities and contradictions of the evidence were succinctly summarized by Tom Brown over forty years ago and recently readdressed by Tommaso di Carpegna Falconieri.[83] It is not always clear whether the army is one based in Rome or whether contingents are sent from Ravenna. *Dux* is usually understood to refer simply to a military command. It has optimistically been taken further and interpreted as a Byzantine creation of an official with territory comprising Rome and representing imperial or exarchal secular power; some scholars have even located this Byzantine official representative on

---

[81] *Corpus Inscriptionum Latinarum* VI, No. 1199 for Narses's restoration of the Ponte Salaria, and see *LP* I, Life 64, pp. 305–7.

[82] Guillou 1971, with illustration at p. 155, and Maskarinec 2018, pp. 58–9 and illustration in Figure 9.

[83] Brown 1984 and Carpegna Falconieri 2012, pp. 43–5.

the Palatine in Rome.[84] Yet between the reference to Narses and these eighth-century episodes there is no unequivocal reference to any military official with the title of *dux* associated with Rome, in any extant source. The *cartularius* is explained by Tom Brown, for example, as a subordinate official in charge of the garrison in Rome (*c*.640), but the *cartularius* Maurice in league with the Exarch of Ravenna who, according to the Life of Pope Severinus (May–August 640), tried to rob the Lateran treasury appears to have been a Ravennan military officer rather than a Roman one.[85] Brown suggests that Rome may have had its own *dux* in 712 who may have had administrative functions and may also have been subordinate to the pope, not least as the power of the exarchs themselves was undoubtedly waning fast in the early eighth century. An alternative interpretation has been to accept that the *cartularius* and the *dux* were indeed Byzantine appointments in Rome. If the *dux* is understood to be a substantial office, one possible explanation is that the military function of *dux* could be both temporary and itinerant, so that the description of his responsibilities in relation to Rome could have been a short-term expedient. Another possible interpretation is that the title was simply a newly coined honorific of a military commander to distinguish him from the Exarch of Ravenna, without implying an actual political role over a specific territory. It may originally have been an official who was an adjunct within the Exarchate, and actually had no real power within Rome at all. It may subsequently have been adopted in the course of the eighth century as the title of a military commander under the pope's control in Rome.[86] It is significant furthermore that if any support is offered the Byzantine officials, it is made to look as if it is the magnanimity of the Bishop of Rome towards a political peer, as in the case of Pope John V. In addition to the military administration there is also the possibility of secular officials to consider. While there were undoubtedly people with Greek names and with eastern family background acting as secular administrators in Rome, such as the famous instance of Plato,

[84] For discussion of the archaeological indications of the use of buildings on the Palatine see Augenti 1996 and 2000, and Coates-Stephens 2006.

[85] *LP* I, Life 75, cc. 2–3, pp. 331–2.

[86] See *LP* I, p. 403 and Bavant 1979, Brown 1984, pp. 53–56, and Delogu 2001, at pp. 20–1. See also Gantner 2014, pp. 64–8 and Hartmann 2006, pp. 39–40.

father of Pope John VII,[87] there is no clear unequivocal evidence of Byzantine secular officialdom being based in Rome itself, let alone of the pope's subordination to such people.

Despite the ambiguities of the evidence, Italy and Rome in the period from the end of the Gothic wars until the middle of the eighth century are sometimes referred to as 'Byzantine'.[88] Quite how misleading such a notion is becomes clear when one attempts to understand the occasional references in the *Liber pontificalis* to the relations with the emperor. Topics such as the question of whether the notice of papal election sent to Constantinople was a requirement or a courtesy, and thus whether the emperor actually had the right to approve the choice of pope or not;[89] whether the claims to revenues from lands in Italy were those of a landlord or of a ruler;[90] whether legally to transform a secular building into one for sacred use, as in the conversion of the Pantheon into the church of Santa Maria ad martyres in 609 or 613, actually still required the permission of the emperor, or whether this was an instance of the pope and his legal advisers hedging their bets in relation to the shreds of old Roman law on the topic: all these questions merit far fuller discussion than can be pursued here.[91]

Similarly, the extent of papal ecclesiastical jurisdiction remains ill defined, partly due to the far wider and ever-growing compass of the pope's spiritual authority as a source of guidance and judgement that is evident from the papal letters and decretals.[92] The Bishop of Rome's ecclesiastical jurisdiction was described at the Council of Nicaea in 325. In the version reported by Rufinus in his extension of Eusebius's *Historia ecclesiastica,* it comprised the following: Rome and the *regiones suburbicariae,* that is, the city of Rome itself, Campania, Tuscany, Umbria,

---

[87] *LP* I, Life 88, c. 1, p. 385, and the epitaphs of Plato and his wife Blatta once in the church of Santa Anastasia are discussed by Duchesne, *LP* I, p. 386, note 1.

[88] See above, p. 7, note 24.

[89] See, for example, the statements in the Lives of Popes Severinus, Vitalian, Eugenius, Agatho, and Benedict II, *LP* I, pp. 341, 343, 350, and 363.

[90] *LP* I, Life 91, c. 16, p. 403: Maiuro 2007.

[91] *LP* I, Life 69, c. 2, p. 317: Loschiavo 2015, pp. 83–108. For discussion of the significance of *dedicatio* in Roman law see Linderski 1985, Orlin 1997, and briefly below, Chapter 4, p. 130.

[92] See further below, pp. 147–57.

suburbicarian Picenum, Samnium, Apulia, Calabria, Sicily, Bruttii and Lucania, Corsica and Sardinia.[93] The ninth-century Byzantine chronicler Theophanes claims that the Byzantine emperor took Dalmatia, Illyricum, and southern Italy with Sicily away from the Roman church province in 715.[94] In ecclesiastical terms, therefore, the pope was understood to have jurisdiction over all the bishops of the cities in these regions, and in principle would have had a role in their consecration. The references in the *Liber pontificalis* to such issues are at best opaque.[95] The many indications of eastern Mediterranean cultural influence, furthermore, especially in the wonderful frescoes and mosaics of the seventh and eighth centuries in Rome, do not prove that any region of Italy apart from the Exarchate was under direct imperial control from Constantinople.[96]

A precise understanding of Rome's political or legal obligations in relation to Eastern imperial government has to be in the context of a superlatively cosmopolitan and multilingual city. Rome was a home, refuge, or spiritual goal for soldiers, ordinary lay families, clerics, monks, religious refugees, migrants, merchants, diplomats, artisans, tradesmen, artists, mosaicists, stoneworkers, brick-makers, sculptors, builders, labourers, city officials, farmers, market gardeners, aristocrats, foreign ambassadors, and pilgrims. They came from Constantinople, Syria, Dalmatia, Thrace, Palestine, Egypt, North Africa, and Sicily, and there were many people from elsewhere in the Eastern and Western Mediterranean as well as from Frankish Gaul and England.[97] Latin and Greek for all these people, whatever their mother tongues, were the dominant languages of communication.[98] A glimpse of the diversity of Roman society is offered,

---

[93] Eusebius–Rufinus, *Historia ecclesiastica,* ed. Schwartz and Mommsen, Latin text ed. Mommsen, pp. 966–7; on Nicaea see McKitterick 2020a.

[94] Theophanes, *Chronicon,* dates this later: s.a. 6224 (= 731/2), trans. Mango, Scott, and Greatrex, pp. 567–8. This confiscation is not mentioned in extant papal sources. The older literature is summarized by Noble 1984, p. 39 and note 124 and Davis, *Eighth-Century Popes,* p. 21, note 13. See also Costambeys 2000, p. 386 and note 734, following Marazzi 1998, p. 137.

[95] McKitterick 2016a and 2018c.

[96] For full discussion of the art historical evidence see Osborne 2020. I am very grateful to John Osborne for allowing me to read his book in advance of publication.

[97] For a fresh perspective see Winterhager 2016. See also Neil and Allen (eds.) 2015.

[98] Adams 2003, Adams, Janse, and Swain (eds.) 2002, and Adams and Vincent (eds.) 2016.

for example, by the seventh-century Latin inscription in Santa Cecilia in Trastevere commemorating Theodore, together with his baby grandson. Theodore was described as a Greek from Byzantium and friend of many Roman magistrates.[99] How thoroughly bilingual the Roman church may have been, moreover, is suggested by the first version of the Lateran decrees of 649 being issued in Greek, and the many Greek-speaking popes in the seventh and early eighth century, such as Pope Leo II (682–3), praised for his proficiency in Latin and Greek by his biographer.[100]

Doctrinal Schism and Dispute

In addition to the political uncertainties, contested areas, and legal ambiguities, the potential for doctrinal tension with *homoion* and catholic Christians coexisting in Italy was exacerbated by the personal involvement of the Eastern emperor in theological matters that manifests itself as a public responsibility. The first major rupture in the late fifth century was the 'Acacian schism'. Named after the Patriarch Acacius of Constantinople (471–89), it disrupted ecclesiastical and political relations between Rome and Constantinople from 482 to 519.[101] The dispute centred on the refusal of the popes to accept the *Henotikon* of the Emperor Zeno, supported by Patriarch Acacius. This Eastern formulation had failed explicitly to affirm both the Council of Chalcedon's definition in 451 of the two natures of Christ in one person, and Pope Leo I's *Tome* in which the Chalcedonian position, the gold standard of Western orthodoxy, was expounded.[102]

Yet the dust of the Acacian schism had hardly settled before a new furore was created by the Emperor Justinian's condemnation of the 'Three Chapters' which also compromised the former papal clarity concerning Chalcedon. The 'Three Chapters' were the works of the Eastern theologians Theodore of Mopsuestia, Ibas of Edessa, and

---

[99] Hunsacker and Roels 2016.
[100] *Concilium Lateranense a. 649 celebratum*, ed. Riedinger; Price, Booth, and Cubitt 2014, pp. 59–68; *LP* I, p. 359. On Greek-speaking popes see also Gantner 2014, pp. 88–90 and Gantner 2013b, pp. 33–49.
[101] Kötte 2013.   [102] For guidance on the issues see Gray 2005.

Theodoret of Cyrrhus. Their work had been explicitly approved at the Council of Chalcedon in 451, so this posthumous condemnation was interpreted in the western Mediterranean as a rejection of the Council of Chalcedon's authority. Justinian's attempt to force Pope Vigilius to agree to the condemnation was ostensibly successful; Vigilius's prevarication in resisting imperial pressure ended with his endorsing the condemnation of the Three Chapters in 553, an embarrassing endorsement his successor Pelagius I then maintained while simultaneously insisting that he was faithful to Chalcedon. The dispute, not least because of the inconsistency of the late sixth-century popes on the matter, created schism within Italy, as well as in the Mediterranean region more generally, with the church of North Africa and the sees of Milan and Aquileia both maintaining the Council of Chalcedon's authority and also opposing the condemnation of the Three Chapters.[103] Theological disharmony between Rome and Byzantium was then reinvigorated still more explicitly with the challenge offered by the Eastern formulations of Monophysitism (one nature) and Monothelitism (one will) as alternatives to orthodox definitions of Christ's two natures, divine and human. Even with the condemnation of Monothelitism at the Lateran council of 649, accepted in Constantinople in 680, there were further ructions in the relations between the popes and the Eastern church when the Quinisext Council in the East of 692 suggested that Eastern ecclesiastical disciplinary practices should also be observed in Rome. This was rejected out of hand by Pope Sergius I (687–701).[104] From the middle of the eighth century the popes also resisted Eastern attempts to ban figural representations in Christian art.[105]

The Arsenal of the Past: Dating the Sixth-Century *Liber pontificalis*

The *Liber pontificalis* is, as we shall see in the following chapters of this book, both a distinctive commentator on the complex interweaving of events and ambitions indicated above, and an essential part of its fabric.

---

[103] Chazelle and Cubitt (eds.), 2007.   [104] *LP* I, Life 86, cc. 6–7, pp. 372–3.

[105] *LP* I, Life 96, c. 23, pp. 476–7, Noble 2009 and Brubaker and Haldon 2011, and see below, p. 161.

The exact historical context of its composition therefore becomes all the more important to determine.

The compilation of the *Liber pontificalis* appears to have been completed during and in the immediate aftermath of the reign of Pope Agapitus (535–6), who ruled in the year after the murder of the Ostrogothic Queen Amalasuintha, King Theodoric's daughter, in April 535. Agapitus is the first pope in the Ostrogothic era not to have his years in office dated by the *Liber pontificalis* authors, either according to the regnal years of the kings of Italy or the Eastern emperor.[106] Instead, after the standard formula of parentage (Roman, the son of the priest Gordian), his own time in office (eleven months and eighteen days) is stated. Agapitus is described as starting his pontificate by destroying the anathema against Dioscorus that a recent predecessor Pope Boniface II (530–2) had extorted from the clergy. The reference to Dioscorus is to the man ordained pope at the same time as Boniface, but Dioscorus had died before the conflict could be resolved. Boniface had forced the Roman clergy to sign an anathema against his rival. It is this document Agapitus is recorded as destroying, but the account of Agapitus's initiation into office ends with the significantly generalized statement that Agapitus 'released the entire church from the malice of faithless men' (*et absolvit totam ecclesiam de invidia perfidorum*).[107] In an entirely fitting climax, the Life of Agapitus ends with a triumphant visit of the pope to Constantinople. Agapitus had been sent by the new Gothic king, Theodohat, so the *Liber pontificalis* reports, 'because the emperor was infuriated with King Theodohat for killing King Theodoric's daughter Queen Amalasuintha; she had entrusted herself to Justinian and he had made Theodohat king'. On arrival in Constantinople, however, Agapitus concentrated on upholding the orthodox understanding of Christ's two natures in a single person, upon which the emperor 'abased himself before the apostolic see and prostrated himself before the blessed pope Agapitus'.[108] It is in the Life of Agapitus's successor Pope Silverius

---

[106] See also McKitterick 2018c.
[107] *LP* I, p. 287. For Life 57 of Boniface see *LP* I, p. 281 and Duchesne's discussion, *LP* I, pp. 282–4.
[108] *LP* I, Life 59, cc. 2 and 5, pp. 287 and 288, trans. Davis, *Pontiffs*, p. 51: *Quia eodem tempore imperator domnus Iustinianus Augustus indignatus est Theodato regi; eo quod occidisset reginam*

(536–7), whom Theodohat had forced upon the people of Rome, that the launching of Justinian's campaign 'to free all of Italy from occupation by the Goths' by the general Belisarius is reported in a style so very different from the preceding Lives that, as I suggested above, it reads far more like a retrospective reconstruction.[109]

The disputed papal election between the rival candidates Symmachus and Laurentius known as the 'Laurentian schism', three decades before these events, has sometimes been proposed as one local context for the initial composition of the *Liber pontificalis*.[110] The Laurentian schism undoubtedly caused a major rift among the various aristocratic families, factions, and interest groups in Rome, and precipitated a 'pamphlet war' still to be seen in the compilations known as the 'Symmachan apocrypha' preserved in both the *Collectio Avellana* letter collection, compiled *c*.553, and the *Sanblasiana* collection of canon law, also thought to be an early sixth-century compilation.[111] The Symmachan apocrypha included a number of concocted texts to try and establish precedents for the resolution of the election dispute. According to the *Liber pontificalis*, the Laurentian dispute had reached such an impasse that the arbitration of King Theodoric in Ravenna was sought. King Theodoric decided in favour of the person first elected, who happened to be Pope Symmachus (498–514). Rather than the *Liber pontificalis* being part of the resistance to too great a control of the papal office by aristocratic families, an alternative impetus for the composition of the *Liber pontificalis* has been seen in the Acacian schism with Constantinople, with an interpretation of the *Liber pontificalis* as primarily a text designed to emphasize the pope's orthodoxy and primacy.[112]

Certainly, the Acacian schism and Laurentian dispute are part of the historical and intellectual background from which the *Liber pontificalis* emerged, and provided important precedents in their use of texts as

---

Amalasuenta filiam Theodorici regis commendatam sibi, qui eum regem fecerat . . . Tunc piissimus Augustus Iustinianus gaudio repletus humiliavit se sedi apostolicae et adoravit beatissimum Agapitum papam.

[109] Useful background in Arnold, Bjornlie, and Sessa (eds.) 2016.   [110] Cohen 2015.

[111] Wirbelauer 1993, *Collectio Avellana*, ed. Guenther, Blair-Dixon 2007, and see further below, pp. 30–1.

[112] Deliyannis 2014.

weapons.[113] Averil Cameron has explicated the notion of 'texts as weapons' in relation to the technique of literary debates in Byzantium. These took the form of piling up citations and providing the exegesis of texts in florilegia designed to demonstrate the proofs of an argument, appealing to authority and tradition.[114] The compilations of dossiers of texts in sixth- and seventh-century Rome are similar to the Byzantine florilegia. Thus, the power of the *Liber pontificalis* depended as much on its content as on the effectiveness of its production and distribution, the receptiveness of the audience, and the contemporary expectations about how debate might be conducted.[115] The text in itself is important evidence to support assumptions about audience expectation, simply because it appears to anticipate and respond to such expectations in how it presents its subjects. The *Liber pontificalis* was also bolstered by the sheer bulk of contemporary written texts in other genres produced and distributed by the popes. The huge volume of papal correspondence, for example, documents the determined campaigns to elicit support for particular papal arguments in what Andrew Gillett has described as 'central' and 'lateral' communication.[116]

The texts devised in relation to the disputed election of Laurentius and Symmachus and the Acacian schism, however, are only two instances among an impressive barrage of texts and arguments produced in the first half of the sixth century; all might be characterized as the assembly of an arsenal of the past. This resource can be understood to form three groups of texts of various types, both from the popes and from those serving the Ostrogothic kings, responding to the opportunities and challenges of the decades after 476. The first of these, for the most part concentrated at the beginning of the sixth century, takes the form of the texts produced in the 'pamphlet war' associated with the Laurentian schism already mentioned, together with attention to codifying conciliar material and incorporating papal 'decretals' such as the historically ordered compilation of 'canon law' made by Dionysius Exiguus between

---

[113] I take my cue from Bowman and Woolf 1994 and Cameron 1994.

[114] For suggestive comments on some of the texts created see Wessel 2012. See further below, pp. 32–5.

[115] See Whiting 2015.   [116] Gillett 2012.

500 and 520.[117] Further manifestations of this 'culture of compilation' are the Rule of St Benedict of Nursia, whose approach to the monastic life was effectively publicized by Pope Gregory the Great in his *Dialogues*, the monastic Rule of Eugippius, and Eugippius's voluminous florilegium of extracts from the works of Augustine.[118] All witness to what has been described as a 'network of textual exchange' in Italy in these early decades of the sixth century.[119] In this early phase the writings of Ennodius, Bishop of Pavia, written while he was still a deacon in Milan, might be included as contributions from the Ostrogothic regime, together with the lost *Chronicle of the Goths* by Cassiodorus, written between 526 and 533, and King Theodoric's provision of an amalgamation of different customs and traditions based on Roman civil laws in his *Edictum*.[120]

The second group is in response to the crisis of the military invasion led by the Byzantine general Belisarius. As already argued above, the consequent political upheaval precipitated the *Liber pontificalis* in Rome, but also from Rome there is Arator's poem *De actibus apostolorum*. A versified rendering of the Acts of the Apostles and publicly performed in Rome in 544, it has a marked emphasis on how Saints Peter and Paul, the 'two lights of the world' chose Rome as their city.[121] Cassiodorus's *Variae*, the massive dossier of official correspondence from the Ostrogothic rulers, is most probably also to be associated with the end of the first phase of the Gothic wars after 540.[122]

The third group comprises texts produced in Rome and in Constantinople in the later 540s and early 550s, some of them composed within or for the circle of Italian refugees in the immediate aftermath of the Gothic wars.[123] These are mostly historical narratives and appear to confirm Peter Van Nuffelen's observation that historiography was one

---

[117] Pitz 1990, Jasper and Fuhrmann 2001, Dunn 2015a, 2015b, Campiani 2018, Graumann 2018, Hoskins 2015, Leyser 2019.

[118] Benedict of Nursia, *Regula*, ed. de Vogüé and Neufville; Eugippius, *Excerpta Augustini*, ed. Knoll, and *Regula* 1, ed. Villégas and de Vogüé.

[119] Leyser 2001 and see also Gorman 1982.   [120] Lafferty 2013, pp. 54–100.

[121] Arator, *De actibus apostolorum*, ed. Orban; also ed. MacKinlay; English trans. Schrader, Roberts, and Makowski. See also Hillier 1993, and below, pp. 63–5.

[122] Cassiodorus, *Variae*, ed. Mommsen. The date of compilation is inevitably a matter of dispute; see Barnish 1992, Bjornlie 2013, and Arnold, Bjornlie, and Sessa (eds.) 2016.

[123] Croke 1983, 2001, 2005.

of the ways in which the literati of Constantinople responded to the political and ecclesiastical crisis of these years.[124] They include the portrait of Theodoric written by the 'Anonymus Valesianus', a Catholic author probably based in Ravenna or Verona.[125] From Constantinople there is the championing of the history of the Goths by Jordanes in the *Getica* as well as his *Historia Romana,* which can be read as a critique of Justinian's military and religious policies.[126] The *Gothic Wars* of Procopius, and the Latin translation and compilation from three Greek ecclesiastical histories by Sozomen, Socrates, and Theodoret in the *Historia ecclesiastica tripartita* produced by Cassiodorus and Epiphanius between 544 and 551, are also part of this historiographical commentary, though the latter work was produced in Cassiodorus's retirement at Vivarium in Italy. It is significant in gauging Cassiodorus's theological position that the Greek historian Theodoret was also one of the authors of the condemned 'Three Chapters'.[127]

From Rome, in addition to the earliest of the *Gesta martyrum* composed during this period,[128] the vast dossier of chronologically arranged papal and imperial letters known as the *Collectio Avellana* was probably compiled soon after 553.[129] The collection comprises 243 letters dating from the late fourth to the mid-sixth century. There is as yet little agreement on this date, nor by whom and for what purpose the collection was made. The offices of both the city prefect and the popes have each been credited with the assembly of the material, and it has variously been seen as compiled for the Laurentian schism, as guidance in the course of the Acacian schism, or as an exercise in the self-definition of the papacy in the middle of the sixth century. Most follow the editor Guenther in seeing it as a whole from the mid-sixth century rather than as a collection initially formed at the beginning of the sixth century in relation to papal politics.[130] Guenther saw it as an assembly of a number

---

[124] Van Hoof and Van Nuffelen 2017.
[125] Anonymus Valesianus, ed. König, and Adams 1976.
[126] Jordanes, *Getica,* ed. Möller and ed. Mommsen, and Van Hoof and Van Nuffelen 2017.
[127] Cassiodorus, *Historia ecclesiastica tripartita,* ed. Hanslik and Jacob; Scholten 2015.
[128] See p. 11 and note 43 above.
[129] *Collectio Avellana,* ed. Guenther, Viezure 2015, Lizzi Testa and Marconi (eds.) 2019.
[130] Blair-Dixon 2007, updated and expanded in Clemente 2017.

of different dossiers: two (Letters 1–40) relate to the disputed papal elections between Damasus and Ursinus, and Boniface and Eulalius, and Letters 56–243 all relate in one way or another to the Acacian schism. The collection also includes material from a Carthage archive concerned with Pelagianism, from the register of Pope Leo I's letters on the problems of the church of Alexandria dated to 17 and 18 June 460, and letters exchanged between the Emperor Justinian and Popes Agapitus and Vigilius between 536 and 553 (Letters 82–93). It is conceivable, such are its bulk and signs of editorial guidance in the compilation as a whole, that the entire collection might best be interpreted as the deliberate formation of an historical archive in itself.

One clue to this may be the letters in the *Collectio Avellana* concerning Ennodius, Bishop of Pavia (474–521). Despite being more usually associated with the regime of Theodoric the Ostrogoth, Ennodius was no stranger to papal politics. Letters in the *Collectio Avellana* indicate that he served as a papal envoy to Constantinople in 515 and 517, that is, during the Acacian schism. The instructions for the legates in 515 (Letter 116) contain precious indications of the functions of an historical dossier when matters of doctrine and jurisdiction were being discussed by legates, and serve to justify such a collection. As Kennell comments, 'the combination of obsessive stage management, absolute certitude and quasi-Socratic method is formidable'.[131] All letters carried by the emissaries had to be brought to the attention of the emperor in discussions of the exact nature of Christ, conduct of previous emperors, the statement at Chalcedon and *Tome* of Leo, and the condemnation of Nestorius and Eutyches.

In comparison to all of these texts the *Liber pontificalis* constructs a far more comprehensive and historical argument than would be appropriate for an immediate, let alone an ephemeral, response to a specific issue. It was not a dossier of letters and edicts like most of the compilations mentioned above, but a determined narrative. The difference also lies in its widespread distribution, as we shall see in Chapter 6. The *Collectio Avellana,* by contrast, is extant in only one eleventh-century manuscript, and the *Variae* had a very limited circulation in the early

---

[131] Kennell 2000, pp. 215–16.

middle ages; not even the other histories match the *Liber pontificalis* in the extent of its dissemination. Placing the *Liber pontificalis* in the context of specific doctrinal or ecclesiastical debates certainly accords it an important role as an ideological statement in internal disputes and theological debate, but nevertheless both the Laurentian dispute and the Acacian schism are too narrow as contexts for the immediate production of the *Liber pontificalis*. Instead, it should be seen as a specifically papal and Roman response to the political crisis engulfing the whole of Italy, with the sudden invasion of a hostile army challenging the regime that had ruled Italy peacefully for the past two generations.

At this point, the evidence of the so-called 'Verona fragment' needs to be considered, for it contains the best known of the preliminary, independent, or possibly even rival versions of two Lives in the *Liber pontificalis*. The Verona fragment contains the last part of a Life of Pope Anastasius (496–8) and the whole of a Life of Pope Symmachus (498–514), and is an integral part of an entire codex produced in the second half of the sixth century. Script and contents indicate a date soon after 555.[132] Both in itself and in its codicological context, this extract from the *Liber pontificalis* is of crucial importance for our understanding of the earliest decades of production and reception of the *Liber pontificalis*. The book is written in a confident half-uncial usually located to Verona. A similar, if not the same, script occurs in a number of other manuscripts, containing related texts, such as the Acts of the Council of Chalcedon (451) and the *Apostolic Constitutions,* a set of very early canons of which Dionysius included the first fifty in his canon law collection.[133] In the current first folio of the Verona codex, the beginning of the *Vita Symmachi* is indicated as the fifty-second pope (not the fifty-third), with a prominent Roman numeral in a manner familiar from later copies of the *Liber pontificalis*. The customary formula concerning *natio* and parentage is absent. At the end of this Life is a list of popes, apparently made by the same scribe as the rest of the text, including the length of their pontificates. This included Pope Vigilius (537–55) and a note that he had died

---

[132] Verona XXII (20) (*CLA* IV, 490).

[133] Verona LIII (51), LIX (57), BAV Vat. lat. 1322 and Paris, BnF lat. 12214 + St Petersburg, Q.I.4 (Augustine, *De civitate dei*), (*CLA* IV, 506, 509; *CLA* I, 8, and *CLA* V, 635).

in Syracuse. Quire marks suggest that an entire eight-leaf quaternion and one further leaf, eighteen pages in all, are missing. At twenty-five lines per page, this is possibly sufficient to have contained the entire narrative before the Life of Pope Anastasius (496–8). The version of the Life of Symmachus in the Verona fragment omits most of the detail about his gifts to churches. Abbreviation of a longer Life by omitting other details about the building and endowment of churches, such as that of Life 34, of Silvester I, is not excluded, so that the original text in the Verona codex may simply have been rather leaner.

There are various possible interpretations of the contents of the compilation in relation to the existence of a full text of the *Liber pontificalis* and how far it extended. One possibility is to accept the allocation of completion of a text of the *Liber pontificalis* (**LP I**) to the period of Pope Hormisdas, Symmachus's successor, in which this less positive version of Symmachus's Life was either the original or a substitute. Another is that the version received in Verona was the whole **LP I** as described above, but that the copyist chose not to include Lives 54–59 of Popes Hormisdas, John I, Felix IV, Boniface II, John II, or Agapitus. The listing of popes to Silverius and Vigilius might imply more than knowledge of their reigns, but there are later *Liber pontificalis* manuscripts from the eighth and ninth centuries that also have more popes listed than biographies represented in the text. Lastly, this alternative and allegedly 'pro-Laurentian' version of Symmachus's Life could indeed be regarded as the remnant of the 'pamphlet war' during the so-called Laurentian schism.

Which interpretation is the most plausible cannot be settled on the basis of this Verona codex. But it is worth noting that the Verona version of the Life of Pope Symmachus is better described as an alternative, more legally and document-oriented approach to writing a papal biography than as an anti-Symmachan or pro-Laurentian text. The remaining lines of the Life of Pope Anastasius refer to a letter written by the pope to the emperor stating that because of the degree of corroboration from heavenly Scripture, the persistence of so atrocious a schism between the Eastern and Western churches is 'quite pointless'. The Life of Pope Symmachus certainly includes some derogatory comments about Symmachus's private life and public actions but these are mostly framed as part of the report of the rumours in circulation.

The striking difference presented in the Verona alternative Life lies in the detail about the hearings of the case by King Theodoric, the charges against Symmachus, what the accusations against Symmachus were, and how many of the bishops and senators went to his defence in order to consider the legal issue of whether a Roman pontiff could be judged. Yet the Roman pontiff was judged. It is this summary of the legal issue that is the crucial one, and it is omitted in the version in the full text of the *Liber pontificalis* as we now have it. That version fudges the entire issue by referring merely to a synod of 115 bishops who acquitted Symmachus of the 'false charges' against him. Nor does it seem particularly pro-Laurentian to say, in an obviously rhetorical formulation, that Laurentius was in Rome four years but that the author prefers not to say anything about the 'civil wars and terrible murders' of that period, thus succinctly doing precisely that. Fuller details of the horrors of these four years are in the standard full text of the *Liber pontificalis,* and the Life of Symmachus is further extended with a description of Symmachus's building activity and destroying the 'Manichaeans'.[134]

In other words, the balance of the Lives is different in the kind of information provided, and to label them as pro-Symmachan or pro-Laurentian is neither helpful nor convincing. One might compare these two narratives with the Lives of Damasus and Sixtus III in the *Liber pontificalis,* or the Life of Boniface II.[135] The first two are both very allusive in reporting that charges were brought against each pope and that they were acquitted, and the third is outspokenly critical of the pope.

That there should be disparities in particular texts once they were reproduced in new books for new audiences perhaps should not surprise us. That there should be various opposing views and emphases about popes in circulation should also not be a surprise, for the viciousness of the disputed papal elections alone, quite apart from such corpora as the Symmachan documents studied by Eckhart Wirbelauer,[136] alert us again to the articulation of different bodies of opinion, factions, and interest

---

[134] For the suggestion that this might be understood as a generic reference to 'heretics' see Cohen 2015.

[135] *LP* I, Lives 32 and 42, pp. 212 and 232.   [136] Wirbelauer 1993.

groups in Rome and beyond.[137] These were by no means confined to the clergy, for as Samuel Barnish has argued, the Roman aristocrats were just as keenly involved in events in Rome as different groups, both lay and ecclesiastical, within the Lombard-controlled areas.[138] Whether the version in the Verona fragment or the more formulaic version of the Life of Pope Symmachus found in the later manuscripts was the original remains a puzzle. Certainly the Verona codex is a precious witness to the liveliness of the manuscript tradition of the *Liber pontificalis* in Italy.[139] Because the end of the preceding Life of Pope Anastasius II in the Verona fragment also differs from the version found in later manuscripts, the Verona fragment may well be a remnant of the original version from Rome. If that were the case, then the later manuscripts could well preserve an edited version made, perhaps in the seventh century, at the point when the text was resumed, updated, and further edited.[140]

Conclusion

Both the format and content of the first section of the *Liber pontificalis*, therefore, need to be read in the light of the political crisis of the late 530s. The text was precipitated by more than local schism or as part of Roman propaganda wars, though it can indeed be considered as contributing to a wider argument in the first few decades of the sixth century, conducted in the form of historical texts, in which the perception of the imperial past was transformed by the popes themselves.[141] To credit the authors of *Liber pontificalis* with using writing as an instrument of persuasion, and offering a new mode of argument deliberately structured to evoke imperial comparison, endows the *Liber pontificalis* itself with power as a text. The particular account of the past in the *Liber pontificalis* was intended in the first instance to play a role in the politics of the sixth century and in a milieu in which there was a marked respect for texts and their authority. The *Liber pontificalis* is potentially a key piece of evidence for the consolidation of the ideological position adopted by the papacy

---

[137] See also above, p. 17. [138] Barnish 2008. [139] See further below, Chapter 6.
[140] See above, pp. 14–15. [141] See McKitterick 2011.

in the new political configuration of the former Western Roman Empire. This involved far more than Rome's primacy and the pope's role as St Peter's successor, crucial elements though these were, as we shall see in the following chapters.[142]

In the rest of this book I shall address, through the prism of the *Liber pontificalis*, the politics and ideology of Rome's transformation from imperial city to Christian capital, and how it became the focus of secular and religious politics in relation to the Ostrogoths, Byzantine Greeks, Lombards, and Franks. I shall examine how the *Liber pontificalis* depicts Rome as the holy city of Christian martyrs and the residence of the pope, the goal of pilgrims, artists, and craftsmen, all of which coexisted with Rome's antique and imperial past as a physical presence and as an idea. How does the *Liber pontificalis* reflect the way the popes developed their power and control within the city? How does papal patronage manifest itself in the text, and how was it orchestrated? How did the *Liber pontificalis* contribute to the establishment of the pope's spiritual authority within and beyond Rome? My suggestion here is that for those who can be shown or inferred to have had access to the text in the early middle ages, the understanding, memory, and perceptions of Rome and the writings of the earliest popes were greatly influenced, if not actually shaped, by the *Liber pontificalis* from the middle of the sixth century onwards. We cannot properly understand the early medieval popes unless we appreciate the invention of the papacy within the papal administration itself in which the popes were arguably complicit, and in which the *Liber pontificalis* apparently played such a key role. The problem of the participation of the subjects of representation in that representation's creation, and the extent to which the popes in their public role live up to their textual representation, is further complicated by the successive extensions to the text and, most obviously, the creation of a multiplicity of models for emulation.[143]

I shall present my cumulative argument as follows. In Chapter 2, I shall discuss the *Liber pontificalis* and the city of Rome. I then address

---

[142] See below, Chapters 2 and 3.

[143] For the models of King David and the Emperor Theodosius see Jong 2009, pp. 112–18, and McLynn 1994, pp. 291–8 and 315–30.

in Chapter 3 the *Liber pontificalis*'s representation of the apostolic succession from St Peter and the construction of the Christian past of Rome as a holy city of Christian saints and martyrs. In the fourth chapter, I shall examine the degree to which the *Liber pontificalis* presents the Bishop of Rome as establishing visible power within the city, and the indications the text offers of the campaign to replace or emulate the Roman emperors as rulers of the city. Subsequently, in Chapter 5, I shall consider the image of the pope projected by the *Liber pontificalis* and the spiritual and ministerial role of the bishop in Rome. Lastly, in Chapter 6, I turn to the question of audience implicit throughout the book and trace the potential power of the text by investigating its manuscript transmission and reception, especially in Italy and Francia, in the early middle ages and thus who may have had access to the *Liber pontificalis*.

2

The *Liber pontificalis* and the City of Rome

Introduction

THE *LIBER PONTIFICALIS* COULD SIMPLY BE DESCRIBED as a history of Rome from the very particular perspective of the Christian church and the popes. Yet it is a far richer and less straightforward narrative than that, and it would not have been the first text to have enchanted readers with a vision of Rome. Think of the Greek geographer Strabo, writing during the reign of the Emperor Augustus: 'If you were to pass back through the ancient forum and were to behold one forum ranged after another and the royal stoas and temples, and were to see the capitol and all the monuments on it and the Palatine and the Porticus of Livia, you might easily forget everything outside the city.'[1]

Not only is the *Liber pontificalis* one possible means, simply because it has ostensibly datable references to particular places, of charting remnants of the city's ancient topography and the transformation of the ancient city in late antiquity and the early middle ages. It is also worth asking whether the text itself can be interpreted as part of the very process of the transformation of the city, in the sense that it offers a narrative of that process to orient perceptions of the city on the part of its readers. This might be rephrased as a question about the degree to which the contexts in which the text was written and transmitted helped to determine the role the city of Rome played in the narrative. Further, how might one appraise the role of Rome and the Roman people in the text? It is therefore the way the *Liber pontificalis* constructed and

---

[1] Strabo, *Geography* 5.3.8, quoted by Woolf 2003, p. 204.

communicated presentations of Roman identities and Rome as a city that I wish to explore in this chapter. To what extent does the *Liber pontificalis* reflect the transformation of the city that has been documented in relation to other categories of evidence? Further, how might the impression the text creates have effected a transformation of perceptions in the minds of its readers?

There are all kinds of ways one can investigate this. One is to focus systematically on life in the city, identifying particular ways the text emphasizes the importance of belonging to Rome and deploys topics involving the people of Rome. A simple example is the highlighting by the *Liber pontificalis* of the Roman or at least Italian *natio* of the greater majority of its bishops by means of its formulaic note of their *natio*. The word can be understood to be a reference not to where a pope was born, but what his family origin or what we might now describe as 'nationality' was understood to be. How else it might be defined is obviously dependent on context, historical, geographical, and philological; Davis renders it as 'of Roman (or Tuscan, African etc.) origin'. The difficulties highlight the dangers of imposing modern understandings of how people were defined and perceived onto descriptions in the past. Altogether the *nationes* of fifty-six out of the 109 earliest popes to the late ninth century were described as Roman,[2] and the 'origins' of twenty were attributed to elsewhere in central Italy, namely Campania, Tuscany, Tivoli, and Albano, as well as Sicily. The biographies in the *Liber pontificalis* make it clear how many of those whose *natio* was not described as Roman were nevertheless trained in Rome.[3] Thus, Pope Theodore (642–9), although described as 'Greek', was the son of Theodore, a bishop from Jerusalem; Pope John V (685–6), described as a Syrian from the province of Antioch, when still a deacon had been sent by Pope Agatho (678–81) as a papal representative at the sixth ecumenical council in Constantinople; Pope Conon's father had been a soldier in one of the Byzantine Empire's military regions, the Thracesian Theme, but Conon himself

---

[2] Popes 3, 4, 7, 8, 16–19, 21–4, 27, 30, 31, 34–8, 40, 41, 44, 46, 50, 52, 57, 61–6, 68, 70, 73, 77, 79, 80, 83, 91,94, 95, 97–108, 112. For a discussion of the 'Greek' and 'Syrian' descriptors and their implications see above, pp. 23–4.

[3] See Noble 2014, p. 81; Davis sometimes translates *natione* as 'born in' and sometimes as 'of . . . origin'. Loomis 1916 chose to render it 'by nationality a . . .'.

had been educated in Sicily and served in the church of Rome before becoming priest; Pope Sergius (687–701), 'of Syrian origin', also from the region of Antioch, but born in Sicily, had been a member of the Roman clergy since the pontificate of Pope Adeodatus (672–6); Pope Gregory III (731–41) was of Syrian origin but is described as proficient in Greek and Latin and a member of the Roman clergy.[4] All popes, therefore, whatever their 'origin', were selected from among the Roman clergy. This can be set out in the following table:

A. *Popes up to the mid-sixth century (earliest section of* LP*), Lives 1–59 (one is 'unknown')*

Roman	29
From elsewhere in Italy	11 (incl. Campania, Tuscany, Etruria, Albano, Tivoli, Samnium)
Greek	9
African	3
Sardinian	2
Spanish	1
'Antiochene'	1
Syrian	1
Dalmatian	1

B. *Popes c.536 to 715, Lives 60–90*

Roman	13
From elsewhere in Italy	9 (Campania, Tuscany, Abruzzo, Sicily)
'Greek'	4
Syrian	4
Dalmatian	1

C. *Popes 715 to 891, Lives 91–112 (3 not recorded; Life 96 records 2)*

Roman	16
From elsewhere in Italy	2 (Constantine II; Stephen III)
'Greek'	1
Syrian	1

The extant manuscripts carefully retain all these notices of papal origin. One, Leiden, VLQ 60, even lists the *natio* beside each name in the table of popes at the beginning of the codex. At face value, the record of

---

[4] *LP* I, Lives 75, 84, 85, 86, and 92, pp. 331, 366, 368, 371, and 415.

nationes is a ringing endorsement of the Romanness of the popes, but we should also consider why the authors included this information and what they were trying to communicate. An obvious question is whether the *Liber pontificalis* author/authors adapted the note concerning the origin of the subject of each Life from the imperial biographical models indicated in the preceding chapter. There, however, it may be necessary to distinguish between Suetonius and the later imperial histories in order not to elide a possible change between the second and the fourth centuries in the formulation of perceptions of identity. It does seem to be from the fourth century that the *natio* begins to have more prominence. In the *Lives of the Twelve Caesars,* Suetonius's main concern is with family parentage and pedigree. In his discussion of the grammarians and rhetoricians in his *De viris illustribus,* it is social rank – free, freed, or slave – that is prominent in the information. Only for the six poets does Suetonius mention their origin and, when known, their parentage as well as their rank. If we compare the discussion of each emperor in the *Historia Augusta* and accept the most recent arguments that it is the work of a single author, there is certainly an interest in the origins of each emperor, but again the emphasis is more on ancestry and family, and the formula *X natione Y* is not used. Of the 135 authors Jerome describes in his *De viris illustribus* in the fourth century, itself modelled on the *De viris illustribus* of Suetonius and serving as another structural model for the *Liber pontificalis,* only twenty-four actually have their origin specified. Most are simply described as the Bishop of X. The consistent use of the formulaic phrase *X natione Y,* therefore, is peculiar to the *Liber pontificalis.* Reading the list for its variety rather than to identify how many 'Roman' or 'Greek' popes there were yields men from the Holy Land, Syria, Greece, Africa, Spain, Dalmatia, Sardinia, Sicily, and many regions of Italy as well as Rome itself. Rather than being simply ethnic markers, they could also act as imperial symbols; they reflect the cosmopolitan character both of the successors of St Peter and of the city of Rome.

The practical focus on the people of Rome, therefore, forms the first part of this chapter. Thereafter, the extent to which the *Liber Pontificalis* creates a mental map of Rome, or virtual Rome, in the minds of readers will be explored.

The People of Rome

Despite the undoubted decrease in both the density of population and numbers of people in the city in the fifth and sixth centuries, there remained a substantial urban population in Rome, albeit concentrated in particular areas of the city.[5] The citizens of Rome, most usually referred to as the *populus* or *plebs* and sometimes as *Romani* or *fideles*, and often paired with the clergy (*clerus et populus*) are represented as playing an essential role as protagonists in the narrative. In this respect, their active presence accords with Shane Bobrycki's demonstration of how crowds continued to regulate social and religious life in the early middle ages, and belies the claims that after the Roman period crowds only again became 'vehicles of popular participation in public events' in the eleventh century.[6]

In the earliest sections of the *Liber pontificalis*, Roman citizens are described as being martyred for their faith. In Life 38 of Felix II (355–65), who had dared to proclaim Constantius son of Constantine to be a heretic, for example, the text reports how the bishop was beheaded with many of the clerics and faithful in secret close to the city walls, alongside the Aqueduct of Trajan.[7] The *Liber pontificalis* created a record of the Christianization of the past of many of Rome's families by the simple process of identifying so many of them as martyrs, with relics of those now accorded holy status brought from their extramural cemeteries into the city from the seventh century and increasingly, from the time of Paul I onwards, installed in many new shrines and churches. Paul's donations of the relics of many saints to San Silvestro in Capite, for example, are corroborated in two lengthy inscriptions mounted on either side of the current entrance to the basilica.[8] Similar lists preserved in an eighth-century inscription record the relics translated by the *primicerius* Theodotus to Sant'Angelo in Pescheria in 767. This includes Roman male and female martyrs alongside angels and apostles, biblical figures, and a small number of Syrian or eastern saints, presumably

---

[5] Meneghini and Santangeli Valenzani 2004, pp. 21–8.
[6] See Bobrycki 2018 and Brown 1998, pp. 76–89; compare Pizarro 1998. On the eleventh century see Moore 2016.
[7] *LP* I, Life 38, c. 3, p. 211.   [8] *LP* I, Life 95, c. 5, p. 464.

introduced to Rome in the course of the seventh century. One of the new Roman saints listed on Theodotus's inscription is Petronilla, mistakenly identified as the daughter of St Peter, whose translation from the cemetery of Achilleis and Nereis and installation in the former mausoleum of Honorius beside St Peter's basilica is recorded at length in Frankish interpolations in the Lives of Popes Stephen II (752–7) and Paul I (757–67).[9] Other relics were translated to Old St Peter's between 757 and 767.[10] The most famous and spectacular mass translation is that of the relics of over 2000 saints by Pope Paschal I to his newly built basilica of Santa Prassede, recorded in another lengthy inscription now mounted on one of the piers in the nave of the church.[11]

Such attention to the dead on the part of the living, and the restoration and custodianship of cemeteries, are constant themes in the *Liber pontificalis,* and are fundamental aspects of the way the text builds the impact of Christianity into Roman identity. Thus Pope Leo II (682–3) 'built a church in Rome close to St Bibiana's where he deposited the bodies of saints Simplicius, Faustinus, Beatrice and other martyrs, and dedicated it in the name of the apostle Paul on the 22nd Day of February'.[12] The pre-Christian populace of Rome thus become the martyrs and saints for Christian Rome and are inserted into the city's topography as well as into the city's festive calendar.[13] Thus the *Liber pontificalis* authors in the sixth century further elaborated the work of Pope Damasus and possibly provided inspiration for the relic translations of the eighth century.[14]

[9] *LP* I, Lives 94, c. 52 and 95, c. 3, pp. 455 and 464, Cardin 2008, Tavola 47 and pp. 68–9; on Petronilla and the Frankish connection see Goodson 2015 and McKitterick 2018a, but note an earlier reference to Petronilla in the cemetery of Nereis and Achilleis in the Via Ardeatina in the Monza relic labels from the seventh or eighth century, ed. Glorie after Valentini and Zucchetti, 'Pittacia (oleorum modeotiana)', in *Itineraria,* ed. Valentini and Zucchetti, p. 294.

[10] Cardin 2008, pp. 68–70 and Tavole 48, 49, 54. Rubeis 2001. See also Thacker 2007b, pp. 13–15 and Maskarinec 2018.

[11] Goodson 2010, pp. 228–30, and Goodson 2007.

[12] *LP* I, Life 82, c. 5, p. 360, trans. Davis, *Pontiffs,* p. 77: *Hic fecit ecclesiam in urbe Roma iuxta sancta Viviana, ubi et corpora sanctorum Simplici, Faustini, Beatricis atque aliorum martyrum recondidit, et ad nomen beati Pauli apostoli dedicavit sub die XXII mens februar.*

[13] See also below, Chapter 4, pp. 123–5.

[14] See below, pp. 69–70 and the useful summary in Thacker 2014.

The current citizens are also represented as active in the politics of the city in the narrative of the *Liber pontificalis*. Thus, Pope John III (561–74) had requested the Byzantine general Narses to come to Rome from Naples. The political situation is represented as being so grim that

> The Romans driven by malice petitioned Justinian (=Justin II) and Sophia 'it would be better for the Romans to serve the Goths than the Greeks when the eunuch Narses is a ruler who subjects us to slavery and our most pious prince does not know it. Either deliver us from his hand or we and the Roman citizenry will serve the barbarians.'[15]

As noted in the previous chapter, further political ructions in Rome, at least in the seventh and early eighth century, were often presented by the *Liber pontificalis* authors as fomented by the Byzantine Exarch in Ravenna seeking to influence or even take over the political life of Rome. Occasionally, pretenders to the Exarchate are represented as seeking to invoke Roman support, such as the patrician and chamberlain Eleutherius whose short career and downfall is recorded briefly in the Lives of Popes Deusdedit (615–18) and Boniface V (619–25), Lives 70 and 71.[16] The political implications of these seventh-century lives as far as the ambiguities of Rome's position in relation to both the Exarch in Ravenna and the emperors in Constantinople have already been discussed above, but the dramatic story of the plundering of the Lateran in 640, in the Life of Pope Severinus (28 May – 2 August 640), who held the see for only two months and four days, is one tantalizing glimpse of the volatile politics of the city. Even before Severinus had been consecrated, Maurice the *cartularius* had enlisted support from both '*iudices* and armed men who chanced to be in Rome, from youths to old men' and Isaac the Exarch had sent the 'church dignitaries' (*misit omnes primatos ecclesiae*) into exile (*in exilio*) 'so that there would be none of the clergy to resist' (*ut non fuisset qui resistere debuisset de clero*) before the Lateran *episcopium*

---

[15] *LP* I, Life 63, c. 3, p. 305, trans. Davis, *Pontiffs*, p. 58: *Tunc Romani invidia ducti suggesserunt Iustiniano et Sophiae quia 'expedierat Romanis Gothis servire quam Grecis, ubi Narses eunuchus imperat et servitio nos subiecit; et piissimus princeps noster haec ignorat. Aut libera nos de manu eius, aut certe et civitate Romana et nos gentibus deservimus.'*

[16] *LP* I, Life 71, c. 2, p. 319.

was plundered of its wealth by Isaac's men and some of the booty sent to the Emperor Heraclius in Constantinople.[17]

The *Liber pontificalis* may well be misleading its readers about the negligible extent to which the Byzantine Exarchate could assert, let alone exert, any authority in Rome,[18] but it is nevertheless significant that for the most part the narrative presents such attempts as intrusion and depredation, often roundly resented and even resisted by the people of Rome. It might be objected that citizens' resentment of taxation is too common to occasion comment. Given the desperate straits of the Byzantine government in the face of the military disasters of the 640s,[19] it is conceivable that Italy and Rome itself may have been especially targeted by Constantinople.

Even more dramatic are the incidents in which the people of Rome are portrayed as acting as witnesses to or protestors against political acts of the pope. In the very first life of all, of Peter, the text notes that the apostle held many debates with Simon Magus, both before the Emperor Nero and before the people.[20] Pope Boniface II (530–2) had won election despite the greater support given his rival Dioscorus, who had died only a few weeks after his consecration.[21] Boniface had subsequently attempted to determine the manner of his succession in favour of the deacon Vigilius. But the *sacerdotes* decided this was 'against the canons' and Boniface thereupon burnt the decree in front of the *confessio* of St Peter and in the presence of all the *sacerdotes,* clergy, and senate.[22] The people generally were allegedly still more energetic in the Life of Pope Vigilius (537–55), who was possibly the same former deacon whom Boniface II had tried to promote. Here the Romans are described as sending their petitions against Vigilius to the Emperor Justinian and the Empress Theodora, saying he had dealt harshly with the emperor's servants the Romans, his (the pope's) very own people (*cum ipsa plebe sua*). The narrative continues:

[17] *LP* I, Life 73, c. 4, p. 329.   [18] See above, pp. 20–4.
[19] See Haldon 1990, pp. 41–63; and specifically on taxation Brubaker and Haldon 2011, pp. 475–82, and Wickham 2005, pp. 64–5.
[20] *LP* I, Life 1, c. 5, p. 118.   [21] Moreau 2015.   [22] *LP* I, Life 57, cc. 3 and 4, p. 281.

Vigilius was arrested as he distributed the gifts to the people, and they took him down to the Tiber and put him on a ship. The *plebs* and the populace followed him, shouting to have a prayer from him. When he had given them a prayer the whole people replied 'Amen' and the ship cast off. When the Roman people saw the ship in which Vigilius was sitting on the move they started to throw stones, branches and cooking pots after him and to say 'Take your famine with you! Take your deaths with you! You treated the Romans badly; may you meet evil where you are going!'[23]

Further, in an attempt to appease the populace on the election of Vigilius's successor, Pope Pelagius I (556–61) and Narses are credited with the adoption of a plan:

When the litany had been given out from St Pancras they processed with hymns and spiritual chants to St Peter's. Pelagius held the gospels and the Lord's cross above his head and went up on the ambo; in this way he satisfied the entire populace and *plebs* that he had caused Vigilius no harm.[24]

The people are even more prominent in the accounts of the political factions that sometimes formed in relation to the election of a new pope. The incident associated with Pope Boniface II and his rival Dioscorus has already been mentioned, but the most famous disputed elections are those of Pope Boniface I (418–22) vs Eulalius, Pope Symmachus (498–514) vs Laurentius, Pope Conon (686–7) vs Theodore, and Pope Sergius I (687–701) vs the Archpriest Theodore making a second bid, as well as the Archdeacon Paschal. In Boniface I's case, with Eulalius installed in the Constantinian basilica and Boniface I outside the walls

---

[23] *LP* I, Life 61, c. 4, p. 297; trans. Davis, *Pontiffs*, p. 56: *Et munera eum erogantem ad populum, tentus est et deposuerunt eum ad Tiberim; miserunt eum in navem. Plebs et populus sequebatur eum, adclamantes ut orationem ab eo acciperent. Data oratione respondit omnis populus: 'Amen'; et mota est navis. Videntes Romani quod movisset navis in qua sedebat Vigilius, tunc coepit populus iactare post eum lapides, fustes, caccabos, et dicere: 'Famis tua tecum! Mortalitas tua tecum! Male fecisti Romanis, male invenias ubi vadis!'*

[24] *LP* I, Life 62, c. 2, p. 303; trans. Davis, *Pontiffs*, p. 58: *data laetania ad sanctum Pancratium, cum hymnis et canticis spiritalibus venerunt ad sanctum Petrum apostolum. Qui Pelagius tenens evangelia et crucem Domini super caput suum in ambone ascendit et sic satisfecit cuncto populo et plebi quia nullum malum peregisset contra Vigilium.*

in the basilica of St Agnes, the *Liber pontificalis* reports that the Western emperors Valentinian III and Honorius intervened to appoint Boniface as bishop. Nevertheless, when Boniface died it was the clergy and people who asked for the recall of Eulalius. The *Liber pontificalis* claims that Eulalius himself refused to return.[25]

In the other disputes, the clergy and people are cited, in different factions, as determining the outcome. In the case of the 'Laurentian schism' clergy and senate were divided, and when King Theodoric suggested that the winning candidate should be whoever had been ordained first and whose faction was the largest, Symmachus was duly installed. His position was subsequently challenged. Acquitted of various charges by a synod, Symmachus 'was gloriously reinstated to sit in St Peter's as prelate of the apostolic see by all the bishops, priests and deacons, the whole clergy and the people'.[26] The refusal of Laurentius's faction to accept this outcome caused much bloodshed within the city. Similarly, in the case of Conon, the army, clergy, and people were all cited as involved. The contest had originally been between the Archpriest Peter (the clergy's candidate) and Theodore, supported by the army. Negotiators for each side 'came and went for a long time' (*irent diutius et redirent*). The *sacerdotes* and the *clerus* then produced a new candidate, Conon, and in due course the *iudices* and the leaders of the army recognized him, and the rest of the army followed suit once they had seen the unanimity of *clerus* and *populus*.[27]

The disputed election of Pope Sergius I (687–701) apparently produced a similar array of antagonists. The *Liber pontificalis* reports that 'as usually happens, the Roman people divided into two factions' (*ut fieri solet, populus Romane urbis in duas partes divisus est*). These comprised the judges, the Roman soldiers (*inito consilio primati iudicum exercitus Romane militiae*), many of the clergy and *sacerdotes* and a crowd of citizens (*civium multitudo*).[28] The narrative accorded a role to the Exarch of Ravenna, who also attempted to influence the election by supporting the

---

[25] *LP* I, Life 44, c. 4, p. 227.

[26] *LP* I, Life 53, c. 4, p. 260; trans. Davis, *Pontiffs*, p. 43: *Tunc ab omnibus episcopis et presbiteris et diaconibus et omni clero vel plebe reintegratur sedis apostolicae beatus Symmachus cum gloria apud beatum Petrum sedere praesul.*

[27] *LP* I, Life 85, c. 2, p. 368.   [28] *LP* I, Life 86, c. 2, p. 371.

candidacy of Paschal the Archdeacon. In a further disruption of the city's affairs the army, including the Ravennate soldiers, and people are represented as supporting Sergius's resistance to the emperor's attempt to force Pope Sergius to sign synodal definitions of the Christian faith formulated in Constantinople. According to the *Liber pontificalis*, the chief *spatharius* Zacharias was sent to arrest Sergius but was terrified into taking refuge from the mob (*turba militiae*) by hiding under the pope's bed. The Life of Sergius concludes this episode by stating that 'the pope received the common soldiers and the people who had come to see him ... they did not give up picketing the patriarchate until they had expelled the *spatharius* out of Rome with injuries and insults'.[29]

Very occasionally the city and the people were under siege. The fullest narrative, comprising one of two exceptionally full descriptions of warfare, is at the beginning of the Gothic wars in the Life of Silverius (ordained June 536, deposed March 537). It is so different from the style of the narrative up to this point as to indicate not only a new author,[30] but also possible quotation from an existing Latin narrative.

> **c. 4** Belisarius surrounded and fortified the city [Rome] with garrisons and defences, by work on the walls and repair of the earthworks.
>
> **c. 5** During those days the city was under such a siege as totally to prevent anyone leaving or entering it. All private, state and church property was destroyed by fire, while men were put down by the sword. The sword killed those it killed, famine killed those it killed, pestilence killed those it killed. Even churches and bodies of the holy martyrs were destroyed by the Goths. So great was the hunger within the city that even water would have had to be paid for had not springs provided relief ... [Belisarius] gave protection to the Romans and delivered the city and the name of Rome through his garrison.[31]

---

[29] *LP* I, Life 86, c. 9, p. 374; trans. Davis, *Pontiffs*, p. 83: *egressus vero idem beatissimus pontifex foris basilicam ... generalitatem militiae et populi qui pro eo occurrerant honorifice suscepit ... iam a patriarchii custodia non recesserunt quousque denominatum spatharium cum iniuriis et contumelis a civitate romana foris depellerunt.*

[30] See above, p. 12.

[31] *LP* I, Life 60, cc. 4 and 5, pp. 290–1, trans. Davis, *Pontiffs*, p. 53: c. 4 *Custodiis et monitionibus vel fabricis murorum aut reparationem fossati circumdedit civitatem Romanam et munivit ... c. 5 His diebus obsessa est civitas ut nulli esset facultas exeundi vel introeundi. Tunc omnes possessiones*

Although the *Liber pontificalis* praises the Byzantine general Belisarius at this point, the Gothic king Totila is praised in his turn in the Life of Vigilius (537–55) when, after he had entered Rome by St Paul's Gate, 'To prevent the Romans dying by the sword he had a war-trumpet sounded all night until the whole people fled or hid themselves in the churches. The king stayed with the Romans like a father with his children.'[32]

At many points in the *Liber pontificalis* the contemporary citizens or *populus* are portrayed as recipients of preaching, alms, or food rations.[33] Thus, in the life of Gelasius I (492–6) the bishop delivered the city of Rome from danger of famine and was 'a lover of the poor' (*hic fuit amator pauperum*).[34] When there was a risk of famine, Boniface II (530–2) came to the clergy's assistance with much giving of alms.[35] In the time of Benedict I (575–9), Rome was the recipient of foreign aid when the Lombards were invading Italy, for the *Liber pontificalis* reports that the Emperor Justin II had ships sent from Egypt to relieve Rome with ships laden with corn.[36]

The pope is portrayed as responsible for relieving the people of their afflictions, though not always as generously as might have been assumed; or else only the disasters are mentioned and not any relief. Thus, in the Life of Pope Sabinian (604–6), peace was made with the Lombard people, but there was serious famine in Rome. Sabinian ordered the church's granaries to be opened and corn put on sale at a *solidus* for thirty *modii* of wheat. Resentment at this ostensible lack of generosity has sometimes been invoked to account for the circuitous route of Sabinian's funeral procession reported by his biographer.[37] This is on the

---

privatas vel fisci vel ecclesiae incendio consumptas sunt; homines vero gladio interempti sunt: quos gladius gladius, quos famis famis, quos morbus morbus interficiebat. Nam et ecclesias et corpora martyrum sanctorum exterminatae sunt a Gothis. Intra civitatem autem grandis famis ut aqua venundaretur pretio, nisi nympharum remedius subvenisset ... [Vilisarius] protexit Romanos vel civitatem custodia sua liberavit et nomen Romanum.

[32] *LP* I, Life 61, c. 7, p. 298; trans. Davis, *Pontiffs*, p. 57: *Tota enim nocte fecit bucina tangi usque dum cunctus populus fugeret aut per ecclesias se celarent, ne gladio Romani vitam finirent. Habitavit rex cum Romanis quasi pater cum filiis.* Compare Procopius, *Wars* IV.22, and the implicit comparisons between Totila's speech and Pericles's last speech from Thucydides: see Pazdernik 2015.

[33] Neil 2011.   [34] *LP* I, Life 51, c. 2, p. 255.   [35] *LP* I, Life 57, c. 3, p. 281.

[36] *LP* I, Life 64, c. 1, p. 308.   [37] *LP* I, Life 67, c. 1, p. 315.

assumption that what Sabinian was selling was grain normally distributed free to the poor. Duchesne cited Gregory of Tours's observation that the church warehouses in Rome (*horrea ecclesiae Romane*) stored grain for distribution to the poor. It is not clear to whom Sabinian had offered the grain at this price, nor whether a *solidus* for thirty *modii* was cheap or exorbitant. Too little is known about both prices and weights in the early seventh century. The Anonymus Valesianus commented, for example, that in the time of Theodoric the Great one *solidus* could buy sixty *modii* of grain and thirty amphorae of wine. This may not be any guide at all to the prices in Rome seventy years later, but merits a little more consideration. The *modius* as a unit of measurement is also problematic, but one suggestion from Byzantine comparisons is that it was equivalent to 12.8 kilos. Prices similarly in Byzantine sources offer fifteen *modii* of wheat for one *nomisma* in the late sixth century. A *nomisma* can be equated with a *solidus* and this gold currency remained remarkably stable between the fourth and the eleventh centuries. Apart from the *Liber pontificalis* and Anonymus Valesianus, the comparisons are mostly with prices from Egypt, where they are generally much higher, and not all of them are famine or crisis prices. Even regular prices would have been subject to seasonal and local variation. It is possible, therefore, that the stored grain may have been offered cheaply rather than exorbitantly in Rome, perhaps to people other than the poor. The unusual route for Sabinian's funeral procession remains a puzzle but, with the comment about the granaries, the *Liber pontificalis* author may have been making a point about the pope's practical use of a resource to help the people of the city.[38]

During the reign of Pope Boniface IV (608–15) there were plagues, floods, and a very serious famine, and under Pope Deusdedit (615–18) in August 618 there was a major earthquake 'and afterwards ensued a disaster for the people, affliction with the scab, so no one could recog-

---

[38] Duchesne, *LP* I, p. 315, note 3. See *Anonymus Valesianus pars posterior,* 73, ed. and trans. Rolfe, pp. 554–5, Ashtor 1984, and Morisson and Cheynet 2002, pp. 817 and 822. I am grateful to Chris Wickham for discussion of the economic context and Rory Naismith for his guidance on the prices and currency values.

nize his deceased'.[39] Under Pope Agatho (678–81) there was such great mortality in Rome and its environs that the *Liber pontificalis* claimed that it was much greater than anyone could remember occurring under any other pope, and added that it was so serious that 'parents and their children, brothers and their sisters, were taken in pairs in biers to their graves'.[40] In Pope Constantine I's time (708–15) there was a three-year famine in Rome but thereafter great plenty.

More regular provision of food was also made. Pope Eugenius I (654–7) is reported as giving the customary stipend to the clergy and supplying alms to the needy so that he ordered the full priestly allowances to be distributed to the poor, the clergy, and the household even on the day he died.[41] Pope Sisinnius (Jan.–Feb. 708) 'had a resolute mind and was concerned for the inhabitants of this city', even if the text does not tell us how this concern manifested itself.[42] The author may simply have offered what he perceived as a general virtue as something to augment the entry for such a brief reign. Of Pope Zacharias (741–52), on the other hand, it is noted that

> this blessed pope laid down that on frequent days the victuals and provisions which are even now called *eleemosyna* should be taken from the venerable patriarchate by the cellarers and dispensed to the poor and pilgrims who doss at St Peter, and he decreed that this *eleemosyna* of provisions should likewise be distributed to all the destitute and the sick living in this city of Rome's region.[43]

---

[39] *LP* I, Life 69, c. 1, and Life 70, c. 3, pp. 317 and 319, trans. Davis, *Pontiffs*, p. 61: *Post haec secuta est clades in populo, percussio scabearum, ut nullus poterat mortuum suum cognoscere.*

[40] *LP* I, Life 81, c. 16, p. 350, trans. Davis, *Pontiffs*, p. 72: *ut etiam parentes cum filiis atque fratres seu sorores binati per lecta ad sepulchra deducerentur.*

[41] *LP* I, Life 77, c. 1, p. 341.

[42] *LP* I, Life 89, c. 1, p. 388; trans. Davis, *Pontiffs*, p. 87: *Erat tamen constans animo et curam agens pro habitatoribus huius civitatis.*

[43] *LP* I, Life 93, c. 27, p. 435; trans. Davis, *Eighth-Century Popes*, p. 49: *Hic beatissimus papa statuit et crebris diebus alimentorum sumptus quae et elymosina usque nunc appellatur, de venerabili patriarchio a paracellariis pauperibus et peregrinis qui ad beatum Petrum demorantur deportari eisque erogari, necnon et omnibus inopibus et infirmis per universas regiones istius Romane urbis constitutis eandem similiter distribui ipsam alimentorum constituit elimosynam.*

A variant of such alms is the redemption of captives: Pope Symmachus (498–514) is said to have ransomed prisoners in the north of Italy and supported exiled bishops from Africa and Sardinia with both money and clothing.[44] Pope John IV (640–2) was praised for having sent an Abbot Martin to John's native country Dalmatia in order to redeem captives.[45]

Divine intervention could be called to assist the Romans in bad weather. During the prolonged rain and thunder in the reign of Pope Adeodatus (672–6), for example, 'it was only because the Lord was placated by the Litanies which took place every day that men were able to thresh the grain and store it in granaries'.[46] Similarly, both the earlier and later versions of the Life of Pope Gregory II (715–31) report that there was a major flood of the Tiber, described at unusual length and in precise terms; prayers and litanies were offered for seven days, after which the floods subsided.[47]

Very occasionally there is an indication of works being carried out for the benefit of the people. Pope Symmachus (498–514), for example, is credited with setting up another fountain outside in the open at St Peter's and St Paul's. He is also described as providing accommodation for the poor at St Peter's, St Paul's, and St Laurence's.[48] According to an early eleventh-century insertion made in the Life of Pope Honorius (625–38) in manuscripts associated with Ademar of Chabannes, the pope built a water mill and made other repairs to conduits for the water supply in Rome 'at the place of Trajan close to the city wall' (*in murum in loco traiani*).[49] In a Frankish addition to the later version of the Life of Pope Gregory II, the pope is said to have ordered the burning of lime to restore the city's walls at the gate near San Lorenzo fuori le mura. Burning lime to repair the walls was also the one thing the *Liber*

---

[44] *LP* I, Life 53, c. 11, p. 263.

[45] *LP* I, Life 74, c. 1, p. 330. On captives see Serfass 2006, pp. 86–8, and Rio 2017, pp. 19–41.

[46] *LP* I, Life 79, c. 5, pp. 346–7; trans. Davis, *Pontiffs*, p. 71: *Post cuius transitum tantae pluviae et tonitrua fuerunt quales nulla aetas hominum memoratur, ut etiam homines et peculia de fulgore interirent.*

[47] *LP* I, Life 91, c. 6, p. 399.   [48] *LP* I, Life 53, cc. 7, 8, and 11, pp. 262–3.

[49] *LP* I, Life 72, c. 5, p. 324 in Paris, BnF lat. 2268 and 2400. See Coates-Stephens 2003a and 2003b, and Francesco 2017.

pontificalis was able to suggest for the activities of Pope Sisinnius during his twenty-day reign in 708.[50]

Most of the *Liber Pontificalis's* comments about the liturgy concern clerical dress, particular prayers, or ritual performance, as we shall see in Chapter 5, but very occasionally there is a glimmer of the processional impact of the liturgy within the city and how much the lay citizens may have been involved. Pope Honorius (625–38), for example, is said to have introduced a Saturday litany with hymns and chants in which the whole people were to join (*populus omnis occurri debeat*) in procession from St Apollinaris to St Peter's.[51] It is obvious that such papal liturgical display in procession would have taken the place of imperial processions, and no doubt intentionally so.[52] The presence of the people at the liturgy was also perceived and presented by the authors of the *Liber pontificalis* as one of the oldest of papal traditions, for it is to Pope Zephyrinus (198/9–217) that the requirement that the ordination of a cleric, deacon, or *sacerdos* should take place in the presence of all the clerics and the faithful laity is attributed and, in a rather more obscure phrase, that after the celebration of Mass 'a consecrated ring should be given to the people'.[53] Pope Miltiades (310–14) decided that the faithful should not fast on a Thursday or Sunday, because those were the days on which pagans fasted.[54] Pope Sergius I (687–701) is just one of a long line of popes who is celebrated for his contributions to the participation of the people in the liturgy within the churches of Rome.[55] Thus Sergius 'determined that both the clergy and people should sing' his new addition of the *Agnus Dei* to the Mass and envisaged the people joining the processions for all the Marian feasts, starting out from Sant'Adriano in the Forum and finishing in Santa Maria Maggiore. When Sergius found a piece of the Cross in a dark corner of St Peter's basilica, moreover, 'from

---

[50] *LP* I, Life 91, c. 2 and Life 89, c. 1, pp. 396 and 388, and see Meneghini and Santangeli Valenzani 2004, pp. 54–69 at p. 54 and compare pp. 133–42.

[51] *LP* I, Life 72, c. 4, p. 323.

[52] See Liverani 2013 and Humphries 2007. John Romano also stresses this point on the basis of the evidence in *Ordo Romanus* I in Romano 2014.

[53] *LP* I, Life 16, c. 2, p. 139 and see Duchesne's note 2, ibid., pp. 139–40.

[54] *LP* I, Life 33, c. 2, p. 168.   [55] See McKitterick 2017.

that day ... this is kissed and worshipped by all Christian people on the day of the Exaltation of the Holy Cross'.[56]

All these topics in the narrative serve to affirm the role allotted to the people of Rome, of all ranks, as active and essential protagonists. They endured suffering in the face of the elements or warfare, enthusiastically supported or contested particular popes, candidates for, or indeed pretenders to the papal throne, vociferously denounced malpractice, formed liturgical congregations, received papal munificence and charity, benefitted from administrative and pastoral organization, emulated the bishop in the endowment and ornamenting of church buildings, manifested devotion to the saints and martyrs of Rome, and affirmed orthodoxy. The people of Rome as a Christian community are a constant presence in the text, are motivators of political action, and provide an essential complement to the biographies of the bishops. The very vocabulary used to refer to the people is an element in the construction of the city's identity. This citizenry, therefore, was also implicated in the distinctive transformation of the identity of the city.

The City of Rome

The city of Rome itself is portrayed in many different ways in the text. Although remarkably few of the distinguished visitors who came to Rome are noted by the *Liber pontificalis* authors, they begin to appear more often in the seventh-century sections, as if to emphasize the distinctiveness of the Bishop of the See of St Peter being visited by his secular peers. Thus, in the Life of Deusdedit (615–18) the patrician Eleutherius came to Rome and was received by the pope, and during the reign of Pope Theodore (642–9), Pyrrhus, the former Patriarch of Constantinople, arrived in Rome. He presented a signed declaration (*libellus cum sua subscriptione*) of his previous errors against the orthodox faith in the presence of the whole clergy and people (*in praesentia cuncto clero et populo*).

---

[56] *LP* I, Life 86, c. 10, p. 374; trans. Davis, *Pontiffs*, p. 83: *ex die illo pro salute humani generis ab omni populo christiano, die exaltationis sanctae crucis in basilicam salvatoris quae appellatur Constantiniana osculatur ac adoratur;* also Life 86, c. 14, *LP* I, p. 376. On the *Agnus Dei* see also below, pp. 138–9.

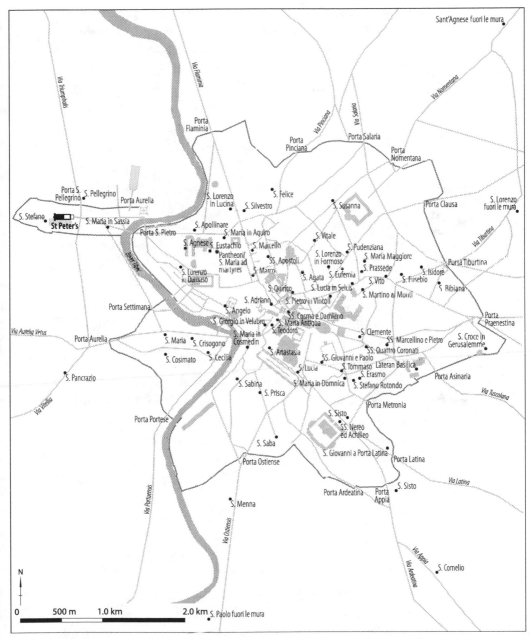

Map 1 Rome in the early middle ages

Theodore made him distribute gifts to the people (*fecit eum munera erogare in populo*).[57] The most infamous visit is that of the Emperor Constans recorded in the Life of Pope Vitalian (657–72), which relates the formal reception of the emperor and his military entourage by the pope at the sixth mile from Rome, all of whom then visited the basilicas of St Peter, San Paolo fuori le mura and Santa Maria Maggiore. The emperor bathed, and dined with the pope at the Lateran palace on the first Saturday of his visit; on the following Sunday he attended the stational Mass at St Peter's. As portrayed in the *Liber pontificalis* it was a remarkable abuse of the hospitality he had received, as well as what can only have been a considerable deployment of his soldiers, that the emperor then apparently spent twelve days pillaging Rome of the public sculptural decor of the city; he even contrived the extraordinary feat of engineering to have the bronze tiles removed from the roof of Santa Maria ad martyres, the former Pantheon, and sent to his imperial city 'with various other things he had dismantled' (*cum alia diversa quae deposuerat*) before proceeding to Sicily where 'he imposed many afflictions on the people'. Arabic sources record, however, that the Roman loot actually remained in port at Syracuse and was later captured by Arabs and dispersed to Alexandria, Damascus, Basra, and India. Such an unsympathetic account may well distort an emperor's exactions. Interpreting this resentment, however, depends on the degree to which the emperor still actually had any right in the late seventh century to make such exactions. The incident may be a hint either that direct intervention was no longer perceived in Rome as appropriate, or that this manifestation of it was extreme.[58]

The most dramatic interventions by the popes in the city, however, are the structural and material changes they wrought. Firstly, the popes effected a major transformation of the city by dividing it into seven new regions. The *Liber pontificalis* credits Popes Clement (*c.*95), Fabian (236–50), and Gaius (282–95) with the creation of these seven diaconal, that is, ecclesiastical, regions. Fabian, for example, is described as having 'divided the regions among the deacons and created seven subdeacons

---

[57] *LP* I, Lives 70, c. 1 and 75, c. 3, pp. 319 and 332.
[58] *LP* I, Life 78, cc. 2–3, p. 343; see Coates-Stephens 2017.

who were to watch over the seven notaries so that they would faithfully collect the complete acts of the martyrs'.[59] This papal redivision could be taken as a deliberate readjustment of the fourteen Augustan regions of Rome created in 7 BC.[60] The regions were subsequently subdivided into twenty-five *tituli,* that is, with churches regarded as the property of the Roman church that were endowed with liturgical equipment and sufficient revenue to maintain a building, celebrate the liturgy, and support clergy.[61] Evaristus and Marcellus are credited with the organization of the *tituli* churches within Rome; recent scholarship has confirmed the involvement of the bishop in the endowment of the *tituli.*[62]

A second major intervention in the topography attributed to the popes was the provision of cemeteries in close proximity to the major roads out of the city.[63] Such provision had previously been a civic responsibility. Pope Fabian (236–50), for example, also ordered many works to be carried out in the cemeteries and Pope Marcellus (305/6, exiled 306/7) built the cemetery on the Via Salaria.[64]

Thirdly, the most visible and dramatic alteration to Rome's sacred topography and skyline was of course the construction of the Christian basilicas. After the conversion of Constantine and from Life 34 of Silvester onwards, the scattering of earlier references to Christian cemeteries in the *Liber pontificalis* was augmented by a steady catalogue of major basilicas within Rome, many credited to Constantine himself. The narrative charts how the imperial city gradually became a holy city of Christian basilicas and saints' and martyrs' shrines, the residence of the pope, an international city of pilgrims, artists, and craftsmen, and a major focus of secular and religious politics. I shall discuss the implications of this astonishing building programme more fully in a subsequent chapter, but here I wish to emphasize that allusion is made to these Christian

---

[59] *LP* I, Life 21, c. 2, p. 148; trans. Davis, *Pontiffs,* p. 8: *Hic regiones dividit diaconibus et fecit VII subdiaconos qui VII notariis inminerent, ut gestas martyrum in integro fideliter colligerent.*

[60] See Neil 2012.   [61] Guidobaldi 2000 and Map on p. 126.

[62] *LP* I, Lives 6, c. 2 and 31, c. 2, pp. 126 and 164. See Hillner 2007 and 2006 adjusting Pietri 1976, pp. 95–6. See also Thompson 2015b.

[63] See Rebillard 1994/2009; Costambeys 2001 and 2002. On one instance of a 'private' cemetery see Tronzo 1986.

[64] *LP* I, Life 26, c. 2 and Life 31, c. 2, pp. 157 and 164.

basilicas with the clear assumption that the sixth-century readers have already accommodated them and are familiar with these landmarks in their minds' eyes.

For the most part, indeed, the directives to readers and visitors for orientation in terms of landmarks are largely in terms of cemeteries or existing basilicas, in proximity to the major roads into the city, notably (clockwise from the north): Via Flaminia, Via Salaria, Via Nomentana, Via Tiburtina, Via Praenestina/Via Labicana, Via Latina, Via Appia, Via Ardeatina, Via Ostiensis/ Laurentiana, Via Portuensis, and Via Aurelia, and the road within the city Via Lata (now the Corso), or prominent Roman monuments.[65] In the lives of the fourth-century popes Silvester, Mark, Julius, Liberius, Felix II, Damasus and Anastasius, Christian churches and cemeteries are logged in relation to secular city landmarks. St Peter's basilica is stated as being located at the Temple of Apollo, Santa Croce 'in Jerusalem' is in the Sessorian Palace, the basilica of Santi Marcellino e Pietro is on 'the land between the two laurels', the mausoleum for Helena is on the Via Labicana at the third mile. Silvester (314–35) himself contributes the *titulus* of Equitius 'close to Domitian's baths', that is, San Martino ai Monti, and endowed it with, among other things, property within the city, namely a house with a bath in the region of Sicininum, a garden in the region *Ad Duo Amantes*, and a house in the region Orpheus. At Pope Mark's petition (*c.*336), Constantine presented a cemetery on the Via Ardeatina. He himself built a basilica on the Via Ardeatina and another 'in Rome close to the Pallacinae'. Pope Julius (337–52) 'built two basilicas, one in Rome close to the Forum, the other across the Tiber, and three cemeteries': on Via Flaminia, Via Aurelia, and Via Portuensis. Liberius (352–66) lived at the cemetery of St Agnes with Constantine's sister. Pope Liberius built the basilica which bears his name close to the Market of Livia; Pope Felix II (355–65), who had been ordained to serve as Bishop of Rome while Liberius was in exile, lived on his small estate on the Via Portuensis, but built a basilica on the Via Aurelia; he was beheaded close to the city walls alongside the Aqueduct of Trajan. Pope Damasus (366–84) built two basilicas, one to St Laurence close to the Theatre and the other on the Via Ardeatina. Anastasius built

---

[65] I draw in this paragraph on McKitterick 2015.

a basilica called Crescentiana in the 2nd region of Rome on the Via Mamurtini.

Later Lives, both in the first portion of the text up to the sixth century and in its seventh- and eighth-century continuations, offer a similar set of topographical indicators. In the time of Pope Leo I (440–61) 'God's handmaid' Demetrias built a basilica to St Stephen on her estate at the third mile of the Via Latina; Pope Leo built a basilica to the bishop and martyr Cornelius near the cemetery of Callistus on the Via Appia. Pope Simplicius (468–83) dedicated the basilica of St Stephen (San Stefano Rotondo) on the Caelian Hill in Rome, another basilica of St Andrew close to the basilica of St Mary, another basilica of St Stephen close to the basilica of St Laurence and, close to the Licinian Palace, a basilica of Santa Bibiana. Pope Felix IV (526–30) built the basilica of Cosmas and Damian in Rome in the area called the Via Sacra, close to the Temple of the City of Rome. Pope John I (523–6) rebuilt cemeteries on the Via Ardeatina and Via Salaria. Pope Gelasius (492–6) dedicated basilicas on the Via Labicana at the Villa Pertusa and built a basilica of St Mary on the Via Laurentina on the farm Crispinus.

One mark of the attempt to create threads of narrative continuity is that this process of topographical Christianization in association with Roman landmarks is maintained by the later continuators. It is said of Pope Gregory I (590–601), for example, that he dedicated the church of the Goths in the Subura in the name of St Agatha the Martyr.[66] The funeral procession of Pope Sabinian (604–6) was taken out by St John's Gate and conducted outside the walls via the Milvian Bridge before his body was interred in St Peter's basilica.[67] Boniface IV (608–15) asked the Emperor Phocas 'for the temple called the Pantheon and in it he made the church of the ever virgin Mary and all martyrs'.[68] Pope Honorius (625–38) built the church of Hadrian 'at the Three Fates' (*in Tribus Fatis*, that is, in the Forum);[69] Pope Adeodatus (672–6) dedicated the church

---

[66] *LP* I, Life 66, c. 5, p. 312.

[67] *LP* I, Life 67, c. 2, p. 315. On this incident see the comment above, pp. 49–50.

[68] *LP* I, Life 69, c. 2, p. 317, *petiit a Focate principe templum qui appellatur Pantheum in quo fecit ecclesiam beatae Mariae semper virginis et omnium martyrum*. See McKitterick 2016a, pp. 254–5 and further below, p. 130.

[69] *LP* I, Life 72, c. 6, p. 324, and p. 326, note 18; see Bordi 2011.

of St Peter on the Via Portuensis close to the Pons Meruli, and enlarged the monastery of Erasmus on the Caelian Hill.[70]

This juxtaposition of pre-Christian imperial monuments and Christian churches is also the guiding principle of a pilgrim guide to Rome from the late eighth or early ninth century known as the Einsiedeln Itinerary. This guide set out twelve walks for pilgrims, noting the pagan and Christian monuments as well as topographical landmarks on the way.[71] This is in contrast to the routes offered in the seventh- or eighth-century *Notitia ecclesiarum urbis Romae* and *De locis martyrum quae sunt foris civitatis Romae* preserved in Vienna, ÖNB 795, which are simply arranged to take the pilgrim to the city and suburban martyrs' shrines clockwise and anticlockwise according to the principal roads out of the city.[72]

Some of the Christian basilicas erected from the time of Pope Callistus onwards and in great abundance in Pope Silvester's reign and thereafter are recorded as paid for by emperors or other lay patrons. Increasingly, however, they were credited to the pope, creating the illusion of a papal monopoly of church building in the city. Within the narrative, these buildings provide a new topography within which the reader of the *Liber pontificalis* can locate the events described. The *Liber pontificalis* maps how the geography of the city, its religious ritual, and its rulers are all connected with the cyclical and public religious observance of the citizens. Thus, the *Liber pontificalis* created a virtual Rome for its readers. It was a Christian city, but the narrative skilfully grafts its new rulers, the bishops, onto the foundations of the ancient city.

'Textualizing' the City of Rome through Narrative

What then are the implications of all this? It is self-evident that memory and the markers of identity in the past are embodied in texts and objects, but such texts and objects are far from passive. They may themselves have been created in order actively to articulate as well as to form identity and shape memory. More than a decade ago, Greg Woolf insisted on our imagining the sheer amazement of visitors in the ancient world on seeing

---

[70] *LP* I, Life 79, c. 2, p. 346.   [71] Walser 1987. See also McKitterick 2006, pp. 43–4.
[72] *Itineraria*, ed. Valentini and Zucchetti, pp. 303–22.

Rome, and reminded us that most readers, even of Strabo's famous description mentioned above, would not actually have seen the city, but only have read about it. Greg Woolf went on to talk about the rewriting of the city in Latin texts from the first to third centuries AD and what he refers to as the 'representation of Rome as a *cultural capital* to the readers of Latin literature'. These readers were not necessarily provincials or even far from Rome, but an audience targeted with a representation of the city of Rome as a literary capital and cultural centre. Woolf suggested that readers were inculcated with a sense of 'cultural alienation' by means of an 'assault course' of literary allusion and esotericism.[73] There were also alternative representations, characterized by Woolf as a debate about the nature of aristocratic virtue within the context of 'un-literary' Rome. To this notion of cultural capital can of course be added Rome's historical status as political centre and as religious capital. The latter is summarized by the speech Livy puts in the mouth of the general Camillus:

> We have a city founded by auspices and augury; there is not a corner of it that is not full of our cults and our gods; our regular rituals have not only their appointed places, but also their appointed times.[74]

Greg Woolf's work exposes the apparent gulf between the self-defined cultural elite of pre-Constantinian Rome and the Rome represented in the *Liber pontificalis*. Yet readers of the *Liber pontificalis* in the sixth century were themselves conditioned by their reading of Rome in the Latin literature of the early period that they would have encountered in the course of their schooling.[75] The *Liber pontificalis* therefore arguably added an extra layer to the imaginative understanding of the city; it did not provide a substitute, but augmented Rome's past and enhanced its religious significance. Even a textual transformation of the city does not mean underlying characteristics of the city as symbol and elements of

---

[73] Woolf 2003.

[74] Livy, *Ab urbe condita* V.52.2, in Foster (ed. and trans.), pp. 174 and 175: *Urbem auspicato inauguratoque conditam habemus; nullus locus in ea non religionum deorumque est plenus; sacrificiis sollemnibus non dies magis sati quam loca sunt, in quibus fiant.*

[75] Marrou 1948/1956, Riché 1976/1962, and Dickey 2016.

its history are abandoned; there are some constant elements in its sacred past, not least religion.

A further strand in scholarship, adapting geographical ideas of space and place to the interpretation of medieval texts,[76] has suggested the notion of 'textualising territory through narrative'.[77] This means more than providing a written description of a place and extolling its buildings or commenting on the impressive statistics about the quantities of bricks, tiles, concrete, gems, textiles, and marble, or counting all the gates, towers, windows, and privies on the Aurelian Walls, however fascinating such a description as provided, for example, in the Einsiedeln manuscript, mentioned above, might be.[78]

All this is necessary background to thinking about the way the *Liber pontificalis* constructs the popes and disseminates a particular representation of their history and their role against the backdrop of the city of Rome, in which the city itself is gradually transformed. There are a number of obvious questions to consider. How might one characterize the city of Rome as it appears in this text? How is the city of Rome transformed in the text? What role does the city of Rome play in the text as a narrative strategy? The *Liber pontificalis*'s composition coincides with that of two other texts in particular.[79] At this stage we might look briefly at these texts, written more or less at the same time as the first section of the *Liber pontificalis*.

The first is from the *Gothic Wars* of Procopius, written in Constantinople in *c.*555, in Greek, and long after the events they describe, namely, Belisarius's letter to the Gothic king Totila:

> Now among all the cities under the sun Rome is agreed to be the greatest and the most noteworthy ... little by little [many companies of the best men] have built the city such as you behold it, thereby leaving to future generations memorials of the ability of them all, so that insult to these monuments would properly be considered a great crime against the men of all time; for by such action the men of former generations are robbed of

---

[76] Nicolet 1991, Gautier Dalché 1997, Lozovsky 2000, Merrills 2005, Blaudeau 2006, 2012a, and 2012b.

[77] I adapt here a phrase from Foot 2019.   [78] Walser 1987, pp. 213–17.

[79] See also above, Chapter 1, pp. 29–30.

the memorials of their ability, and future generations of the sight of their works . . .

Yet the Romans love their city above all the men we know, and they are eager to protect all their ancestral treasures and to preserve them, so that nothing of the ancient glory of Rome may be obliterated. For even though they were for a long period under barbarian sway, they preserved the buildings of the city and most of its adornments, such as could through the excellence of their workmanship withstand so long a lapse of time and such neglect. Furthermore, all such memorials of the race as were still left are preserved even to this day, and among them the ship of Aeneas, the founder of the city, an altogether incredible sight.[80]

The second text is a versified rendering in Latin of the Acts of the Apostles by another sixth-century author, Arator, who was resident in Rome and presented his poem at the church of San Pietro in Vincoli near the Forum in 544, that is, during the Gothic wars, to an audience of clergy, lay nobles, and the people of Rome, with the written version presented publicly and dedicated to Pope Vigilius.[81] According to the preface supplied by Surgentius, the *primicerius* of the notaries, as he entered the codex into the papal register of publicly read letters (preserved in a number of manuscripts of the poem), Arator first performed his poem over a period of four days (punctuated by demands for repetition) to a large crowd of noble laity and the people of Rome.

Arator had served as *comes domesticorum* under King Athalaric before entering the Roman clergy, possibly as early as 536, but only attaining the rank of subdeacon. Sotinel has commented on the similarity of an occasion celebrating the anniversary of imperial accession with the possibility that this poem was designed to mark the anniversary of Vigilius's election as pope. She herself concedes that this is rather tenuous, for Vigilius had been consecrated on 29 March 537 and the poem was delivered on 13 April.[82]

---

[80] Procopius 7.22.9–14 and 8.22.4–6, ed. and trans. Dewing, IV, Books 6.16–7.35, p. 347, and V, Book 7.36–8, p. 279. Compare Kaldellis (revised translation), pp. 424–5 and 511–12.

[81] Arator, *De actibus apostolorum*, ed. Orban, pp. 213–15; trans. Schrader, Roberts, and Makowski, pp. 21–2. See also MacKinlay 1942 and Green 2006.

[82] Sotinel 1989, but compare Hillier 1993, p. 2, note 2.

Rome in Arator's poem is still the mistress of the world but the city's power is founded now on its new twins Peter and Paul instead of Romulus and Remus. The city's physical presence reinforces the power of these two saints, but the extra elements are the church's teaching and the Christian faith. Both Procopius and Arator, therefore, give some notion of the importance of the history and power of Rome, not least as the city of Romulus, Aeneas, and the apostles Peter and Paul, and how important all this still is to the Roman citizens of their own day. The buildings in particular serve as commemorative monuments, as *lieux de mémoire* in Nora's basic sense.[83]

Arator's poem emphasizes above all how Saints Peter and Paul, the 'two lights of the world', chose Rome:

> Peter rose to be leader in the body of the church; turret crowned, she
> [Rome] surrounded her head with the regions of the world; the greatest
> things were gathered to her [Rome] so that all the [episcopal] sees might
> observe the secure heights of the mistress of the world. More justly present
> in this [place than in any other city], the preferred [city] which instructs
> the nation, Paul, chosen to be teacher for the gentiles forever, unleashes
> the power of his eloquence, and whatever he thunders there, the honour
> of the city compels the subject world to hear.[84]

These two texts by Procopius and Arator were written very close to each other in time; each was precipitated by the Gothic wars and the occupation of the city by various armies. Procopius was writing at least seven years after the events which prompted his account of the siege of Rome and the career of Totila, king of the Ostrogoths. His commentary may well be his own retrospective projection of the Romans' attachment to the physical city, its monuments and buildings, and how the city still in his own memory represented evidence of how the Romans had clung to their identity, embodied in these very buildings, despite all the

---

[83] Nora 1984–92.

[84] Arator, *De actibus apostolorum*, ed. Orban, p. 400: *Petrus in ecclesiae surrexit corpore princeps;/ haec turrita caput mundi circumtulit oris;/ conveniunt maiora sibi, speculentur ut omnes/ terrarum dominae fundata cacumina sedes./ Gentibus electus Paulus sine fine magister,/ Aequius huic praesens oris diffundit habenas// Quae gentes praelata monet; quodque intonat istic/ Urbis cogit honor, subiectus ut audiat orbis;* trans. Schrader, Roberts, and Makowski, p. 93.

vicissitudes of history. His attitude to the importance of place was no doubt shaped in part by the knowledge of ancient Greek texts that had formed part of his education, but there is a sense of the very particular importance of Rome nevertheless. Both texts imply how important the special status of Rome, its pagan past, and its Christian present appear to have been to the Roman people's sense of identity as citizens. Here there appears to be an indication of civic identity, and especially the civic sense of ownership and investment in very particular structures and sources of inspiration. Procopius's text claims to speak on behalf of Romans; Arator's was recited publicly before the Roman people in the church of San Pietro in Vincoli. Its reception was reputedly so enthusiastic that one has to assume it struck a chord in the hearts of his hearers and was not just a didactic volley of opinion. As a statement just before the Byzantine army disrupted the peace achieved after 540, it may have served as an affirmation of a reinforced sense of Rome's status.

Conclusion

This deployment of the topography of Rome to express the city's historical identity is not, as we have seen, unique to Procopius or Arator; nor was it new. From the end of the fourth century we also find it in Jerome's Latin translation of Eusebius's original Greek *Chronicon*, which presents itself predominantly as a history of Rome. From the birth of Christ onwards it is an account of the Christianization of Rome and of the Roman Empire, to the extent that the conjoining of Roman and Christian identity and the insertion of the notices of the papal reigns are striking features of the text.[85] Further, the *Liber pontificalis*, the papal history first produced in the middle of the sixth century and extended in seventh, eighth, and ninth century continuations, cumulatively records the topographical transformation of Rome into a Christian city. The text articulated or helped to shape perceptions of a specifically Roman and Christian identity, the investment of its citizens in the Christian church, the Romanness of its bishop, and the Christianization of the past of Roman families by identifying so many of them as saints and martyrs.

---

[85] Eusebius–Jerome, *Chronicon*, ed. Helm and ed. Jeanjean and Lançon.

Roman identity in the early middle ages was transformed into a composite identity in which religious, civic, and historical elements were equally important.[86]

Texts such as Procopius, Arator, and Eusebius–Jerome can be interpreted as communicating particular representations of Rome that accommodated change over a millennium and a half of the city's history. The *Liber pontificalis*'s record of the transformation of Rome's topography, moreover, carries with it a transformation of Rome's identity. The impact of the city of Rome in the *Liber pontificalis* is not only to be measured in its ancient monuments, for the evolving sacred topography of the city is a major element of post-Constantinian Rome.[87] The *Liber pontificalis* includes statements about the function, history, and identity of Rome and its inhabitants, as well as evocations of the memory of place and emotional response.[88] As George Shuffleton has commented (though with reference to London): 'A city continuously occupied self-evidently connects the past to the present.'[89] Following this line of thinking, one way of framing any question about the role of Rome in the *Liber pontificalis* might indeed be to ask whether the *Liber pontificalis* can be said to 'textualise Rome through narrative', for it expresses a past reality to which any reader would have access by means of this text.

In addition to the wider notion of textualising space, I have suggested in this chapter the extent to which the *Liber Pontificalis* can be said to map the city space in writing and thus create a mental map, or virtual Rome, in the minds of readers. But it is not simply the virtual Rome created by late antique and early medieval itineraries, and the reality of a place made always present by its description and circumscription in a text. The *Liber pontificalis* adds the bishops and the people of Rome itself. It creates an historical context, a narrative, and an insistence on the Christian identity of the city in which the significance of its topography can be communicated and understood. To readers in a more distant time and place it matters that the city in which the popes live and work is Rome.[90] Conversely, the history of the popes is inextricably bound up with both the ancient and the Christian city and its past. The text makes the city

---

[86] McKitterick 2018d.   [87] Edwards and Woolf 2003.
[88] Edwards 1996 and Purcell 1992.   [89] Shuffleton 2019.   [90] See below, pp. 201–6.

accessible in an utterly distinctive form. The text both creates and reflects a deliberate construction of a Christian city to sit alongside the evocative representations of the city's power as a political symbol, its physical structures, religious cults, its history, and the history of the Christian institution at its heart. It is to that history, therefore, that I shall turn in my next chapter.

3

Apostolic Succession

Introduction

I HAVE SUGGESTED SO FAR THAT THE *LIBER PONTIFICALIS* offers a very particular portrait of the Bishop and people of Rome. Further, the text creates a mental map or virtual Rome in the minds of its readers, and invokes the imperial history of the city. The text thereby provides an essential framework for the history of the bishops and the formation of the Christian community in Rome.

The *Liber pontificalis* starts with a Life of St Peter, first Bishop of Rome, which is of fundamental importance in establishing the agenda and aims of the *Liber pontificalis* as a whole. As I explained in the introductory chapter, the Lives after Peter are numbered in sequence in all the earliest manuscripts. The history of Rome is presented as a continuous sequence of its bishops. Their time in office, therefore, as well as the ostensible exactitude in recording the length of the vacancy between popes, creates a new Petrine chronology of Roman time. This new chronology also reflects a particular understanding of the history of the bishops of Rome as an unbroken succession of Christian leaders from St Peter onwards. When first written, the succession record was for half a millennium, but then was extended by the continuators of the *Liber pontificalis* for a further three centuries. Many manuscripts of the *Liber pontificalis* add names to the papal list at least until the series of biographies was resumed in the twelfth century. The fourteenth-century *Gesta episcoporum* attributed to Jacques Zeno (Brussels, Bibliothèque royale MS 14814), and the fifteenth-century *Vitae pontificum* of Bartolomeo Platina in their turn drew on the original *Liber pontificalis* of the earlier

Lives and followed their format.[1] Papal historians thereafter invariably included the *Gesta pontificum* and sequential lists of the popes in their compilations.[2] All these continuators thus reinforce, in the historiographical genre and format they adopted, the potency of the apostolic succession.

The prefatory letters purporting to be from Jerome to Pope Damasus further enhance this Petrine chronology, for the history is presented as a response to a request to the pope for

> an orderly account of the history enacted in [the] see from the reign of the Apostle Peter down to [his] own time, so that in humility I may learn which of the bishops of your see deserved the crown of martyrdom and which of them is reckoned to have transgressed against the canons of the apostles.

Damasus responds that he is sending Jerome 'what I have been able to find out about its history'.[3]

These two prefatory letters are in all the earliest complete manuscripts. However improbable the connection with Damasus and Jerome claimed for the initial compilation of the *Liber pontificalis* may appear to modern readers, this is a classic way to claim authority and enhance the link with an older tradition.[4] The association is one that is familiar from the explanatory letters *Plures fuisse* and *Novum opus* exchanged between Damasus and Jerome about the latter's translation of the Bible, included in the prefatory material in many Bible and Gospel manuscripts throughout the middle ages.[5] The association with Damasus as a promoter of a history of Christian Rome may also have been given greater plausibility

---

[1] See Bauer 2006 and Märtl 2016–18.   [2] For a useful survey see Franklin 2017.

[3] *LP* I, p. 117; trans. Davis, *Pontiffs*, p. 1: *ut actus gestorum a beati Petri apostoli principatum usque ad vestra tempora, quae gesta sunt in sedem tuam, nobis per ordinam enarrare digneris; quatenus vostra humilitas sentire cognoscat, qui meruit episcoporum supradictae sedis martyrio coronari, vel qui contra canones apostolorum excessisse cognoscatur ... Tamen quod gestum est quod potuimus repperire nostrae sedis studium.*

[4] See Grafton 1990. Jerome's Latin translation and continuation of Eusebius's *Chronicon* as a resource for the authors of the *Liber pontificalis* is considered in McKitterick 2015.

[5] See for example Paris, BnF lat. 8850 fols 1r–4r and 4r–6r, accessible in digital facsimile on the Gallica website (https://gallica.bnf.fr/ark:/12148/btv1b8452550p/f21.image), and see Cain 2009, pp. 43–52.

by the visibility of his epitaphs for the martyrs in Rome itself, for Damasus was the pope who had promoted the memory of particular Roman martyrs in his campaign of inscribed epitaphs in 'memory theatres' around the city of Rome.[6] Damasus also commissioned the Vulgate Latin translation of the Bible from Jerome. Jerome himself was an historian as well as translator, exegete, and theologian.[7] The letters have the further function of underlining the effort made by the sixth-century compiler(s) to draw on a range of historical sources and earlier histories to create the new narrative, and reminding the readers thereof. A suggestion by means of these letters that the project may have been conceived during Damasus's pontificate is consistent with serial authorship and augmentation of other historical texts in late antiquity, not least Jerome's Latin version of Eusebius's *Chronicon* and Rufinus's edition of Eusebius's *Historia ecclesiastica*. As intimated in the previous chapter, moreover, the letters may also be a subtle way of affirming papal involvement in the narrative project of the *Liber pontificalis* itself.[8]

Frankish copyists of the *Liber pontificalis* made much of these prefatory letters attributed to Damasus and Jerome. The late eighth-century scribe of the St Amand copy of the *Liber pontificalis,* Leiden, VLQ 60, for example, elaborated this association with a dramatic orchestration of decorated initials, fancy capitals, and title pages over four pages at the beginning of the codex. The initial letters provided for the Life of Peter, moreover, are reminiscent of the incipit pages of many early medieval Gospel books. The prefatory letter exchange at the beginning of the *Liber pontificalis* thus effectively presents the text as a continuation of the Gospels and Acts of the Apostles, with a particular focus on Peter and his successors. Acts itself was the foundation story for the Christian movement and is generally credited to St Luke, quite apart from serving as an inspirational model for early medieval writers of historical narrative.[9]

---

[6] For a critique of the spectrum of interpretations of Damasus's work see Denzey Lewis 2018, Sághy 2000, Curran 2000, pp. 148–56, and Maskarinec 2015. For the notion of 'memory theatre' see Trout 2003 and 2015.

[7] Kelly 1975 and Kamesar 2013.   [8] See above, p. 9.

[9] See Rothschild 2004 and Parker 2013.

As I stressed in the previous chapter, the earliest section of the *Liber pontificalis* was composed in the middle of the fourth decade of the sixth century. The first section of the *Liber pontificalis* charted the transformation of a small, persecuted Christian minority in Rome into a strong institution, and drew on the combined resources of historiography, liturgy, and law to effect the transformation in the bishop's status. The text thus appears to be an opportunity seized both to offer an historical interpretation of Christian Rome and to adopt a particular political position. By emphasizing the strength of the papacy's traditions, the text provided a wider and longer context for the conditions of the 530s. The very production of the *Liber pontificalis,* quite apart from its content, belies the customary assumption challenged above, that the papacy remained politically subordinate to the Eastern Empire even while asserting its ecclesiastical primacy.[10] I have proposed that the *Liber pontificalis* can be seen as representing a deliberate emulation of the style of Roman imperial biography and a dramatic Christianization of Roman history. If also seen as a continuation of the Acts of the Apostles, with its emphasis on Christian teaching and community, the *Liber pontificalis* becomes a further episode in the foundation story of Christianity, now decisively relocated in Rome. In this respect one might also reflect on the degree to which the *Liber pontificalis* provides an epitome of the thinking about the Bishop of Rome's role up to each author's own day.

Despite the plurality of authorship over 300 years and the potential for many different perspectives, moreover, there is a notable thematic and narrative consistency in a text manifestly designed to assert the popes' upholding of Christian orthodoxy, the provision and organization of pastoral ministry, and the particularities of the pope's role in Rome and the Western church, as well as in relation to Byzantium. The *Liber pontificalis,* as I have already emphasized, is ostensibly a repository of factual information, but actually offers very particular representations of the popes and the city of Rome, and very far from disinterested

---

[10] See above, pp. 20–5. For discussion of the historical context I am grateful to colleagues involved in the Universität Frankfurt SFB 1095 Schwächerdiskurse und Ressourcenregime, led by Hartmut Leppin and Christian A. Müller, for their comments on a seminar paper in Frankfurt, 7 June 2017. See also McKitterick 2018c.

narrative strategies in its deployment of information. As well as the topographical transformation I highlighted in the previous chapter, the *Liber pontificalis* offers a history of the early Christian community in Rome as a steady organizational process in which the emergence of episcopal leadership is central. Yet I suggest too that the *Liber pontificalis* reflects, in however opaque a manner, an important indication of a very diverse community, the vulnerability of the Christians within the pre-Constantinian city of Rome, and, above all, the multilayered identity of Rome in late antiquity and the early middle ages. The specific use of, and careful selection from, its textual sources to do this are significant, as we shall see in this chapter. It is within this sixth-century ideological, historical, and textual context, therefore, that the Life of Peter in the *Liber pontificalis* and the importance of the apostolic succession need to be considered.

St Peter

To appreciate the diversity of the content of the Life of Peter it may be helpful to compare it with the formulaic structure and details of most of the papal biographies in the earliest section of the text. As I explained in the previous chapter, each Life contains at the outset standard details about the *natio* and father of the bishop concerned, his length of time in office, and information about his election. The Lives, then, contain a variable amount of information about the religious and political life of the city as well as, regularly from Life 34 of Silvester I at least, the bishop's patronage of building activity in Rome.

Let us compare in particular the lives of two third-century popes, Lucius and his successor Stephen I. In the case of Lucius, born in Rome, son of Porphyrius, who held the see 'three years, three months, and three days', the extra information supplied is that he was exiled, and entrusted the leadership of the church to Stephen before he was beheaded under the Emperor Valerian. In Stephen's case, also born in Rome, the son of Jovius, who held the see 'six years, five months, and two days', the text supplies the extra information that he was martyred, but while he was bishop issued a decree about ecclesiastical vestments. The final formulaic information provides the number of ordinations of deacons, priests, and bishops any pope performed, his death, and the length of the vacancy before the next pope took office. Thus, Lucius ordained four priests, four deacons, and 'for various places seven bishops', and was buried in the cemetery of Callistus on the Via Appia. The bishopric was then vacant for thirty-five days. Stephen ordained six priests, five deacons, and 'for various places three bishops', was also buried in the cemetery of Callistus, and the bishopric was vacant for twenty-two days before Pope Sixtus II, described as having been born in Greece and formerly a philosopher, succeeded him.

By contrast, the Life of St Peter has a strikingly full catalogue of extra information, though this has the character of a carefully judged summary rather than an assembly of mere scraps. It can be baldly presented schematically as follows:

SUMMARY OF THE LIFE OF ST PETER IN THE *LIBER PONTIFICALIS*
Name and *natio*: Peter, son of John from Bethsaida in Galilee,
Length of reign: bishop twenty-five years, two months, and three days,
Writings: wrote two Epistles and Mark's Gospel, and confirmed all four Gospels.
Co-workers: He ordained Linus and Cletus as co-bishops;
Event: he debated with Simon Magus;
Provision for succession: he consecrated Clement as his successor;
Death: he was martyred under Nero,
Burial: and buried on the Vatican hill.
Ordinations: He ordained three bishops, ten priests, and seven deacons.

It should be noted from this summary that there is no reference to St Paul in this Life of Peter, but I have discussed elsewhere the *Liber pontificalis*'s narrative strategy concerning St Paul and its interesting contrasts and subtle comparisons, omissions and understatements.[11]

I consider the topics in Peter's life now in turn.

Name and *natio* and Comparison with Jerome's *De viris illustribus*

At the beginning of the Life, Peter is described as apostle and *princeps apostolorum,* an Antiochene, the son of John, from the village of Bethsaida in the province of Galilee, the brother of Andrew. The ideological

[11] McKitterick 2013a.

implications of the designation of Peter as *princeps apostolorum* ('first' or 'prince of apostles') do not need spelling out,[12] but the *Liber pontificalis* is here repeating more or less verbatim the description of Peter from Jerome's *De viris illustribus.* Jerome's text was written *c.*392, deliberately emulating Suetonius's *De viris illustribus,* and with the aim of demonstrating the great number of excellent Christian writers who 'founded, built, and adorned the church'. Of the 135 ecclesiastical *scriptores* in Jerome's text, it is significant and fitting, in relation to the association the *Liber pontificalis* author created with Jerome, that St Peter is the first.[13] Jerome included Peter's origins and that his brother was Andrew, though Jerome had added other elements not taken over by the *Liber pontificalis* author, such as the story about Peter's crucifixion upside down. Jerome also expanded Peter's career to include his preaching to Jews in Pontus, Galicia, Cappadocia, Asia, and Bithynia before he arrived in Rome in the reign of Claudius.

The *Liber pontificalis,* however, continues with the information that Peter first occupied the episcopal *cathedra* at Antioch for seven years before arriving in Rome. Although the *Liber pontificalis* states that Peter went to Rome when Nero was Caesar, it immediately contradicts itself when it then states that he occupied the episcopal *cathedra* for twenty-five years, two months, and three days, and was bishop in the time of Tiberius, Gaius (Caligula), Claudius, and Nero. In this respect, the *Liber pontificalis* fills in the time between Peter's escape from prison as recorded in the Acts of the Apostles and his death. The *Liber pontificalis* author may have been attempting to reconcile one tradition about Peter's martyrdom under Nero with the length of reign offered in a source or sources similar to, but not the same as, the fourth-century Roman 'Chronograph of 354'; it differs slightly from the latter (twenty-five years, one month, and nine days), a source about which I shall have more to say in the following chapter.[14]

---

[12] Scholz 2006 and Borgolte 1995.

[13] Jerome, *De viris illustribus,* ed. Bernouilli, p. 6, and ed. Richardson, pp. 1–2.

[14] As guides to the vast literature on St Peter see Vinzent 2014, Eastman 2015, and Demacopoulos 2013.

Texts by Peter

Peter's writings are described next. Peter is credited with the writing of two epistles 'called catholic' (*quae catholicae nominantur*).[15] This is of course important for the further confirmation of the canonical status of both the Epistles 'of Peter'. The First Epistle in particular, a rallying cry for all Christians, appears to have been widely acknowledged as part of the New Testament canon from the third century onwards, even if its origin and Petrine authorship are no longer regarded as certain.[16] The confirmation of the canonicity of this epistle was also taken from Jerome's *De viris illustribus*.

Again, the *Liber pontificalis* author does not include Jerome's itemization of the various apocrypha associated with Peter, such as the *Acta* of Peter (despite the use Jerome himself had clearly made of it!) or the so-called Apocalypse of Peter, the text of his 'preaching', and the *Judicium*. In what appears to be an allusion to 1 Peter 5.12, where Peter refers to Mark as his 'son', the *Liber pontificalis* does relate, however, that Peter also wrote the Gospel of Mark 'because Mark was his hearer and his son by baptism'. The *Liber pontificalis*'s author echoed both Jerome and Eusebius–Rufinus in this, for Rufinus had retained Eusebius's discussion of Mark's Gospel in the widely disseminated Latin translation made in the early fifth century of Eusebius's original Greek text. The claim that St Mark's Gospel, now understood by modern scholars to be the earliest of the four Gospels, really represents Peter's recollections of Christ's ministry, thus making him the ultimate source of Mark's text, is still uncertain, and robustly rejected as a proposition by some. So too, many doubt whether Mark's Gospel was actually written in Rome by a member of the new generation of Christians.[17] Others have been less dismissive.

---

[15] *LP* I, Life 1, p. 118.

[16] Three of the earliest extant witnesses to these Epistles, in the Old Latin and the Vulgate, are Italian: Naples, Biblioteca Nazionale Lat. 2 (Vindobon. 16) fols 42*, 43–56, 71–5, written in sixth-century half-uncial but palimpsested, probably at Bobbio in the eighth century (*CLA* III, 395); Paris, BnF lat. 6400G, fols 131–45 (*CLA* V, 566), in fifth-century uncial; and the sixth-century Victor Codex that was written apparently for Victor of Capua (541–54) but was in Fulda by the eighth century, Fulda, Landesbibliothek, Codex Bonifatianus 1 (*CLA* VIII, 1196). See Houghton 2016, pp. 176–81.

[17] Gamble 1995, p. 57.

Joosten, for example, has commented not only on the grammatical interference of a Semitic language and Aramaic in the language of the text, but also on what he refers to as the frequent 'use of lexical Latinisms in the original Greek text'. These he interprets, nevertheless, not as an indication of an author from Roman Palestine or Alexandria writing Greek in Rome. Instead he regards them as merely a sign that the author, probably of modest social status, had 'no feeling for *belles lettres*' but had simply repeated common Latin colloquialisms used in contemporary 'vulgar Greek'. Joosten suggests that such borrowings from Latin were too widespread in colloquial Greek to make Mark's usage significant.[18]

In the *Liber pontificalis*, the claim for Peter's association with the Gospel of Mark functions as a further strengthening of the elevation of Rome as the continuation of the Christian evangelism inaugurated at Pentecost. One further indication of a strand of tradition that associates Peter with St Mark's Gospel is the so-called shorter ending of Mark's Gospel, with the language slightly garbled, in which allusion is made to statements made by 'those with Peter': 'But those who were also with the boy (a misreading for *Petro*/Peter?) told in brief everything which they had been instructed' (*Omnia autem quaecumque praecepta errant et qui cum puero erant breviter exposuerunt*).[19]

To audiences in Rome, however, even without an authorial link to Peter, Mark's Gospel may well have been more familiar for its strong representation of the life and ministry of Jesus as the fulfilment of Old Testament prophecies, and for its narrative in the very first chapter of John the Baptist's teaching, the baptism of Jesus, and Christ's calling of Simon, later called Peter, and his brother Andrew from their work as fishermen on the Sea of Galilee. It is probably from the reference in this Gospel to the healing of Peter's mother-in-law (Mark 1.30), furthermore, that a story about Peter having a daughter was later extrapolated in such texts as the *Acta* of Nereis and Achilleis. This may have contributed to the

---

[18] Joosten 2013, pp. 39–41.

[19] Houghton 2016, pp. 160–2 and p. 210. Only one extant manuscript of the pre-Hieronymian Old Latin version preserves this 'short ending'. It is 'VL 1', that is, Turin, Biblioteca Nazionale Universitaria 11163 (G.VII.15), thought to have been written in Africa, in fourth-century uncial (*CLA* IV, 465).

identification reported in the early eighth century of relics from the cemetery of Achilleis and Nereis in Rome as those of Petronilla, a supposed daughter of Peter.[20] Mark's narrative, furthermore, has a strikingly strong presence of Peter, with Peter as a witness to many of the miracles, and present at many of the key events, not least the meeting of Jesus with Elijah and Moses, the reproach to Peter in the Garden of Gethsemane, Peter's denial of Christ, and the message from Christ to Peter and the other disciples, sent via Mary by the angel in the tomb, on Easter morning after the Crucifixion.

The *Liber pontificalis* makes the further claim that Peter was responsible for confirming the content of all four Gospels: 'later he was the complete source of the four gospels – when he was questioned, Peter confirmed them by his testimony. Whether in Greek, Hebrew or Latin they are in agreement, and it was by his testimony they were confirmed'.[21] This sixth-century Roman understanding of the composition of all four Gospels and Peter's confirmation of the validity of their account of the career, Passion, and teaching of Christ are significant reminders of the emergence of the written word within the Christian movement; these texts constituted a crucial element in Christian identity. Their propagation was perceived as a central task for all Christian evangelists.[22] The dissemination of core Christian texts also applied to the Pauline and catholic epistles. The *Liber pontificalis* author appears here to have absorbed information from Eusebius in the Latin version of his *Historia ecclesiastica* made by Rufinus, where he explains that those who heard Peter preach in Rome

> were not satisfied with just listening but all of them begged his disciple Mark to write down what he was preaching, that they might have a permanent record of it and be able to continue reflecting on his words at home and away. Nor did they stop begging him until they got what they

---

[20] *LP* I Life 92, c. 13, p. 420 and note 26, p. 424. For Petronilla see above, p. 43 and below, p. 211.

[21] *LP* I, Life 1, c. 2, p. 118: *Post omnem quattuor evangeliorum fontem quae ad interrogationem et testimonio eius hoc est Petri firmatae sunt dum alius Grece, alius Ebraice, alius Latine consonent tamen eius testimonio sunt firmatae.*

[22] See Gamble 1995, and Hurtado and Keith 2013.

wanted. This is why the gospel 'according to Mark' came to be written. Peter, when he discovered through the Holy Spirit that his spiritual property had been filched from him, was delighted by the faith they had shown thereby, and considering their devotion, he confirmed what had been done and handed on the writing to the churches to be read permanently ... Papias adds that Peter, in his first letter, which he writes from the city of Rome, and in which he calls Rome 'Babylon' figuratively, mentions Mark when he says, 'the chosen one in Babylon greets you, as does Mark my son'.[23]

The *Liber pontificalis* recast Eusebius's account in a way that reinforced the fundamental aspects of Peter's role as Bishop of Rome. In every respect the author of the *Liber pontificalis* augmented his sources or offered a different perspective on the information they contained. The subsequent direct reference to Antioch and the allusion to Mark are perhaps also to be taken as an oblique reference to Alexandria. This might be taken, moreover, as a subtle enhancement of Rome's relationship with that see and what Philippe Blaudeau has referred to as Rome's 'géo-ecclésiologie'.[24] In this respect, with the implied superiority of Rome over Antioch and Alexandria, two of the principal patriarchal sees of late antiquity, it might also be read as echoing the sixth clause in the account of the Council of Nicaea, that Rufinus offered in his translation and extension of the *Historia ecclesiastica* of Eusebius. Rufinus notes Alexandria's responsibility for Egypt and the Bishop of Rome's charge of the suburbicarian churches of Italy.[25]

---

[23] Eusebius–Rufinus, *Historia ecclesiastica* 2.15.1, ed. Mommsen, pp. 139–41: *ita ut cottidie audientibus eum nulla umquam satietas fieret unde neque auditio eis sola sufficit, sed Marcum discipulum eius omnibus precibus exorant, uti ea, quae ille verbo praedicabat, ad perpetuam eorum commonitionem habendam scripturae traderet, quo domi forisque in huiuscemodi verbi meditationibus permaneret nec prius ab obsecrando desistunt, quamquae oraverant imperarent et haec fuit causa scribendi quod secundum Marcum dicitur evangelium. Petrus vero, ut per spiritum sanctum religioso se spoliatum conperit furto, delectatus est fidem eorum per haec devotionemque considerans factumque confirmavit et in perpetuum legendam scripturam ecclesiis tradidit ... Papias qui et hoc dicit quod Petrus in prima epistula sua, quam de urbe Roma scribit, meminerit Marci, in qua tropice Romam Babylonam nominarit cum dicit 'Salutat vos ea, quae in Babylone electa est et Marcus filius meus';* trans. Amidon, p. 78.

[24] Blaudeau 2012a and 2012b.

[25] Eusebius–Rufinus, *Historia ecclesiastica*, ed. Mommsen, p. 969; trans. Amidon, p. 388.

Most of the details of Peter's career so far could be culled from the Acts of the Apostles, the Epistles of Peter, the Chronograph of 354, the *De viris illustribus* of Jerome, and the *Historia ecclesiastica* of Eusebius–Rufinus. All these texts were available in Italy from at least the fifth century. All reinforce the authority and standing of Peter, and by implication of the city of Rome over which the *princeps apostolorum* presided, in relation to the rest of the Christian world. By offering the *Liber pontificalis* as an implicit continuation of the Acts of the Apostles, and by presenting Peter as the apostle who was the final guarantor responsible for the truth of the Gospel texts, therefore, the *Liber pontificalis* author neatly made Rome and its first bishop into instrumental safeguards and champions of both Christian identity and the texts underpinning it.

Rather more particular in its implications for both the claims being articulated on the Bishop of Rome's behalf in the *Liber pontificalis*, and the author of the *Liber pontificalis*'s access to other texts, however, is the paragraph relating to Peter's debates with Simon Magus. It is on these and their implications that I shall focus for the next section of this chapter.

Peter and Simon Magus

The *Liber pontificalis* relates that Peter 'held many debates with Simon Magus, both before the emperor Nero and before the people, because Simon was using magical tricks and deceptions to gather those whom Peter had gathered into Christ's faith. When their disputes had lasted a long time, Simon was struck down by God's will.'[26] Sixth-century readers accustomed to doctrinal arguments may well have registered the appositeness of a story about the representation of discussion and disputes between the Christians and pagans in Rome precipitated by Christian efforts at conversion, and that these involved imperial authorities and people, if not the emperor himself. They may also have been familiar with the far fuller details about the career and nefarious teachings of

---

[26] *LP* I, Life 1, c. 4, p. 118: *Hic cum Simone mago multas disputationes habuit tam ante Neronem imperatorem quamque ante populum ut quos beatus Petrus ad fidem Christi adgregabat, ille per magias et deceptiones segregabat. Et dum diutius altercarent, Simon divino nutu interemptus est;* trans. Davis, *Pontiffs*, p. 2.

Simon Magus available in other texts, not least the Acts of the Apostles, of which the *Liber pontificalis* makes such a brief summary. The main point of presenting Peter in debate with the arch-heretic Simon Magus appears to be to reinforce the role of the Bishop of Rome as the champion of orthodoxy from the outset.

The most famous work of heresiology compiled in late antiquity is probably the vast *Panarion* of Epiphanius.[27] Epiphanius had been in Rome in 382 with Paulinus and Jerome to attend Damasus's council. His text is often described as an encyclopaedia of heresies. In it, Epiphanius aimed to convert and protect Christians and provide them with antidotes against the serpents and beasts of the heretics. His sects begin with Adam and extend into the fourth century AD. There are twenty sects identified in the pre-Christian period and sixty after Christ. The first sect in the latter category is that of Simon Magus and his followers. Epiphanius's structure was consistent: he first provided the sect's name and relation to preceding sects; he then summarized its beliefs and practices before refuting them, emphasizing their noxiousness and making comparisons with other nefarious beliefs.

Although it is conceivable that the *Liber pontificalis* author was familiar with the *Panarion*, it is more likely that he was drawing, just as Eusebius–Rufinus had drawn in the *Historia ecclesiastica*, on the earlier catalogues and descriptions of heresies in the *Syntagma* of Hippolytus of Rome, pseudo-Tertullian's *Praescriptio haereticorum*, a third-century epitome of the *Syntagma*, and by Irenaeus of Lyon.[28] The *Contra haereses* of Irenaeus indeed, written *c.*190, originally in Greek but only extant in a defective Latin translation, is thought to have been addressed to readers in Rome. It appears to have been the fullest account of Simon Magus, and the presence of the text is attested in Italy by the sixth century. It is Irenaeus who thought of Simon Magus as the father of all heretical sects. While the definition of Simon Magus's beliefs and teaching are supplied in these encyclopaedias of heresies, fuller accounts of the debate between Simon and St Peter in Rome are to be found in the *Acta Petri*, probably originally compiled in Greek in Asia Minor in the second century but

[27] Epiphanius of Salamis, *Panarion*, ed. Williams, 1 (sects 1–46). See also Kim 2015.
[28] Irenaeus of Lyon, *Contra haereses*, ed. Unger and Dillon, 1.23, pp. 81–4.

translated into Latin, possibly in North Africa, in the third or fourth century.[29]

It is the latter that survives in a Vercelli manuscript of the seventh century, presumably based on an earlier exemplar. It is consequently sometimes known as the *Actus Vercellenses*. Hilhorst suggested that the *Acta* were copied into the original compilation with the pseudo-Clementine *Recognitiones* in order 'to complete a dossier about the confrontation between the apostle Peter and Simon Magus, with a greater focus on magic and trickery than had been provided by either Irenaeus or Epiphanius'.[30]

The *Acta* is a six-part drama, as follows: in preparation for the competition with Simon Magus and Peter, Paul leaves Rome. Simon Magus comes to Rome and disrupts Paul's missionary work. God then sends Peter to Rome to prevent the ruin of Christianity in the city. Peter arrives in Rome. Simon is staying at the house of the senator Marcellus, who was a lapsed Christian. Peter sends a talking dog to the house and Simon receives a challenge to a debate in the Forum. Peter prays for strength in his competition with Simon and addresses the Christians of Rome. Marcellus has a dream, the Forum debate takes place, and the Roman official Agrippa gives Simon and Peter a man to kill and revive. Simon kills him by whispering something in his ear, but Peter raises him from the dead. Simon flees. Peter prays to Christ to make Simon fall. Simon breaks his leg and dies. It is the emphasis on magic that is echoed by the *Liber pontificalis*. The *Liber pontificalis* also seems to take over the element of verbal debate between Simon and Peter from Hippolytus, rather than the competitive display of strength in a miracle contest related in the *Acta*. By paring down the details so drastically, the *Liber pontificalis* also contrives to highlight the involvement of the imperial authorities, if not the emperor himself, and the people of Rome in discussion and disputes between the Christians and pagans in Rome within a context of conversion.

---

[29] Bremmer (ed.) 1998; Vercelli, Biblioteca Capitolare CLVIII (*CLA* IV, 468a) and compare Turner 1931, who favoured the third/fourth century as the date of composition. On the manuscript see Döhler 2017, pp. 3–6. For a summary of the legends see also Ferreiro 2005, pp. 55–81 and Demacopoulos 2013.

[30] Hilhorst 1998.

The Succession: Linus and Cletus

Peter's pastoral work in Rome is briefly described in the context of his ordaining two bishops, Linus and Cletus, to be 'present in Rome to provide the entire sacerdotal ministry for the people and for "visitors" while Peter himself was free to pray and preach, to teach the people'.[31]

Despite the reference to Peter's appointment of Linus and Cletus as his co-workers, both Linus and Cletus were counted formally in most subsequent papal succession lists as Peter's immediate successors in sequence rather than as his assistant bishops. In a possible attempt to reconcile conflicting traditions, the sixth-century author of Life 4 of Clement is then careful to explain that Linus and Cletus are recorded before Clement because they were ordained bishops by the *princeps apostolorum* himself in order to provide the sacerdotal ministry.[32] Clement, however, was given the management of the church by Peter, who is quoted in Life 1 as saying to Clement: 'As the power of government, that of binding and loosing, was handed to me by my lord Jesus Christ, so I entrust it to you.'[33] This is of course an allusion to Matthew 16.19: 'I will give you the keys of the kingdom of heaven; whatever you bind on earth will be bound in heaven, and whatever you loose on earth will be loosed in heaven.' It is significant that the choice for the Roman Gospel Lectionary reading for the feast of St Peter on 29 June was also precisely this text.[34]

The pastoral role of the bishop remains a crucial consideration: Peter's admonition to Clement concludes that Clement is 'to ordain those who are to deal with various cases and execute the church's affairs', and echoes the description of Peter's ministry in suggesting that Clement should 'not be caught up in the cares of the world but ensure you are

---

[31] *LP* I, Life 1, p. 118; trans. Davis, *Pontiffs*, p. 2: *Qui praesentaliter omne ministerium sacerdotale in urbe Roma populo vel supervenientium exhiberent beatus autem Petrus ad orationem et praedicationem populum erudiens;* Loomis 1916, p. 5, offers 'strangers' for 'visitors' as a translation of *supervenientium*.

[32] *LP* I, Life 4, p. 123.

[33] *LP* I, Life 1, p. 118; trans. Davis, *Pontiffs*, p. 2: *Sicut super mihi gubernandi tradita est a domino meo Iesu Christo potestas ligandi solvendique, ita et ego tibi committo.*

[34] See the full list in the Godescalc Lectionary of *c.*781, Paris, BnF n.a.lat. 1203, fol. 86r; the antiphon for Lauds and Vespers on this feast is *Tu es Petrus*, cf. csg 359, pp. 123–4.

completely free for prayer and preaching to the people'.[35] The ministry entrusted by Christ to Peter and by Peter to Clement is alluded to further in Life 4 of Clement, with the comment that Clement, on St Peter's instruction, 'undertook the pontificate for the governing the church, as the *cathedra* had been handed down and entrusted to him by the Lord Jesus Christ'. That Life adds that 'you will find in the letter written to James (by Clement) how the church was entrusted to him (that is, Clement) by Peter'.[36]

This reminder of the bishop's pastoral role and sacerdotal ministry in Rome, and the way in which Peter himself determined his succession, augmented by the reference to Christ's injunction to Peter, is further reinforced by the formulaic reference at the end of the Life to the number of ordinations Peter performed: three bishops, ten priests, and seven deacons. Peter's successors continue to extend the body of the clergy. The three bishops are presumably Linus, Cletus, and Clement. Every subsequent Bishop of Rome adds to the numbers of priests. Whether this reference to Peter's ordination of seven deacons could be read as an allusion to the seven regions of Rome to which seven deacons, one for each, were subsequently allocated is possible, but it is to Clement that the creation of the seven regions is credited. Reference to the seven deacons is made soon thereafter in Life 6 of Pope Evaristus (c.100–9), but without specifying any connection to the regions. It is Pope Fabian (236–50) who is said to have 'divided the regions among the deacons and created seven subdeacons who were to watch over the seven notaries so they would faithfully collect the complete acts of the martyrs'.[37]

The formulaic and repetitive reiteration of the details of pope after pope reinforces the apostolic tradition. Reports of a process of election

---

[35] *LP* I, Life 1, p. 118; trans. Davis, *Pontiffs*, p. 2: *ut ordinans dispositores diversarum causarum, per quos actus ecclesiasticus profligetur et tu minime in curis saeculi deditus repperiaris; sed solummodo ad orationem et praedicare populo vacare stude.*

[36] *LP* I, Life 4, c. 2, p. 123; trans. Davis, *Pontiffs*, p. 3: *Hic ex praecepto beati Petri suscepit ecclesiae pontificatum gubernandi sicut ei fuerat a domino Iesu Christo cathedra tradita vel commissa tamen in epistola quae ad Jacobum scripta est qualiter ei a beato Petro commissa est ecclesia repperies.*

[37] *LP* I, Life 21, p. 148; trans. Davis, *Pontiffs*, p. 8: *Hic regiones dividit diaconibus et fecit VII subdiaconos qui VII notariis inminarent ut gestas martyrum in integro fideliter colligerent;* and compare Life 20, p. 147, which reports that Pope Anteros (235–6) sought the acts of the martyrs from the notaries.

are rare in the *Liber pontificalis* before the eighth century, at which point election by the whole Roman people in unanimity and concord becomes an important rhetorical strategy.[38] In this early period, however, successors to Clement, notably those going to their execution, entrust their responsibilities to one of the priests or deacons in the style of Peter designating his successors. Thus, the *Liber pontificalis* notes that Pope Lucius (253–4) appointed Stephen the Archdeacon, Pope Gaius (283–96) designated Pope Marcellinus, and Pope Stephen I (254–7) in a later interpolation is said to have handed over the sacred vessels or care of the money chest to his archdeacon;[39] that person subsequently became Stephen's successor as Pope Sixtus II.[40]

The *Liber pontificalis* was not the first to display this powerful sense of the past and of a continuing tradition and responsibility that was both maintained and cumulative. The logging of the succession of imperial reigns in relation to those of the popes in Jerome's Latin translation of Eusebius's *Chronicon*, and Eusebius's own insistence on the apostolic origins and succession of the sees of Rome, Antioch, and Alexandria, had established the particular significance of apostolic foundation and succession. A later instance is the *History of the Coptic Patriarchs of Alexandria* in the seventh century, preserved in an eleventh-century Arabic version of the text. It was probably compiled in the context of the Arab incursions into Egypt, for the benefit of the vulnerable Christian community, in order to strengthen their sense of community in the face of adversity.[41] Like the *Liber pontificalis*, the focus is on the leader, the Bishop of Alexandria. In both the *Liber pontificalis* and the history of the Patriarchs, that leadership is given a long and illustrious pedigree in the text, with the claims of a direct line of apostolic succession from St Peter and St Mark respectively.

---

[38] See Daileader 1993, who links it with what he describes as papal political 'independence', which he suggests was achieved after 731.

[39] *LP* I, Life 24, p. 154; the interpolation is in the eleventh-century manuscript E 1, BAV Vat. lat. 3764.

[40] *LP* I, Lives 23, 29, and 24, pp. 153, 161, and 154.

[41] *History of the Patriarchs of the Coptic Church of Alexandria Attributed to Sāwīrus ibn al-Muqaffaʿ, Bishop of el-Ashmunein*, ed. and trans. Evetts, 1, fasc. 2 and 4; 5, fasc. 1; 10, fasc. 5 (Paris, 1904–14). I am grateful to Christian Sahner for conversation about this text.

The Burial of St Peter

Thus far, the details so deftly summarized in the Life of Peter have identifiable sources. The account of Peter's burial on the Vatican Hill, however, is one of the most puzzling contradictions in the text. The note in St Peter's Life is apparently unequivocal: Peter's burial is recorded as follows: 'he was buried on the Via Aurelia at the temple of Apollo, close to the place where he was crucified, and to Nero's palace on the Vatican, and to the triumphal territory, on 29th June'.[42] This may be a somewhat clumsy attempt to report the status quo in the sixth century, given the significance of the Life and Peter in the text as a whole. One cautionary note to be voiced here is that none of the extant manuscripts containing the full text of Peter's Life is earlier than the late seventh century. We cannot be certain that it was Peter's burial, as distinct from his death, that was located on the Vatican Hill in the sixth-century original. The early epitomes known as the Felician and Cononian, however, both refer to his burial being close to the place where he was crucified. In Life 22 of Pope Cornelius (251–3), moreover, the pope is described as taking up the bodies of both Paul and Peter 'from the catacombs' (*de catacumbas*) at night and putting the bodies close to the places of their execution, that is, respectively, on the Via Ostiensis and with the bodies of the holy bishops at the Temple of Apollo on the Mons Aureus on the Vatican Hill at Nero's palace on 29 June.[43] The contradictions between this story of a third-century translation of the apostle Peter's relics, presumed to be from the Via Appia to the Vatican Hill, the *Depositio martyrum* in the Chronograph of 354,[44] the reference in the Life of Pope Damasus (366–84) in the *Liber pontificalis*, to the catacombs (*ad catacombas*) as being the place where the bodies of the apostles Peter and Paul lay,[45] and the ambiguous archaeological evidence in the Vatican necropolis itself, have of course been discussed many times, among others by

[42] *LP* I, Life 1, c. 6, p. 118; trans. Davis, *Pontiffs*, p. 2: *Qui sepultus est via Aurelia, in templum Apollinis, iuxta locum ubi crucifixus est, iuxta palatium Neronianum, in Vaticanum, iuxta territurium triumphalem, III kal. Iul.*
[43] *LP* I, Life 22, p. 150.
[44] Chronograph of 354, *LP* I, pp. 1–12. Divjak and Wischmeyer 2014.
[45] *LP* I, Life 39, p. 212.

Jocelyn Toynbee and John Ward-Perkins, Engelbert Kirschbaum, Henry Chadwick, Paolo Liverani, and most recently by Nicola Camerlenghi.[46] The precise relationship between the original burial place, the third-century translation, and the construction of the basilica of St Peter and the apostle's *confessio* remains ambiguous. Certainly, by the time St Peter's basilica was built in the fourth century, there was an established tradition of the presence of Peter's relics at the site.[47]

What can be said here is that the claim made in the Life of Peter served to enhance the status of St Peter's basilica and the shrine of St Peter. Although it anticipates a later translation, and credits this to a third-century pope, when considered in the context of the entire Life of St Peter in the *Liber pontificalis,* and its role in setting the themes of the text as a whole, the placing of Peter's body on the Vatican Hill has the effect of instantly locating and confirming the major cult site of the saint for its readers.

The telegraphic format of the first Life in the *Liber pontificalis* appears to have assumed not only a familiarity with the traditions associated with St Peter and the topography of the city, but a knowledge, in sixth-century Rome at least, of the various Latin versions of the texts that supplied the information: Paul's Epistle to the Galatians, the Acts of the Apostles, the Gospel of Mark and two Epistles of Peter, the letters of Clement, the *Contra haereses* of Irenaeus, the *Syntagma* of Hippolytus, the pseudo-Clementine *Recognitiones,* the *De viris illustribus* of Jerome, the *Chronicon* of Eusebius–Jerome, the *Acta Petri,* and the *Historia ecclesiastica* of Eusebius in Rufinus's edition and Latin translation. All these were available in Latin by the sixth century. There is no reason to suppose that they were not available to the writers of the *Liber pontificalis,* and there are besides clear instances of these texts having been used. These texts were presumably also available to other writers and thinkers in sixth-century Italy, but the *Liber pontificalis* authors chose to construct a very different text from

---

[46] Chadwick 1957, Toynbee and Ward-Perkins 1956, Kirschbaum 1959, Liverani and Spinola 2010, Camerlenghi 2018, pp. 23–40. See also Bowersock 2005 and Brandenburg 2011a.

[47] I have discussed the story of Peter's initial burial and translation in the context of a wider consideration of the significance of the representation of St Peter's basilica in the *Liber pontificalis* in McKitterick 2013b.

these resources in comparison with the work of their contemporaries.[48] In this respect the text of the Life in the *Liber pontificalis* could even be described as a mnemonic, acting as a prompt or a representative summary of the rich traditions associated with the *princeps apostolorum*. For readers unfamiliar with this range of texts, the *Liber pontficalis* could be regarded as an ingenious distillation of a wealth of older traditions.

This first Life of Peter thus contrives to offer many of the facets of Christian identity subsequently developed further in the rest of the text: Peter's teaching; his organization of the clergy; the sharing of the stories of the Gospels and the placing of these texts as both central to the Christian faith and confirmed by the *princeps apostolorum*; the recognition of both Epistles of Peter as part of the New Testament canon; the dramatic affirmation of faith in the face of imperial persecution by Peter because he was martyred; his disputation with Simon Magus and rejection of the latter's herctical views as an indication of the maintenance of an accurate and orthodox Christian faith; Peter's provision for his succession; Rome's primacy in relation to the ancient sees of Antioch and Alexandria; and Peter's major cult site in Rome.

The Early Christian Community in Rome

The Life of Peter and the subsequent Lives of his successors in themselves offer a further common history and Christian identity, especially for the people of Rome. In the next section of this chapter I wish to suggest that the *Liber pontificalis* provides an authoritative narrative about the Christian community and its bishops in the time of the pagan Roman emperors, as well as under the leadership of Pope Silvester and his successors in the aftermath of the conversion of the Emperor Constantine.

Again, the sparseness of the narrative has to be set against the wealth of interpretations of new excavations, burial practices, the development of martyr cults, liturgy and ritual, the variety of pagan as well as Christian experience and communities, processes of conversion and Christianization, the diversity of social organization, and the very gradual nature of

---

[48] See above, Chapter 1, pp. 25–35.

the encroachment of Christian buildings within the Aurelian Walls of the city of Rome as well as on the principal roads out of the city.[49] Recent studies have very convincingly disrupted the old but improbable notions of a neat displacement of homogenized pagans by united Christians in both physical and institutional terms with the conversion of Constantine at the beginning of the fourth century. This makes the version of events offered in the *Liber pontificalis* all the more fascinating.[50]

A dominant theme in the lives of the thirty-three popes before Pope Silvester and the conversion of the Emperor Constantine is their championing of the Christian faith. The most obvious manifestation of this is the recurrent resistance to state power on the part of the Christians in Rome, a phenomenon described even more generally by Burrus and Lehmann as 'a public stance of political resistance to empire'.[51] The consequences of such resistance were grim. Of those thirty-three popes before Silvester, the *Liber pontificalis* records twenty-four as being crowned with martyrdom (*martyrio coronatur*): Peter, Linus, Cletus, Clement, Evaristus, Alexander, Sixtus I, Telesphorus, Anicetus, Victor, Callistus, Urban, Pontian, Anteros, Fabian, Cornelius, Lucius, Stephen I, Sixtus II, Felix I, Eutychian, Gaius, Marcellinus, Marcellus.

Only rarely are others besides the bishop mentioned. Peter was crowned with martyrdom along with Paul (*c.* AD 67);[52] the priest Eventius and the deacon Theodulus died alongside Pope Alexander (*c.* AD 110); The priest Maximinus accompanied Pope Anteros (235–6); after Pope Fabian's death (236–50), the priests Moyses and Maximus and the deacon Nicostratos were imprisoned.[53] Pope Urban (222–30), praised for his teaching and the number of converts to Christianity he had achieved, suffered death along with many others.[54] Bishop Marcellus

[49] Wienand (ed.) 2015, Burrus and Lehmann 2012, Cameron 2011; Bonamente, Lenski, and Lizzi Testa (eds.) 2012; Lizzi Testa (ed.) 2013; Salzman, Sághy, and Lizzi Testa (eds.) 2015; Behrwald and Witschel (eds.) 2012, and Guidobaldi and Guiglia Guidobaldi (eds.) 2002.

[50] I draw in the next few paragraphs on a paper delivered in Helsinki in November 2016, McKitterick in press b.

[51] Burrus and Lehmann 2012, p. 7.   [52] *LP* I, Life 1, c. 6, p. 118.

[53] *LP* I, Lives 1, 7, 20, 21, pp. 118, 127, 147, 148.

[54] *LP* I, Life 18, p. 143 (the dating in the time of Diocletian does not correspond to either the list of consuls or of emperors): *Hic sua traditione multos convertit ad baptismum et*

(305/6–306/7), according to the *Liber pontificalis,* was 'caught and held because he made arrangements for the church, and arrested by Maxentius to deny he was a bishop and be brought low by sacrificing to demons. He kept despising and spurning the pronouncements of Maxentius and was condemned to the Catabulum.'[55] From there, 'his entire clergy came and rescued him at night'.[56]

Both Pope Cornelius (251–3) and Pope Sixtus II (257–8) were killed in the Decian persecutions. Six members of Sixtus's clergy were killed at the same time: the deacons Felicissimus, Agapitus, Januarius, Magnus, Vincent, and Stephen. After Sixtus's passion, his archdeacon Laurence suffered the same fate, along with Claudius the subdeacon, Severus the priest, Crescentius the reader and Romanus the doorkeeper. Pope Gaius (282–95), noted as a member of the Emperor Diocletian's family, was nevertheless martyred along with his brother Gabinius the priest.[57] The most extreme case of persecution in the *Liber pontificalis* is recorded in Life 30 of Marcellinus (295–303). During the reigns of Diocletian and Maximian, the *Liber pontificalis* alludes to the horrific scale of the killing: 'when there was so great a persecution that within thirty days 17,000 persons of both sexes were crowned with martyrdom as Christians in various provinces'.[58]

Again, the *Liber pontificalis* may be summarizing other, fuller accounts of the fifth and early sixth centuries, such as the *Gesta martyrum* and *Passiones.*[59] A hint of the further details such sources may have contained is suggested by some of the later manuscripts of the *Liber pontificalis,* such

---

credulitatem, etiam et Valerianum, nobilissimum virum, sponsum sanctae Ceciliae; quos etiam usque ad martyrii palmam perduxit et per eius monita multi martyrio coronati sunt; trans. Davis, *Pontiffs,* p. 7.

[55] *LP* I, Life 31, c. 3, p. 164; trans. Davis, *Pontiffs,* p. 13: *Hic coartatus et tentus eo quod ecclesiam ordinaret et comprehensus a Maxentio ut negaret se esse episcopum et sacrificiis humiliari daemoniorum. Quo semper contemnens, deridens dicta et praecepta Maxenti, damnatus est in catabulum.*

[56] Ibid., p. 164; trans. Davis, *Pontiffs,* p. 13: *mense autem nono noctu venerunt clerus eius omnis et eruerunt eum noctu de catabulo.*

[57] *LP* I, Life 29, p. 161; trans. Davis, *Pontiffs,* pp. 11–12: *propter filiam Gavini presbiteri.*

[58] *LP* I, Life 30, c. 2, p. 162; trans. Davis, *Pontiffs,* p. 11: *intra XXX dies XVII milia hominum promiscui sexus per diversas provincias martyrio coronarentur Christiani . . . Ab eodem die cessavit episcopatus ann. VII m. VI d. XXV persequente Diocletiano Christianos.*

[59] Dufourcq 1900–7, Lanéry 2010, and Gioanni 2010.

as BAV Vat. lat. 3764 of the eleventh century, in which the scribes added extra names of martyrs. According to this manuscript, with Stephen I (254–7) in prison before execution, for example, were nine priests, two bishops (Honorius and Castus), and three deacons (Sixtus, Dionysius, and Gaius).[60] As already mentioned, it was while he was in prison that Stephen designated one of the deacons, Sixtus (Pope Sixtus II), also later martyred, as his successor.[61] Another hint of knowledge of other sources on the part of the *Liber pontificalis* author is indicated in the account of the dispute between Pope Cornelius and the Emperor Decius, in which Cornelius (251–3) refers to letters he had received, containing not treasonable words but 'spiritual advice for redeeming souls'.[62] The letters thus alluded to were from Cyprian and are still extant.[63]

The resting places of the bodies of these papal martyrs, like that of St Peter, are meticulously recorded and became in due course cult sites attracting pilgrims. The *Liber pontificalis* may even have had as one of its aims to play a definitive role in claiming these resting places for the martyrs and creating a legitimating pedigree for them. The author or authors of the *Liber pontificalis* may have intended his or their work to function in some respects as a pilgrim guide, giving an outline of the circumstances and location of the various Roman martyrs to whom their devotion was to be directed.[64] Clement (*c*.95) for example, was buried in Greece but his body was brought back to Rome.[65] The cemetery of Callistus harboured a concentration of papal bodies, namely, Sixtus, Fabian, Lucius, Stephen, Dionysius, Felix, Eutychian, Gaius, Eusebius, Miltiades, and Julius,[66] possibly all in the chamber now known as the Crypt of the Popes, for which Pope Damasus commissioned the scribe and stonecutter Filocalus to inscribe one of Damasus's verse epitaphs.[67]

---

[60] See below, p. 193.   [61] *LP* I, Life 24, p. 154. Mommsen, *LP*, p. 33 and above, p. 73.

[62] *LP* I, pp. 150–1; trans. Davis, *Pontiffs*, p. 9: *Ego de corona Domini litteras accepi, non contra rempublicam, sed magis animas redimendas.*

[63] Cyprian, *Epistolae*, ed. Clarke and Diercks, and Bevenot 1961.

[64] McKitterick 2006, pp. 46–51.   [65] *LP* I, Life 4, p. 123.

[66] Blaauw 2016, Picard 1969, and Borgolte 1995.

[67] Gray 1956, Morison 1972, pp. 94–5, Cardin 2008, pp. 16–18, Trout 2015, and Denzey Lewis 2018.

Similarly, the sanctity of other Roman cemeteries, some provided by the popes, others apparently the gift of pious laymen and women such as the cemeteries of Praetextatus on the Via Appia and of Priscilla on the Via Salaria,[68] was enhanced by the presence of martyred popes and their clergy.[69] In the cemetery of Praetextatus, for example, were buried the six deacons executed at the same time as Pope Sixtus II (257–8), as well as Pope Urban (222–30). Laurence was buried in the cemetery of Cyriaces on the Ager Veranus in the crypt with many other martyrs,[70] and Pope Eutychian (275–83) was said to have buried 342 martyrs in various places with his own hands.[71] Pope Zephyrinus (198/9–217) was buried in his own cemetery, near the cemetery of Callistus.[72] With this careful construction of a topography of sanctity, the *Liber pontificalis* also enhanced the holiness of the successors of St Peter. They too had won the martyr's crown and joined the congregation of saints.

Occasionally there are hints in the text of the reception of new converts to Christianity and how that may have been regulated. There was a community of Jews in Rome, among whom Peter may have worked.[73] Pope Pius (c.145), moreover, is credited with a decree 'that a heretic coming from the heresy of the Jews should be received and baptized',[74] and Pope Victor (c.195) with a decision 'that in case of necessity anyone coming from paganism might be baptized wherever he happened to be, whether in a river, or in the sea or in springs, provided only that his confession of faith as a Christian be delivered clearly'.[75] The establishment of *tituli* in Rome 'for the baptism and

---

[68] *LP* I, p. 162; trans. Davis, *Pontiffs*, p. 12: *Et post hoc factum iacuerunt corpora sancta in platea ad exemplum christianorum dies XXV ex iussu Diocletiani.*

[69] *LP* I, Life 18, p. 143.   [70] *LP* I, Life 25, p. 155.   [71] *LP* I, Life 28, p. 159.

[72] *LP* I, Life 16, p. 139.

[73] Rutgers 1995, 2000, and 2009. Currently Rutgers is directing two international projects, one entitled *Reconfiguring Diaspora: The Transformation of the Jewish Diaspora in Late Antiquity* and another excavation project focussing on the origins of Christianity in Rome.

[74] *LP* I, Life 11, c. 3, p. 132; trans. Davis, *Pontiffs*, p. 5: *Hic constituit hereticum venientem ex Iudaeorum herese suscipi et baptizari.*

[75] *LP* I, Life 15, c. 2, p. 137; trans. Davis, *Pontiffs*, p. 6: *Et constituit ut necessitate faciente, ut ubiubi inventus fuisset, sive in flumine, sive in mari, sive in fontibus, tantum christiano confessione credulitatis clarificata quicumque hominum ex gentile veniens ut baptizaretur.*

repentance of many converts from paganism' is mentioned in the Life of Pope Marcellus (305/6–306/7).[76] A further indication of the variety of belief among the people of Rome in the fourth century is the decree attributed to Pope Miltiades (310–14) forbidding the faithful to fast on Sundays or Thursdays 'because the pagans kept these days as a holy fast',[77] Pope Eusebius (*c*.308) is said to have 'discovered heretics in Rome and reconciled them by the laying on of hands'.[78] One group at least of these 'heretics' is specified as Manichaeans in the Lives of Eusebius's successors, Popes Miltiades, Gelasius (492–6), and Hormisdas (514–23), though Samuel Cohen has suggested that 'Manichaean' may have functioned as a general label for heretics by the sixth century.[79]

The *Liber pontificalis* portrays a cosmopolitan population as well as one with a great diversity of religious belief. The memory of pagans at least was preserved in some aspects of the daily rhythms of life in Rome as well as the topography.[80] Throughout the fourth century, many pagan traditions and sacred sites were maintained, at least until the repressive decrees of Theodosius. Groups from Palestine, Syria, Egypt, Greece, Dalmatia, and North Africa, as well as those referred to collectively as Goths, settled in Rome.[81] Pilgrims and exiles, and men from Sicily, Spain, Sardinia, and elsewhere in the Italian peninsula in pursuit of a clerical career also converged on Rome. The international profile of Rome's clergy was taken for granted. I mentioned how many popes are claimed as Roman or from Italy in the *Liber pontificalis* in the previous chapter. Even so, seventeen of the first fifty-nine popes were immigrants from Christian communities in the Holy Land, Syria, Spain, Dalmatia, Africa, and Greece. Of the ten popes described as Greek, two seem to have had Jewish fathers. Their very inclusion in the *Liber pontificalis* and their

---

[76] *LP* I, Life 31, c. 2, p. 164; trans. Davis, *Pontiffs*, p. 12: *propter baptismum et paenitentiam multorum qui convertebantur ex paganis.*

[77] *LP* I, Life 33, c. 2, p. 168; trans. Davis, *Pontiffs*, p. 13: *Hic constituit nulla ratione dominico aut quinta feria ieiunium quis de fidelibus agere, quia eos dies pagani quasi sacrum ieiunium celebrabant.*

[78] *LP* I, Life 32, p. 167; trans. Davis, *Pontiffs*, p. 13: *Hic hereticos invenit in urbe Roma quos ad manum inpositionis reconciliavit.*

[79] *LP* I Lives 33, 51, and 54, pp. 255 and 270, and Cohen 2015.

[80] See Marazzi 2000 and Humphries 2007.

[81] See the prosopography of Goths in Italy in Amory 1997, pp. 348–485.

eligibility to become pope effectively Romanized them. At the same time, the varied backgrounds of these popes is expressive of the expansion of Christianity and reinforces the *Liber pontificalis*'s function as the next instalment in the Acts of the Apostles.

The community of Christians in Rome is not obviously presented as a small and vulnerable group before the conversion of Constantine, but this is certainly what emerges from the text. More crucially, it is the status of the sole bishop among the many Christian groups in Rome that is promoted, with very little indication of the variety and possibly divided loyalties that may have existed between the different groups of Christians. In modern patristic scholarship, this emphasis on a single leader is described as the emergence of a 'monarch bishop'. The alternative leadership and vision of the Christian life offered by Hippolytus in Rome, for example, is not even acknowledged; he was merely mentioned in the *Liber pontificalis* as a priest exiled by the imperial authorities at the same time and to the same place as Pope Pontian (230–5).[82] Similarly, the challenge Novatian presented to the leadership of Popes Fabian (236–50) and Cornelius (251–3) is barely alluded to, and other *loci* of spiritual authority within Rome are ignored.[83] In Rome at the time these may have been strong personal rivalries, but they are subsumed in the narrative of the popes' martyrdom. The story of the translation of Peter and Paul in the Life of Pope Cornelius appears to reinforce the stewardship of their apostolic founders by their successors, and thus enhances still more the authority of the Bishop of Rome.[84]

Disagreements within, or tensions between, communities in the seven regions and twenty-five *tituli* in Rome may have had as much to do with different liturgical practices, emphases in morality and charity, social incompatibility, and doctrinal variation in relation to the Chalcedonian definition of the Trinity, as with the alleged 'political' rivalries within the city. The *Liber pontificalis*, as we saw in the previous chapter, presents us with disputed elections and opposing factions disrupting the elections of

---

[82] *LP* I, Life 20, p. 147. Brent 1995. See also Curran 2000, Dunn (ed.) 2015, and Fear (ed.) 2013.

[83] *LP* I, pp. 148, 150–1. See also Gülzow 1975, and Papandrea 2008.

[84] See McKitterick 2013b, and the references cited above, pp. 85 and 86, notes 43 and 47.

Popes Damasus, Boniface II, and Symmachus.[85] Such accounts, however, highlighting enthusiastic partisans and family members, may well be the same kind of telegraphic and generalized reporting we observed in the Life of Peter, with the Laurentian schism even within the living memory of some readers. The Verona fragment, for example, the alternative version of the Life of Symmachus discussed in Chapter 1, refers to 'such an enormous and savage disagreement that took hold of the clergy and Roman people that neither the thought of God nor the fear of the king could prevent the factions colliding'.[86] No reason is given for the disagreement. The narrative mentions at a later stage that some of the senators and bishops went to Symmachus's defence and more select clergy and senators supported Laurentius. The *Liber pontificalis*'s version also records that clergy and senate were split, though again without indicating why. It then goes to the length of recording the ex-consuls Festus and Probinus and their 'battle' with another ex-consul Faustus, and how their malice 'caused slaughter and murder among the clergy'.[87] By reinforcing the history of the see and its apostolic origins, the *Liber pontificalis* authors may also be buttressing a case against too much aristocratic interference in the episcopal office.

Any reference to heretics, Arians, Manichaeans, Donatists, and the embattled complications resultant on the Acacian schism with Byzantium between 484 and 519 are generally only alluded to by the *Liber pontificalis* as an aspect of the bishop's triumph over error and dissent. The bishops had proved themselves steadfast under the pagan emperors and remained the champions of orthodoxy as the sole leaders of the Christian community in Rome. There will be more about how the *Liber pontificalis* contrives to emphasize this in relation to the bishop's authority below,[88] but here I wish to emphasize the *Liber pontificalis*'s description

---

[85] Wirbelauer 1993, Llewellyn 1976, and Blair-Dixon 2007.

[86] Verona, Biblioteca Capitolare XXII (20) (*CLA* IV, 490); ed. *LP* I, pp. 43–6 at p. 44; trans. Davis, *Pontiffs*, p. 95: *tantaque clerum ac populum romanum discordia feralis invaserat, ut nec divina consideratio, nec metus regius partes a propria conlisione cohiberet*, and see above, pp. 32–5.

[87] *LP* I, Life 53, c. 5, pp. 260–1; trans. Davis, *Pontiffs*, p. 43: *et caedes et homicidia in clero ex invidia*. On the historical context, the personalities identified here, and details see Wirbelauer 1993 and earlier commentary by Llewellyn 1976 and Moorhead 1978.

[88] See Chapter 4, below.

of the institutional structure the bishops introduce to what appears, even from this laconic text, to have been a small, vulnerable, and mostly poverty-stricken community. The bishop had a loyal and steadfast little band of clergy supporting him, though as we have seen, we hear most about them when they are martyred alongside their bishop; the entourage executed with Pope Sixtus II (257–8), for example, looks like the personnel of just one small establishment.[89]

Conclusion

I have argued in this chapter that the *Liber pontificalis* was a determined representation of Rome's anchoring of the Christian faith in the work of the *princeps apostolorum* and his successors in written form. It was a text, moreover, which drew on other traditions which were also in written form. The *Liber pontificalis* embedded the innovations of the sixth-century bishops of Rome in a 500-year-old past. It stressed the inheritance and careful stewardship of a legacy. It provided an example to sustain and instruct those bishops' successors. It reinforced the authority and standing of Peter within the church and by implication in Rome, over which the *princeps apostolorum* presided, in relation to the rest of the Christian world.

I suggested at the end of the previous chapter that the *Liber pontificalis* can be understood as a means by which the perceptions and memory of Rome were reshaped and its past restructured.[90] A distinctive aspect of many texts in the early middle ages is their dynamic relationship with late antiquity. This is particularly the case with the *Liber pontificalis*, whose presentation and reception of versions of the past, written in the early middle ages but with reference to late antiquity, have much to tell us about the formation of identities or, at least, about how particular individuals may have endeavoured to shape collective identities. As we have seen, the original *Liber pontificalis* and its continuations can be interpreted as an attempt to frame a new identity for Christians within a narrative of the transformation of Rome from pagan to Christian city. In this respect, the text is an essential component of the formation in

[89] *LP* I, Life 25, p. 155.   [90] Gantner, McKitterick, and Meeder (eds.) 2015.

early medieval Europe of cultural memory in the sense defined in the work of Jan Assmann and Aleida Assmann.[91] I have endeavoured to demonstrate how to assess the relationship between the very particular narrative of the *Liber pontificalis* and the realities both of the early stages of the formation of Christian Rome and of the emergence of the bishop or pope as sole leader of the Christian community in Rome. It is to the question of imperial emulation and the representation of the popes as the new rulers of Rome, therefore, that I shall turn in the following chapter.

[91] Assmann, J. 1999/2011; Assmann, A. 1999/2011.

4

Establishing Visible Power

Introduction

I N THE PREVIOUS CHAPTER, I EMPHASIZED THE WAYS IN which the sixth-century Roman history of the popes in the *Liber pontificalis* used the work of Peter, *princeps apostolorum,* and his successors to anchor the Christian faith in Rome, and how it thereby shaped the memory of the early stages of the formation of Christian Rome and the emergence of the bishop or pope as leader of the Christian community before the conversion of Constantine. I turn in this chapter to consider the implications of the means the text employs, from the narrative covering the beginning of the fourth century onwards, to enhance the pope's power still further.

The Life of Pope Silvester in the *Liber pontificalis* and its Implications

The Life of Pope Silvester (314–35) in the *Liber pontificalis,* Life 34, introduces a major and significant change in character to the content of the Lives. It starts in the customary manner with the note of Silvester's origin. Like fifteen of his martyred predecessors, Silvester was a Roman and born in Rome. He is described as the son of Rufinus, about whom nothing more is known,[1] and as bishop in the time of the consulship of

---

[1] A number of Roman clerics named Rufinus are mentioned in sources from the late third and the fourth century but no more appears to be known about Silvester's parentage. Compare Duchesne, *LP* I, p. 187, who notes that the name of Silvester's mother Iusta, and of his teacher Cyrinus, rather than the name of his father, are mentioned in the *Vita* or

Constantius and Volusianus. He was exiled or had fled from Constantine's persecution. He returned *in gloria* and baptized Constantine, whom 'the Lord cured from leprosy' (*quem curavit Dominus a lepra*).

Thus far, this might appear to be a conventional summary of disparate sources. Certainly, the garbled information about the consular years appears to have been gleaned from the Chronograph of 354.[2] The claim that Silvester baptized Constantine, however, is not what is recorded in Jerome's Latin continuation of Eusebius's *Chronicon* from the later fourth century, a text that was, as we have seen, one of the resources of the author of the *Liber pontificalis*. Jerome had placed the Emperor Constantine's baptism at the end of his life in Nicomedia and at the hands of the Arian bishop Eusebius, and stated that there was much discord in the church thereafter.[3] Rufinus, in his extension to his translation and edition of Eusebius's *Historia ecclesiastica*, only reports Constantine's death 'in a suburban villa in Nicomedia' and says nothing about his baptism.[4] Silvester's act is thus the first hint that the *Liber pontificalis* is offering not only an alternative version of the relationship between Silvester and the Christian emperor who made Christianity a legal religion within the Roman Empire, but also a more positive understanding of Constantine himself.

An earlier text, the *Actus Silvestri*, had already elaborated the story of Constantine's being cured of leprosy and baptized by Silvester in Rome.[5] Although its contents are usually regarded as mostly fictional, the

---

Actus Silvestri. See also Rupke and Glock 2008, pp. 871–2, who merely repeat Duchesne's information.

[2] See Duchesne's comparison, *LP* I, pp. 1–12

[3] Eusebius–Jerome, *Chronicon*, ed. Helm, pp. 233–4, and ed. Jeanjean and Lançon, p. 80: *Constantinus extremo vitae suae tempore ab Eusebio Nicomedensi episcopo baptizatus in Arrianum dogma declinat. A quo usque in praesens tempus ecclesiarum rapinae et totius orbis est secuta discordia.* See Bardill 2012, pp. 304–5 for the standard account, apparently passing over these undercurrents. Eusebius's *Vita Constantini* was not known in the West in a Latin version until the eleventh century. Even the Greek text had very limited circulation: see Fowden 1994. Constantine was not the first Christian emperor. That description was applied to Philip the Arab (244–9) by Jerome in his translation of Eusebius's *Chronicon* as well as Eusebius in his *Historia ecclesiastica*, 6.3. See also Liverani 2008.

[4] Eusebius–Rufinus, *Historia ecclesiastica*, 10.12, ed. Schwartz and Mommsen, p. 978. English trans. Amidon, p. 402.

[5] See Cameron 2015; the leprosy story is perhaps a metaphor for the taint of paganism.

anti-*homoion* and political point of placing Constantine in Rome for his baptism at the hands of the orthodox Bishop of Rome is obvious.[6] The *Actus Silvestri*, in Pohlkamp's opinion, may have been produced in Rome as early as the late fourth or early fifth century, though Tessa Canella prefers a fifth-century Greek origin and has suggested that the later Latin version may not have circulated in the West until the late fifth or early sixth century. Unfortunately, the manuscripts of this Latin version, of the ninth and the twelfth centuries (Vat. lat. 5771 and Vat. lat. 1194 respectively) are too late to be helpful, but the *Actus Silvestri* is first mentioned in the early medieval list of approved and prohibited books sometimes attributed to Gelasius and known as the *De libris recipiendis et non recipiendis:* 'likewise the acts of blessed Silvester bishop of the apostolic seat, although the name of whoever wrote [them] is unknown, [but] we know [them] to be read by many catholics in the city of Rome and because of the ancient use of the multitude this is imitated by the church'.[7]

The Roman version of the story of Constantine and Silvester in the *Liber pontificalis*, therefore, is a combination of historical reconstruction, deliberate selection, and political use of fiction, and is unequivocal in its claims on Pope Silvester's behalf.

Silvester is then described as building a church in the city of Rome itself, in the 3rd region, 'close to the baths of Domitian' (*iuxta termas Domitianas*) and probably on the site of the present church of San Martino ai Monti on the Esquiline.[8] He was not quite the first pope the *Liber pontificalis* records as having built a church. One in Trastevere is credited to Pope Callistus (217–22),[9] and another is Felix I's (268–73) basilica on the Via Aurelia outside the walls at the second mile from Rome, though the text also attributes this same basilica, perhaps more plausibly, to Felix II (355–65).[10] Yet Silvester's new church is not only more precisely located and defined; the text also gives details of the

---

[6] Pohlkamp 1984; Canella 2006 and Amerise 2005.

[7] *De libris recipiendis et non recipiendis*, ed. von Dobschütz, pp. 9–10: *item actus beati Silvestri apostolicae sedis praesulis, licet eius qui conscripserit nomen ignoretur, a multis tamen in urbe Roma catholicis legi cognovimus et pro antiquo usu multae hoc imitantur ecclesiae.* On this decree and the possibility that it might be a Frankish compilation, see McKitterick 1989, pp. 202–5.

[8] *LP* I, p. 170, and note 4, p. 188.   [9] *LP* I, Life 17, pp. 141–2, note 5.

[10] *LP* I, Lives 27 and 38, pp. 158 and 211.

wealth Silvester bestowed upon it. It was 'on the estate of one of his priests and he established it as a Roman *titulus*' (the *titulus* of Silvester and Equitius);[11] Silvester endowed his new church with gold, silver, and bronze liturgical vessels, including 'a silver *patena* (a broad shallow dish) weighing 20 lbs from the gift of the emperor Constantine', lights and candlesticks, a number of farms in the Sabine and Cora territories, two houses with a bath, and a garden. Such an endowment, placing the pope among the ranks of wealthy landowners and benefactors, is another sign of the dramatic change in status of the Bishop of Rome.

In stating thereafter that Silvester 'issued a decree about the whole church', moreover, the *Liber pontificalis* deftly credits Silvester with the convening of the Council of Nicaea, the exposition of the catholic faith, and the condemnation of the Arian heretics. At another council in Rome, this time convened 'on Constantine's advice', the condemnation of the heretics was repeated. A number of other measures were passed, whose implications I shall consider in more detail in the following chapter.

From being the leader of a persecuted minority, therefore, the Bishop of Rome in the person of Silvester is presented as the instrument of conversion of the Roman emperor himself, the bishop ultimately respon-sible for the definition of orthodoxy at Nicaea in 325, retrospectively claimed as a major benefactor of the church in Rome, and defined as a legislator for the church both within and beyond Rome. It is of further significance that Silvester's is the first Life in the *Liber pontificalis* that fully replicates, by incorporating the building and patronage activity, the structure of an imperial biography I outlined in the first chapter above. In this chapter, therefore, I shall explore the *Liber pontificalis*'s account of the bishops' endowments and construction of churches in Rome as one crucial aspect of the sixth-century text's campaign, taken up by the seventh- and eighth-century continuations, to represent the visible estab-lishment of papal power in Rome.[12]

---

[11] *LP* I, p. 170 and see Hillner 2006, pp. 59–68 and discussion of San Martino ai Monti's strangely contradictory archaeology. On the *tituli* see also above, Chapter 2, p. 57.

[12] See above, p. 14.

The Emperor Constantine's Churches in Papal Rome

The biographical section of Silvester's career is completed in many respects with the decrees Silvester promulgated in Rome, and the note of Silvester's ordinations at the end of chapter 8 of Life 34. But a long section was then added, comprising chapters 9–33, on the construction and endowment of the churches credited to the Emperor Constantine, and entirely omits any reference to Constantine's own agenda for the destruction of the memory of the Emperor Maxentius.[13] The long additional section in Life 34 is usually thought to have been the work of Duchesne's hypothetical reviser who compiled the 'second edition' of the *Liber pontificalis*. As I indicated briefly in my introductory chapter above, the notion of a 'second edition' is problematic. The Felician epitome's omission of the buildings of Constantine cannot necessarily be understood as a sure indication of the absence of these details from the 'first edition', so much as the epitomizer's sacrifice of text that did not materially alter the points already made in his abridgement. The Cononian epitome in any case includes references to the buildings in an abridged form and, like the 'E' version of the full text, adds that the building of St Peter's basilica was at the request of Silvester (*ex rogatu Silvestri episcopi*). These brief references suggest that the lengthy account of Constantine's endowments was already part of the *Liber pontificalis* when the epitomes were made. As Paolo Liverani has argued, moreover, the formulaic phrasing of the text of this section of the Life suggests that it is based on an authentic estate record in a *libellus* containing details of the original foundations. He proposes that it was either from the imperial chancery or from a copy or version retained in the papal writing office, to which a number of clearly identifiable insertions were added by the sixth-century compiler of the *Liber pontificalis*.[14] I too regard this addition as part of the original text rather than the work of a reviser;[15] they have the effect, moreover, of making it look as if the emperor were

---

[13] For Constantine and Rome see Curran 2000, pp. 70–115, and Moralee 2018, pp. 39–51.

[14] Liverani 2019, pp. 169–217. I am very grateful to Michele Salzman for drawing my attention to this article. See also below, pp. 199–201.

[15] Geertman 2003a and 2003b at p. 291, note 11. Compare Duchesne, *LP* I, pp. cxli–cxliv, clxii, and Pietri 1976, p. 79.

following the pope's example, and lend a new significance to the eight opening chapters. With the exception of Leiden, VLQ 60, the earliest manuscripts from the eighth and ninth centuries even present the endowments in chapters 9–33 as if they were a continuation of the narrative of papal ecclesiastical organization, rather than the orderly separate lists devised by Duchesne for his edition.

Constantine's churches, therefore, serve the important function of placing the first major interventions made to the topography of Rome in Silvester's reign. Crucially, the pope is associated with the beginning of the transformation of the city, both by the building of his own church and with the claim that it was he who had made Constantine a Christian. The gifts from Constantine emphasize the substantial imperial patronage the bishops of Rome now enjoyed, in great contrast to the sorry catalogue of imperial anger and persecution in the preceding lives.

Chapters 9–33 of Life 34 list in exhaustive detail the gifts of the Emperor Constantine and the construction of many churches in Rome, Ostia, Albano, Naples, and Capua, and their equipment with lights, liturgical furniture, and gold, silver, and bronze liturgical vessels such as chalices and patens, *amae, metretae* (jars or flasks of some kind), crowns, and censers, many of them embellished with jacinth, chryso-phrase, and pearls. The endowment of these churches was lavish, with estates granted in Italy as well as further afield in the Holy Land, Sicily, Egypt, other Mediterranean islands, and Greece; houses, shops, and gardens in Antioch and Alexandria; revenues from estates noted in hundreds of *solidi;* and renders in kind such as papyrus stalks, Cyprus oil, cloves, papyrus (*charta*),[16] linen, spices, nard oil, balsam, cassia, storax, pepper, and saffron.[17] How accurate any of this is, whether it may be a reflection of papal estates acquired by various means by the sixth and seventh centuries rather than by imperial gift in the early fourth century, or indeed whether some of these estates even existed, is all beside the point, for the impression created is of stupendous imperial

---

[16] Davis, *Pontiffs,* p. 20 translates *chartae* as 'paper'. It is likely that this refers to blank rolls of papyrus ready for writing. The papal chancery continued to use papyrus for its legal documents and correspondence until the eleventh century; compare below, Chapter 6, pp. 176–8.

[17] I discuss the significance of these endowments further in McKitterick 2013a and 2020c.

munificence.[18] The church of Rome had become a major landowner and landlord. Imperial gifts follow the initial donation made by Silvester, especially in relation to St Peter's, the earliest basilica of San Paolo fuori le mura, and the seat of the popes at the Lateran. Further Constantinian churches were built at the Sessorian Palace, dedicated to the Holy Cross (Santa Croce in Gerusalemme), and at the burial sites of St Agnes, and of Saints Marcellinus and Petrus, where Constantine also erected the mausoleum for his mother Helena. In Ostia, Constantine paid for the construction of the church dedicated to Saints Peter, Paul, and John the Baptist. In Capua, he paid for the church of the Apostles, and in Albano, the church of St John the Baptist. At the end of the Life the information about Silvester's *titulus* is repeated, but this time, the gifts enumerated are from Constantine himself to Silvester's church, with many additional farms, and silver and bronze liturgical vessels for use in the church.

Many of the churches founded before 500, both inside and outside the walls of Rome, are described in the *Liber pontificalis* either as endowed by the popes or, if by emperors, then enriched by further gifts made by the popes. The descriptions of the endowment, building, and decoration of church buildings, and the donation of gold, silver, and bronze liturgical vessels, lights, screens, and silk hangings may well have drawn their information from inventories kept in the papal account books and estates' registers in the office known as the *vestiarium*.[19] In the text at least, the Christian bishops replace the pagan emperors in Rome as principal benefactors in the city, assisted materially by the recently converted emperors themselves. Closer scrutiny of the *Liber pontificalis*'s record of the subsequent intervention in the Constantinian structures by the popes, however, augmented by comparison with the extant buildings themselves, exposes new manifestations of papal power.

The Constantinian Basilica

Let us consider first the Constantinian basilica, later known as St John Lateran, and the Lateran Baptistery, to serve as an illustration of an initial imperial construction subsumed into papal patronage.

---

[18] Fuhrmann 1959, Liverani 1988, Marazzi 1995, and Montinaro 2015.
[19] Krautheimer 1980/2000 and *Corpus*.

The two buildings were, with Santa Croce in the Sessorian Palace, the only buildings that Constantine built within the walls of the city. Constantine razed the barracks of the *Equites singulares* (the mounted imperial guard) to the ground, and the Constantinian basilica was built using the basement rooms of the barracks as platform and foundation for the church. This was in itself a dramatic marker of the new Christian order, for the Lateran complex with church, episcopal residence, and baptistery, was not at first designed as a shrine for a saint; rather its very substantial endowment, far greater than that for either St Peter's or San Paolo fuori le mura,[20] appears to have been designed to assist the bishop to establish the Lateran as his base for his work as bishop, with a staff of clergy.[21] The *Liber pontificalis* certainly records continued imperial generosity towards the Constantinian basilica, but usually qualifies the gift, making it a result of a papal request. The Emperor Valentinian, for example, constructed a silver *fastigium* (what this was or looked like remains disputed) at Bishop Sixtus's request.[22] Far more prominent are the papal gifts, such as those of Pope Leo I (440–61). Thus, 'after the Vandal disaster', Pope Leo I is said to have

> replaced all the consecrated silver services throughout all the *tituli*, by melting down six water jars, two at the Constantinian basilica, two at the basilica of St Peter, two at St Paul's, which the emperor Constantine had presented, each weighing 100 lb. From these he replaced all the consecrated vessels [i.e. 600 lbs silver] ... He renewed St Peter's basilica and the apse vault; and he renewed St Paul's after the divine fire [that is, lightning]. He also constructed an apse ceiling in the Constantinian basilica.[23]

---

[20] I draw here on McKitterick 2020c.

[21] For details of the new excavations and reconstruction of the Lateran and the baths, barracks, and Roman *domus* found underneath the present building see the contributions by Lex Bosman, Ian Haynes, and Paolo Liverani to Bosman, Haynes, and Liverani (eds.) 2020. On the palace see Ballardini 2014. See the description in *Corpus* V (1977), pp. 1–92. See also Bauer 2004, pp. 61–80.

[22] *LP* I, Life 46, c. 4, p. 233.

[23] *LP* I, Life 47, c. 6, p. 239; trans. Davis, *Pontiffs*, p. 37: *Hic renovavit post cladem Wandalicum omnia ministeria sacrata argentea per omnes titulos, conflatas hydrias VI basilicae Constantinianae, duas basilicae beati Petri apostoli, duas beati Pauli apostoli, quas Constantinus*

Other papal gifts comprising decoration of various kinds, silver and gold vessels, silk veils or curtains, are referred to from time to time in the later seventh- and eighth-century sections of the *Liber pontificalis,* such as the gifts of Pope John IV (640–2),[24] and of Pope Hadrian I (772–95). The latter apparently carried out major restoration work on the fabric of the basilica as well as adorning it with rich silk hangings and gifts of silver and gold vessels.[25] It is in the ninth-century sections that the Lives of Popes Leo III (795–816) and Sergius II (844–7) contain the most detailed lists of embellishments, in the form of new church furniture, liturgical vessels, ornaments, hangings, glass windows, canopies, railings, and pictures to the churches of Rome, not least to the Constantinian basilica and the baptistery.[26] Gifts to the Constantinian basilica even emerge by the middle of the ninth century as a conventional way for the pope to mark the beginning of his pontificate, for this is mentioned in extravagant terms in the Lives of Popes Sergius II, who, 'burning with love from on high . . . completed a work of wondrous beauty in the Saviour's basilica called Constantinian',[27] and Benedict III (855–8), in almost exactly the same words: 'In the Saviour's basilica called Constantinian he provided an icon of wondrous beauty of the Redeemer our Lord Jesus Christ himself, trampling the lion and serpent underfoot of fine silver swathed in gold, weighing sixteen and a half pounds.'[28]

Augustus obtulit, qui pens. sing. lib. centenas; de quas omnia vasa renovavit sacrata. Hic renovavit basilicam beati Petri apostoli et beati Pauli post ignem divinum renovavit. Fecit vero cameram in basilica Constantiniana. See Salzman 2019.

[24] *LP* I, Life 74, c. 2, p. 330. [25] *LP* I, Life 97, cc. 49, 70, 84, pp. 500, 507, 510–11.

[26] Leo III, *LP* II, Life 98, cc. 8, 31, 51, 82, pp. 3, 9, 14, 25; Sergius II, *LP* II, Life 104, cc. 19, 25, 26, pp. 91 and 93. See also Gregory IV, *LP* II, Life 103, cc. 37 and 41, pp. 81 and 82.

[27] *LP* II, Life 104, c. 19, p. 91; trans. Davis, *Ninth-Century Popes,* p. 83: *In primo quidem pontificatus sui exordio, superno amore exardescans, in basilica Salvatoris quae Constantiniana nuncupatur mire pulchritudinis opus explevit.*

[28] *LP* II, Life 106, c. 21, p. 144, trans. Davis, *Ninth-Century Popes,* p. 177: *In primo quidem pontificatus sui exordio, superno exardescans amore, in basilica Salvatoris quae Constantiniana dicitur, ipsius redemptoris domini nostri Iesu Christi mire pulchritudinis ex argento purissimo auroque perfusam fecit iconam, leonem draconemque pedibus conculcantem, pens. lib. XVI semis.* The Life of Pope Nicholas I (858–67) does not use the phrase, but the record of gifts comes immediately after the elaborate chapters on the festivities accompanying his consecration: *LP* II, Life 107, cc. 11–14, pp. 152–3.

In the sixth-century section of the *Liber pontificalis*, the Constantinian basilica is accorded a determining role in confirming the legitimacy of contenders for the papal throne; Liberius's (352–66) restoration during the reign of the heretic Emperor Constantius was confirmed by his being given charge of the churches of St Peter, San Paolo fuori le mura, and the Constantinian basilica.[29] The basilica played a significant role in the claims of both Eulalius and Dioscorus to the see, in that each had been consecrated by their supporters in the Constantinian basilica, even though their respective rivals, Boniface I (418–22) and Boniface II (530–2) were each ordained in the basilica of Julius and were recognized as the legitimate popes in due course.[30] In the Laurentian schism, furthermore, it was Symmachus's consecration in the Constantinian basilica that was one of the things that appeared to work in his favour.[31] In the course of the seventh and eighth centuries, the Constantinian basilica is presented as becoming the site of an essential stage in the creation of a new pope, for it was there that the actual election took place before the candidate was installed in the Lateran palace and thereafter consecrated in St Peter's basilica.[32]

The Constantinian basilica in the later seventh- and eighth-century continuations is represented as playing an ever larger part in Roman politics and the liturgy. It enhanced thereby the central role of the Lateran in relation to the pope's authority and activities as bishop. It became a regular venue for synods, not least the Lateran Synod of 649,[33] the ritual deposition of Pope Constantine II,[34] and judicial hearings.[35] It was described as the site for the ceremonial burning of heretical books by Popes Gelasius, Symmachus, and Hormisdas.[36]

---

[29] *LP* I, Life 37, p. 208.   [30] *LP* I, Life 57, p. 281.

[31] *LP* I, Life 53, c. 2, p. 260. For full commentary see Wirbelauer 1993.

[32] See McKitterick 2013b.

[33] *LP* I, Life 76, c. 3, p. 336, and see Price, Booth, and Cubitt 2014.

[34] McKitterick 2018b.   [35] McKitterick 2020b.

[36] *LP* I, Lives 51, c. 1; 53, c. 5; and 54, c. 9, pp. 255, 261, 270–1.

The Lateran Baptistery

The remodelling of the Constantinian basilica in the seventeenth century has obscured most of its late antique details, but far more of the late antique and early medieval structures of the Lateran Baptistery are still visible. The Lateran Baptistery's font is identified in the *Liber pontificalis* as the site of Constantine's baptism, described as 'of porphyry stone covered with the finest silver on every side'. Other details in the text, however, emphasize the rite of baptism itself, such as the seven silver stags (presumably evoking the stag in the baptismal Psalm 41(42)), the golden basin on a porphyry column in which 200 lbs of balsam was burnt at Eastertide, the lamb of gold, silver statues of Christ and John the Baptist and the inscription (now lost) from St John's Gospel 1.29: BEHOLD THE LAMB OF GOD BEHOLD HIM WHO TAKES AWAY THE SIN OF THE WORLD.[37]

By the time the *Liber pontificalis* was written, the baptistery had been remodelled by Pope Sixtus III (432–40) and the text reports, in a mixture of historical reconstruction and omission, the eight porphyry columns 'that had been gathered from the time of the Emperor Constantine' (*quas a tempore Constantini Augusti fuerunt congregatas*), and Sixtus's erection of them with the architrave and adornment with verses. These verses are not copied into the *Liber pontificalis,* but they comprise a series of distychs on the significance of baptism for the rebirth of a Christian and the promise of eternal life in the heavenly kingdom, usually attributed to the young archdeacon who was to become Pope Leo.[38]

According to the *Liber pontificalis,* Pope Hilarus (461–8) was the next to intervene, and considerably enhanced the sacred space of the baptistery by adding three side chapels or oratories dedicated to John the Baptist, John the Evangelist, and the Holy Cross, 'all of silver and precious stones' (*omnia ex argento et lapidibus pretiosis*). In the oratories of both the Saints John he added 'bronze doors chased with silver' (*ianuas aereas argentoclusas*), and in each of the oratories a *confessio,* richly

---

[37] The texts are conveniently reproduced in Webb 2001, pp. 46–7. See also on the *Agnus Dei* below, pp. 138–9.

[38] *LP* I, Life 46, c. 7, p. 234; see Webb 2001, pp. 46–7.

decorated in gold and silver. The use of the word *confessio* is sometimes used to mean the burial place of a martyr, or the tomb of a martyr under an altar, so in this instance can probably be interpreted as a special altar with a relic. The gifts from Pope Hilarus, for example, included a piece of wood from the True Cross, though the oratory itself is no longer extant.[39]

The Life of John IV (640–2) reports that John 'built a church for the martyrs Saint Venantius, Anastasius, Maurus and many other martyrs whose relics he had ordered to be brought from Dalmatia and Istria; he deposited them in that church close to the Lateran Font and the oratory of St John the Evangelist; he decorated it and presented various gifts'.[40] These included silver arches and liturgical vessels. There were subsequent restorations in the ninth and twelfth centuries and extensive redecoration in the seventeenth century. The mosaics in this chapel indicate that Pope Theodore (642–9), John IV's successor, completed this chapel, for both popes are depicted in the apse mosaic: John IV holds a model of his chapel and Theodore holds a casket; on either side of the representation of the Virgin Mary are Saints John the Baptist, John the Evangelist, Peter, and Paul, and above them Christ with two angels. As we shall see, this is not the first instance of the presentation of the pope in saintly company, as if he were himself on the threshold of heaven. In this instance, however, as Gillian Mackie has stressed, the other saints depicted in this mosaic, on either side of the apse, are the Dalmatian saints whose remains have been gathered together and brought from their homeland and original burial sites to Rome to enrich this collective new shrine.[41] The saints commemorated in the mosaic images as well as the inscription, moreover, are precisely those referred to in the *Liber pontificalis*.

---

[39] *LP* I, Life 48, pp. 242–5. *LP* I, Life 51, c. 5, p. 255. See Johnson 1995, and on the terminology see Mackie 2003, p. 5.

[40] *LP* I, Life 74, p. 330; trans. Davis, pp. 64–5: *Eodem tempore fecit ecclesiam beati martyribus Venantio, Anastasio, Mauro et aliorum multorum martyrum, quorum reliquias de Dalmatias et Histrias adduci praeceperat, et recondit eas in ecclesia suprascripta iuxta fontem Lateranensem, iuxta oratorium beati Iohannis evangelistae quam ornavit et diversa dona optulit.*

[41] Mackie 2003, pp. 212–15. And see further below, pp. 116–20.

St Peter's Basilica

The next major construction attributed to Constantine in the *Liber pontificalis* is St Peter's basilica. Although the Emperor Constantine built a new basilica to St Peter the Apostle at the Temple of Apollo where he sealed the tomb containing Peter's body and decorated it, the *Liber pontificalis,* as noted in the previous chapter, had already claimed for two earlier popes, Anacletus and Cornelius, the initial creation of a memorial to St Peter on the Vatican Hill as well as the translation of Peter to his final resting place.[42] Pope Damasus (366–84) subsequently, moreover, is described as adorning a tablet with verses at the catacombs where the bodies of Saints Peter and Paul lay.[43] The early chronology for the initial construction of St Peter's basilica, and its imperial connections over the years from the 320s to the 340s, seems clear from the evidence of the archaeological excavations (notably those carried out in 1844 and 1945), inscriptions, and brick stamps.[44] The basilica itself was an extraordinary feat of engineering, built on a massive platform created by filling in an older Roman necropolis that was still in use in the third century.

The basilica was a large rectangular hall in shape, with an apse and aisles marked out with massive columns supporting a clerestory with windows. Two rotundas were added on the south side in the early fifth and the early sixth century respectively, also built on top of earlier structures. One was built as a mausoleum for the Emperor Honorius and for other members of his family. The second was the building, dedication, and endowment of the other rotunda to Peter's brother Andrew by Pope Symmachus (498–514); it included oratories dedicated to the saints Cassian, Protus and Hyacinth, Apollinaris and Sossus. The *Liber pontificalis* also reports that Symmachus constructed oratories in the main basilica dedicated to the Holy Cross, St John the Evangelist, and John the Baptist, which have been interpreted as an attempt on Symmachus's part to mirror the three oratories of the Lateran Baptistery as a major element of his building campaign.[45] Meaghan McEvoy has

---

[42] *LP* I, Lives 5 and 22, pp. 125 and 150–1. [43] *LP* I, Life 39, c. 2, p. 212.
[44] Liverani 2006, 2008, and 2013. See also Gem 2013 and Liverani and Spinola 2010.
[45] *LP* I, Life 53, c. 6, p. 261; see Alchermes 1995, and for a general description, *Corpus* V (1977), pp. 165–285.

suggested that the mausoleum of Honorius was an effort on Honorius's part to strengthen the imperial association, even in death, with the apostle, and thereby renew imperial commitment to the city of Rome.[46] This suggestion needs to be seen in relation to Honorius's simultaneous embellishment of the church of St Laurence in Ravenna, his new imperial city.[47] It could also have been a demonstration of Honorius's rivalry with the pope for an association with St Peter. The *Liber pontificalis* says nothing of this.

The mausoleum of Honorius was definitively taken over by the popes in the middle of the eighth century and converted into a chapel dedicated to Petronilla, claimed in the narrative of her translation as St Peter's daughter.[48] Despite the number of aristocratic burials in the basilica, moreover, of which only one, that of the family of Bassus, is mentioned in passing in the Life of Sixtus III (432–40) in the *Liber pontificalis*,[49] the narrative systematically reports instead how from Pope Leo I's death onwards, the basilica of St Peter's itself became the papal necropolis. This has as much to do with the politics of papal burial, to trump imperial and aristocratic claims to a special relationship with St Peter, as with the cult of St Peter himself.[50]

The basilica of St Peter acted as a strong force field for the city.[51] The *Liber pontificalis* records how St Peter's was subsequently repaired, embellished, equipped with many further oratories, monasteries to house attendant clergy, and facilities for pilgrims.[52] Many more rich papal gifts of gold, silver, and bronze vessels and silk hangings were made, by Popes Sixtus III (432–40), Leo I (440–61), Hilarus (461–8), Simplicius (468–83), Symmachus (498–514), Hormisdas (514–23), Pelagius II (579–90), Gregory I (590–604), Honorius (625–38), Severinus

---

[46] McEvoy 2013.

[47] Deliyannis 2010, pp. 46–51 and compare her account of Honorius's sister Galla Placidia's lavish patronage in Ravenna, ibid., pp. 62–86.

[48] McKitterick 2018a and Goodson 2015.

[49] *LP* I, Life 46, p. 232: reporting how Bassus was buried by the pope at St Peter's in his parents' tomb chamber (*sepellivit ad beatum Petrum apostolum, in cubiculum parentum eius*). On the famous sarcophagus of Junius Bassus, prefect of Rome, ancestor of the fifth-century Bassus, see Elsner 1998, pp. 193–7 and see also Thacker 2013, pp. 141–4.

[50] On the papal burials see Picard 1969, Borgolte 1995, and McKitterick 2013b.

[51] Liverani 2013, pp. 33–4.   [52] Santangeli Valenzani 2014.

(May–August 640), Benedict II (684–5), and Sergius I (687–701). Particular attention was given to the *confessio* of St Peter between the fifth and seventh centuries.[53] During the reign of Pope Hormisdas, several kings are recorded as making gifts to St Peter. Thus, Clovis, king of the Franks, gave a jewelled crown; the 'orthodox emperor' Justin presented gold and silver liturgical vessels, and King Theodoric gave two silver candlesticks weighing 70 lbs to St Peter.[54] In the reign of Vitalian (657–72) the visit of the Emperor Constans at least began conventionally, with gifts to St Peter.[55] The basilica rapidly became the place for papal ceremonial, not least the consecration of each new pope. In the subsequent papal biographies, St Peter's basilica was rapidly absorbed into the orchestration of papal ceremonial and processions: it became a key focus of the stational liturgy, a venue for councils, a major pilgrimage site, art treasure, and holy place. All these themes were deployed by the *Liber pontificalis* authors to enhance and promote papal authority. In other words, the text actually used the basilica and its functions to forge the essential link between St Peter and his successors.[56]

San Paolo fuori le mura

The *Liber pontificalis* states that at Silvester's petition the Emperor Constantine and, according to a number of the early manuscripts, his son the Emperor Constantius as well, built a basilica to St Paul. The remains of a small church, possibly that built by Constantine and his son, were discovered during excavations in 1850 and 2002–6.[57] It was allegedly on the site where Paul had been executed, and to which Paul's body was supposedly translated in the third century by Pope Cornelius and the lady Lucina from the *memoria apostolorum* at San Sebastiano on the Via Appia.[58] In keeping with the highlighting of the role of Silvester and his successors, however, the author chose not to mention either the

---

[53] *LP* I, Life 83, c. 2; Life 86, cc. 10–11; Life 46, cc. 4 and 8; Life 47, c. 6; Life 48, c. 7; Life 49, c. 5; Life 53, cc. 6 and 7; Life 54, c. 11; Life 65, c. 2; Life 66, c. 4; Life 72, c. 1; pp. 363, 374, 233–4, 239, 243, 249, 261–2, 271, 309, 312, and 323.

[54] *LP* I, Life 54, c. 10, p. 271.   [55] *LP* I, Life 78, cc. 2–3, p. 343.

[56] McKitterick 2013b, Thacker 2013, and Humphries 2007.

[57] Camerlenghi 2018, pp. 23–31.   [58] *LP* I, Life 22, p. 150.

construction of the massive new church of San Paolo fuori le mura under the Emperors Valentinian II (375–92), Theodosius I (378–95), and Arcadius (395–408), or the triumphal arch at San Paolo paid for by Galla Placidia (388–450). Other imperial endowments elsewhere in Rome are also ignored, such as the Empress Eudoxia's foundation of San Pietro in Vincoli. San Paolo fuori le mura has two earlier surviving inscriptions which assert Pope Siricius's (384–99) claims of association with the construction of the building: *Siricius episcopus tota mente devotus* ('the Bishop Siricius [to Christ] with all the devotion'), though again there is no matching claim in the *Liber pontificalis*'s Life of Siricius.[59]

The mosaic decoration with Christ the evangelist and angels at San Paolo fuori le mura includes two inscriptions:

THEODOSIUS C[O]EPIT PERFECIT [H]ONORIUS AULAM
DOCTORIS MUNDI SACRATAM CORPORE PAULI

Theodosius began and Honorius finished the Hall made sacrosanct by the body of Paul.

PLACIDAE PIA MENS OPERIS DECUS OMNE PATERNI
GAUDET PONTIFICIS STUDIO SPLENDERE LEONIS

Placidia's devoted heart is delighted that all the dignity of her father's work shines resplendent through the zeal of Pope Leo.[60]

Despite these highly visible statements in the church itself, the *Liber pontificalis* merely observes that Leo I (440–61) renewed St Paul's 'after the divine fire' (*post ignem divinum*). San Paolo was severely damaged in another fire, in 1823, but descriptions and drawings made of it before this, as well as the remarkably faithful restoration completed after the fire, make it relatively easy to imagine the visual impact of the original, a

---

[59] *LP* I, Life 40, p. 216. Webb 2001, p. 211; *Corpus* V (1977), pp. 93–164. See also Kinney 2011.

[60] I follow Duchesne's rendering, *LP* I, p. 195, note 71; trans. Webb 2001, p. 212. The nineteenth-century reconstruction of this inscription is illustrated in Camerlenghi 2018, p. 93 (fig. 3.11), where OMNE in the second phrase on the mosaic was spelt HOMNE.

process now greatly assisted by Nicola Camerlenghi's computer-aided reconstructions.[61]

A dramatic statement of papal presence, moreover, was the series of papal portraits added above the arches in the nave, with the entire sequence of popes from St Peter. They act as a visual complement to the *Liber pontificalis* text itself. A few of the original paintings survived the fire of 1823 and used to be dated, ostensibly on stylistic grounds, to the late fifth century or early sixth century. Fortunately, a further source of information is the entire cycle copied into an imperial folio volume in 1634 by Antonio Eclissi.[62] It is possible that the sequence was begun or augmented by Pope Leo I (440–61) and continued further by Laurentius in the brief four years between 498 and 502 in which he occupied the see, or so the inclusion of Laurentius's portrait, rather than that of his rival Symmachus, in the sequence might suggest. Camerlenghi, however, has mounted a compelling case for the first forty-two portraits culminating in Pope Innocent I (401–17), on the south wall of the nave, having been part of the original decorative scheme of the basilica, set in panels underneath the sequence of representations of Heavenly Jerusalem, forty-four large-scale figures of the Prophets, Old Testament scenes from the Creation to the Plagues of Egypt, and New Testament scenes, mostly recording Paul's exploits from the Acts of the Apostles. It was Pope Innocent who had dedicated the Theodosian church. The nave of St Peter's basilica apparently had a similar cycle, described by Grimaldi in 1619. These were attributed, without any substantial justification, to fresco painters during the reign of Pope Liberius, whereas Gerhard Ladner credited them to Pope Leo I. It would be more logical to see them as part of the same display of confidence, or bravado, that prompted Leo I's extension of the San Paolo portraits.[63] Yet they also can be seen as an emerging substitute, not only for the now defunct display of imperial statues in public fora in Rome that had been on the wane since the end of the fourth century, but also in competition with the briefly revived

---

[61] *LP* I, Life 47, c. 6, p. 239, and Camerlenghi 2018, pp. 82–118 and
https://rcweb.dartmouth.edu/CamerlenghiN/VirtualBasilica/.
[62] See McKitterick 2013a.
[63] BAV Barberini lat. 2733: Grimaldi 1972, pp. 138–57 and Figs 52–8. Ladner 1941.

fashion for public statues of the ruler during the reign of Theodoric the Ostrogoth.[64] These sets of papal portraits offer a visual history of the apostolic succession, consolidated within the *Liber pontificalis* itself.

San Lorenzo fuori le mura

The idea of displaying papal portraits in close proximity to the saints, and in a new kind of sacred space, was subsequently developed further. The original Constantinian funerary hall at San Lorenzo fuori le mura has been identified as the structure excavated in 1957 in the adjoining city cemetery. The site of St Laurence's martyrdom had received a great deal of papal attention before that. The first account of his death is in the Life of Pope Sixtus II (257–8) and took place during the Decian persecutions. In the wake of the Constantinian endowment, further buildings and gifts dedicated to Laurence are recorded. San Lorenzo fuori le mura was chosen as a site for particular liturgical rites or as a burial place by Popes Damasus (366–84), Zosimus (417–18), Sixtus III (432–40), Hilarus (461–8), and Simplicius (468–83).[65] The Constantinian church of San Lorenzo fuori le mura was superseded by a magnificent new building, mentioned briefly in the *Liber pontificalis* as 'built from the ground up' (*a fundamento*) by Pope Pelagius II (579–90).[66]

Part of the nave and the triumphal arch preceding the original apse of Pelagius's church survived the radical alteration and reorientation carried out by Pope Honorius III (1216–27) in the thirteenth century. The iconography anticipates the similar message of the mosaic depicting Popes John IV and Theodore in the Lateran Baptistery, in that Pope Pelagius is depicted presenting his church to St Laurence, and is in the company of Saints Peter and Paul, Stephen and Hippolytus, all flanking Christ enthroned on the world and with representations of Bethlehem and Jerusalem. There is a lengthy mosaic inscription, spelling out Pelagius's achievement in building the church and reinforcing the imagery:

---

[64] Machado and Ward-Perkins 2013, Machado 2010, pp. 237–58. See also the 'The Last Statues' database http://laststatues.classics.ox.ac.uk.

[65] *LP* I, Life 49, c. 2, p. 249.

[66] *LP* I, Life 65, c. 2, p. 309; see the discussion in *Corpus* II (1959), pp. 1–145.

PRAESULE PELAGIO MARTYR LAURENTIUS OLIM

TEMPLA SIBI STATUIT TAM PRETIOSA DARI

MIRA FIDES GLADIOS HOSTILES INTER ET IRAS

PONTIFICEM MERITIS HAEC CELEBRASSE SUIS

TU MODO SANCTORUM CUI CRESCERE CONSTAT HONORES

FAC SUB PACE COLI TECTA DICATA TIBI.

Under Pelagius's prelateship it was once decided that this sanctuary, so precious, should be set up to the martyr Laurence. A wonderful faith that the pope by his merits would complete the church despite the weapons and the passions of his enemies. Now Laurence, make the building that is dedicated in your name subject to the peace of heaven, since it is decreed that you will share in the communion of the saints.[67]

Sant'Agnese fuori le mura

Sant'Agnese fuori le mura was also credited to Constantine in Life 34 of the *Liber pontificalis*. Only the shell of the vast funerary hall, possibly as early as the reign of Constantine, is still visible, but traces of an earlier church, discernible behind the current apse of the church, may be those of a construction later in the fourth century. Pope Liberius (352–66) commissioned a monument to honour Agnes, and fragments also remain of Pope Damasus's poem in honour of the saint inscribed in the fine capital letters known as Filocalian.[68] Here again the *Liber pontificalis* records a steady increase in papal care of this martyr's shrine. Pope Symmachus (498–514) is described as renewing 'the apse of St Agnes which was liable to collapse and the whole basilica',[69] while Honorius I (625–38) is said to have replaced the church completely, for 'he built

---

[67] Duchesne's rendering, *LP* I, p. 310, note 5, from the inscription in its present position (see Krautheimer, Josi, and Frankl 1952); trans. Webb 2001, p. 244; the imagery is illustrated in Brandenburg 2004, p. 237.

[68] See Gray 1956, pp. 5–13, Trout 2015, and Aste 2014. On the building see *Corpus* I (1937), pp. 14–38.

[69] *LP* I, Life 53, c. 10, p. 263; trans. Davis, *Pontiffs*, p. 45: *Hic absidam beatae Agnae quae in ruinam inminebat et omnem basilicam renovavit.*

from the ground up the church of St Agnes the martyr at the 3rd mile from Rome on the Via Nomentana where the body rests. He decorated it to perfection on every side and there he put many gifts.'[70]

The text does not mention the apse portrait of Pope Honorius, depicted with Pope Symmachus on either side of the saint herself, with Honorius holding a model of his church,[71] nor the flamboyant dedicatory inscription which concludes with the injunction:

SURSUM VERSA NUTU QUOD CUNCTIS CERNITUR UNO

PRAESUL HONORIUS HAEC VOTA DICATA DEDIT

VESTIBUS ET FACTIS SIGNANTUR ILLIUS ORA

[LUCET ET] ASPECTU LUCIDA CORDA GERENS

What all can see in a single upward glance are the sacred offerings dedicated by Honorius. His portrait is identified by robes and by the building. Wearing a radiant heart, he radiates in appearance also.[72]

Donor Portraits: Reaching to Heaven

Such a depiction of the pope in an apse mosaic, in the company of the saints, and portrayed as donor, seems first to have been devised in Rome at about the same time as the production of the first section of the *Liber pontificalis*. That is, coinciding with the early stages of the Ostrogothic wars, it appears to be part of the same assertion of very particular power and an appeal to the support of the saints on the popes' part. Felix IV is represented in the apse of Santi Cosma e Damiano as a donor holding his church. His new church was built 'in the area called the Via Sacra, close to the temple of the city of Rome'. This was the first church to be established in the Forum, and was converted from an apsed hall by adding a mosaic depicting Christ's second coming in power and glory,

---

[70] *LP* I, Life 72, c. 3, p. 323; trans. Davis, *Pontiffs*, p. 62: *Eodem tempore fecit ecclesiam beatae Agne martyri, via Numentana miliario ab urbe Roma III, a solo, ubi requiescit, quem undique ornavit, exquisivit, ubi posuit dona multa.*

[71] Grig 2005, and see also Wirbelauer 2014.

[72] In Duchesne's rendering, *LP* I, p. 325, note 9; trans. Webb 2001, p. 248; illustrated in Brandenburg 2004, pp. 244, where the alternative reading AECETET ASPECTU is visible.

with St Peter, the two martyrs Cosmas and Damian, the martyr Theodore, St Paul, and on his right Pope Felix IV, presenting a model of his church, though that image, alas, was painted over in the seventeenth century.[73] Beneath is a mosaic inscription which concludes with the statement that Felix has made to the Lord this offering, worthy of the Lord's harvest, that he may be granted life in the airy vault of heaven:

OPTULIT HOC DNO FELIX ANTISTITE DIGNUM MUNUS
UT AETHERIA VIVAT IN ARCE POLI.

Later portraits of popes from the ninth century, of Paschal I in Santa Prassede, Santa Maria in Dominica, and Santa Cecilia, and of Pope Gregory IV in San Marco, are part of this symbolic tradition in every respect.[74] Such a representation of the pope offering a model of the church to the saint predates, and may even have inspired, the depiction of Archbishop Ecclesius in the church of San Vitale in Ravenna. Ecclesius is one of a sequence of four bishops of Ravenna portrayed in the apse of that church, probably in the process of its completion under Archbishop Maximian in c.547.[75] Although the construction of the church began under Bishop Ecclesius in 526, the man who paid for the building appears to have been the layman Julius Argentarius. In this context, the portrait of Ecclesius has more the function of reminding the congregation of the building's history. The subsequent addition of the two panel mosaics on either side of the apse depicting the Emperor Justinian flanked by Archbishop Maximian, and Empress Theodora and her retinue, function as a virtual presence for rulers who never actually visited Ravenna, rather than as donor portraits; the imperial entourages are portrayed in the church as if they were participating in the processional liturgy.[76]

The donor portrait of the bishop within a church, offering a model of that very church to Christ and/or Mary and the saints, has no parallel in Roman imperial imagery. That is, there are no representations of Roman

---

[73] *LP* I, Life 56, c. 2, p. 279; trans. Davis, *Pontiffs*, p. 49: *in urbe Roma, in loco qui appellatur via sacra, iuxta templum urbis Romae.* For illustrations see Brandenburg 2004, pp. 222–30.

[74] Bolgia 2006, Goodson 2010.   [75] See James 2017, pp. 236–45.

[76] See the illustrations in David 2013, pp. 141–67.

emperors presenting the temples to the gods; the dedication of temples is more usually depicted in an iconography of sacrifice. Although there are many representations of the emperor receiving crowns, sceptres, globes, or thunderbolts from the gods, emperors giving gifts to gods are far rarer, though there are a few from Egypt dating to the reign of Trajan. Further, the only representations of deities holding temples known to me are on a handful of eastern (Thrace, Smyrna, Edessa) provincial, non-imperial coins of Septimius Severus, Severus Alexander, Julia Domna, and Gallienus. That of Caracalla actually represents Tyche on the reverse holding a model building in each hand.[77]

These papal donor images with their churches cannot be read simply as representations of gift-giving and patronage, though they are that too of course. The gift in such representations has been seen in general terms as anticipating a counter-gift, namely, the saint's help for the donor in heaven, so that the image is a visualization of a hoped-for transaction of exchange.[78] As a consequence of the gift, the church thereafter might be said to belong to the saint. Beatrice Leal, for example, has commented how such 'architectural donor portraits belong to the visual language of partnership with the saints . . . [T]he imagery can be understood as the saints introducing the pope to Christ in return for the dedication of the church.'[79]

Further, there is the symbolism of the spiritual transformation effected by the image. Indeed, Rico Franses has argued that the figures in what he prefers to describe as 'contact portraits' (of which 'donor portraits' are a subset) are dynamic elements of interactive supplication, rather than merely images of passive 'relations' between the human and the divine. They portray, because it is an encounter between the human and the heavenly, a demand for judgement and forgiveness.[80] His

---

[77] Schoenert-Geiss 1965, Perinthos 596. See also Varbanov 2005–7, Nos. 173, 235; Schultz and Zahle 1981–2, Cop. 219, 1410; Poole 1873, pp. 284, 390. I am very grateful to Dennis Jussen, Ketty Iannantuono, and Olivier Hekster, all of Radboud University, Nijmegen, for these examples and for conversation on this point. See also Burgersdijk and Ross (eds.) 2018, Ewald and Noreña (eds.) 2015.

[78] Brubaker 2010.

[79] See Leal 2016, pp. 148–60, especially p. 151. I am very grateful to Bea Leal for kindly letting me see a copy of her thesis. See also an earlier survey by Lippsmeyer 1981.

[80] Franses 2018, pp. 6–8. See also Ševčenko 1994, and compare Elsner 1995.

arguments are largely based on painted representations in Byzantine manuscripts from the later ninth to the eleventh centuries, and stress the way the portraits 'show the barrier between human and divine being breached'.[81] The mosaic representations of the popes with their model churches, in the apse or on the triumphal arches of early medieval Roman basilicas, suggest that such a demand is surely affected by the status of the individual portrayed, how it is imagined such divine help might be delivered, and what form it would take. Not all the benefits may have been envisaged as only to be received in the afterlife. The saints themselves, as well as the papal donors, are historical figures with terrestrial pasts, anchored in terrestrial memories, which, as we have seen, are often spelt out in the inscriptions associated with the mosaic images.

The proximity of pope and saint in the image, even with the titular saint embracing the pope, and the way the pope is portrayed as bridging the gap between earth and heaven with the church in his arms, however, also transports the entire congregation within the church with him. The pope is the head of the congregation and has a representative and intercessory function for his people.[82] The people participating in the liturgy, and the liturgy itself, essentially a ritual of offering,[83] are symbolically inside, or embodied in, the little model church carried in the pope's arms to heaven. While the image as a whole can count as a particular representation of the initial dedication, it is continually renewed and invigorated with further meaning every time the liturgical rituals in honour of God and his saints are enacted within the building. For their part, the saints as well as the pope are a continuous virtual presence in the church, fulfilling what Franses conceives to be the function of the donor portrait. That is, they show not so much the barrier between the human and the divine being breached in any simple sense, but 'generate the charged, laden, miraculous belief in that impossible event'.[84]

Other papal foundations between the fifth and seventh centuries, made by Popes Felix II, Damasus, Anastasius, Boniface I, Celestine I,

---

[81] Franses 2018, p. 15. [82] Franses 2018, p. 85.
[83] See the apt description of the Eucharist as a 'reciprocity of giving' in Ganz 2010, at p. 18.
[84] Franses 2018, pp. 221–2.

Leo I, and Hilarus, may have lacked such papal portraits. The record of their buildings catalogued in the *Liber pontificalis* are none the less indicative of a papal forging of a special papal relationship with particular saints as well as the more prosaic papal stepping into the void created by the absence of imperial patronage. Pope Simplicius (468–83), for example, dedicated a basilica on the Caelian Hill to St Stephen, as well as a basilica dedicated to St Andrew the apostle close to the basilica of St Mary, another church dedicated to St Stephen close to the basilica of St Laurence, and the church of St Bibiana.[85] The holiness of San Stefano Rotondo was further enhanced under Pope Theodore (642–9), who had the bodies of the martyrs Prius and Felician brought from their original burial place in the Via Nomentana and deposited in a new resting place in a side chapel, also the burial place of his own father Theodore, a former Bishop of Jerusalem, with a mosaic depicting the saints above the altar.[86]

The Cult of Mary the Virgin

Santa Maria Maggiore, moreover, symbolizes the beginning in Rome, in the aftermath of the decree of the Council of Ephesus of 431 which declared Mary to be Mother of God (*Theotokos*), of an extended Roman appropriation and promotion of the cult of St Mary the Virgin and 'Mother of God'. In stressing Roman devotion to Mary, I here depart from the widespread assumption of an 'adoption of a Byzantine *Theotokos* cult' in Rome. If there were such a 'Byzantine' *Theotokos* cult in Italy one would expect to see rather more evidence for it in Ravenna than there is. Apparently only one fifth-century basilica, Santa Maria Maggiore, was dedicated to Mary in Ravenna, and Mary as either Virgin or Mother is not especially prominent in the mosaic imagery of the churches of the city.[87] The church of Santa Maria Maggiore in Rome was first described as a foundation by Pope Liberius (352–66) but it was either restored and

---

[85] *LP* I, p. 249. On all this papal building summarized above see in particular Geertman 2004, Blaauw 1994a, and Bauer 2004.

[86] *LP* I, Life 75, c. 4, p. 332. See Davis-Weyer 1989, *Corpus* IV (Vatican City, 1970), pp. 213–17.

[87] Ephesus 431. Compare Moralee 2018, pp. 94–109, and his references, and Osborne 2008.

augmented or replaced by a new building by Pope Sixtus III (432–40) nearly a century later.[88] The *Liber pontificalis* records rich gifts of estates and revenues from Sixtus III, as well as liturgical vessels and furniture, including 'a silver stag at the font pouring water weighing 20 lbs, and all the silver vessels for baptism weighing 15 lbs'.[89] It was built on a magnificent scale. The apse mosaic was replaced in the thirteenth century, but the triumphal arch mosaics are from the fifth century. They depict the Annunciation and the earliest years of the life of Christ (Epiphany, Massacre of the Innocents, Flight into Egypt, King Herod visited by the Magi, the Presentation in the Temple) and the cities of Jerusalem and Bethlehem. Depicted in the long entablature of the clerestory on both sides of the nave is a series of Old Testament scenes, including many battles, in mosaic. These too were made in the fifth century, though some were replaced with painted copies in the sixteenth century.[90] Beneath a representation on the arch of the saints Peter and Paul, on either side of a throne containing the book with the seven seals from the Book of Revelation and four Evangelist symbols, is a short inscription. It makes the uncompromising statement XYSTUS EPISCOPUS PLEBI DEI (Sixtus the bishop to the people of God).

Further instances of the growing cult of St Mary are the famous consecration of a hitherto secular building to Christian liturgical use with the transformation of the Pantheon into the church of Santa Maria ad martyres in 609 or 613 by Pope Boniface IV: 'At that time he asked the emperor Phocas for the temple called Pantheon and in it he made a church of the ever Virgin Mary and all martyrs.'[91]

There is also the remarkable construction and frescoed decoration of Santa Maria Antiqua, constructed within the vestibule of a palace on the Palatine Hill, patronized by a succession of popes and papal officials from the sixth to the end of the eighth century, notably Pope John VII at

---

[88] *LP* I, Lives 37 and 46, pp. 208 and 232, and see *Corpus* III (1967), pp. 1–60.

[89] *LP* I, Life 46, c. 3, p. 233: *cervum argenteum fundentem aquam, pens. lib. XX; omnia vasa baptismi sacrata argentea, pens. lib. XV;* trans. Davis, *Pontiffs,* p. 35.

[90] Warland 2003 and Miles 1993.

[91] *LP* I, Life 69, c. 2, p. 317: *Eodem tempore petiit a Focate principe templum qui appellatur Pantheum, in quo fecit ecclesiam beatae Mariae semper virginis et omnium martyrum;* trans. Davis, *Pontiffs,* p. 61. Marder and Wilson-Jones (eds.) 2015, and on the date of the consecration Thunø 2015, p. 234.

the beginning of the eighth century. These are currently the subject of intensive studies by colleagues, so I shall say no more about them here.[92] I discuss the use of former public buildings in Rome further below.

The *Liber pontificalis* records and could even be interpreted as making a case for what amounts to papal monopoly of church building, despite the ample physical evidence to the contrary.[93] The bishop emerges as the primary patron of church building in Rome,[94] with a steady expenditure in the fifth, sixth, and seventh centuries on churches both within Rome and beyond the walls, as well as a notable provision of cemeteries to accommodate the presumably ever-increasing number of Christian burials.[95]

Only rarely does the *Liber pontificalis* concede that private citizens or members of the clergy also endowed churches, as in the reference to Santa Sabina, backed up by a magnificent mosaic inscription in the church itself. The Life of Pope Sixtus III (432–40) records that in his time the bishop Peter built in Rome the basilica of St Sabina, where he also built a font. The inscription, however, says Peter was a priest and that the church was built in the time of Pope Celestine.[96] Sometimes too there is a tribute to the support of wealthy patrons in cooperation with the pope, such as the widow Vestina for the building of a basilica dedicated to the saints Gervase and Protasius,[97] the handmaid Demetrias for the building of a basilica dedicated to St Stephen on her own estate,[98] and the *matronae* Priscilla and Lucina, who gave land for cemeteries. Lucina also made her own house into a *titulus.*[99]

---

[92] Andaloro, Bordi, and Morganti (eds.) 2016; Bordi, Osborne, and Rubery (eds.) 2020; and Osborne 2020. As noted above, I am very grateful to John Osborne for letting me read drafts of his chapters in advance of publication.

[93] Coates-Stephens 1997.

[94] A similar argument about papal monopoly of church building is mounted, on the basis primarily of the inscription evidence, by Behrwald 2016.

[95] Meneghini 2000, Costambeys 2001, and for general context, Rebillard 1994/2009.

[96] *LP* I, Life 46, p. 235. For a transcription and description of the inscription see Webb 2001, p. 173.

[97] *LP* I, Life 42 (Innocent I, 402–4), p. 220.   [98] *LP* I, Life 47 (Leo I, 440–61), p. 238.

[99] See Machado 2019. I am very grateful to Carlos Machado for kindly allowing me to see his monograph in advance of publication. See also Cooper 1999, Kudock 2007, and Grig 2004.

The Communion of Saints

I have emphasized the essential association between the popes and church-building that the *Liber pontificalis* charts, but there is a further and obvious link to stress, and that is the saints to whom these churches were dedicated and with whom as we have seen they are sometimes portrayed in triumph. The stories behind the saints memorialized by these new churches, moreover, are preserved in the earliest pre-fourth-century biographies in the *Liber pontificalis*. It is hardly news that the popes promoted the cults of Roman saints and especially of Roman martyrs, for this has been a constant theme of scholarship over the past century and half.[100] Nevertheless the *Liber pontificalis* insists, time and time again, on the papal association with particular saints, their devotion to them, their building of shrines and basilicas dedicated to them, the provision of communities of clergy to observe the liturgical commemoration of them, and the translation and veneration of a multitude of new saints brought from the catacombs and installed in special new resting places in the city. The umbrella term 'cult', in other words, involves a great range of activities and manifests itself in an enormous diversity of evidence. The references to translations especially increase in momentum in the eighth-century Lives. In this respect the *Liber pontificalis* is acting as both a publicizing text on behalf of pope and saint alike, and as a complementary source. It documents the great range of activities that the 'cult' of a saint entails and cannot be regarded simply as propaganda. The *Liber pontificalis* essentially corroborates the inscription evidence. An example from the eighth century is Paul I's list of the saints, already referred to in Chapter 2 above, that he brought to his new church of San Silvestro in Capite,[101] in which the *Liber pontificalis* describes Paul's translation of saints and the construction of San Silvestro. It is worth quoting this description in full:

> He observed that very many locations in these cemeteries of the saints had
> been largely demolished through the neglect and carelessness of antiquity

---

[100] Most recently see Maskarinec 2018, Moralee 2018, pp. 87–109, and 185–208. See also Goodson 2010.

[101] San Silvestro inscription in Cardin 2008, p. 68 and Tavola 48.

and were now nearly reduced to ruin, so he forthwith removed the saints' bodies from these destroyed cemeteries. With hymns and spiritual chants he brought them inside this city of Rome and he took care to have some of them buried with fitting honour around the *tituli*, deaconries, monasteries and other churches.

c. 5 This holy prelate constructed from the ground up a monastery in his own house in honour of St Stephen the martyr and pontiff and of St Silvester another pontiff and confessor of Christ. He built a chapel onto this monastery's upper walls and with great veneration he deposited their bodies there. Within the monastery's enclosure he constructed from the ground up a church of wondrous beauty ... and there with great respect and reverence he deposited the bodies of the uncounted saints he had removed from the demolished cemeteries.[102]

The inscription at San Silvestro in this instance acts as corroborating detail for this account in the *Liber pontificalis*. The most extravagant claim is the ninth-century inscription recording Paschal I's improbable multitude of saints translated to his new basilica of Santa Prassede, which again serves as supporting detail for the *Liber pontificalis*'s narrative:

This holy and distinguished pontiff sought out, found and collected many bodies of saints lying in destroyed cemeteries, with dutiful concern that they should not remain neglected; and with great affection and veneration he removed and buried them in the Church of Christ's said martyr St Praxedes, which he had wonderfully renewed and constructed, with

---

[102] Compare above, Chapter 2, pp. 42–3. *LP* I, Life 95, cc. 4–5, pp. 464–5: *unde cernens plurima eorundem sanctorum cymiteriorum loca neglectu ac desidia antiquitatis maxima demolitione atque iam vicina ruine posita, protinus eadem sanctorum corpora de ipsis dirutis abstulit cymiteriis. Quae cum hymnis et canticis spiritalibus infra hanc civitatem Romanam introducens, alia eorum, per titulos ac diaconias seu monasteria et reliquas ecclesias cum condecenti studuit recondi honore.* [c. 5] *Hic sanctissimus presul in sua propria domu monasterium a fundamentis in honore sancti Stephani, scilicet martyris atque pontificis, necnon et beati Silvestri, idem pontificis et confessoris Christi construxit. Ubi et oraculum in superioribus eiusdem monasterii moeniis aedificans, eorum corpora magna cum veneratione condidit. Infra claustra vero ipsius monasterii ecclesiam mirae pulchritudinis a fundamentis noviter construxit ... illicque innumerabilium sanctorum corpora quae de praefatis demolitis abstulit cymiteriis maximo venerationis condidit affectu;* trans. Davis, *Eighth-Century Popes*, pp. 82–3.

the assistance of all the Romans, bishops, priests, deacons and clerics chanting psalms of praise to God.[103]

Imperial Emulation?

A far more speculative and subjective element is the impact of the physical bulk and material of the buildings themselves and the question of whether the textual replacement of emperors with popes as patrons and benefactors in the *Liber pontificalis* has a material counterpart. Even a brief allusion in the text might be supposed to have the power to evoke the physical building in the imagination of its readers both within and perhaps especially outside Rome, but it is important to remember how many of the early churches were erected well over a century before the earliest portion of the *Liber pontificalis* was compiled. The way the text adds steadily to the popes' contributions to the buildings over decades, as well as observations about particular buildings, could echo both the statements about the founders and benefactors' inscriptions with which many of the buildings were adorned. All combined to express verbally the impact of the buildings themselves and reflect the enormous wealth in terms of material, artisan skill, and building labour expended on these buildings.

Reports of repairs such as new tiles or replacement of roof beams were just as important as a textual display of papal stewardship of the city, and this is evident too in the physical repairs to the Aurelian Walls, first mentioned as prompted by a pope in the Life of Pope Sisinnius, who was pope for only twenty days and who is credited with ordering lime to be burnt for the repair of the walls.[104] Papal upkeep of an imperial monument has an obvious symbolic resonance for us, but the appreciation of it

---

[103] *LP* II, Life 100, c. 9, p. 54: *Hic enim beatissimus et praeclarus pontifex multa corpora sanctorum dirutis in cimiteriis iacentia, pia sollicitudine, ne remanerent neglecte, querens atque inventa colligens, magno venerationis affectu in iamdictae sanctae Christi martyris Praxedis ecclesia, quam mirabiliter renovans construxerat, cum omnium advocatione Romanorum, episcopis, presbiteris, diaconibus et clericis laudem Deo psallentibus, deportans recondidit;* trans. Davis, *Ninth-Century Popes,* pp. 10–11, and see Goodson 2010. See also Costambeys and Leyser 2007.

[104] *LP* I, Life 89, c. 2, p. 388, and compare above, Chapter 2, p. 53. See also Dey 2011, pp. 32–70, and Coates-Stephens 2012.

at the time may have been more pragmatic. This twelve-mile (19 km) rampart circuiting the city was first constructed in the 270s, with a massive second level including arcaded galleries added during the reign of Honorius at the beginning of the fifth century. Traces of repairs and maintenance thereafter are difficult to identify and date, though some inevitably have been allocated to the course and immediate aftermath of the Gothic wars; the repairs of the eighth and ninth centuries appear to be less controversial.[105]

In its mapping of the new Christian topography of Rome, the *Liber pontificalis* might be regarded as the textual counterpart to what Jaś Elsner has described as Christianity's exploitation of material culture in Rome 'to upstage that of traditional paganism'. Elsner generalized the transformation of Roman topography as 'one of Christianity's most brilliant acts of outplaying its polytheistic rivals at the very game which they had themselves pioneered and mastered'.[106] As I suggested in Chapter 2 above, moreover, the Christian topography embraces and augments, even while it transforms, the older Roman topography. The *Liber pontificalis* author does not emphasize its pagan character. While the process of Christianizing Rome is far from passive, it is not obviously antagonistic towards the pagan past. The popes had new things to say, as is clear from the art which adorned many of their churches, for the popes are participants in what Elsner elsewhere referred to as 'visual hagiography'.[107] But this is more than a 'continuation of an imperial tradition of display and religious devotion' as I rather inadequately have described it previously.[108] The papal appropriation of martyrs to augment the perception of papal power is far more comprehensive than the initial endowment of the churches by Constantine. Under papal patronage, the basilicas become a material manifestation of the pope's ideological claims; they offer a physical articulation of the ideological and practical position of the popes in Rome.

The construction of these churches could be said to be straightforwardly imperial in terms of marble columns, bases, the decorative

---

[105] Coates-Stephens 1999.   [106] Elsner 2003, p. 70.
[107] Elsner 2003, p. 73. See also Mathews 1993, Finney 1994, and Brent 1995.
[108] McKitterick 2018c.

schemes of *opus sectile* in the marble floors, revetments on walls, mosaics, frescoes, and internal furnishings and equipment, all using expensive stone and other materials. There is ample modern scholarly discussion to this effect. Comparisons, say, with the Aula of Trier, are obvious for the scale of the buildings. There is an easy comparison to be made, as I suggested above, between the increasing incidence of papal portraits paralleling, albeit in a different medium, the imperial distribution of self-portraying statues around the city, even though the papal portraits communicated sacred power more than secular, and placed the popes in an historical sequence of time.[109] Yet there are further considerations.

The first is the vexed issue of the use of spolia, and its purported symbolic and ideological significance as opposed to the practical economy of reusing building material available in plentiful supply from ruined or disused buildings, ever since the ravages created by the construction of the Aurelian Walls in the third century.[110] Spolia in modern discussion is not so much about the large-scale recycling of bricks so evident, for example, in the late antique churches of Ravenna, the burning of marble to make lime, the use of rubble from older buildings as infill, or even funerary slabs built into walls.[111] Instead there is an assumption that there was a selection made of particularly expensive stone and well-made parts of buildings, such as columns, bases, capitals, carved architraves, decorative panels, and marble *opus sectile* from walls and floors. Recent work, moreover, has emphasized the spoliation of public buildings for private use well into the sixth century. In Rome, or so Cassiodorus claims, such plundering was carried out by the aristocrats of the city themselves, and Cristina La Rocca has argued how such destruction and rebuilding provides 'material evidence for political competition and disagreement'.[112] For the pope to join and augment late imperial aristocratic and Ostrogothic building activity to create new monumental assertions of power can be read as a calculated move.[113] The new churches were prominent statements of the new order in the landscape,

---

[109] Moralee 2018, Machado 2017, Behrwald and Witschel (eds.) 2012.

[110] Coates-Stephens 2006, Dey 2011, and Dey 2015.

[111] Coates-Stephens 1998 and 1999.   [112] See La Rocca 2014 and 2018.

[113] See also the suggestions made by Dey 2019.

with the important extra dimension insisted upon in the *Liber pontificalis* that these buildings were primarily to honour the saints and Christ.

Nevertheless, the question remains of whether the particular recycling of columns, capitals, bases, marble, and other architectural fragments of older Roman buildings conveys particular messages to subsequent users, in what Maria Fabricius Hansen has called the 'eloquence of appropriation'. How deliberate was it? Practical and symbolic use can coexist of course, though their interpretation has also to be filtered through our own modern preconceptions.

Maria Fabricius Hansen suggested, for example, in building the Lateran Baptistery, especially the remodelling under Pope Sixtus III (432–40), that the Christians deliberately reused massive purple porphyry marble for the narthex of the baptistery and composite second-century capitals and white marble bases from the first century. She described these as imperial 'badges of grandeur and rank'. Further, she suggested that the capitals may even have been taken from the Temple of Venus Genetrix in the Forum of Caesar both to underline their new Christian purpose and to signal an exalted status. Hansen also thought that the entablature and *opus sectile* revetment of the building could be interpreted as a conscious reuse, not simply of imperial decorative elements in a new Christian context, but as material conversion to Christian use of building elements from pagan temples.[114]

A hint of nuance in detecting deliberate use is the passing reference in the *Liber pontificalis* that Pope Sixtus III 'set up the hard porphyry columns, eight in number, that had been gathered from the time of the Emperor Constantine'.[115] This seems to suggest, at least in building practice and reuse of architectural fragments, a more general appropriation of antiquity and occasional recognition of earlier specific associations.[116] Hansen's case for an aesthetic in late antiquity and the early middle ages that included recontextualizing aspects of the imperial past raises more than the question of reuse of spolia. It also invokes the

[114] Hansen 2003, and compare Kinney 2012, Brandt and Guidobaldi 2008, and McKitterick 2018c.

[115] *LP* I, Life 46, c. 7, p. 234.

[116] See Kinney 2011, Esch 2011, Liverani 2011, Brandenburg 2011b, Ng and Swetnam-Burland (eds.) 2018.

aesthetic of emulation and the persistence in Rome of antique notions of *decorum* or appropriateness articulated in the context of moral behaviour by Cicero and for the design of buildings by Vitruvius.[117] Ellen Perry has shown how Vitruvius's ideas also invoked the notion of *auctoritas,* the personal taste of the individual as well as socially accepted norms. She suggested that this conceptual framework embraced the pluralism of contemporaneous style to be observed in Roman art but also determined the choice or commissioning of works of art that were appropriate for their particular contexts. In other words, eclecticism, which left room for innovation as well as emulation, was embedded in Roman art and architecture and was an essential element of its aesthetic.

I suggest that these ideas can be applied to the new buildings created to honour the Christian saints and accommodate Christian ritual. In structure and materials they evoked an ancient and imperial past but simultaneously offered new spaces with new functions, images of Christ and his saints, and of the popes, decorative sequences of new and recycled marble columns, elaborate floor and wall mosaics and revetments, and extended series of narrative cycles illustrating the biblical and hagiographical texts of the Christian religion.

Further, there was a symbolic resonance to the transformation of Roman public buildings into churches by Christians. The case assembled by Claudia Bolgia for the first church on the Capitol in the sixth century is a striking instance of this. The gradual encroachment of churches into the Forum, not least the creation of the church of Santi Cosma e Damiano, the conversion of the Roman Curia into the church of Sant'Adriano under Pope Honorius (625–38), and the establishment of Santa Maria Antiqua in the vestibule of the imperial palace on the Palatine are usually regarded as part of the same development. Such a development appears to be a continuation of the process of the privatization of public monuments in Rome during the reign of Theodoric recorded by Cassiodorus in the *Variae.*[118]

---

[117] I adopt here the concept so usefully invoked and explored by Perry 2005.
[118] Discussed by La Rocca 2018.

Conclusion

The *Liber pontificalis* appears to be a witness to a gradual transference of the control of many such formerly public buildings into the hands of the popes as well as those of local aristocrats, with or without any formal negotiation with a secular public authority. As I mentioned earlier, Pope Boniface IV, for example, is said to have asked the Emperor Phocas for permission to convert the Pantheon to Christian use, but it is impossible to establish how necessary such a negotiation may have been. It may be an attempt to indicate that legal formalities had been observed in a context where the question of public ownership was uncertain; but the matter would merit further investigation.[119] The legally significant word *dedicavit* (dedicated) to indicate a public or private building being dedicated to sacred use is not deployed in this brief entry, though it is used in relation to many of the other church buildings associated with the pope.[120]

The conversion of the Pantheon into the church of Santa Maria ad martyres in 609 or 613 was described by Bede only a century later, in reaction to the account in the Life of Boniface IV in the *Liber pontificalis,* as the conversion of a pagan temple and the elimination of abominations.[121] Such a reading on Bede's part is an interesting example of preconceptions governing understanding, but the Pantheon's new use raises the crucial question of the function of all the buildings I have discussed in this chapter. A special liturgy was composed for the dedication of Santa Maria ad martyres. The texts of the *Alleluia* and verse from Psalm 137.2, *Adorabo ad templum, sanctum tuum et confitebor nomini tuo* ('I will worship toward Thy holy temple and praise Thy name'), and from Chronicles, invoked the temple of Solomon and celebrated the building as a gateway to heaven.[122] A spectacular Roman building was

---

[119] See above, Chapter 1, p. 22. Geertman 1975, p. 190 and Voelkl 1964. I am grateful to Caroline Humfress for a conversation about this issue.

[120] On the legal discussion see Linderski 1985, Tatum 1993, Orlin 1997, pp. 163–89. See also Davis-Weyer 1989 and Goddard 2006, p. 283.

[121] See Bede, *Historia ecclesiastica gentis Anglorum,* II.4, ed. Colgrave and Mynors, pp. 148–9, Marder and Wilson Jones (eds.) 2015, pp. 1–48 with the redating of the consecration to 613 (from 609), and Blaauw 1994b. For further discussion see McKitterick 2016a.

[122] Rankin 2011.

thus incorporated into the public liturgy of the pope within the city. It is to the presentation of the liturgy as part of the construction of the popes, therefore, that I shall turn at the beginning of my next chapter, before considering the popes as legislators, and the reception of the *Liber pontificalis* in the early middle ages more generally.

5

Bishop and Pope

Introduction

SO FAR IN THIS BOOK I HAVE HIGHLIGHTED PARTICULAR themes in the *Liber pontificalis* presented by the authors of the sixth-century portion of the narrative and its continuations. These can be summarized as follows: the transformation of the city of Rome in imagination and text; the construction of a distinctively papal and apostolic past in early Christian Rome; and the visible display of papal power in Rome in the building and embellishment of churches in honour of the saints. All these themes combine to convey a very particular understanding of the history of the popes and of the Christian city of Rome. There is no inevitability in the development of the papacy. All the papal building projects, for example, constructed particular places for collective and regular Christian observance and devotion. They were spaces which acted as the venues where many Christians gathered, that belonged to their communities, were associated with particular saints who were part of the history of the city, and were where the institutionalized liturgical rituals of belonging took place. I have explored the way the authors exploited existing knowledge and reframed it, shaping the way subsequent readers would remember and understand the popes' role in the city and in relation to its Christian inheritance. Indeed, I have suggested that the *Liber pontificalis* needs to be seen as complementing and corroborating both the contemporaneous visual and material evidence and other categories of written text. Not only that: the narrative offers a persuasive, chronologically ordered framework into which the other categories of text and material evidence could be fitted and their credentials understood. We cannot read the *Liber pontificalis* in isolation from these other texts and the wider physical context whose existence the *Liber pontificalis* implies. This is particularly the case for the liturgy, the pope's definitive statements about Christian orthodoxy, and his interventions in canon law.

In this chapter, therefore, I shall discuss each of these topics in turn before offering some reflections on their implications in relation to textual authority and conceptualization of the past. First of all I offer a consideration of how liturgy is used by the *Liber pontificalis* authors to define and emphasize the bishop's ministry and pastoral role.

Liturgy in the *Liber pontificalis*

Although most of the earliest extant liturgical manuscripts of Mass texts, calendars, lectionaries, *ordines,* and antiphonaries are actually of Frankish origin from the late seventh century onwards, many of these texts claim, and can be shown to have had, Roman origins.[1] The *Liber pontificalis* offers an understanding of the Christian observance documented in all these texts within the historical framework it creates for the liturgy. As we shall see, the *Liber pontificalis* simultaneously extends that role to embrace the pope's responsibility for the organization of the church and the maintenance of orthodoxy.

I have already provided many indications in this book of how often the *Liber pontificalis* is frustratingly selective and improbably inventive, as well as how that very selectiveness and inventiveness nevertheless can make strong points. One manifestation of this is the enumeration of bishops, priests, and deacons ordained by the pope added in a formulaic phrase at the end of every Life. Up to the early eighth century, the popes are credited with the systematic creation of clerical personnel on an industrial scale. In the six centuries from Peter to Silverius, the ordination of 1294 bishops, 388 priests, and 335 deacons is claimed. Between 537 and 715, when one might suppose the records were more accurate, the thirty popes during that period ordained 1002 'bishops for various places', 284 priests, and 114 deacons. In the next century, nine popes

---

[1] See below, p. 174.

added 646 bishops, 171 priests, and 43 deacons. The ninth-century Lives from Paschal I to Stephen V often lack these details and some, such as those for Sergius II and Hadrian II, only had them added in eleventh-century recensions. The pattern of far more bishops (462) than priests (48) and deacons (28), however, is maintained. These figures can be set out schematically:

PAPAL ORDINATIONS RECORDED IN THE *LIBER PONTIFICALIS*

	BISHOPS	PRIESTS	DEACONS
Peter to Silverius	1294	388	335
537–715	1002	284	114
715–816	646	171	43
816–895	462	48	28
TOTAL	3404	891	520

The deacons are presumably not only the men who subsequently were ordained priests, but also those who occupied the increasingly illustrious posts of the seven deacons in Rome, first referred to in the Life of Pope Clement I, and described as 'cardinal deacons' in Life 96 of Pope Stephen III. The priests, similarly, are probably those officiating in the many *tituli* churches in Rome.[2] Participation in ordinations for other suburbicarian dioceses defined as within papal jurisdiction at the Council of Nicaea may also be indicated.[3] The superabundance of bishops, taking the multitude of sees (well over one hundred) thought to exist in late antique and early medieval suburbicarian Italy into account, and assuming the pope had no role in consecrating bishops within the archdioceses of Milan or Ravenna, may be less of a puzzle. First of all, it can be presumed that the Bishop of Rome was responsible for the appointment to all the suburbicarian bishoprics, whereas he would be consecrating priests and deacons only within the city of Rome itself. Very occasionally might these have been bishops consecrated for work elsewhere, such as Augustine, sent to preach to the English by Pope Gregory (590–604), though it was Eleutherius, Archbishop of Arles, who actually

---

[2] On the *tituli* churches see above, Chapter 3, p. 93.
[3] See Carpegna Falconieri 2002, pp. 37–45.

consecrated Augustine at Gregory's request.[4] Other examples are Damian, Archbishop of Ravenna, Beorhtwald, Archbishop of 'Britain' (i.e. Canterbury), and Clement-Willibrord, Archbishop of the Frisians, described as ordained by Pope Sergius I (687–701). In addition, Boniface of Mainz was consecrated by Pope Gregory II (715–31), though the *Liber pontificalis* does not say this explicitly.[5] Secondly, the short incumbencies of so many of the popes might be taken as a guide to the time in office of the bishops and thus to the apparently high rate of turnover.

There may have been some administrative registers to provide a basis for the estimates, but the function of these notes of ordination credited to the popes may have been perceived as more symbolic than real. It is not as if most readers would have been in a position to argue with these statistics, let alone check them. They witness to the source of episcopal office, the popes' unfailing attention to the continuity of the clergy, and how ordination from the very beginning of the Christian church was an essential element in the consolidation of the church as an institution.[6] The formula reinforced a reader's sense of the pope's systematic provision for priestly succession, pastoral care, and liturgical services both within Rome and in all other areas under his direct jurisdiction.

In addition to the provisions of clergy, standard elements of church organization within Rome and subdivisions such as the regions, *diaconiae,* and *tituli* in which daily and weekly liturgical devotions were observed are credited to the earliest popes in order, first of all, to lend a sense of antiquity to the major ecclesiastical structures.[7] Secondly, they are a way of presenting Christian Rome as ruled and administered, in ecclesiastical terms, by the pope and his officials. As I noted in a previous chapter,

---

[4] On Augustine compare Bede, *Historia ecclesiastica gentis Anglorum,* I.27, ed. Colgrave and Mynors, p. 78.

[5] Willibrord's consecration is also reported in the marginal note in his Calendar in Paris, BnF lat. 10837, fol. 39v: *fuit ordinatus in Romae episcopus ab apostolico viro domno Sergio papa.* On Boniface, *Epistolae,* ed. Rau, Ep. 20: Pope Gregory to Charles Martel reports that his legate presents to Charles: Boniface *a nobis episcopum consecratum,* p. 72.

[6] For an instance of a later epitomizer choosing to preserve all these ordination details see McKitterick 2014 and below, p. 202.

[7] On *tituli* and *diaconiae* see Hillner 2006 and 2007, Thacker 2007a, Dey 2008 (but his assumptions about the Rule of St Benedict vitiate his argument somewhat). See also above, p. 93.

Popes Clement (*c*.95), Fabian (236–50), and Gaius (283–96) created the seven regions under the seven deacons, subdeacons and notaries; their subdivision into *tituli* is reported as the work of Popes Evaristus (*c*.100–9) and Marcellus (305/6–306/7).[8] To Gaius is further credited the ecclesiastical grades in a decree that 'anyone who might deserve to be bishop should be doorkeeper, reader, exorcist, acolyte, subdeacon, deacon, priest before being ordained bishop'.[9] The stipulation that the three bishops of Ostia, Albano, and Portus are to consecrate the Bishop of Rome is credited to Pope Mark (336) and referred to as standard procedure in the Life of Pope Leo II (682–3).[10] The communities serving oratories and churches founded by later popes were required to follow the model of the liturgy of St Peter's basilica.[11]

Far more revolutionary than the steady substitution of clerical and papal administrative districts and personnel in place of the structures and officials of the imperial bureaucracy was the impact on time and its measurement documented in terms of papal interventions and liturgical feasts.[12] In addition to a new understanding of the progression of time in terms of the successive episcopal reigns since St Peter, the *Liber pontificalis* reinforced the commemorative and recurrent annual cycle of liturgical time by constructing a notional chronology for particular papal contributions to this cycle. The bishop fixed fundamental points of the liturgical calendar, not least the date of Easter: the *Liber pontificalis* claimed that Pope Victor emulated Pope Eleutherius in saying Easter should be on a Sunday, but makes no reference to the politically charged issue of the differing calculations of the date in Rome and elsewhere.[13] Further, additions to the structure and prayers of the Mass, and elements of the ritual performance of the liturgy, were all identified as made by the pope.

---

[8] Above, p. 83, and see *LP* I, Lives 4, 21, and 29; and 6 and 31 respectively, pp. 123, 148, 161; 126 and 164.

[9] *LP* I, Life 29, c. 2, p. 161; trans. Davis, *Pontiffs*, p. 11: *si quis episcopus mereretur, ut esset ostiarius, lector, exorcista, sequens, subdiaconus, diaconus, presbyter, et exinde episcopus ordinaretur.*

[10] *LP* I, Lives 35 and 82, c. 6, pp. 202 and 360.

[11] *LP* I, Life 92, c. 9, p. 418; compare Davis, *Eighth-Century Popes*, p. 24.

[12] Compare Salzman 1990.

[13] *LP* I, Life 15, p. 137. Only the Verona fragment, Verona, Biblioteca Capitolare Cod. XXII (20) alludes to Pope Symmachus having failed to celebrate Easter on the same date as everyone else, *LP* I, p. 45 and see Holford-Stevens 2011.

Pope Telesphorus (*c.*130) is said to have introduced the Lenten period of fasting before Easter and the celebration of a night Mass on Christmas Eve.[14] Fasting on Thursdays and Sundays was forbidden by Pope Miltiades on the grounds that pagans had fasted on these days.[15] A fast on Saturdays, on the other hand, according to the Life of Pope Innocent I (401–17), commemorated the fact 'that it was on a Saturday that the Lord had lain in the tomb and the disciples fasted'.[16]

That psalms were to be sung day and night by priests, bishops, and monasteries, was attributed to Pope Damasus (366–84).[17] A further refinement was associated with Pope Celestine (422–32), who is described as issuing a decree that 'before the sacrifice the 150 Psalms of David should be performed antiphonally by everyone, that this used not to be done, but only St Paul's Epistle and the holy Gospel were recited'.[18] Although Pope Gelasius (492–6) is said to have provided 'prefaces and prayers for the sacraments' (*sacramentorum praefationes et orationes*), it is striking that the papal interventions are mostly so specific and occasional, and could be interpreted as insisting on a peculiarly Roman practice. Recent scholarship has vigorously debated the nature and extent of Roman textual and musical contributions to the liturgy, and it is against this complex background that the claims of the *Liber pontificalis* need to be understood.[19]

Thus, particular popes are associated with specific prayers. Besides introducing the Lenten period of fasting, Pope Telesphorus (*c.*130) in the early second century is given the credit for placing the *Gloria* before the set of prayers consecrating the host, even though the text of the *Gloria* or angelic hymn is usually attributed to the fourth-century bishop

---

[14] *LP* I, Life 9, p. 129.

[15] *LP* I, Life 33, c. 2, p. 168: *quia eos dies pagani quasi sacrum ieiunium celebrabant.*

[16] *LP* I, Life 42, c. 7, p. 222; trans. Davis, *Pontiffs*, p. 32: *quia sabbato Dominus in sepulchro positus est.*

[17] *LP* I, Life 39, c. 6, p. 213; trans. Davis, *Pontiffs*, p. 29: *Hic constituit ut psalmos die noctuque canerentur per omnes ecclesias; qui hoc praecepit presbiteris vel episcopis aut monasteriis.*

[18] *LP* I, Life 45, p. 230; trans. Davis, *Pontiffs*, p. 33: *ut psalmi David CL ante sacrificium psalli antephanatim ex omnibus, quod ante non fiebat, nisi tantum epistula beati Pauli recitabatur et sanctum evangelium.*

[19] Jeffery 1984, Dyer 1995, MacKinnon 2000, Page 2010, Hen 2011, McKitterick 2017, Westwell 2017 and 2019.

Hilary of Poitiers. It is then reported that Pope Symmachus (498–514) at the beginning of the sixth century stipulated the singing of the *Gloria* every Sunday and martyr's feast day.[20] Further, the introduction of the prayer 'a holy sacrifice' (*sacrum sacrificium*) in the Mass is mentioned as the work of Pope Leo I (440–61) in the middle of the fifth century, while Pope Gregory I (590–604) at the end of the sixth century added the prayer 'and dispose our days in thy peace etc.' (*diesque nostros in tua pace dispone, et cetera*) to the recital of the canon.[21]

The introduction of the *Agnus Dei* by Pope Sergius I (687–701), who 'laid it down that at the time of the breaking of the Lord's body the clergy and people should sing "Lamb of God, who takest away the sins of the world, have mercy upon us"', is one of a number of demonstrations of papal leadership recorded in that life, and I shall return to Sergius I below.[22] The words of the *Agnus Dei*, however, as well as the references in the *Liber pontificalis* to the introduction of other prayers, rituals, and chant, offer a glimpse of the resources for liturgical composition in Rome as well as how difficult it is to pin anything down in terms of chronology or sources, given the patchy evidence. The phrases of the *Agnus Dei* may simply have been taken from the probably fourth-century 'angelic hymn' known as the *Gloria*, referred to above, for it too has the Lamb of God taking away the sins (*peccata*) of the world rather than the singular sin (*peccatum*) referred to in St John's Gospel 1.29 in the Latin Vulgate.[23] The many sins mentioned in Isaiah 53.12 may also have been influential, or there is perhaps an echo intended of the liturgical section of the *Apostolic Constitutions* in Book 8, possibly known in Italy in the sixth century.[24] Alternatively, this may be an instance of the use in seventh-

---

[20] *LP* I, Life 53, p. 263.

[21] *LP* I, Lives 47 and 66, c. 3, pp. 239 and 312; trans. Davis, *Pontiffs*, pp. 37, 60.

[22] *LP* I, Life 86, c. 14, p. 376; trans. Davis, *Pontiffs*, p. 84: *Hic statuit ut tempore confractionis dominici corporis Agnus Dei qui tollis peccata mundi miserere nobis a clero et populo decantetur.*

[23] Capelle 1949, and see Chapter 4 above for the inscription in the Lateran Baptistery, p. 107.

[24] The *Apostolic Constitutions* are supposedly fourth century in date and thought possibly to be Antiochene in origin, but Book 8 may be earlier; little appears to be certain. See Brock 1982, pp. 1–4, and *Didascaliae apostolorum canonum ecclesiasticorum traditionis apostolicae versiones latinae*, ed. Tidner, based on Verona, Biblioteca Capitolare Cod. LV (53) (*CLA* IV, 508), written before 486. See also Connolly 1929.

century Rome of an Italian strand of the *Vetus Latina* tradition of St John's Gospel, with the plural reading 'sins'.[25] The suggestion made by Eamon Duffy, among others, that Sergius, because his parents came from Antioch, may have been invoking Syriac liturgy or been influenced by a Syriac translation of the Gospel is unlikely; the *Agnus Dei* is not attested in the early Syriac liturgy, and all Syriac, Coptic, Greek, and other eastern texts maintain the singular 'sin' for John 1.29.[26] The choice on Sergius's part of the less abstract plural form 'sins' (implying specific sins) may possibly reflect a greater attention to the bishop's pastoral role.[27] Less compellingly, a reaction to the Eastern prohibition against portraying Christ as a lamb rather than in human form, in the Council of Trullo (691/2), was tentatively suggested by Duchesne, but this seems to overlook the significance of Trullo's endorsement of 'the Lamb who takes away the sin of the world, Christ our God'.[28] The earliest copies of a Mass text to incorporate the *Agnus Dei* appear to be from Francia. The *Missale Gallicanum vetus*, for example, inserts it in the Mass for the fourth day of Easter week.[29] Similarly, ninth-century Frankish manuscripts of *Ordo Romanus* I, a Roman text thought to date from the first half of the eighth century, include the chanting of the *Agnus Dei* at the fraction of the host.[30]

---

[25] See Shaker 2016 and see also the *Vetus Latina* online edition of St John's Gospel, ed. Burton, Balserak, Houghton, and Parker, www.iohannes.com. The plural *peccata* is recorded in their catalogue of manuscripts 2, 9A, 9C, 11A, 15, and 30, which include manuscripts of fifth-century Italian as well as eighth-century insular origin, the latter presumably in their turn based on earlier Italian exemplars.

[26] Duffy 1997, p. 67. For help with the Greek, Syriac, Coptic, and Gothic (from a commentary on John, for there is no Gothic John 1 extant) texts of John 1.29, all of which use the singular for 'sin' (the Armenian of John 1, however, uses the plural, and the word for 'sin' is not attested in the singular), I am grateful to Christian Askeland, James Clackson, Robert Crellin, Nevsky Everett, Patrick James, and Lucy McKitterick.

[27] *LP* I, Life 86, c. 1, p. 376; I am grateful to John Morrill and Rowan Williams for conversation about this.

[28] *LP* I, p. 381, note 42, and followed by Andrieu (ed.), *Ordines Romani*, pp. 48–50, and Romano 2014, pp. 71–3. For Trullo see *Concilium Constantinopolitanum a. 691/2 in Trullo habitum (Concilium Quinisextu)*, ed. Ohme.

[29] BAV pal. lat. 493, fol. 84r (*CLA* I, 93) in Frankish uncial of the second half of the eighth century.

[30] *Ordo Romanus* I, ed. Andrieu, p. 101. A new edition is in preparation by Peter Jeffery. Compare Atchley (ed.), pp. 159 and 177, and Romano 2014, pp. 219–48 and clause 105 at p. 245.

The rhythm of liturgical observance within the city, according to the *Liber pontificalis*, was also determined by the bishop. In the later fifth century, Pope Simplicius (468–83) supposedly introduced 'the weekly turns at St Peter's, St Paul's and St Laurence's so that priests should remain there for penitents and for baptism: from region 3 at St Laurence's, region 1 at St Paul's, regions 6–7 at St Peter's'.[31] According to the *Liber pontificalis*'s authors, Pope John III (561–74) took this further by insisting that 'every Sunday at the martyrs' cemeteries the offering, the vessels, and the lighting should be serviced from the Lateran'. This implies a little group of clergy setting out each Sunday in procession from the Caelian Hill to the martyrs' shrines on the Via Nomentana, Via Tiburtina, Via Salaria, Via Ostiensis, and elsewhere.[32] An invocation of the liturgical past[33] is in the Life of Pope Leo III (795–816), where 'according to ancient tradition the litany had been announced in advance by a notary of the holy church at the church of Christ's martyr St George on his feast day and all the men and women devoutly crowded into the church of Christ's martyr St Laurence in Lucina to join the gathering announced to take place there'.[34] In a further attempt to reconstruct a chronology for the liturgy, the *Liber pontificalis* dates to the time of Pope Miltiades (310–14) at the beginning of the fourth century the distribution of the *fermentum*, that is, the host consecrated by the pope, to the churches of Rome as a symbol of unity of a bishop, his priests, and their congregations.[35]

---

[31] *LP* I, Life 49, p. 249; trans. Davis, *Pontiffs*, p. 40: *Hic constituit ad sanctum Petrum apostolum et ad sanctum Paulum apostolum et ad sanctum Laurentium martyrem ebdomadas ut presbyteri manerent, propter penitentes et baptismum: regio III ad sanctum Laurentium, regio prima ad sanctum Paulum, regio VI vel septima ad sanctum Petrum.*

[32] *LP* I, Life 63, p. 305; trans. Davis, *Pontiffs*, p. 58: *Hic instituit ut oblationem et amula vel luminaria in easdem cymiteria per omnes dominicas de Lateranis ministraretur.*

[33] For the 'liturgical past' invoked in a Byzantine and early Rus context see Griffin 2019, from whom I adapt the phrase.

[34] *LP* II, Life 98, c. 11, p. 4; trans. Davis, *Eighth-Century Popes*, p. 184: *et sicut olitanam traditionem a notario sanctae Romane ecclesiae in ecclesia beati Georgii Christi martyris in eius natale ipsa letania praedicata fuisset, omnes tam viri quamque femine devota mente catervatim in ecclesia beato Christi martyris Laurenti quae appellatur Lucine, ubi et collecta praedicta inherat occurrerent.* The churches referred to are San Giorgio in Velabro, a *diaconia* in the sixth century with a church built in the seventh century, and San Lorenzo in Lucina, built in the fifth century on the site of a fourth-century *titulus*.

[35] *LP* I, Life 33, p. 168.

The fixing of the feast of Saints Peter and Paul on 29 June is attributed to Pope Cornelius (251–3) in the third century,[36] and the provision for the liturgical commemoration of St Peter and his shrine in St Peter's basilica was augmented by Pope Gregory I (590–604) at the end of the sixth century.[37] Devotion to the Cross was enhanced in the aftermath of Sergius I's finding of a fragment of the Cross in St Peter's basilica.[38] Sergius I (687–701) also laid it down that on the principal Marian feasts 'a litany should go out from St Hadrian's and the people should meet up at St Mary's'.[39] In the ninth century, Leo IV added to the growing number of Marian commemorations in Rome by introducing the Octave day of the Assumption, 'never before kept at Rome' (*quae minime Romam antea colebatur*).[40]

Papal performance of the liturgy in public ceremonial evolved into the regular cycle of Masses in the stational basilicas developed from the Roman churches designated for the 'weekly turns', mentioned earlier.[41] The celebration of papal liturgy in a succession of Roman churches in this way anchored papal ritual to Roman topography and Roman saints. Very little of the detail of this cycle can be reconstructed from the *Liber pontificalis,* however. For that we are dependent on the Gospel Lectionary of the set readings throughout the liturgical year, in conformity with Roman practice. A Würzburg list of the Gospel readings survives from the second half of the eighth century. Würzburg, Universitätsbibliothek M.p.th.f.62 is written in a rapid and confident insular minuscule, and was probably copied by an insular scribe working for one of the three earliest bishops of Würzburg.[42] It contains an introductory section on fols 1r–2v listing the principal Roman feasts and many of the stational churches for the readings throughout the liturgical year, 212 in all. That is, the entire

---

[36] *LP* I, Life 22, p. 150, and McKitterick 2013b.

[37] *LP* I, Life 66, p. 312, and see Jeffery 2013.

[38] *LP* I, Life 86, c. 10, p. 374; trans. Davis, *Pontiffs*, p. 83: *die Exaltationis sanctae crucis in basilicam Salvatoris quae appellatur Constantiniana osculatur ac adoratur,* and see Ó Carragáin 2013, pp. 185–7.

[39] *LP* I, Life 86, c. 14, p. 376; trans. Davis, *Pontiffs*, p. 84: *letania exeat a sancto Hadriano et ad sanctam Mariam populus occurrat.*

[40] *LP* II, Life 105, c. 26, p. 112, and compare above on the Roman cult of Mary, Chapter 4, pp. 120–2.

[41] Baldovin 1987.   [42] McKitterick in press b.

set of readings is orchestrated according to the stational churches of Rome. During Holy Week, for example, the Gospel and Epistle during the Mass for the day were read in sequence from Monday to Saturday in the basilicas of Santa Prassede, Santa Prisca, Santa Maria,[43] Santa Croce in Gerusalemme, the Lateran or Constantinian basilica, and on Easter Sunday itself at Santa Maria Maggiore. In Easter week the readings were at St Peter's, San Paolo fuori le mura, San Lorenzo fuori le mura, the basilica ad apostolos, Santa Maria ad martyres (formerly the Pantheon), and the Lateran. A list of 255 Epistle pericopes with incipits and explicits follows on fols 2v–10v, and thereafter an incomplete list of the Gospel pericopes, many of them without numbers. This is undoubtedly a Roman list of readings and it is in marked contrast to the Neapolitan character of the lections recorded in the Northumbrian Gospel Book as well as the Lindisfarne Gospels, and added in the eighth century to the sixth-century Burchard Gospels.[44]

It took centuries for the set of readings and the practice of scriptural readings within the liturgy, especially of the Mass, to be agreed in the Western church. Many different choices were made, with considerable variation within Italy as well as in Gaul and Spain. The structure of *temporale* and *sanctorale*, with the designation of the vigils and major feasts and saints' days, emerged in Rome in the course of the sixth century, but the process and chronology by which Roman practice was adopted either in Rome, Francia, or England is still insufficiently understood.[45] The Würzburg *comes* may offer some indication of this. Fuller evidence for the readings, with even more details concerning the stational churches included, is set out in the Lectionary compiled by the court scribe Godescalc working for Charlemagne in 781, still extant in Paris, BnF n.a.lat. 1203. Godescalc included the designation of the location of the

---

[43] Here not more specifically indicated.

[44] The essential groundwork on the annual cycle of lections is Frere 1930–5; Klauser 1935 and Lietzmann 1927. On liturgical readings see Vogel 1986, pp. 291–355. See London, British Library MS Royal I.B.VII (*CLA* II, 213, London, British Library MS Cotton Nero D.IV (*CLA* II, 17), and Würzburg, Universitätsbibliothek M.p.th.f.68 (*CLA* IX, 1423a and 1423b).

[45] For a useful summary of past discussions by the liturgical scholars G. Morin, A. Wilmart, T. Klauser, W. H. Frere, A. Chavasse, and others see Thurn 1968.

Gospel readings throughout the year in the information he supplied as the heading for each Gospel extract.[46] Thus, the Christmas reading from St Matthew's Gospel (1.18–21) is signalled to be read *ad sanctam Mariam*, that is, Santa Maria Maggiore, which is also specified for Easter Sunday. The Lectionary, like the *Liber pontificalis* itself, could thus recreate the physical reality of Rome far from Rome and create a virtual Rome to reinforce, with the names of the Roman saints to whom the Roman churches were dedicated, their virtual presence and place in the liturgical memory. This worked for anywhere beyond Rome, but I have argued elsewhere that the Franks appear to have been particularly receptive. Their adoption and propagation of these located liturgical readings in the form in which Godescalc had assembled them boosted not only the authority of Rome itself but the creation of a mental map of Rome's sacred topography.[47]

Processions and 'litanies' were not merely a dramatic and public form of papal display, but were also a further extrapolation of the pope's pastoral role as bishop. The bishop's function as intercessor with God and his saints for the people of the city is the most obvious aspect of this. Prayer is, above all, a formulaic ritual of communication between the bishop, clergy, and people and God and his saints, with the latter's aid, intervention, and mercy sought for the former groups. A famous example of such intercession is recorded, for instance, in the Life of Adeodatus (672–6):

> After he passed away there was rain and thunder such as no one however old could remember; even men and cattle were destroyed by lightning. It was only because the Lord was placated by the Litanies which took place every day that men were able to thresh the grain and store it in the granaries.[48]

---

[46] Crivello, Denoel, Mütherich, and Orth 2011.

[47] McKitterick 2018a, and see also Chapter 2, above.

[48] *LP* I, Life 79, c. 5, pp. 346–7; trans. Davis, *Pontiffs*, p. 71: *Post cuius transitum tantae pluviae et tonitrua fuerunt quales nulla aetas hominum memoratur, ut etiam homines et peculia de fulgore interirent. Et nisi per letanias quas cotidie fiebant Dominus est propitiatus ut potuissent homines triturare vel in horreis frumenta recondere.*

Another comprehensive example is the blessing of the new Leonine Walls of Rome, which were extended to embrace St Peter's basilica in the ninth century:

> [Pope Leo IV] ordered with the devotion of a great spirit and in joy of heart that all the bishops, *sacerdotes*, deacons and all the orders of the holy catholic and apostolic Roman church should, after litanies and the chanting of the Psalter, with hymns and spiritual chants go with him round the whole circuit of the wall barefoot and with ash on their heads.
>
> ... The venerable pontiff himself pronounced three prayers over this wall with much weeping and sighing, asking and beseeching that this city might both be preserved for ever by Christ's aid and endure safe and unshaken from every incursion of its enemies by the guardianship of all the saints and angels.[49]

So far, I have argued that the many different elements of the liturgy in the *Liber pontificalis* narrative, of which I have given only a few illustrative instances, established a new religious and civic rhythm in Rome. Roman liturgy and the ecclesiastical control of time emerge as a very particular and visible expression of the cultural memory of the city, orchestrated daily in its major basilicas, lesser churches, martyrs' shrines, and monasteries, but also adopted and adapted throughout Christian Europe. The attention paid to liturgy in the *Liber pontificalis* further reinforced the theme of imperial emulation and substitution, for the emperor's devotion to religious matters had been a central aspect of the public role of the emperor, as portrayed in the biographies of Suetonius and the *Historia Augusta*. An extra element, however, is the degree to which the pope himself is represented as contributing so much to the liturgy in

---

[49] *LP* II, Life 105, cc. 72–3, p. 124; trans, Davis, *Ninth-Century Popes*, pp. 141–2: *iussit cum magna animi devotione cordisque letitia ut omnes cum eo episcopi pariter ac sacerdotes, immo levite et universi ordines clericorum sancte catholicae et apostolicae Romane ecclesiae, post letanias et psalterium decantatum, cum hymnis et canticis spiritalibus, per totum murorum ambitum, nudis pedibus, cinerem portantes in capite, circuirent ... Ipse autem venerabilis pontifex ore suo tres super eundem murum orationes multis cum lacrimis ac suspiriis dedit, rogans ac petens ut sepedicta civitas et Christi conservaretur in aevum auxilio et sanctorum omnium angelorumque praesidio ab universo inimicorum secura et inperterrita perduraret incursu.*

Rome; he is far from a passive participant, but instead is the leading celebrant.

There is no suggestion, nevertheless, that the popes are doing anything more than tailoring an inherited tradition, in terms of organization and structure, to reflect new emphases in theology. The reception of the narrative in the *Liber pontificalis,* therefore, needs to be seen in relation to everyday experience and knowledge of the liturgy in Rome and elsewhere in the West, as well as to the extant Mass texts, *ordines,* and collections of liturgical readings, prayers, and sermons. Liturgical organization, innovation, and commemoration are ways in which the pope's position was emphasized as public and visible. The authors had to take account of, as well as imply, a body of knowledge and practice that was the inheritance of the Christian church as a whole. Consequently, they shaped a particularly Roman understanding of the Bishop of Rome's contribution to Christian observance.

Doctrine and Law

I turn now to the topics of doctrine and law as presented in the *Liber pontificalis* The bishop's legal interventions, like the liturgical contributions, were presented as of universal applicability, from Silvester's time onwards, at least in the West, alongside the decisions of the early church councils. Yet they were simultaneously a manifestation of the Bishop of Rome's leadership of the church as pope. With respect to the formulation of canon law collections, the *Liber pontificalis* is as oddly sketchy and allusive as it is for so many other topics. Even Pope Hormisdas's request to Dionysius Exiguus in the early sixth century, to gather together a collection of the earliest conciliar decrees of the Greek councils in Latin translation, is not mentioned.[50] This appears to be another instance of the *Liber pontificalis* both complementing other contemporary texts and assuming knowledge of them, but I shall return to this point below.

The agenda of synods in which ecclesiastical legislation was formulated often included pronouncements on Christian doctrine. The period

---

[50] See the discussion in Somerville and Brasington 1998, pp. 23–7 and 47–9. *Collectio Dionysiana,* ed. Strewe, and Kéry 1999, pp. 9–13.

from the fifth to the ninth centuries was one in which there were long-running and bitter Christological disputes and irreconcilable positions adopted on the veneration of images, often involving outright schism between Rome and Byzantium, excommunication of the patriarch by the pope, anathema, removal of names from the diptychs, and exclusion from Communion.[51] Affirmations of orthodoxy and the definition of Christ at Chalcedon in 451 as one person with two natures, human and divine, are the most usual contexts in which the pope's and Rome's relationship with the Byzantine Empire was articulated. Such universal claims to orthodoxy were upheld and even strengthened through these disputes, in which churches north of the Alps were increasingly involved.[52] Subsequent observations concerning papal decrees address the definitions of faith, often in reply to challenges from the emperors and patriarchs of Constantinople, and the ecclesiastical treatment of heretics. The pope's upholding of orthodoxy is reiterated time and time again in the *Liber pontificalis*. I have addressed this topic in more detail elsewhere.[53] Subsequent observations concerning papal decrees address the definitions of faith, often in reply to challenges from the emperors and patriarchs of Constantinople, and the ecclesiastical treatment of heretics. Illustrative examples are Pope Leo's 'frequent confirmation of the Synod of Chalcedon in his letters',[54] and Agapitus's confrontation with the Emperor Justinian I in Constantinople in 536, in which 'the blessed bishop Agapitus consistently gave him a response about the Lord Jesus Christ as God and Man which accorded with the apostolic faith, namely that there are two natures in one Christ'.[55]

In the seventh century, the *Liber pontificalis* reports that Pope Martin I (649–53)

---

[51] Chazelle and Cubitt (eds.) 2007 and Price 2009.   [52] See, for example, Esders 2019.

[53] McKitterick 2016a and 2018c.

[54] *LP* I, Life 47, c. 5, p. 238; trans. Davis, *Pontiffs*, p. 37: *Hic firmavit frequenter suis epistolis synodum Calcedonensem.*

[55] *LP* I, Life 59, c. 2, p. 287; trans. Davis, *Pontiffs*, pp. 51: *Cui beatissimus Agapitus episcopus constantissime fidei apostolicae responsum reddidit de domino Iesu Christo Deum et hominem, hoc est duas naturas in uno Christo.*

gathered 105 bishops in Rome and, following the teaching of the orthodox fathers, he held a synod in the church of the Saviour close to the Lateran *episcopium*. In session were the bishops and priests with the deacons and the whole clergy in attendance. They condemned Cyrus of Alexandria, Sergius, Pyrrhus, and Paul, patriarchs of Constantinople, for daring to contrive novelties against the unsullied faith ... This synod is kept today in the church archive. [Martin] made copies and sent them through all the districts of East and West broadcasting them by the hands of the orthodox faithful.[56]

The attendance lists at the Lateran Synod are preserved with the rest of the *Acta*. This was by no means an ecumenical council: the bishops in attendance were primarily from Rome and the suburbicarian dioceses, that is, from Sardinia, Corsica, Italy, Sicily, and Istria (Aquileia and Pola). However extravagant the claims to have sent copies of the Council to East and West may seem, the Latin copies of the decrees did at least reach England and Francia, and the Council was reported in Constantinople.[57] In a letter to Bishop Amandus of Maastricht, Pope Martin states that he has taken steps to ensure that the volumes of the synodal acts have been sent to Amandus.[58]

At the earlier Synod of Trullo in Constantinople in 680,

the synodal letter of the holy pope Agatho was read out ... So great was the grace of Almighty God granted to the envoys of the apostolic see, that to the joy of the people and the holy council in the imperial city, on Sunday the octave of Easter in the church of St Sophia, John bishop of Portus (the papal legate) celebrated a public mass in Latin before the emperor and

---

[56] *LP* I, Life 76, c. 3, pp. 336–7; trans. Davis, *Pontiffs*, p. 67: *et congregavit episcopos in urbe Roma numero CV et fecit synodum secundum instituta patrum orthodoxorum in ecclesia Salvatoris, iuxta episcopio Lateranense, resedentibus episcopis, presbiteris, adstantibus diaconibus et clerum universum. Et condemnaverunt Cyrum Alexandrinum, Sergium, Pyrrum et Paulum patriarchas Constantinopolitanos, qui novitates contra immaculatam fidem praesumpserunt innectere ... Quem synodum hodie archivo ecclesiae continetur. Et faciens exemplaria, per omnes tractos Orientis et Occidentis direxit, per manus orthodoxorum fidelium disseminavit.*

[57] See Price, Booth, and Cubitt 2014, pp. 103–8, 114–15, 385–8; but compare Delogu 2000, pp. 199 and 208–9. Laon, BM Suzanne Martinet, MS 199 of Latin text is a ninth-century codex. See further below, Chapter 6, pp. 178 and 214.

[58] *PL* 87, cols 137–98, and see Price, Booth, and Cubitt 2014, pp. 408–12.

patriarchs. With one heart and one voice they made their acclamations of praise for the victories of the pious emperors, this too in Latin.[59]

The Life of Pope Sergius I (687–701) describes how he rejected the 'erroneous novelties' to which the Emperor Justinian II had wanted him to subscribe. The clear affirmation of the leadership of the apostolic see in orthodox doctrine, moreover, is stated in relation to a dispute between Sergius I and the Archbishop of Aquileia. Those who were previously held by wickedness and error were enlightened by the doctrine of the apostolic see; now that they were peaceably in harmony with the truth (*cum pace consonantes veritati*), they were allowed to go home.[60] It is in relation to Constantinople's assertions of status above all, moreover, that the scattering of statements about Rome's primacy are made. Boniface III (February–December 607), for example, 'obtained from the Emperor Phocas that St Peter's apostolic see should be head of all the churches' and the climax of the Life of Pope Constantine I (708–15) portrays a triumph of orthodoxy and of the pope, in which the Emperor, 'crown on head, prostrated himself and kissed the feet of the pontiff'.[61]

The cumulative claims to universal ecclesiastical authority emerge from the legal prescriptions relating to ecclesiastical discipline, clerical organization, dress, conduct, eligibility, and hierarchy. The phrases *Hic constituit* ('he decreed') or *Hic fecit constitutum de ecclesia* ('he issued a decree about the church') are consistently used by the *Liber pontificalis* authors to introduce the legislative acts which cumulatively emphasize pope's overall responsibility and authority for the church in Rome and as a whole. Thus Clement, the fourth pope, is said 'on St Peter's instruction' to have undertaken 'the pontificate for governing the church, as the

---

[59] *LP*I, Life 81, cc. 10 and 15, pp. 352 and 354; trans. Davis, *Pontiffs*, pp. 74 and 75: *synodica sanctissimi Agathonis papae relecta est . . . tanta gratia divina omnipotentis concessa est missis sedis apostolicae ut ad letitiam populi vel sancti concilii qui in regia urbe erat, Iohannes epsicopus Portuensis dominicorum die octava paschae in ecclesia sanctae Sophiae publicas missas coram principe et patriarchas latine celebraret et omnes unanimiter in laudes et victoriis piissimorum imperatorum idem latine vocibus adclamarent.*

[60] *LP*I, Life 86, cc. 7 and 15, pp. 373 and 376.

[61] *LP*I, Life 68, c. 1, p. 316; trans. Davis, *Pontiffs*, p. 60: *Hic obtinuit apud Focatem principem ut sedis apostolica beati Petri apostoli caput esset omnium ecclesiarum,* and *LP*I, Life 90, c. 6, p. 391; trans. Davis, *Pontiffs*, p. 88: *cum regno in capite sese prostravit et pedes osculans pontificis.*

cathedra had been handed down and entrusted to him by the Lord Jesus Christ'.[62] It is Pope Silvester (314–35), the Bishop of Rome during the reign of the Emperor Constantine I, who is described not only as responsible for summoning the Synod of Nicaea, but also as convening a synod in Rome and there issuing a comprehensive decree 'about the church'.[63]

Pope Siricius (384–99) 'issued a decree about the whole church and against every heresy and he broadcast it through the whole world (*exparsit per universum mundum*) to be kept in the archive of every church for rebutting every heresy'. Pope Hilarus (461–8) too 'issued a decretal and broadcast it through the whole of the east (*et per universam orientem exparsit*), and letters on the catholic faith, confirming the three synods of Nicaea, Ephesus and Chalcedon, and the Tome of the holy archbishop Leo'.[64] Of Pope Felix III (483–92) it was reported that after his death a decree 'about the whole church was issued by the priests and deacons', and Pope Gelasius I (492–6) also issued a decree 'about the church' (*de omnem ecclesiam*).[65]

The *Liber pontificalis* occasionally includes descriptions of procedure in its account of particular synods convened to discuss ecclesiastical matters and doctrinal issues that are entirely consistent with the procedure described in surviving synodal *acta* as well as in imperial legislation from the reign of Theodosius. The structure of conciliar proceedings and their *Acta* had been established since the fourth century. Their records are to be found both in separate codices and in the canon law collections compiled from the end of the fifth century onwards discussed

---

[62] *LP* I, Life 4, c. 3, p. 123; trans. Davis, *Pontiffs*, p. 3: *Hic ex praecepto beati Petri suscepit ecclesiae pontificatum gubernandi, sicut ei fuerat a domino Iesu Christo cathedra tradita vel commissa.*

[63] *LP* I, Life 34, cc. 4–8, pp. 171–2; trans. Davis, *Pontiffs*, pp. 15–16.

[64] *LP* I, Lives 40, c. 1 and 48, c. 1, pp. 216 and 242; trans. Davis, *Pontiffs*, pp. 29 and 37: *Hic constitutum fecit de omnem ecclesiam vel contra omnes hereses et exparsit per universum mundum ut in omnem ecclesiae archibo teneantur ob oppugnationem contra omnes hereses* and *Hic fecit decretalem et per universam orientem exparsit*. Note the spelling of 'archive' with 'b' rather than 'v', as an instance of 'betacism'.

[65] *LP* I, Lives 50, c. 5 and 51, c. 1, pp. 252 and 255: *Et post transitum eius factum est a presbiteris et diaconibus constitutum de omnem ecclesiam;* trans. Davis, *Pontiffs*, p. 41.

below.[66] They are also the form in which they would presumably have been available to the authors of the *Liber pontificalis* as they constructed the summaries and brief notices included in the papal biographies.

The *acta* of councils are set out as a report of the sessions, day after day. They often include an overall summary which comes immediately after the record of those attending. In the case of the Lateran 649 Council only the Greek version includes the summaries, and some of these in any case may be much later additions. The *acta* which follow are summaries of the debates, often with each protagonist named and direct speech reported, in which the person speaking alludes to or quotes from, often at length, many biblical passages and patristic authorities in support of his arguments. Documents are often requested, produced, and read out to those assembled. Each day's session usually ends with an indication that the discussion will continue, until the council finishes, which usually takes the form of a summary of the final conclusions reached, issued as a decree. In the case of Lateran 649, for example, there are nineteen concluding points and an affirmation of faith. Thus, Lateran 649 finishes: 'now that you have repelled every heretical innovation and confirmed the whole orthodox faith'. At the end of the decree there is a list of signatories, of all the attending bishops, confirming that they enact the decrees of the council and sign to indicate their consent.[67] It is clear from the surviving reports of other councils, such as Chalcedon (451) or Constantinople (453), that the provision of the official record, and the work of the secretaries trying to record in shorthand all that was said and decided, was far from straightforward.[68] That for the Council of Trullo (680) in the Life of Pope Agatho (678–81), for example, describes how the codices were brought to the synod by the protagonists in the debate about the nature and wills of Christ and 'how an enquiry into those codices was held and thus [the synod] found that there were freshly inserted forgeries'.[69] The Trullo proceedings, however, were especially concerned with doctrine, and the texts brought to the synod

[66] See below, pp. 151–7.   [67] Price, Booth, and Cubitt 2014, pp. 383–88.
[68] See Price and Gaddis 2005, pp. 64–68. Compare also Hess 2002, and Graumann 2018.
[69] *LP* I, Life 81, cc. 6–10, pp. 351–2: *inquisitione de ipsos codices facta, ita repperit falsa noviter addita fuisse;* trans. Davis, *Pontiffs,* pp. 77–8.

for discussion were theological treatises and commentaries, and statements on Christology by theologians such as John of Constantinople, Cyril, Athanasius, Basil, Gregory, Hilary, Ambrose, Augustine, and Leo, and most probably the records of the earliest conciliar statements from Nicaea, Constantinople, Ephesus, and Chalcedon as well.

Textual Authority

These procedures and methods of argument centre on textual authority. Because the *Liber pontificalis* offered reports of papal confirmations of orthodox doctrine and summaries of synodal proceedings, as well as an accumulation of authoritative statements about liturgy and the ecclesiastical hierarchy, albeit in the form of a narrative summary, it effectively made its own claim for textual authority. The whole history became an instrument for the propagation of the notions of institutional authority and orthodoxy. The text is a classic instance generally, quite apart from specific cases of summaries of synodal proceedings within the *Liber pontificalis,* of how law and narrative history can overlap in terms of acquiring authority.[70]

In this respect, the allusions to the particular popes who 'issued a decree about the whole church' acquire even greater significance, for they can be understood as signalling a text or categories of text that act as supporting documents for the *Liber pontificalis* itself. A case in point is the reference I cited above to Siricius, whose 'decree' was to be kept 'in the archive of every church'.[71] The *Liber pontificalis* entry thereafter appears to be drawing on a knowledge of Siricius's letters generally, of which only seven are now extant.[72] It is possible, however, that this 'decree' can be identified as the famous letter of Pope Siricius to Bishop Himerius of Tarragona of 385.[73] Zechiel-Eckes suggested that such early papal letters

---

[70] For a full discussion of the Synod of Rome in 769, also recorded in the *Liber pontificalis,* for example, see McKitterick 2018b, and the different perspective offered in Verardi 2019.

[71] *LP* I, Life 49, p. 216: *ut in omnem ecclesiae archibo teneantur.* Compare p. 149, note 64 above.

[72] The literature on papal letter collections is too copious to be cited here, but a useful starting point is Jasper and Fuhrmann 2001, and Allen and Neil (eds.) 2015. See also the introduction to Thompson 2015a, and Sogno, Storin, and Watts (eds.) 2017.

[73] Zechiel-Eckes 2013.

were originally composed as exhortation and instruction in response to queries or reports from a bishop elsewhere, and not necessarily intended to be 'legal' in either function or tone. Siricius's request to Himerius that he make known to all his fellow bishops and not just those in Himerius's region what he wrote back in response to his questions, however, suggests a papal consciousness of the weight and definitiveness of his guidance. One of Siricius's successors, Pope Innocent I (401/2–417), moreover, has been characterized by Bronwen Neil as using papal letters in emulation of imperial decretals in order to offer opinions on disciplinary and dogmatic issues.[74] In the Life of Pope Leo I (440–61), the *Liber pontificalis* alluded to the frequent confirmations of Chalcedon in his letters. In other words, by the time the first section of the *Liber pontificalis* was compiled, a papal letter had come to be regarded as a precept or command, and eligible to be included alongside the decrees of the early councils and synods of the church as part of its body of 'law'. The significance of this development needs further comment, for it has important implications for both the construction and the reception of the *Liber pontificalis* narrative.[75]

I am not referring here to the compilations of papal letters made from the time of Leo I onwards, on which there has been so much excellent scholarship. In this respect, concentration on papal letter transmission, notably the dissemination of Pope Leo's letters, has proved invaluable, but risks overlooking the wider implications of the codicological context. These letter collections appear to have been designed to assemble material for particular theological arguments, though their codicological context still needs more thought.[76] Still less am I referring to the phenomenon of individual letter collections, such as those of many of the patristic writers and the fifth- and sixth-century bishops Sidonius Apollinaris, Ennodius of Pavia, Avitus of Vienne, Ruricius of Limoges, or the seventh-century Desiderius of Cahors. Instead I am particularly interested in the recurrence of a specific set of papal letters which acquired the status of decretals and become a standard element of what I label for convenience with the umbrella term early

---

[74] Neil 2017.   [75] *LP* I, Life 47, cc. 2–3, p. 238. For earlier discussion see Getzeny 1922.
[76] Mordek 1991 and Hoskins 2015. See also Evers 2019.

medieval 'canon law collections'.[77] The greater majority of such collections combine the decisions of early church councils and a selection of particular papal letters and are in late eighth- and ninth-century manuscripts from the Carolingian Empire. Many of the sequences of conciliar and papal statements, rightly or wrongly,[78] are credited with Roman or at least Italian origins as collections.[79] As many before me have emphasized, compilers were making serious claims of legitimacy and authority in invoking the popes.

Although often regarded as the 'first papal decretal', Siricius's letter was included from the sixth century onwards at the head of the newly defined papal 'decretals' in many of the independent compilations known as canon law collections, the earliest extant manuscripts of which are all from Frankish Gaul. These include the *Collectio Corbeiensis* in Paris, BnF lat. 12097, *Collectio Coloniensis* in Cologne, Dombibliothek 212 from the sixth century, and the *Collectio Albigensis* in Toulouse, Bibliothèque d'étude et du patrimoine MS 364 from the seventh century, as well as the more famous *Dionysiana*.[80] Dionysius Exiguus, already famous for his work on the date of Easter reckoning and the invention of the *Anno Domini* dating system we still use,[81] is thought to be the first to combine conciliar decrees with papal decretals. He extended his collection with the letters of Popes Innocent I, Zosimus, Boniface, Celestine, Leo I, Gelasius I, and Anastasius I. Quite apart from providing a useful core set of texts for subsequent compilers of the collections modern scholars tend to lump together as 'canon law', it is probable that such inclusion influenced the subsequent development of a far more self-conscious production of decretals by the popes themselves.[82] It has perhaps not been sufficiently recognized hitherto how much the allusive phrasing of the *Liber pontificalis* actually reflects the rich archival resources, including papal letters and synodal proceedings, available in Rome. The allusions

---

[77] McKitterick 2020b.   [78] Turner 1916.

[79] For a reassessment of the evidence for Italian canonical collections see Moreau 2019.

[80] McKitterick 1985, Dunn 2015a, and D'Avray 2019. Compare Jong 2019, pp. 203–5, and the discussion of Wala and Paschasius Radbert presenting writings confirmed by the holy fathers and Pope Gregory IV's predecessors to the pope.

[81] See Declercq 2000. On the implications see Warntjes and Ó Cróinín (eds.) 2017.

[82] See Moreau 2010.

to Siricius's decree, Leo's letters, and the synods of Silvester and Sixtus III, among many others scattered throughout the text, imply considerable cross-referencing to canon law collections and papal letters on the part of the *Liber pontificalis* authors, and these serve to enhance the authority of the text. The so-called *canones apostolorum* included in so many of the early canon law manuscripts, moreover, were often attributed to Clement, and could be regarded as a demonstration of his carrying out the charge laid on him by St Peter to 'govern the church' reported in the brief summary in Life 4 of the *Liber pontificalis*.[83]

In addition to the legitimization provided by the legal dimension of the papal narrative summarized above and rightly stressed by Antonio Verardi,[84] the *Liber pontificalis* offers a particular conceptualization of history as incorporating a dialogue with the past by reference to texts. Yet the *Liber pontificalis* authors were doing far more than defining or summarizing an authoritative tradition and rehearsing elements of disciplinary and liturgical requirements introduced by the popes that were to become part of a body of law. They were also engaged in a very precise dialogue with the past, making specific selections and constructing a chronology that actually established the authority of their own narrative.[85] In presenting such legal traditions within a narrative and biographical framework, the authors not only simultaneously acknowledged and recorded historical change and instilled the pope's role in effecting such change in the readers' minds, but implied the historical solidity of the papal archive on which their record rests.

One simple manifestation of the effectiveness of this record is the formative structural influence apparently exerted by the framework of papal history in the *Liber pontificalis* on the compilers of canon law collections and their conceptualization of authority, especially in Frankish Gaul. Any assessment of such an influence has to be tentative in the light of the manuscript evidence. While there are some sixth-century manuscripts extant, a great many collections thought by Frederick

---

[83] *LP* I, Life 4, p. 123. For example, Berlin, Deutsche Staatsbibliothek, Hamilton 32 and Modena, Biblioteca Capitolare O.I.12; see below, pp. 186–7.

[84] Verardi 2016 and 2019.

[85] I here invoke the notion of communication with the past discussed in McKitterick 2005.

Maassen to be of fifth- or sixth-century origin are only extant in late eighth- or ninth-century manuscripts, and the greater majority of these codices are Frankish.[86] The structural influence nevertheless is baldly displayed in the inclusion of the lists of popes. Some of these lists were usefully assembled by Duchesne, though his interest was more in the sequence of popes and the parity between the length of reign recorded in the various lists than the function of the lists in the codices in which they are to be found. Thus, the Frankish manuscript of the second half of the sixth century, Cologne, Dombibliothek 212, has such a list, on its final pages, fols 168v–169r. Written in the same hand as the preceding compilation of early church councils in the Dionysian Latin translation, papal decretals of Siricius, Innocent, and Celestine, Gallican councils from the sixth centuries, interspersed with a further selection of letters from the Popes Siricius, Innocent, Celestine, Leo, Zosimus, and Symmachus addressed to various bishops in Frankish Gaul and Spain, it appears to have been planned as a climax to the book. The original list with details of the length of reign of each pope stopped at Agapitus (535–6). The youngest conciliar record in the codex is that of the Council of Orleans from 549. Soon after 590, the names of the popes from Silverius to Gregory appear to have been added as a group, but Gregory lacks his years in office. This suggests that the first list could have been extracted from the information in a copy of the first redaction of the *Liber pontificalis*, ending with Agapitus. The names at the end of the list raise interesting questions about how such information may have been transmitted to Gaul.[87]

Other early collections of canon law include these papal lists, whether as introductory statements at the beginning of the codex, as in the *Collectio Corbeiensis*,[88] after the contents list, as in the Arras collection,[89] between the contents list and the rest of the compilation of conciliar canons and papal decretals, as in the Albi collection,[90] or at the end of a

---

[86] For a summary see McKitterick 2004b, pp. 245–56 and Kéry 1999.
[87] See below, pp. 186–7.
[88] Paris, BnF lat. 12097, fols 1r–1v: *LP* I, pp. xi–xxiv and cxvi–cxxx.
[89] Arras, BM, MS 672 (641) fols 2r–3r.
[90] Albi, BM, MS 2, a ninth-century copy of Toulouse, BM, MS 364 which has lost its first eight leaves.

collection.[91] The collections in these manuscripts have papal material and Roman synods as integral and often substantial elements of their contents. I have cited the earliest collections because the palaeographical evidence confirms their compilation in the sixth and seventh centuries. Other eighth- and ninth-century manuscripts containing canon law collections may more properly be regarded as newly created eighth- and ninth-century compilations, but they nevertheless affirm the recognition of papal authority. Papal lists serve to endorse the authority all these texts represent. Papal history and the authority of the apostolic see, moreover, are the most obvious principles of organization in the systematically chronological Carolingian pseudo-Isidore decretal collections of the mid-ninth century. In this respect, the famous 'forgers' were simply following a long-standing convention in compilation and method of selection,[92] for the papal orientation and chronological organization of canon law is evident in the earliest manuscript collections from the sixth century onwards. Criteria of inclusion, the predominance of earlier popes, and the absence of Pope Gregory's statements in most of the canon law collections extant (an exception is the *Collectio Frisingensis* in its second part) are significant in this respect and would merit further consideration. The *Liber pontificalis* itself may well have played a role, by highlighting particular topics, in determining the selection of material. Essential questions for each of these manuscripts remain those of who did the compiling, when, where, and for whom?

The authenticity of elements of these collections is not as important as how the genuine and supposedly forged texts together can manipulate signs of authority and identity to gain acceptance by an audience.[93] Yet, in a sense acting as intermediary, the *Liber pontificalis* created the historical and conceptual framework in which such law, emanating from Rome, could be 'invented', applied, and understood in a new context. The complex codicological association of conciliar records, canon law, papal decretals, and many early manuscript copies of the *Liber pontificalis*

---

[91] Berlin, Deutsche Staatsbibliothek, Phillipps 1743 (fols 293v–294r).

[92] See Harder 2014. I differ here from Leyser 2016, p. 191.

[93] See McKitterick 2005, pp. 941–79. For discussion, and on forgery as an extension or exaggeration of the genuine, see Hiatt 2004, Hathaway 1978, and Grafton 1990.

within an essentially historical context has also much to reveal about the conceptualization of ecclesiastical authority.[94]

The Liturgical Past and Papal History

A striking confirmation of the effectiveness of the *Liber pontificalis* and its representation of the popes' authority and the importance of Roman precedent takes us back to the liturgy I discussed at the beginning of the chapter. There my emphasis was on how liturgy is used by the *Liber pontificalis* authors to define and emphasize the bishop's ministry and pastoral role. But, as with canon law, there is a further dimension, that of a dialogue with the past, that needs to be considered. Of particular significance in this respect are the comments made by the Carolingian scholar Walafrid Strabo in the 840s, with specific reference to the papal contributions to the liturgy.

In his *Libellus de exordiis et incrementis quarundam in observationibus ecclesiasticis rerum*, addressed to readers and hearers, *studiosi* and *auditori*, Walafrid Strabo observed that:

> What we do today in a complex liturgy of prayers, readings, chants and consecrations, we believe the apostles and their immediate successors did simply with prayers and the commemoration of the Lord's Passion as he Himself taught ... Subsequently the Faith gained more ground, and Christians elaborated the liturgy of the Mass because either the stability which peace brought further spread the Church's limits, or the growing Christian practice multiplied the number of saints. We have already said that the same sort of development also took place in the construction and embellishments of sacred buildings.
>
> ... Therefore, many of the Greek- and Latin-speaking people set up the order of the Mass as they thought best for themselves; and the followers of the Roman tradition particularly, taking over the practice of observances from blessed Peter the principal apostle, each in their own generation added what they judged appropriate. The reason why so many nations followed the Roman usage in the liturgy is twofold: such important

---

[94] Neil 2015. For further discussion of the manuscripts see below, pp. 178–220.

instruction is illustrious because it originates from the apostolic head, and no other church throughout the entire world has remained as free from heretical taint in all past ages as that of Rome.[95]

In these passages, Walafrid placed ninth-century Frankish liturgical practices in a long but evolutionary relationship with the prayers and commemorative practices first recorded in the Gospels, Acts of the Apostles, and early Christian church, as well as in the wider historical context of Christian history. He referred to the multiplicity of liturgical texts used in his day, which we can identify from extant manuscripts as the Sacramentaries, Epistle and Gospel Lectionaries, Antiphonaries, and other books of chant texts and hymns, prayers for specific rites and occasions such as baptism, ordination of priests and bishops, and the consecration of churches, litanies, votive Mass texts, benedictions, and collections of *ordines,* that is, the descriptions of rituals to accompany the texts. Walafrid also acknowledged the development of specifically liturgical spaces and buildings. He emphasized the Romanness of the liturgy because its sources were both apostolic and orthodox. Throughout the text of the *Libellus* there is clear evidence of Walafrid using the *Liber pontificalis* to try and work out how the structure of the liturgy evolved. He does so from the vantage point of his own experience of the liturgy of the Mass in particular, but also tries to make sense of the divergent references in his sources.

Walafrid's text illustrates not only the historical approach to early medieval commentaries on the liturgy but also the ways in which a history of the liturgy could be constructed: the sources from which it was

---

[95] *Quod nunc agimus multiplici orationum, lectionum, cantilenarum et consecrationum officio, totum hoc apostoli et post ipsos proximi, ut creditur, orationibus et commemoratione passionis dominicae, sicut ipse praecepit, agebant simpliciter . . .*

    Proficiente dehinc religione eo amplius aucta sunt a Christi cultoribus officia missarum, quo vel pax praestita latius terminos propagavit ecclesiae vel sanctorum copia usu facta est convalescente frequentior . . . Multi itaque apud Grecos et Latinos missae ordinem, ut sibi visum est, statuerunt; et Romani quidem usum observationum a beato Petro principe apostolorum accipientes suis quique temporibus, quae congrua iudicata sunt, addiderunt. Quorum morem ideo in sacris rebus tam multae gentes imitantur, quia et tanti magysterii ex apice apostolico primordiis clarent et nulla per orbem ecclesia aeque ut Romana ab omni faece hereseon cunctis retro temporibus pura permansit, trans. Harting-Corrêa, pp. 127–9. All the page references to Harting-Corrêa indicate the Latin on the even-numbered pages and the English on the odd-numbered pages.

constructed and the contexts, both codicological and textual, in which the history of the liturgy might have been disseminated and received.

Walafrid Strabo is celebrated as a scholar of the middle Carolingian period, educated at the major cultural and religious centres of Reichenau and Fulda. After Walafrid had left the royal court, he became Abbot of Reichenau. There he remained, apart from a brief period in exile between 840 and 842, until his death by accidental drowning in the River Loire in 849 while on a diplomatic mission. Walafrid displayed a rich assortment of learning in the texts he gathered together in his famous *vade mecum* or commonplace book, still extant in csg 878.[96] Yet it is his *Libellus* on the origins and developments of aspects of ecclesiastical matters, mostly concerned with the liturgy, which provides a remarkable display, not only of Walafrid's learning, but also of his critical historical understanding. It was completed by 842, for it was listed by Reginbert of Reichenau in his additions to the Reichenau library catalogue.[97] Walafrid may have begun compiling it while still acting as tutor to the young prince, later king, Charles the Bald (840–77), at the court of Louis the Pious. It survives in a number of manuscripts, of which the earliest, csg 446, of the third quarter of the ninth century, is regarded as already at two removes from the lost original. This codex includes Walafrid's *Libellus* alongside *ordines* and other discussions of the liturgy, Scripture, and the sacraments, including Jerome's long response, designed for Latin readers and explaining Greek and Hebrew words, to the series of questions on discrepancies in the translation of the 'Gallican Psalter' posed by the Gothic priests Fretela and Sunnia,[98] Alcuin's commentary on Baptism,[99] and the episcopal statutes of Theodulf of Orleans and Haito of Basle.[100]

Although the *Libellus de exordiis et incrementis quarundam in observationibus ecclesiasticis rerum* has often been understood as a history of liturgy or a handbook of liturgical history, such a description does insufficient justice to Walafrid's conceptualization of the liturgy in its historical context.[101] Walafrid reflected on current liturgical practice in Francia,

---

[96] Bischoff 1967 and Corradini 2014. [97] Lehmann (ed.), p. 262.
[98] McKitterick 2004a. [99] Keefe 2002. [100] *Capitula episcoporum*, ed. Brommer.
[101] Harting-Corrêa (ed.), p. 1, but compare Pössel 2018.

but always with the intention of tracing its origins as well as any record of alternative practice. Walafrid stated at the outset, in the preface addressed to Reginbert of Reichenau: 'I shall write with whatever ability God has given me about the beginnings and causes of some ecclesiastical matters, and I shall indicate from what source this or that has come into use, and how it developed as time passed.'[102]

The sources for Walafrid's discussion of the various topics he chose to address in the *Libellus* are thought to have been derived from the books he consulted at the Carolingian royal court as well as those in the libraries of the monasteries of the Reichenau and St Gallen. They include Augustine's *Confessiones, Enchiridion,* Sermons, and *De peccatorum meritis,* Bede's *De tabernaculo* and *De templo,* the Rule of St Benedict, Cyprian, Gennadius's *De ecclesiasticis dogmatibus,* Gregory the Great's *Dialogues,* Isidore's *Etymologiae* and *De differentiis rerum,* Jerome's letters, and the *Ordines Romani,* as well as the work of Walafrid's contemporaries Hraban Maur and Amalarius of Metz. Rather more copious use is made of particular conciliar decisions drawn apparently from the *Dionysio-Hadriana,* and the *Hispana* collections of canon law, and a number of histories, such as Bede's *Historia ecclesiastica gentis Anglorum,* Cassiodorus–Epiphanius's *Historia ecclesiastica tripartita,* Eusebius–Rufinus's *Historia ecclesiastica,* Gregory of Tours's *Historiae,* Josephus's *Antiquitatum libri* and *De bello Judaico,* and Orosius's *Historiarum adversus paganos libri VII.*

Walafrid's principal source in his discussions of the history of certain practices and prayers, however, diligently cited throughout his text and especially in chapter 23 of his work, was the *Liber pontificalis.* In this chapter Walafrid explored at length 'the arrangements of the Mass and the reason for offering it' (*de ordine missae et offerendi ratione*), which had been preceded by discussions of various lengths on the following topics: origins of buildings for worship – pagan, Jewish, and Christian; comparison of different religions; the progress of the Christian religion; the direction to be faced by those praying; on bells and explanation of other

---

[102] *Scribam igitur in quantum Dominus dederit facultatem, sicut ex authenticorum dictis, quae adhuc attigimus, addiscere potui, de quarundam ecclesiasticarum exordiis et causis rerum, et unde hoc vel illud in consuetudinem venerit, quomodo processu temporis auctum sit, indicabo, habiturus,* trans. Harting-Corrêa, pp. 48/9.

names for sacred objects; German names for the house of God; images and pictures; consecration of churches and activities allowed or forbidden in them; the manner of praying and diversity of voices; who does or does not profit from the liturgy; God's desire for offerings and virtues; discussion of sacrifices in the Old and New Testaments; sacraments; what should be offered at the altar, and taking of Communion; on the Mass; vessels and vestments; canonical hours, kneeling, hymns, chants; baptism; tithes; litanies; sprinkling (and blessing) of water; blessing of the Easter candle; a comparison of the ecclesiastical and secular orders.

In elucidating his theme of how Frankish liturgy emulates Roman practice, considered from both an historical and an ideological perspective, Walafrid uses the *Liber pontificalis* to try and work out how the structure of the liturgy evolved. He does so from the vantage point of his own experience in Francia of the liturgy of the Mass in particular, but also tries to make sense of the divergent references in his sources. In his discussion of church orientation, for example, he referred to the variety of orientation for altars in Constantine's church in Jerusalem. His information here was presumably from Arculf's *De locis sanctis* preserved in Adomnán's narrative. He also discussed the Pantheon, consecrated by 'blessed' Boniface, for which the information was derived from the *Liber Pontificalis* and Life 69 of Pope Boniface IV (608–15), and the church of St Peter in Rome, where the information appears to have been gained from contemporary Frankish descriptions.[103] In his discussion of images and pictures, Walafrid observed, displaying knowledge of the eighth-century section of the *Liber pontificalis,* that it was under Pope Gregory II that the Emperor Constantine abolished images in Constantinople, and that a synod convened in Rome by Pope Gregory III affirmed that images of saints were to be restored 'according to the ancient use of the universal church'.[104] In his chapter devoted to offerings at the altar, he cited the Life of Pope Eutychian about only offerings of beans and grapes being permitted,[105] and drew extensively on various lives in the *Liber*

---

[103] Ed. Harting-Corrêa, pp. 60/1. Compare *LP* I, Life 68, p. 285.

[104] *Secundum priscum catholicae ecclesiae usum restituerentur,* trans. Harting-Corrêa, pp. 76/7, and compare *LP* I, Lives 91, c. 23 and 92, cc. 2–4, pp. 408 and 416–17.

[105] *LP* I, Life 28, pp. 108–9.

pontificalis on such topics as how frequently Communion should be taken and Mass celebrated, and how the practice of fasting evolved.

In his long chapter on the Mass, chapter 23, Walafrid complained that 'it is not quite clear who first ordered readings from the Apostle and Gospel before the celebration of the sacrifice', but he added his own surmise about the reason for both Gospel and Epistle being part of the Mass: 'the readings from the Gospel should call to mind the foundation of their salvation and faith, and they should receive instruction in the faith and way of life pleasing to God from the Apostle'. He then added the information, quoting directly from the *Liber pontificalis,* that 'Anastasius the 41st pope ruled that whenever the holy Gospel is read aloud priests should not be seated but should stand bowing'.[106] Walafrid offered an extra comment on this provision, that this was 'so that even their body shows the humility the Lord teaches'.[107] In paying particular attention to the reading of the Gospel and Epistle, the reciting of the Creed, and the offertory chant, Walafrid grumbled further about the difficulty of working out when the different elements of the Mass were introduced, saying: 'We see that even today readings and collects and different kinds of praises are being added to an almost superabundance of things.'[108]

At the beginning of this section of his treatise, moreover, Walafrid expressed a general opinion on the development of the liturgy: 'However, as we said before, with the growing practice of the divine religion, the composition of prayers and liturgy for the church was also gradually growing with many additions made – written by people with excellent, mediocre and very little knowledge – which explained things appropri-

---

[106] *Lectiones apostolicas vel evangelicas quis ante celebrationem sacrificii primum statuerit, non adeo certum est . . . ex evangelio salutis et fidei suae recognoscerent fundamentum et ex apostolo eiusdem fidei et morum Deo placentium caperent instrumentum . . . Statuit autem Anastasius XLI papa 'ut quotiescumque sanctum evangelium recitaretur, sacerdotes non sederent, sed curvi starent',* trans. Harting-Corrêa, pp. 135/6, and compare *LP* I, Life 41, c. 1, p. 218.

[107] *Ut videlicet humilitatem, quae a Domino docetur, etiam corpore demonstrarent,* trans. Harting-Corrêa, pp. 134/5.

[108] *Cum videamus usque hodie et lectiones et collectas et diversas laudum species iam paene abundantibus omnibus superaddi,* trans. Harting-Corrêa, pp. 136/7.

ately.'[109] With the help of the information he extracted from the *Liber pontificalis* as well as other sources, Walafrid provided a chronology for the recitation of the Creed and Lord's Prayer in the Mass. He claimed that the Creed began to be repeated in the liturgy of the Mass more widely and frequently after the deposition of Felix the heretic, condemned under the most glorious Charles, ruler of the Franks.[110] Although he is obliged to acknowledge how much of the history of the Mass was obscure, he nevertheless pieced together a chronological development for the canon of the Mass 'as one sees quite often in the *Liber pontificalis*' (*ut in pontificalibus saepius invenitur*).[111] Walafrid further noted, with reference to Life 66 in the *Liber pontificalis*, that Pope Gregory I had added the prayer of the canon 'and dispose our days in Thy peace' (*Diesque nostros in tua pace disponas*) and that Pope Sergius I, '86th bishop of the Roman people, had ruled that the priest and people sing the *Agnus Dei* at the breaking of the Lord's body'.[112]

The most striking example of Walafrid's attempt to deal with contradictions within the *Liber pontificalis* text is his discussion of the *Gloria*. He introduced his explanation of 'the arrangement of the Roman Mass' by noting that: 'We read in the *Liber pontificalis* that antiphons at the introit were established by Celestinus the 45th pope; until his day only one reading from the Apostle and the Gospel were read before the sacrifice.'[113] This can be compared with the *Liber pontificalis*'s version: 'He issued many decrees, including one that before the sacrifice the 150 Psalms should be performed antiphonally by everyone; this used not to be done, but only St Paul's Epistle and the holy Gospel were

---

[109] *Crescente autem, sicut praediximus, religionis cultu divinae crescebat etiam paulatim orationum et officiorum ecclesiae compositio multis et ex summa scientia et ex mediocri et ex minima addentibus, quae congrua rebus explicandis videbantur,* trans. Harting-Corrêa, pp. 132/3.

[110] Ed. Harting-Corrêa, pp. 138/9. This is a reference to both the Adoptionist dispute and the argument with Pope Leo III about the inclusion of the *filioque* in the Creed. See on the former Cavadini 1995, and on the latter *Concilium Aquisgranensis* 809, ed. Willjung.

[111] Trans. Harting-Corrêa, pp. 140/1.

[112] Trans. Harting-Corrêa, pp. 142/3: *Agnus Dei in confractione corporis Domini a clero et populo decantari Sergius LXXXVI Romanorum antistes constituit,* trans. Harting-Corrêa, pp. 146/7.

[113] *Antiphonas ad introitum dicere Caelestinus papa XLV instituit, sicut legitur in gestis pontificum Romanorum, cum ad eius usque tempora ante sacrificium lectio una apostoli tantum et evangelium legeretur,* trans. Harting-Corrêa, pp. 128/9.

recited.'[114] After noting the 'litanies', that is, the *Kyrie eleison* and *Christe eleison,* 'believed to have been taken from the Greeks' practice' (*a grecorum usu sumptae creduntur*), Walafrid then launched into a discussion of the 'Hymn of the Angels' and its position in relation to the antiphons and reading of the Epistle and Gospel as recorded in the *Liber pontificalis:* 'Telesphorus the ninth bishop of the Romans decreed [the angelic hymn] should be sung before the sacrifice so that at such a great and holy celebration the souls of the congregation might be soothed by the sweet angelic melody.'[115]

Walafrid then addressed contradictions in these two statements. If Telesphorus said this, he asked, then why does Celestine's life claim that only a reading of the Apostle and the Gospel preceded the sacrifice? Walafrid suggested first that Celestine put the chanting of antiphons from the Psalms of David before these two readings. He made two further conjectures. Telesphorus may have established the singing of the hymn at the beginning of the Mass but his successors did not do it. Or, alternatively, Telesphorus decreed that it was only to be done by bishops at important feasts, so it may sometimes have been done, but not always, until Celestine established the singing of antiphons at the introit. Walafrid then offered a further possible explanation, namely that Celestine could have taught that the *Sanctus* should be said before the Sacrifice because the *Sanctus* might be what is described in the *Liber pontificalis* as the 'Hymn of the Angels', but ignorant people assumed it was *Gloria in excelsis Deo* instead. Walafrid thought this was a better explanation because it made sense of the reference in the Life of Pope Symmachus, whom he noted as the 53rd bishop of the Romans, 'who decreed that on every Sunday and on saints' feast days the *Gloria in excelsis* should be

---

[114] *LP* I, Life 45, c. 1, p. 230; trans. Davis, *Pontiffs,* p. 33: *Hic multa constituta fecit et constituit ut psalmi David CL ante sacrificum psalli antephanatim ex omnibus, quod ante non fiebat, nisi tantum epistula beati Pauli recitabatur et sanctum Evangelium.*

[115] *Thelesphorus IX Romanorum praesul constituit, ut ad tantae sanctitatis caelebrationem congregatorum animi angelica modulationis dulcedine mulcerentur,* trans. Harting-Corrêa, pp. 128–9. Compare *LP* I, Life 9, c. 2, p. 129; trans. Davis, *Pontiffs,* p. 4: *Hic constituit ut . . . ante sacrificium hymnus diceretur angelicus, hoc est, 'Gloria in excelsis deo'* ('He decreed . . . that the angels' hymn, that is, Glory be to God on high should be sung before the sacrifice').

sung'.[116] This is not only a fascinating instance of a Carolingian reader wrestling with the internal contradictions of the evidence offered by his source text, but also implies that Walafrid appreciated that the possible interventions of later scribes, those he describes as 'by ignorant people' (*ab imperitis*), may have distorted the original information in the text.

In addition to specific prayers or structures of the liturgy, Walafrid also reiterated the contributions of the popes and Roman authority more generally. Thus, he stressed that 'Pope Gelasius, the fifty-first pope, is said to have put in order the prayers he had composed as well as those composed by others, and the Gallican churches used their own prayers, still kept by many churches'.[117] Further, on Pope Gregory I's contribution, Walafrid commented that 'Because so many prayers by so many undetermined authors were dubious and lacking in sound meaning, blessed Gregory carefully collected the reasonable ones, setting aside the excessive or inappropriate; he put together a book which is called a sacramentary, shown clearly in its title.'[118] With reference to the *Alleluia* sung before the Gospel, Walafrid also noted: 'Nevertheless when Roman practice recommended its use it then spread to all the churches of the Latin-speaking people.'[119] With reference to plainchant and psalmody, moreover, he observed:

> But the prerogative of the Roman see was observed and the reasoned consistency of its arrangements persuaded almost all the churches of the Latin-speaking world to follow its custom and authority because there was

---

[116] Walafrid: *ut omni dominica vel nataliciis sanctorum 'Gloria in excelsis Deo' diceretur*, trans. Harting-Corrêa, pp. 130/1; compare *LP* I, Life 52, c. 11, p. 263: *Hic constituit ut omne die dominicum vel natalicia martyrum Gloria in excelsis ymnus diceretur.*

[117] *Nam et Gelasius papa in ordine LI tam a se, quam ab aliis compositas preces dicitur ordinasse, et Galliarum ecclesiae suis orationibus utebantur, quae et adhuc a multis habentur*, trans. Harting-Corrêa, pp. 132/3–134/5.

[118] *Et quia tam incertis auctoribus multa videbantur incerta et sensus integritatem non habentia, curavit beatus Gregorius rationabilia quaeque coadunare et seclusis his, quae vel nimia vel inconcinna videbantur, composuit librum, qui dicitur sacrasacramentorum, sicut ex titulo eius manifestissime declaratur*, trans. Harting-Corrêa, pp. 134/5.

[119] *quod tamen postea usu Romano commendatum ad omnes Latinorum pervenit ecclesias*, trans. Harting-Corrêa, pp. 136/7.

no other tradition like it either for following the rules of the faith or in the instruction of obligations.[120]

Walafrid's *Libellus* is an eloquent vindication of the *Liber pontificalis*'s insistence on the papal contributions to the liturgy and the way in which this acted as a further legitimation of papal and Roman authority. His interpretation is also distinctive in a number of other crucial ways in relation to previous expositions of ecclesiastical offices or the liturgy, such as those offered in the seventh century by Isidore of Seville's *De ecclesiasticis officiis*, in the early ninth century by Walafrid's teacher Hraban Maur in the *De institutione clericorum*, or by the Carolingian scholar Amalarius of Metz in his *Liber officialis*.[121] Isidore was more concerned with a general exposition of the shape of a liturgical year, and the significance of some of the feasts and biblical precedents; he was not the least bit interested in Roman practice or bishops of Rome as a source of authority. He made no reference to any pope's innovation in the liturgy, nor did he cite either a papal decretal or the *Liber pontificalis*. Hraban Maur's *De institutione clericorum*, probably written *c.*819, is rather closer to Walafrid's than Isidore's treatise. This is certainly the case with respect to the citation of authorities and precedents from conciliar decrees and papal decretals to underpin and justify certain practices and the structure of the ecclesiastical hierarchy. On liturgical matters Hraban occasionally drew on the evidence of the Frankish sacramentaries and *Ordines Romani* to illustrate his comments, but he had also quite clearly read the *Liber pontificalis*. On Holy Saturday, for example, he noted that it was celebrated as the day the Lord rested in the sepulchre, a comment also made in Life 42 of Pope Innocent I (401–17) in the *Liber pontificalis*.[122] The *Liber pontificalis*

---

[120] *Sed privilegio Romanae sedis observato et congruentia rationabili dispositionum apud eam factarum persuadente factum est, ut in omnibus paene Latinorum ecclesiis consuetudo et magisterium eiusdem sedis praevaleret, quia non est alia traditio aeque sequenda vel in fidei regula vel in observationum doctrina*, trans. Harting-Corrêa, pp. 166/7.

[121] Walafrid could have known all three of these works, for they are extant in St Gallen manuscripts, such as csg 230, containing Isidore's treatise, texts of Amalarius in csg 278 and csg 446, which also contains Walafrid's own work, and a copy of Hraban's *De institutione clericorum*, written in Regensburg but at St Gallen by the middle of the ninth century, csg 286.

[122] *LP* I, Life 42, c. 6, p. 222; Hraban Maur, *De institutione clericorum*, II.38, ed. Zempel, p. 388.

evidently acted as a useful confirmation of papal precedent and authority for particular elements of the liturgy, but Hraban used it much as one would a conciliar decree, that is, as confirmatory evidence. His treatise thus reinforced the authority of Rome, even if by no means as emphatically as Walafrid.

Amalarius of Metz, by contrast with Walafrid and even Hraban Maur, made far more limited use of the *Liber pontificalis*, for his principal focus in the *Liber officialis* was not on tracing the development of the liturgy as an historical exercise, so much as explaining the 'purpose behind the order of our Mass which we celebrate in accordance with established custom' to his contemporary Frankish audience.[123] Only occasionally in his treatise did he quote from or refer to any papal precedents culled from the *Liber pontificalis*. When he does so, one wonders whether these particular associations of particular popes with specific innovations in Christian liturgical observance had become so well entrenched, because of widespread knowledge of the claims of the *Liber pontificalis* in the Frankish world, that we should not be particularly surprised by it. The reference to the establishment by Pope Telesphorus of a seven-week Lenten fast before Easter and the blessing of the Easter candle determined by Pope Zosimus are two such possible instances.[124] On the other hand, it is the *Actus Silvestri* to which Amalarius refers when discussing the anointing of a neophyte's head by the priest, and demonstrates his own knowledge of history as well.[125] Thus, he referred to Bede's exegesis on Acts with the comment 'if priestly anointing were established previously it was redundant for Pope Silvester to establish that it be done in his time'. 'Down to Silvester's time,' he added, 'not everyone was baptized, especially since the emperors and their ministers were pagans'.[126]

---

[123] Amalarius, *Liber officialis*, ed. and trans. Knibbs, Preface, pp. 18 and 19: *ut scirem rationem aliquam de ordine nostrae Missae, quam consueto more caelebramus.*

[124] Amalarius, *Liber officialis*, I.1.18; I.18.1, ed. and trans. Knibbs, I, pp. 40–1 and 192–3; compare *LP* I, Lives 9 and 43, pp. 129 and 225.

[125] Amalarius, *Liber officialis*, I.27.1, ed. and trans. Knibbs, I, pp. 248–9: *ut in gestis pontificalibus legitur.*

[126] Amalarius, *Liber officialis*, I.27.1, ed. and trans. Knibbs, I, pp. 250–1: *Quod si antea agebatur superflue constitutum a sancto Sylvestro quod iam agebatur ... usque ad illud tempus non generaliter omnes baptizabantur, praecipue cum imperatores et ministri eorum pagani erant.* Referring to this same *LP* passage, see also I.27.8, ed. and trans. Knibbs, I, pp. 254–5.

Elsewhere in the text, Amalarius quoted from the *Liber pontificalis* on a number of topics, such as the necessity for clerics to wear consecrated vestments in church only,[127] the introduction of the dalmatics for deacons and the marking of the baptized with chrism by Pope Silvester,[128] and the pattern of ordinations, with Simplicius the first to ordain in February.[129]

On the Mass, the *Liber pontificalis* represented a particularly important source of authority and, like Walafrid after him, the *Gloria* and *Sanctus* struck Amalarius as particularly important elements of the Mass ritual to discuss.[130] Telesphorus's introduction of the angelic hymn and the Mass on the night of the Lord's nativity were also mentioned with specific reference to the *Liber pontificalis:* 'Thus it is written in the Deeds of the bishops'.[131] Similarly, Amalarius repeated the rationale from the Life of Symmachus for the time of Mass on every Sunday and the feasts of the martyrs not being before the third hour, when the Lord ascended the Cross. He referred to the *Liber pontificalis*'s record of particular phrases and prayers being added to the Mass, such as Pope Gregory the Great (Life 66) adding the prayer *diesque nostros in tua pace disponas* and Pope Sergius I's introducing the *Agnus Dei* into the Mass and special litanies on the Marian festivals. On the *Agnus Dei,* Amalarius appears to pick up the significance of the use of *peccata* in the plural rather than *peccatum* (singular) referred to above, and spells out the reference to plural sins, that is, of thoughts and words (*peccata ... scilicet cogitationum verborumque*).[132]

---

[127] Amalarius, *Liber officialis,* II.16.1, ed. and trans. Knibbs, I, pp. 44–5; cf. *LP* I, Life 24, p. 154.

[128] Amalarius, *Liber officialis,* II.21.1, ed. and trans. Knibbs, I, pp. 446–7; see also I.27.15, ed. and trans. Knibbs, I, pp. 260–1.

[129] Amalarius, *Liber officialis,* II.1.18, ed. and trans. Knibbs, I, pp. 368–9; and cf. *LP* I, Life 49, p. 249.

[130] Amalarius, *Liber officialis,* III.21.9, ed. and trans. Knibbs, II, pp. 140–1.

[131] Amalarius, *Liber officialis,* III.41.1, III.42.1, ed. and trans. Knibbs, II, pp. 248/9: *Ita scriptum est in gestis episcopalibus.*

[132] Amalarius, *Liber officialis,* III.23.24, III.27.6, III.33.1, III.43.1, ed. and trans. Knibbs, II, pp. 160–1, 194–5, 220–1, 252–3.

Conclusion

All these Carolingian authors read the *Liber pontificalis* as an authoritative reconstruction of the history of the liturgy, much of it determinedly orchestrated by the popes. An understanding of the *Liber pontificalis* as itself a fabricated history of the liturgy does not detract at all from its effectiveness as a text which mounted a powerful historiographical case for the authority of Rome, the crucial importance of the Petrine succession, and Peter's appointment by Christ as the rock on which he would found his church as the basis for that authority. That authority was further enhanced by the text's insistence on the Bishop of Rome's invincible orthodoxy. Both authority and orthodoxy are reinforced by the presentation of the bishops of Rome as the designers and augmenters of the liturgy. The powerful message of the *Liber pontificalis*, moreover, is not merely appreciated by modern scholars; its argument was absorbed and exploited by early medieval readers of the *Liber pontificalis*, and particularly by Carolingian scholars. It is a point Walafrid Strabo rams home in his discussion, already quoted above, of Rome's position in relation to liturgical development:

> The reason why so many nations followed the Roman usage in the liturgy is twofold: such important instruction is illustrious because it originates from the Apostolic head, and no other church throughout the entire world has remained as free from heretical taint in all past ages as that of Rome.[133]

Walafrid reinforced his readers' understanding of the strength of Rome, the authority of the pope, and the ecclesiastical hierarchy in relation to secular politics with the final chapter of his *Libellus*, in which he offered a comparison of ecclesiastical and secular order from popes and kings down to cantors and secretaries. Despite his caveat that he was 'not unaware that putting rulers and offices in any kind of order has been

---

[133] *Quorum morem ideo in sacris rebus tam multae gentes imitantur, quia et tanti magysterii ex apice apostolico primordiis clarent et nulla per orbem ecclesia aeque ut Romana ab omni faece hereseon cunctis retro temporibus pura permansit,* trans. Harting-Corrêa, pp. 128/9, and above, p. 158.

complicated by the great diversity of races, localities and periods',[134] Walafrid is uncompromising in his statement:

> Just as Roman emperors are said to have held the absolute rule of the entire world, so the head bishop in the Roman see who holds blessed Peter's office is elevated to the highest position of the entire Church.[135]

In ending this chapter with the respectful and critical use made of the *Liber pontificalis* by three Carolingian scholars, the question of the availability of the text in the Frankish kingdoms has obviously been demonstrated in general terms. How the function and purpose of the *Liber pontificalis* may have differed at different stages of its compilation and reception, and how the availability of the text in the eighth and ninth centuries fits specifically into the history of the production and distribution of the manuscripts of the text from the sixth century onwards remain to be explored in the following, and final, chapter.

---

[134] *Quamvis non nesciam ordinationes potestatum et officiorum tanta diversitate pro varietate gentium, locorum et temporum perplexas,* trans. Harting-Corrêa, pp. 188/9.

[135] *Sicut augusti Romanorum totius orbis monarchiam tenuisse feruntur, ita summus pontifex in sede Romana vicem beati Petri gerens totius ecclesiae apice sublimatur,* trans. Harting-Corrêa, pp. 190/1.

6

Transmission, Reception, and Audiences

The Early Medieval Manuscripts of the Liber pontificalis *and their Implications*

Introduction

THE POWER OF THE *LIBER PONTIFICALIS* HAS SO FAR been deduced from its contents. It is now time to address the question of audience, the text's reception, and its potential influence. Rather than speculate further on the intended audiences, whether within or beyond Rome, it makes better sense to focus in this chapter on the actual early medieval audiences indicated by the surviving manuscript evidence.

This entails exploring the implications of the peculiar pattern of survival of the text, for despite its sixth-century Roman origin, most of the earliest surviving manuscripts of the full text were written in the late eighth, ninth, and tenth centuries and are not from Rome, or even from Italy, but from Francia.

When the evidence of knowledge in the early middle ages of the text of the *Liber pontificalis* (whether in full or abridged versions) is added, more gaps can be filled. It can be tracked in the form, firstly, of emulation, such as Gregory of Tours's history of the bishops of Tours included in Book X of the *Histories,* Paul the Deacon's *Liber de episcopis Mettensibus,* the *Gesta episcoporum Autissiodorensium* (Auxerre), Flodoard's *Historia Remensis ecclesiae,* Agnellus's history of the bishops of Ravenna, or the *Gesta* of the bishops of Naples.[1]

---

[1] Gregory of Tours, *Historiae,* X.31, ed. Krusch and Levison, pp. 526–34; Paul the Deacon, *Gesta episcoporum Mettensium,* ed. and trans. Kempf; Flodoard, *Historia Remensis ecclesiae,* ed. Stratmann, Agnellus, *Liber pontificalis ecclesiae Ravennatis,* ed. Deliyannis; *Gesta episcoporum Neapolitanorum,* ed. Waitz, pp. 398–436; Flodoard, *De triumphis Christi,* ed. Jacobsen; see also Roberts 2019.

Secondly, it was used as a source, as in Bede's *Historia ecclesiastica* and *De ratione temporum,* in the eighth century;[2] the *Gesta abbatum Fontanellensium;* the work of Amalarius of Metz and Walafrid Strabo on the liturgy;[3] Flodoard of Reims again, in his narrative poem *De triumphis Christi;* and many other authors in the ninth and tenth centuries.[4]

Thirdly, there are references to the papal history in book lists from Carolingian Francia. The library catalogues of Lorsch, Reichenau, and St Gallen each list the book among their possessions,[5] and Eberhard, Count of the March of Friuli, and his wife Gisela bequeathed a copy of the text to their son Berengar, later emperor.[6] We may not know which recension they possessed, how many Lives these volumes included, whether it was a full text or an abridgement, nor even if the scribe and compiler who presented the text in each manuscript may have intervened in various ways, but the fact that the *Liber pontificalis* in some form was available in these centres and to these people is important in itself. Adding the evidence of manuscripts containing epitomes of the *Liber pontificalis* augments still more the weight in favour of the Frankish dissemination of the text.[7]

What are the implications of this predominantly Frankish survival pattern? Only a beginning can be made in response to this question, but this chapter will consider the possible processes of production and the dissemination of the text from its Roman origins to its widespread dissemination in Francia, and thus how the text was in a position to shape or influence a particular understanding of Rome and the popes both within and beyond

---

[2] On Bede's use of the *Liber pontificalis* see Hilliard 2018.

[3] See above, Chapter 5, pp. 157–66.

[4] *Gesta sanctorum patrum Fontanellensis coenobii,* X.3, ed. Pradié, pp. 120–2; Amalarius of Metz, *Liber officialis,* ed. Hanssens, reprinted with English trans. Knibbs; Walafrid Strabo, *Libellus de exordiis et incrementis quarundam in observationibus ecclesiasticis rerum,* ed. Harting Corrêa. See also above, pp. 166–8.

[5] Lorsch: BAV pal. lat. 1877, fol. 3v; *Gesta pontificum Romanorum in uno codice,* ed. Häse, *Mittelalterliche Bücherverzeichnisse aus Kloster Lorsch,* p. 137; Reichenau: ed. Lehmann, *Mittelalterliche Bibliothekskataloge* I, p. 247; St Gallen: csg 728, p. 11, *Gesta pontificum romanorum,* ed. Lehmann, *Mittelalterliche Bibliothekskataloge* I, p. 76. See also the list of references to the *Liber pontificalis* in medieval library catalogues compiled by Bougard 2009, pp. 147–52. On the possible reference to the *Liber pontificalis* in the book list from Würzburg, *c.*800, see McKitterick in press a.

[6] Will of Eberhard, ed. Coussemaker, reprinted in Schramm and Mütherich 1981, pp. 93–4.

[7] On the epitomes see further below, pp. 195–206.

Rome. In this respect the extant manuscripts, containing the full text as well as abridgements and adaptations, are potentially the most instructive.

Each manuscript needs to be considered as a piece of historical evidence in its own right, not merely as a vehicle for constructing a modern scholarly edition. I offer here, therefore, some comments on the early medieval manuscripts of the *Liber pontificalis* as well as the problems they raise, based on a fresh examination of all the codices dating from before the end of the tenth century.

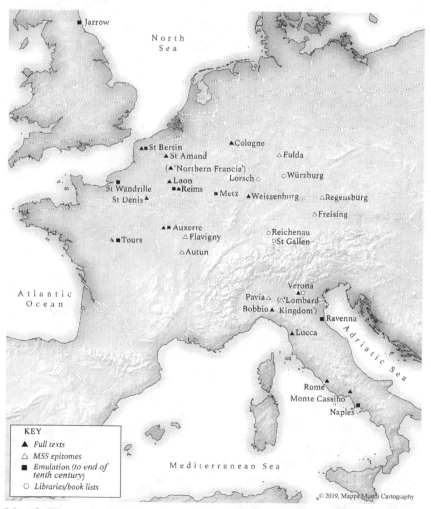

Map 2 The early medieval manuscript distribution of the *Liber pontificalis*

A Roman Text

First of all, as I stated in the introductory chapter, the *Liber pontificalis* is surmised, as a common but not unreasonable assumption from its internal evidence, to be a text produced within the papal administration in Rome. The first portion of the text, furthermore, can be dated to the early sixth century, and probably *c.*536. Nevertheless, we do not know precisely when, where, or by whom it was produced, nor how it was distributed. The manuscript evidence offers no help in determining whether the original text stopped at Life 59 with the Life of Agapitus, as I have argued, or with Life 60 of Silverius, or, as some maintain, closer to the beginning of the sixth century.[8] No sixth-century Roman manuscript of the entire *Liber pontificalis* to that date survives, nor is there even an original manuscript or fragment extant of any text, let alone the *Liber pontificalis,* recognized as emanating from the papal chancery before the later eighth century. This is all the more puzzling because we know from references in the *Liber pontificalis* itself that notaries were part of the papal administration. Pope Julius I (337–52), for example, is said to have 'issued a decree ... that the drawing up of all documents in the church should be carried out by the *primicerius notariorum,* whether they be bonds, deeds, donations, exchanges, transfers, wills, declarations or manumissions, the clerics in the church should carry them out in the church office'.[9] Even if this is a back projection by the sixth-century author or authors of the date of the formation of the papal writing office, the description is entirely plausible in the light of many copies of the copious papal correspondence, of estate and conciliar records from late antiquity and the early middle ages, and references elsewhere both to this correspondence and to administrative work, including that of the notaries themselves.

---

[8] See the discussion above, pp. 12–16.

[9] *LP* I, Life 36, c. 3, p. 205; trans. Davis, *Pontiffs,* p. 27: *Hic constitutum fecit ... et notitia, quae omnibus pro fide ecclesiastica est, per notarios colligeretur, et omnia monumenta in ecclesia per primicerium notariorum confectio celebraretur, sive cautiones vel exstrumenta aut donationes vel commutationes vel traditiones aut testamenta vel allegationes aut manumissiones clerici in ecclesia per scrinium sanctum celebrarentur.*

Roman Script?

A further major obstacle for any assessment of Roman document or book production in the early middle ages is the lack of a secure recognition of Roman scripts by modern scholars. A number of highly plausible conjectures for very late sixth- or early seventh-century Roman uncial and half-uncial were made by Armando Petrucci in a path-breaking article half a century ago.[10] He referred, for example, to codices such as the late sixth- or early seventh-century copy of the *Cura pastoralis* of Gregory the Great, now in Troyes, which E. A. Lowe had conjectured to be a book 'revised under the author's immediate supervision'.[11] Its letter forms resemble those in a handful of other manuscripts dated to the turn of the sixth century and the early seventh century.[12] Paolo Chiesa, however, has cast doubt on the nature of the corrections over erasure and the marginal insertions in Troyes 504. He has suggested that they are in a different style from that of Gregory I, and should be understood as simplifications of the text made by someone else.[13] That of course does not necessarily remove the possibility that the script itself is indeed 'Roman uncial', as Petrucci reaffirmed in 2005.[14]

There is also a tantalizing fragment of a papyrus codex now in London that once contained Gregory the Great's homilies on the Gospels and might also be counted as Roman.[15] It should be noted, however, that the arguments for Roman origin spring more from the content of the text, rather than any impregnable palaeographical judgement; the provenance of this fragment and the codex to which it once belonged before the sixteenth century, moreover, are unknown. Similarly, many of the other early codices or fragments that are thought to offer the possibility of being Roman may only seem so because they contain the works of Gregory; this is not enough to confirm Roman origin. One exception may be the 'Laudian Acts', a bilingual *Vetus Latina* and Greek text of Acts, possibly produced in Rome with a layout of the

---

[10] Petrucci 1971.   [11] Troyes, Bibliothèque municipale 504, *CLA* VI, 838.
[12] *CLA* II 2nd edition, 192, and Petrucci 1971. Compare the summary by Ganz 2002.
[13] Chiesa 2005 and see also Leyser 2010.   [14] Petrucci 2005.
[15] London, British Library, Cotton Titus C.XV: Babcock 2000.

text virtually in glossary format, apparently designed to assist in learning Greek; it had reached Würzburg or Fulda by the eighth century.[16]

Past discussion has sometimes foundered on the dubious and undoubtedly subjective judgements concerning the greater beauty and elegance of the letter forms that are assumed to indicate an Italian rather than Frankish origin.[17] Similarly, grandeur in size, layout, script, decoration, and use of colour, such as gold and silver lettering on purple-dyed parchment, is thought to point to Roman or Ravennan origins. The examples often offered are the Augustine Gospels, possibly brought by Augustine of Canterbury to England at the end of the sixth century, or a sixth-century Psalter written in gold and silver on purple-dyed parchment, now in Paris.[18]

There is a remarkable disjuncture between texts emanating from Rome and the origin of the surviving manuscripts thereof. Why so much has disappeared is perplexing. It needs to be emphasized, however, that the absence of early Roman copies of many texts judged to be Roman is not a peculiarity of the *Liber pontificalis* alone. Most of our earliest manuscript witnesses to Roman liturgy, the *Ordines Romani,* canon law, papal letters and decretals, papal sermons, doctrinal and exegetical works by particular popes, Roman martyr narratives, and Roman legendaries cannot be identified as Roman or even Italian. Instead, the earliest witnesses to the majority of these texts survive in Frankish copies. Not until the eighth and early ninth centuries are there at last clear indications of the survival of Roman book production, with manuscripts such as the Homiliary of Agimund acknowledged as written in Roman uncial script.[19]

Papyrus or Parchment?

To the problems of a survival pattern weighted towards Frankish Gaul, the apparent loss of Italian exemplars, and the additional possibility of particular letter forms becoming redundant and less easy to read for later

---

[16] Lai 2011 and Houghton 2016, p. 233.

[17] See also my discussion of the problem of early medieval uncial in McKitterick 1990 and on Troyes 504 in McKitterick 1981.

[18] Cambridge, Corpus Christi College MS 286 (*CLA* II, 126) and Paris, BnF lat. 11947 (*CLA* V, 616).

[19] BAV Vat. lat. 3835 and 3836 (*CLA* I, 18a and 18b). See Osborne 1990.

generations of scribes and readers, a further point worth registering is what the London papyrus fragment suggests about the material on which books from Rome may have been distributed. So much of what we think we know about Italian manuscripts survives in parchment codices from the northern centres of Verona and Bobbio.[20] It has long been understood that papyrus was used in the papal chancery until the eleventh century. The handful of original charters that survive from the tenth century, for example, are written on papyrus.[21] That papal letters were also written on papyrus is suggested not only by a couple of surviving fragments from the late eighth century,[22] but also by a reference in Charlemagne's preface to the *Codex epistolaris Carolinus*. This famous collection of papal letters to the Carolingian mayors of the palace and kings between 741 and 790 was compiled in 791 on Charlemagne's orders. Charlemagne required the papal letters to be recopied from the originals in the palace archive onto parchment, 'which preserves memory'. In the same codex, the scribe attempting to copy one of the letters of Paul I noted that he had not copied it into the volume because it was so dilapidated.[23]

The remarkable survival of the list of martyrs' shrines in Rome from which oil had been collected into little ampoules, as a gift brought to the Lombard Queen Theodolinda in the time of Pope Gregory I (590–604), is a further indication from the early seventh century of papyrus being the normal writing material in the papal administration. The relic labels and list also incidentally provide an example of early medieval Roman cursive script.[24] Longer texts may also have been produced in papyrus

---

[20] See Zironi 2004.

[21] Of the 325 extant papal charters from the period 896–996, for example, only six survive on the original papyrus; the remainder are later copies on parchment: see Zimmermann (ed.), I: *896–996*, Nos 5, 206, 207, 210, 245, 325, pp. 11, 406, 409, 413, 484, 634, but see also the 'angebliche Original' on parchment, No. 271, p. 532; Bresslau 1888, Giry 1925, pp. 661–72, and Noble 1990.

[22] Paris, Archives nationales K7, No. 9(1) and K7, No. 9(2), facsimile Vezin and Atsma 1986, pp. 59–71; texts ed. Gundlach, pp. 644–55.

[23] Vienna, ÖNB Cod. 449, fol. 1. *Codex epistolaris Carolinus*, ed. Gundlach, pp. 476 and 512; German trans. Hartmann and Orth-Müller, pp. 1 and 152–3; English trans. McKitterick, Pollard, Price, and Espelo; facsimile ed. Unterkircher, and see Hack 2006–7.

[24] Monza, Cattedrale S. Giovanni Battista Sacrista Tesoro s.n., facsimile ed. Petrucci, Tjäder, and Cavallo 1993, No. 863. I am grateful to Massimiliano Bassetti and Marco Stoffella for discussion of this list.

codices. The *Vita sancti Amandi,* for example, refers to a letter from Pope Martin, and a papyrus codex containing the Latin text of the canons of the Lateran Council of 649 sent to Amandus by Pope Martin, which probably served as the exemplar for the now earliest extant copy, a ninth-century parchment codex written in the distinctive Caroline minuscule script associated with the monastery of St Amand.[25] Such an observation has to be set beside the tiny number of papyrus codices or fragments thereof from either Gaul or Italy. Most of the surviving papyrus material is late antique, and from Egypt.[26]

The *Liber pontificalis:* Sequential Production and Distribution?

Such conjectures aside, it is the later copies of the *Liber pontificalis* that witness to its dissemination, so I turn to a second obvious reminder, with crucial implications for the manuscript dissemination, namely that the *Liber pontificalis* is a composite text, written by many authors in stages over a period of three hundred years. The sequential composition opens up the possibility of both progressive updating and continuation of the entire text, as well as the distribution of single biographies or sets of biographies piecemeal. For convenience I repeat here the schematic table of the possible stages of composition I offered in Chapter 1:

LIBER PONTIFICALIS: PHASES OF PRODUCTION

LP I (= Duchesne's 2nd redaction) *c.*536, Lives 1–59/?60: Peter to Agapitus (†536)

LP IIA Lives 60–71: Silverius (†537) to Boniface V (†625)

LP IIB Lives 72–81: Honorius (†638) to Agatho (†681) but possible breaks before 672 and 676–8

LP IIC Lives 82–90: Leo II (†683) to Constantine I (†715)

LP III Eighth-century Lives 91 (two versions), 92, 93, 94 (three versions), 95, 96, 97 cc. 1–44, 97 cc. 45 to end: Gregory II (†731) to Hadrian I (†795)

LP IV Ninth-century Lives 98–112: Leo III (†816) to Stephen V (†891)

Louis Duchesne differentiated a number of recensions of the *Liber pontificalis* text, which he labelled 'A', 'B', 'C', 'D', 'E', and 'G'. The 'A'

---

[25] Milo, *Vita sancti Amandi episcopi,* ed. Krusch, p. 452. See Price, Booth, and Cubitt 2014, p. 79: for the Latin *acta,* Laon, BM Suzanne Martinet, MS 199.

[26] Roberts and Skeat 1983 and Gamble 1995, pp. 42–81.

group comprised essentially the north Italian codex from *c*.800, Lucca, Biblioteca Capitolare Feliniana 490, and its later descendants, and Duchesne chose to use this as the base text for his edition. 'B', 'C', and 'D' are Frankish recensions with representative manuscripts numbered by Duchesne in sequence; the 'B' and 'D' recensions, furthermore, contain Frankish interpolations, especially in Lives 92–5. The significance of these is discussed later in this chapter. 'E' is possibly the Roman and original strand of the tradition, but now represented only in manuscripts of the eleventh century and later. 'G', also Italian from the late tenth or early eleventh century, lacks the Lives before Leo I, needs more work, but will not be considered further here.[27] The principal recensions can be set out schematically for ease of reference as follows:

LIBER PONTIFICALIS: DUCHESNE'S RECENSIONS

A North Italian (Lucca); Duchesne's base text
B Frankish with Frankish interpolations
C Frankish but without Frankish interpolations
D Frankish with Frankish interpolations; related to 'B'
E Italian, probably Roman, possibly original

Theodor Mommsen also argued the case for sequential composition, and divided the manuscripts into three classes, I, II, and III. In most of the surviving manuscripts of the full text the usual contents are **LP I, II A–C**, and **LP III**, at least as far as Life 94, presented as a seamless series of numbered biographies.

An ever diminishing number of early medieval manuscripts contain the papal biographies after Life 94, so that the only surviving ninth-century copy of the Life of Pope Leo III (795–815) is in a codex from Tours.[28] In other words, an understanding of the history of the papacy in Francia at least was predominantly based on the Lives up to the middle of the eighth century, with only a few continuing the story to include Pope Hadrian (†795), and apparently limited availability of the ninth-century biographies. Such a marked respect for the authority of a more distant past is echoed in such works as the Carolingian chronicle by Frechulf and Carolingian biblical exegesis.[29]

The work of François Bougard, Lidia Capo, and Clemens Gantner has highlighted the initial collation of information within the papal

---

[27] *LP* I, pp. clxiv–ccvi.   [28] Paris, BnF lat. 5516.
[29] Frechulf, *Historiae,* ed. Allen, and Ward in press, Pohl 2015, and Jong 2015.

administration required to produce a papal biography.[30] The logistics of composition and distribution may also help to explain why so few texts contain the later eighth-century biographies. Although particular copyists may have copied a base text of **LP I** + **LP IIA–C**, they may well then have used *libelli* (small books or pamphlets) that contained the new biographies in **LP III** as they became available.

There are indications that smaller updating sections may also have been disseminated from Rome, such as the oft-quoted example that before 725 Bede in Anglian Northumbria had received and used the Life of Gregory II in its earlier version in his treatise *De ratione temporum*.[31] Even in the ninth century, moreover, Archbishop Hincmar of Reims wrote to his colleague Wenilo, Archbishop of Sens, in 866, saying he desired a copy of the *Liber pontificalis* with the biography of Pope Sergius II (Hincmar did not tell Wenilo why he wanted it). This might indicate that, whether in the form of progressively updated and extended copies or as *libelli* containing a Life or small batches of Lives, it was necessary to procure copies from Rome.[32] Study of the eighth-century Lives, and especially of the so-called 'Lombard' recension of Life 94 of Pope Stephen II (752–7), has been especially important for what it has suggested about the production and circulation of the contemporary history of individual popes in Lives 91–7. François Bougard has suggested that there is the possible legitimating role a Life of the immediate predecessor, newly composed, might play as a 'carte de visite', or confirmation of the new pope's position. Pope Paul I, for example, may have encouraged a distribution of the text of Life 94 of his brother Pope Stephen II (752–7), or even the entire history, in the early stages of his pontificate.[33]

Further, the interventions by local copyists in these new sections of text expose the manipulation of the text once it had left Rome. Yet this also begs the questions of whether the text's subsequent readers were aware of the different sources of intervention in the text and how far it was actually removed from its original source in the papal

---

[30] Bougard 2009, Gantner 2013a, and Capo 2009.

[31] Bede, *De ratione temporum*, ed. Jones, p. 534 and pp. 777–9. See the brief discussion in Wallis 1999, p. 366.

[32] Hincmar of Reims, *Epistolae,* ed. Perels, p. 194, and see Bougard 2009, p. 134.

[33] Bougard 2009, pp. 135 and 138.

administration. Life 94 of Stephen II, for example, is preserved in no fewer than three different versions: the 'Lombard', the 'Frankish', and the 'Roman'. Clemens Gantner has suggested in this respect that the toning down of the excessive praise of the pope and Pippin III, and the removal of the epithets of opprobrium concerning the Lombards in the 'Lombard' version of Life 94 of Stephen II, may have been an ad hoc decision on the part of one individual in Rome, Farfa, or even Lucca, between 758 and 780.

Gantner, moreover, has identified two strands of the 'Lombard' version, on the basis of the alternative versions of the story of Pope Stephen II travelling to Francia and sighting a celestial sign. His observation invokes the different strands of the manuscript tradition, which need a brief explanation here, but with fuller discussion later in this chapter. In one 'Lombard' version of Life 94, a fireball (*globus igneus*) comes from Gaul towards the Lombard kingdom. In the other version, used in 'A', 'C1', 'G', and 'E', the ball becomes a sword (*gladius igneus*). One codex, dated approximately 790 and probably produced at St Amand in northern France, contained the '*gladius* version' of the text, whereas the other 'Lombard' version of Life 94 in a manuscript dated approximately 810, and produced at the monastery of Weissenburg, contained the variant *globus*.[34] Gantner has surmised that both versions must have been 'in circulation' by the end of the eighth century. He concluded that in general the eighth- and ninth-century Lives in the *Liber pontificalis* were transmitted in heterogeneous ways and forms, and that the Lombard recensions alone disprove all theories claiming a planned and well-controlled distribution of the *Liber pontificalis* from the Lateran or even by the Carolingians.[35] Lidia Capo and Clemens Gantner have indicated furthermore that early medieval scribes combined different text traditions of particular Lives when compiling their versions of a full text.[36] That is, in assessing the distribution and production of the text, the manuscript witnesses indicate that some scribes used more than one

---

[34] The manuscripts are now Leiden, VLQ 60 and Wolfenbüttel, Herzog August Bibliothek, Cod. Guelf. 10.11 Aug.4° respectively in Duchesne's classification, *LP* I, pp. clxiv–ccvi, usefully summarized in Davis, *Eighth-Century Popes*, pp. xv–xvii.

[35] Gantner 2013a, p. 102.   [36] Capo 2009.

exemplar, or added the texts from new *libelli* to the older copies as the former were received.

In a number of the surviving manuscripts of the *Liber pontificalis*, it is sometimes possible to surmise that the whole text, containing the Lives up to and including Life 90 of Pope Constantine I, up to Life 94 of Pope Stephen II, or up to Life 97 of Pope Hadrian I were sent out or received indirectly or unofficially in the form of copies made by visitors to Rome. Some centres may never have received the updated versions or the *libelli* containing new lives. There is a note in the famous Lucca copy of the *Liber pontificalis*, dated *c*.800, at the end of Life 90, for example, stating that 'up to this point it is 129 years and 7 months since the Lombards arrived',[37] and a clear differentiation in the codicological construction of the manuscript between the earlier part of the text to 715 and the eighth-century Lives that follow.[38] This led Duchesne to surmise that a copy of the whole text up to and including the Life of Pope Constantine I (708–15) had been received in Lucca most probably before 774 and the Frankish conquest. It certainly makes sense to think of the scribes in Lucca using one exemplar for the section up to 715, and then using *libelli* of each subsequent life, or possibly a small collection of such *libelli* as they were acquired. A further witness to the circulation of *libelli* with one or only a small selection of Lives is preserved in the EXPLICIT LIBELLUS added at the end of Life 94, the final Life in a ninth-century copy of the *Liber pontificalis* now in Milan.[39]

Indications of the way in which the text was received and reproduced can also be observed in the ninth-century copy of the *Liber pontificalis* in Bern.[40] Apart from what is omitted or added to the text, there is intriguing evidence within this codex that it is drawing on a number of different copies of the text in order to construct its own. An indication of a new text received is possibly fol. 72v–73r, ending at Life 92. The Life

[37] Lucca, Biblioteca Capitolare Feliniana 490. The relevant page is illustrated in *LP* I, Plate II after p. clxii: *Hu[n]c usque CXXVIIII anni sunt quod Langobardi venerunt et VII menses* (= *c*.586).

[38] See further *LP* I, pp. clxiv–clxvi, and Plates II and III, and Schiaparelli 1924, Petrucci 1992, and Unfer-Verre 2013.

[39] Biblioteca Ambrosiana M.77sup. (B6), fol. 93r.

[40] Bern, Burgerbibliothek 408 and see *LP* I, p. cxci.

of Zacharias lacks the end note about ordinations which is only in the 'BD' 'Frankish' group. It has the earlier version of Gregory II. The text from Peter onwards is also abbreviated here and there in distinctive choices on the scribe's part. In the Life of Peter, for example, the sentences concerning Peter's designation of his successors, the debate with Simon Magus, and the reference to Clement are missing, so that the biography is simply about Peter, his writings and association with the Gospel of Mark, and his death and burial. Similarly, the Life of Clement is truncated, with no reference to the Petrine appointments. In the Life of Silvester, on the other hand, a large section appears to have been added to the account of the Constantinian donations in relation to San Lorenzo fuori le mura. The scribe also departs at certain points from the received text. Thus, Victor is said to have determined that Easter should be on a Sunday, just like Eleutherius. In all other versions, the pairing is Pius and Eleutherius. The sequence of popes, names, and number of ordinations sometimes differ.

A possible hint that the scribe of the Bern manuscript was copying an ancient codex rather than a more recent eighth-century exemplar, at least for the earliest portion of the text (**LPI**) is the apparent misreading of the old abbreviation N with a line above, for *noster*, as *non* in Life 9 of Pope Telesphorus: *ante horae tertiae cursum nullus praesumeret missas caelebrare qua ore dominus non* (recte *noster*) *ascendit crucem* ('normally no one would presume to celebrate mass before the office of the third hour, the time that our lord went up on the cross') so that the phrase becomes: 'the time when the lord did not ascend the cross'.[41] Pope John II (533–5), moreover, is referred to as *junior,* which would imply that there was not yet a John III (561–74) when the exemplar was composed.

For the parts after 535 there are also some indications in the manuscript that the scribe may have been working from dictation, and there are also far fewer variant readings. An interesting example in the Life of Pope Pelagius II (579–90) is the sentence *Hic domum suam fecit **tpochium** pauperum senum* ('he made his own house into an almshouse for the aging poor').[42] Other ninth-century codices in the various classes have

---

[41] Lindsay 1915, pp. 143–57.

[42] *LP* I, Life 65, c. 2, p. 309; trans. Davis, *Pontiffs,* p. 59. *Tpochium* should be *ptochium* (another sign of dictation?). *Xenodochium* is found in Duchesne's classification of the

xenodochium, though one, Leiden, VLQ 41 fol. 47r, has the Latin word *hospitium.* Here the scribe either deliberately substituted a Latin word or was working from a different exemplar.

Such occasional indications of a variety of recensions in circulation within the Carolingian kingdom need to be explored more thoroughly, but they confirm the strong impression noted above of how a scribe compiling a text might move from one version to another, most probably from full copies of **LPI** and **LPIIA–C**, augmented by *libelli* for **LPIII**.[43]

Distribution and Reception of the *Liber pontificalis* up to the Eighth Century

The circulation and adaptation of contemporary Lives in the eighth and ninth centuries considered in the previous section could also suggest new ways of looking at the dissemination and use of the earlier sections of the text before 715, that is, Lives 1–90.

The mid sixth-century Verona codex containing part of the Life of Pope Anastasius II and an alternative version of the Life of Symmachus I has already been discussed in the context of the initial production of the *Liber pontificalis.*[44] The compilation then continued with the *De viris illustribus* of Jerome, which, like the *Liber pontificalis,* begins with St Peter.[45] After the *De viris illustribus,* with its emphasis on orthodox Christian writers, there is a significant number of papal letters relating to the Acacian schism in the remaining portion of the codex. As a whole, therefore, it appears to be a dossier produced in Verona concerning the Acacian schism and the papal championing of orthodoxy as a matter of historical record, of which the papal history was a vital component. In other words, this entire manuscript appears to have been designed as a unit, with a collection of testimonies to orthodoxy, authorial legitimacy,

manuscripts 'A1' Lucca 490; 'B2' BnF lat. 13729; 'B3' Cologne 164; 'C1' VLQ 60; 'D' BnF lat. 5516. *Ptochium* and spelling variants are in 'B5' Brussels 8380-9012; 'B7' Milan M.77sup.; ('C4' BnF lat. 5140 has *pitochium*); 'E'; 'G' Italian; 'C2' Wolfenbüttel, Herzog August Bibliothek, Cod. Guelf. 10.11 Aug.4°.

[43] Compare above, p. 180.

[44] Verona, Biblioteca Capitolare XXII (20). See above, Chapter 1, pp. 32–5.

[45] See above, Chapter 3, pp. 72–81.

and papal leadership. Its most likely function was to serve as background information for those involved in the Three Chapters controversy within Italy.[46]

As far as the late sixth- and seventh-century distribution of the text is concerned, again, the extant manuscripts reflect very little, for few survive. The undoubted knowledge of the *Liber pontificalis* in late sixth-century Tours reflected in Gregory's emulation of the biographical catalogue of bishops in his *Historiae,* for example, may have been the outcome of the visit the deacon Agilulf from Tours made to Rome, where he witnessed the enthronement of Pope Gregory I. But no Frankish manuscripts from before the eighth century containing any portion of the *Liber pontificalis* text have been preserved.[47] Other hints at early dissemination are from Italy.

Naples, Biblioteca Nazionale IV.A.8, fols 40–7, is an important Italian copy of the text that breaks off in the Life of Pope Anastasius.[48] The *Liber pontificalis* is the upper script of a set of palimpsested bifolia. Attempts by nineteenth-century scholars to enhance the underneath sixth-century uncial copy of Gargilius Martialis, *De re rustica,* wrought terrible damage to the parchment and has obscured much of both texts. The list of popes on the horribly disfigured first page, fol. 40r, however, ends with Pope Conon. The script of this name is the same as that of the others in the list that finishes at the top of the second column on fol. 40r. The layout of the final fourteen names in this column, themselves in two columns – Honorius to Vitalian, Adeodatus to Conon – suggests that the codex can be dated early in Pope Sergius I's reign (687–701). The palaeography is compatible with this, for it is written in what has been described as 'north-Italian pre-Caroline minuscule' with very distinctive ligatures, a script that is consistent with a late seventh-century date. The scribe also employed many abbreviations, and the entire text was crammed into a

---

[46] Chazelle and Cubitt (eds.) 2007 and above, Chapter 1, pp. 24–5.

[47] Gregory of Tours, *Historiae,* Book X, ed. Krusch and Levison, clearly based his history of the bishops of Tours on the *Liber pontificalis.* See also his references in *In gloria martyrum,* ed. Krusch and Levison, pp. 501–3, 513, 544, *Historiae* X.ii, pp. 477–81. See also Simperl 2016, and McKitterick 2014.

[48] *LP* I, pp. clxxvi and cxxxviii.

single quire of four bifolia.[49] Paolo Radiciotti argued on palaeographical and codicological grounds that this section of Naples IV.A.8 can be connected with Bobbio. The first five quires of the codex contain Charisius, *Ars grammatica* and Sergius, *De centu metris,* written in an insular minuscule. Some of the leaves of this portion are also palimpsest. Radiciotti thought that some of the parchment and lower text of fols 40–7 may have originated in Ravenna, with a further possibility that the upper text had been copied from a manuscript also once in Ravenna. Given the uncertainty about what can be identified as Roman uncial script, a Roman rather than a Ravennan origin for the lower script might be possible.[50] It is conceivable, therefore, that these four bifolia of recycled parchment on which the *Liber pontificalis* was written in a very different type of hand from the first section of the current codex were only bound with the first section at Bobbio at a later stage; they may even have been written in Ravenna, or Rome, during the reign of Pope Sergius I. Whatever the case, the Naples copy of the *Liber pontificalis* with its later Bobbio connections indicates that the text was received at an early stage of its history in northern Italy.

One other late seventh-century Italian fragment of the *Liber pontificalis* that has often been overlooked is the abridgement in Modena.[51] It is possibly to be connected later in its history with the eighth-century Lombard foundation of Nonantola. It is written in a large, distinctively extravagant uncial with some fancy capitals for headings. The

---

[49] The dimensions are 290 x 240 mm and written space 260 x 190 mm, with two columns of between 40 and 46 lines per page, *CLA* IV, no. 403. This manuscript is now too fragile for personal consultation of the original, but high-resolution tiff photographs can be consulted in the Biblioteca Nazionale in Naples. I am grateful to Mariolina Rascaglia of Naples, Biblioteca Nazionale, Sezione manoscritti e rari etc., for her help in providing me with a digital version to study. See *LP* I, pp. clxxvi and cxxxviii and Mommsen, *LP,* pp. lxxxiv–lxxxvi, who included it in his Class II.

[50] Radiciotti 2002, p. 86. I am grateful to Massimiliano Bassetti for discussion of both the lower and upper scripts of the Naples codex.

[51] Modena, Biblioteca Capitolare O.I.12. The text was noted by Duchesne *LP* I, pp. cxcvi–cxcix with a transcription of the *Liber pontificalis* extracts, and subjected to analysis by Fornasari 1966, though his transcription includes quite a lot of text not actually in the manuscript and omits some of the text which *is* in the manuscript. Few apart from Wirbelauer 1993, pp. 184–5, and Verardi 2016, pp. 213, 220–1, have paid attention to it since.

compilation embeds an epitome of the *Liber pontificalis* in a collection of *canones* and papal decretals. It has the character of an individual compilation by and for a specific individual, and in this particular selection has no known duplicates. The extracts from the *Liber pontificalis,* set out in a pope-by-pope format, effectively summarize legislation for which various popes were noted. This is even signalled by a note at the end of fol. 29r, where it writes EXPLICIT CONSTITUTIONES BREVIATAE. The codex also contains the *Apostolic Constitutions*, firmly attributed in the manuscript to Pope Clement, and the texts purporting to be the decrees of the synods convened by Popes Silvester and Sixtus III in Rome. These are also synods mentioned in the Lives of these popes in the *Liber pontificalis*, but in this instance the compiler appears to have drawn on the collection of texts known as the 'Symmachan forgeries', though he departed considerably even from that collection in his sentences about Pope Marcellinus. The papal decretals start with the so-called first papal decretal of Siricius, and include others attributed to Popes Anastasius, Innocent, Zosimus, Boniface, Celestine, Sixtus III, and Leo I. These decretals or extracts thereof effectively act as substitutes for the biographies. All these popes are given their papal numbers as if they were still in the narrative sequence with which the abridged text of the *Liber pontificalis* started. The most recent set of excerpts at the end of the codex is attributed to Pope Gregory I.

The importance of this codex is considerable. Not only does it witness to the distribution of the text of the *Liber pontificalis* to the Lombard kingdom before the late seventh century, but with its emphasis on papal legislation relating to the organization and liturgical development of the church it reflects one way in which the text was understood and adapted to fulfil different objectives by the scribe and compiler. That is, the codicological and textual contexts of the excerpts from the *Liber pontificalis* mean that the *Liber pontificalis* is used to provide the chronological and narrative framework for a particular selection of papal decretals.[52]

The lower script of a fragment now a flyleaf in Turin, Biblioteca Nazionale F.IV.18, seems to be a further significant witness to circulation of the text in Lombard Italy. The fragment's condition is poor as a consequence of attempts to treat it with chemicals in the nineteenth

---

[52] Bischoff 1983.

century. Written in pre-Caroline minuscule, it dates from early in the first half of the eighth century and has tentatively been located in Bobbio's library in the Lombard period.[53] It contains portions of the lives of popes of the Ostrogothic era, Hormisdas and John I, and thus relates to the years between 514 and 526. It too, perhaps, is a remnant of a once complete copy of the text, and its script relates it to an entry of a poem on the Synod of Pavia in 698 made in two other early medieval manuscripts.[54] One of these is a copy of the *Acta* of the Council of Chalcedon and the 'Synod' of Pavia itself, which confirmed the Chalcedonian position. If the *Liber pontificalis*, *Acta*, and this record of the Pavia meeting were indeed all produced in the same place and at the same time, it reflects a consistent level of interest in the particular relevance of the *Liber pontificalis* and its portrayal of the papal upholding of orthodoxy some decades after the Three Chapters controversy had been settled.

So far, I have emphasized the following points. The *Liber pontificalis* is probably of Roman origin, but no Roman manuscripts of it survive before at least the eleventh century. There are only a few fragments surviving from Italy in the sixth, seventh, and eighth centuries, and these raise the problems of the survival of Roman manuscripts generally and whether this might in part be due to the poor survival rate of papyrus. These surviving fragments also indicate dissemination of the text from Rome, and Lucca, Biblioteca Capitolare Feliniana 490 in particular throws some light on when, or at least which, portions of the text may have arrived in Tuscany. There are interesting indications, even in the earliest fragments of the *Liber pontificalis*, of the way the text could be adapted to suit both different political opinions and different understandings of the significance of the Lives. We have also seen that the Verona fragment of Lives 53 and 54, the abridgement of the text in Modena O.I.12, the Turin fragment, and Lucca 490's copies of the eighth-century Lives, especially Life 94, reflect the apparently

---

[53] *CLA* Suppl., 1810: *CLA* III 323b, *CLA* III, **31.

[54] Milan, Ambrosiana C.105inf., fol. 121r–121v and Milan, Ambrosiana E.147sup. + Vat. lat. 5750. *Carmen de synodo Ticiensi*, ed. Bethmann, pp. 189–91. See Markus and Sotinel 2007, p. 277. For Bobbio see Zironi 2004.

contemporary or near-contemporary presentations of the text to fulfil local agendas. The variants in the Verona and Modena manuscripts, furthermore, are more than those that occur in a copying process; they reflect local engagement with papal history in a way that needs to be explored further. Such variant versions also suggest the lack of control that could be exerted by Rome once the text had reached another destination. In its new homes, therefore, the text could fulfil the purpose the authors had intended, but serve other purposes as well. We should welcome this diversity recorded in the manuscripts rather than seek to homogenize it and assume that only one text is the ideal outcome. In a paper published in 2014, Eckhart Wirbelauer rightly reflected on the degree of tension and disagreement actually reflected in the *Liber ponti-ficalis* itself.[55] In this context, the variant versions in the manuscripts possess even greater potential and importance.

Yet ever more questions have emerged. What does this complex pattern of transmission suggest about the possibly changing functions of the text as it continued to be copied? Did the *Liber pontificalis* retain the character of contemporary polemic and political argument that had been such an important aspect of the initial production of its first and subsequent sections? What governed the intentions and interests of the compilers and scribes of the late eighth- and ninth-century copies of the text? Why are there so few copies of the history of the popes which go further than the middle of the eighth century? It is to a consideration of these questions in relation to the late eighth- and early ninth-century manuscript witnesses to the *Liber pontificalis* that I now turn.

Late Eighth- and Ninth-Century Manuscripts Containing the *Liber pontificalis*

As stated at the beginning of this chapter, the majority of the earliest witnesses to the text, as can be seen from the map (Map 2), are in Frankish manuscripts dating from the late eighth and the ninth centuries. One important caveat is necessary: all locations of manuscripts, if made on palaeographical evidence alone, and in the absence of any

---

[55] Wirbelauer 2014, pp. 125–35.

other specific piece of evidence that enables a book to be located to a particular place, such as the book lists of Lorsch, Reichenau, and St Gallen mentioned above, are necessarily approximate.[56] They simply indicate that the book was written by a scribe trained in a particular place or region; the palaeography does not prove the origin of a manuscript.[57] If the book's provenance thereafter suggests that it did not move away from the centre suggested by the evidence of the script, then a little more security can be achieved. An example might be Leiden, VLQ 60, written in early St Amand script, but with no indication that it went further than Reims in the ninth century. From this perspective, each surviving manuscript witness to the *Liber pontificalis* needs to be considered as designed for a particular context, but most of the individual owners and readers of a copy of the *Liber pontificalis* understood it to be a single text about the popes and Rome; they were presumably unaware of variant copies and alternative compilations of texts.

I have already referred to the possibly Tuscan version of Life 94 presented in Lucca, Biblioteca Capitolare Feliniana 490, but the initial codicological context of the entire Lucca codex is significant too for the light it throws on the perception of what kind of text the *Liber pontificalis* was. Luigi Schiaparelli was inclined to see the now unwieldy codex as originally comprising three separate volumes, though more recent assessments see it as one composite, quadripartite volume assembled over the period 787–816.[58] It is more important to acknowledge that these texts were assembled in the same scriptorium over a relatively short period of time by a group of scribes working together. In other words, all the texts were part of the same programme or enterprise of production that incorporated the various instalments of the *Liber pontificalis*. The first three sections of Lucca 490's current contents can be set out as follows:

---

[56] See above, p. 172, note 5.   [57] See McKitterick 2012 and 2016b.

[58] *LP* I, pp. clxiv–clxvi, Schiaparelli 1924, Petrucci 1992, and the important adjustments to the structure suggested by Unfer-Verre 2013 and Pomaro 2015, pp. 257–9. I am very grateful to Dr Unfer-Verre for material she kindly sent me, and for her help on my visit to Lucca. See also the MIRABILE entry for Lucca, Biblioteca Capitolare Feliniana 490, http://sismelfirenze.it, and McKitterick 2015, pp. 241–4.

I Fols 2–31

    fols 2–30 *Chronica Hieronymi*

    fols 30, 31 Antiphonary fragment

II Fols 32–160

    fols 32r–35r *Isidori Chronica*

    fols 36r–48v *Isidori De officiis ecclesiasticis*

    fols 49r–132v *Historia ecclesiastica Eusebii a Rufino versa*

    fols 132v–136v *Rescriptum beati Gregorii ad Augustinum episcopum*

    [between fols 136 and 137 Jerome–Gennadius, *De viris illustribus*][59]

    fols 137r–160v *Liber pontificalis* to Constantine I

III Fols 161–210

    fols 161–9 *Liber pontificalis* Gregory II to Stephen II (*libellus*)

    fols 170–210r *Liber pontificalis* Paul to Hadrian I

The fourth section of the codex is more problematic, and some of its subsections may well have got misplaced, not least fols 236–80, containing the *Sanblasiana,* whose script would seem to indicate it belongs in Part III above.[60] Nevertheless, the work of other scribes responsible for parts of the first three sections also appears in this problematic fourth section.

The entire compilation appears to represent a major project, presumably presided over by the enterprising and politically active Bishop John of Lucca,[61] that included the *Liber pontificalis* text from the beginning to 715, together with the two prefatory letters attributed to Jerome and Pope Damasus. Further portions for Lives 91–4 and 95–7 (that is, for the years 715–57 and 757–95) were appended.[62] As can be seen from the scheme above, the portion of the Lucca codex containing the text of the *Liber pontificalis* to 715 also includes Eusebius–Rufinus's *Historia ecclesiastica,* Jerome–Gennadius's *De viris illustribus,* the *Chronicle* of Isidore, and most probably the historically arranged canon law collection known as the *Sanblasiana,* which incorporated the Symmachan apocrypha.[63]

---

[59] These folios, comprising two quires, were still part of the book in the eighteenth century but no longer part of the codex by the 1880s. They have since re-emerged, reported by Bischoff and Brown 1985, p. 352 at **III 303b. and are now, as ascertained 18 July 2019, in a private collection.

[60] See Unfer-Verre 2013, pp. 58–61 and for some of the texts Caffaro 2003, with, on pp. 166–95, a facsimile of fols 211v, 217r–231r.

[61] On Lucca in this period see Stoffella 2018.

[62] Schiaparelli 1924, pp. 13, 18, 106, but compare Parker Johnson 1939, p. 10.

[63] Kéry 1999, pp. 29–31.

Now also part of the book, if not always intended to be part of it, therefore, is Jerome's continuation of the *Chronicle* of Eusebius and a variety of texts relating to *computus* and ecclesiastical matters, including the so-called Spanish epitome of canon law, also historically arranged. The strong emphasis on the history of Christianity and development of the Christian church is continued in the final text of the codex, the *Liber genealogus,* which is a Donatist world chronicle from fifth-century North Africa. This curious text stakes a claim for the persecuted Donatists to be ranked beside the pre-Constantinian Christian martyrs, and thus presents an alternative perspective from that in the other histories in the codex. In another late eighth-century copy of the *Liber genealogus* from St Gallen, it is even attributed to Jerome.[64]

The assembly of texts in Lucca 490 overall appears to echo the intentions of the original author of the *Liber pontificalis,* as expressed in the main text and the creative prefatory letters attributed to Jerome and Damasus. Thus, the compiler of Lucca 490, like the author of the first edition of the *Liber pontificalis,* explicitly associated the production of the narrative with Jerome and thereby created a number of links, the most important of which are with Jerome and Damasus in connection with an authoritative new translation of the Bible, with Jerome as the definer of orthodox writers in the *De viris illustribus,* and of course with Jerome the historian and continuator of the *Chronicle* of Eusebius.

Unfer-Verre noted one pertinent indication of the possible Roman origin of the exemplars of the eighth-century portions of the *Liber pontificalis,* in the similarity between the style of initial ornament, including a portrait of Paul I in the initial P of his biography on fol. 183r, and initials in a number of codices that have been identified as produced in Rome at the end of the eighth century.[65] To those can be added the lost manuscript 'E6', the 'Farnesianus' in Duchesne's Italian 'E' Class. The 'Farnesianus' was discussed, collated, and illustrated by Bianchini, and at that stage contained Lives 60–97, c. 4, with some chapters of the last four

---

[64] Csg 133, p. 299. See Unfer-Verre 2013, p. 58, *Liber genealogus,* ed. Mommsen, pp. 154–96, and Dearn 2007. The suggestive codicological context of the other copies of this text will be explored elsewhere.

[65] See *CLA* I, 18b (Agimund's Homiliary Book II), Vat. lat. 3836, fol. 64r, and the 'Codex Iuvenianus', Rome, Biblioteca Vallicelliana, MS B.25, fol. 51r, and the examples discussed in Osborne 1990.

Lives missing. The codex has been lost since the eighteenth century.[66] Only late eleventh-century and later copies of this 'E' recension are extant, written at Farfa (such as BAV Vat. lat. 3764) and elsewhere in central Italy. The Farnesianus appears to have been an early ninth-century codex, written in uncial script. It too had the portrait initial at the beginning of the Life of Paul I. Given the character and date of the uncial as well as the initials, moreover, it raises the intriguing possibility that the Farnesianus may also have been a Roman codex. Rather than the 'A' recension chosen by Duchesne, it is the 'E' recension, therefore, that may actually represent the original Roman text of the continuations after Life 59.

An association of ideas led to the pairing of the *Liber pontificalis* with Jerome's *De viris illustribus,* the chronologically ordered list of Christian authors from St Peter onwards, together with a note of their works, in both the sixth-century Verona codex and the ninth-century codex from Lucca, as well as the books containing the epitomes discussed below. This pairing is replicated in an early composite manuscript from central Italy now in Florence, Biblioteca Laurenziana, San Marco 604. This codex has received less attention than it warrants, for it is actually a relatively early witness to the dissemination of the *Liber pontificalis* south of Rome. Duchesne's caution concerning opinions about its date and his own apparent unfamiliarity with the early development of Beneventan script may have contributed to this neglect. Waitz considered San Marco 604 to be a tenth-century codex, and comparisons with more recent judgements in the wake of the pioneering work of E. A. Lowe as well as internal evidence suggest that this codex is indeed to be located to central Italy, possibly the Naples region, in the first half of the tenth century. The codex has now lost at least three quires. It lacks the Lives from John I to Silverius, and stops in the middle of the life of Leo II in the *Liber pontificalis,* only to resume again in the third bio-bibliography, that of Matthew, in the *De viris illustribus.* This too breaks off, and the codex resumes with a text attributed to Augustine on categories of heretic, the decree *De libris recipiendis et non recipiendis,* and an excerpt from

---

[66] Bianchini's was reprinted with illustrations of the 'Farnesianus' in *PL* 127 (Paris, 1852), cols. 224–8. See also his preparatory material in Verona, Biblioteca Capitolare CCCCXXXI, fasc. XV, fol. 1r and Franklin 2017, pp. 620–9 and Figs 3 and 5.

Cassiodorus's *Institutiones* on the books of the Bible. *De viris illustribus* and the *Liber pontificalis* were part of the original codex. The text of the *Liber pontificalis* itself omits much of the description of Constantine's gifts from the Life of Silvester, as well as narrative detail from many of the Lives, but appears to be have been abridged from a full text. An abbreviated version of the *Gesta episcoporum Neapolitanorum* known as the *Catalogus episcoporum Neapolitanorum*, extending from the first Bishop Asper to Bishop Stephen III (898–907) was added very soon afterwards.[67]

Most of the 'B' recensions of the *Liber pontificalis* occupy the entire codex, but a later ninth-century copy of the *Liber pontificalis* in Vienna, ÖNB Cod. 473 is an exception. It is associated with Charlemagne's grandson Charles the Bald. It presents a further context in which the *Liber pontificalis* was prominent; the text of the *Liber pontificalis* up to Life 94 was incorporated into some carefully selected material relating to the history of the Franks. It was probably produced at St Amand in connection with Charles the Bald's coronation at Metz in 869.[68] Its contents are as follows:

Fols 1–85v *Liber pontificalis* up to Life 94, 'B' text, that is, with the Frankish additions included, such as the reference to the papal appeal for help from Charles Martel against the Saracens, the perfidy of Duke Hunuald, and the grant of the pallium to Chrodegang of Metz[69]

Fols 91–107v *Liber historiae Francorum* in the unrevised 'D' version

Fols 108r–114 Continuations of the *Chronicle* of Fredegar to the death of Charles Martel

Fols 116r–143v *Annales regni Francorum*, 'D' version

Fols 144r–151v Einhard *Vita Karoli* excerpts concerning the repudiation of the daughter of King Desiderius of the Lombards by Charlemagne, and Charlemagne's marriage to Hildegard

Fols 152v–169r *Annales regni Francorum* continued

Fols 169r–172v *Genealogiae domus Carolingicae*

The various sections of the *Annales regni Francorum* were divided in this manuscript into sections headed *gesta*, for example, *Gesta Karoli Magni*,

---

[67] *Catalogus episcoporum Neapolitanorum*, ed. Waitz, pp. 436–9. Lowe and Brown 1980, p. 44, dated it to the early eleventh century, but their own illustrations of the development of the Beneventan script contradict this, for the San Marco scripts are closer to the 'formative period' in Monte Cassino 269 (before AD 949) (Plate II).

[68] McKitterick 1998 and 2004b, pp. 120–32; and Reimitz 1999.

[69] On the Frankish interpolations see below, pp. 206–16.

Gesta Hludovici, perhaps emulating the biographical divisions of the *Liber pontificalis.* The codex thus presents the history of the popes as an adjunct to, and historical context for, the history of the Carolingian family. It enhances Carolingian associations with the papacy, provides historical justification for the Carolingian conquest of the Lombards, and reinforces the authority of the popes and Rome in relation to the Franks.

The codicological associations with history and law we have observed in Verona XXII (20),[70] Lucca, Biblioteca Capitolare Feliniana 490, San Marco 604, and Vienna, ÖNB 473 are important evidence of new contexts provided for the full text of the *Liber pontificalis,* and thus new uses found for the papal history. The compilers clearly took their cue from the intentions of the original author(s), but thereby reveal a certain respect for ancient authority and its embodiment in the history of the popes. Abbreviated versions or epitomes of the *Liber pontificalis* also found interesting travelling companions. It is an obvious point, but none the less important to emphasize, that the copying and presence of a text by itself or in a deliberately devised compilation are not necessarily sufficient to determine how a text was read in any one centre. Certainly, annotations are one crucial way to chart this,[71] but abridgements or epitomes are another.

The Epitomes and their Implications 1: the Felician Epitome

Because of the processes of selection and omission, the epitomes have the potential to reflect local engagements with the text and particular themes and topics highlighted in the history of the popes. Why and how would someone set out to create a shorter version of the text? How much of the original delineation of the city of Rome and the original emphases of the text on the physical or material history of the city, apostolic succession, papal orthodoxy, and papal authority are preserved in the

---

[70] See above, pp. 184–5.

[71] I signal here work in progress presented by Andrea Verardi, 'On the margins of the popes: notes, glosses, and marginalia in the manuscripts of the Roman *Liber pontificalis,* 8th–11th century', at the Leeds International Medieval Congress, 1–4 July 2019.

early medieval epitomes? What was their function? What is the signifi-cance of what is retained and what omitted, and of what is summarized and paraphrased? How might we be able to draw on the evidence of the small number of early medieval epitomes to document perceptions, in Francia and Italy between the sixth and ninth centuries, of the late antique and early medieval history of the popes and Rome? An obvious place to start is with two famous early medieval epitomes or abridge-ments of the text, the 'Felician' and the 'Cononian' epitomes, that have been thought to offer information about the initial composition of the *Liber pontificalis*.[72] Not only their content but also their manuscript con-text needs to be taken into account.

These two epitomes in particular were crucial elements for Duch-esne's deduction about the original composition of the text in the sixth century. One stopped with the Life of Felix IV (Life 56) and the other with the Life of Conon (Life 85).[73] Duchesne had deduced the existence of a 'first but no longer extant edition' of the *Liber pontificalis* from differences between these two epitomes and the full text, extant only in manuscripts from the late eighth century onwards, such as the consular dating and aspects of the Lives of the sixth-century popes, Hormisdas and John I. Duchesne suggested that the portions up to Felix IV in these epitomes were two independent abridgements of this now lost hypothet-ical first edition.[74] That both the Felician and the Cononian epitomes are only extant in late eighth- and ninth-century Frankish manuscripts, and in multiple copies, should at least prompt closer scrutiny of Duchesne's position, despite its brilliance as a piece of editorial reconstruction. Doubts about Duchesne's hypothetical 'first edition' came to a head with Herman Geertman's suggestion in 2003, repeated in 2009, that it was time the whole question was re-examined.[75] It has recently been chal-lenged more comprehensively by Andrea Verardi, Matthias Simperl, and myself, though the three of us wrote our initial arguments independently at more or less the same time, each of us unaware of the others' hypotheses.

---

[72] See above, p. 12.

[73] On Epitomes F and K, see *LP* I, pp. xlix–lvii; see also Levison 1913, pp. 513–18.

[74] *LP* I, p. 47.   [75] Geertman 2003a, p. 270 and Geertman 2009.

Andrea Verardi thinks both the Felician and the Cononian abbreviated texts should be seen as alternative and more or less coincidental but independent versions produced by different groups of papal officials in Rome before the full *Liber pontificalis* was composed, all within a very few years in the early sixth century. He also included in his book full discussions of all the manuscripts of these two epitomes and their codicological context, and the many questions they and the texts included in them raise.[76] Matthias Simperl made a case for the Felician epitome being a late sixth-century Frankish abbreviation made at Tours from the full first section of the *Liber pontificalis*,[77] and I have argued that the Cononian recension is an eighth-century Frankish compilation made in the Burgundian diocese of Autun, also abbreviated from a full version.[78]

The later eighth- or early ninth-century copies of the Felician epitome are now in The Hague, Meermanno-Westreenianum Museum 10.B.4, written by someone in the second half of the eighth century at least trained in northern Francia and possibly from the ecclesiastical province of Reims;[79] Paris, BnF lat. 1451[80] and BAV reg. lat. 1127, both from the Tours region; and a lost manuscript from Laon. In these codices, the abbreviated text of the *Liber pontificalis* is part of a compilation that includes a short history of the early councils, emphasizing the popes to whose initiative they were to be credited, various expositions of the Creed and statements of faith, including extracts from the *Histories* of Gregory of Tours,[81] and a list of the ecclesiastical provinces of Gaul.

The order of contents in the manuscript in The Hague differs a little from that in the Paris and Vatican versions. The collection of conciliar decrees and selection of papal decretals in the Paris manuscript appears to be a shortened version of the canon law collection known as the *Collectio Sancti Mauri*. This *collectio* was once, judging from the quire signatures, a separate manuscript, though it may have been added to

---

[76] Verardi 2013 and 2016.

[77] Simperl 2016, and see also proceedings of the Rome 2018 conference on the *Liber pontificalis,* Herbers, Heide, and Simperl (eds.) 2020.

[78] McKitterick 2019.   [79] *CLA* X, 1572a and 1572b.

[80] Paris, BnF lat. 1451 (*CLA* V, 528) and Bischoff, *Katalog* III, 4011. The most recent pope mentioned is Hadrian I (†795).

[81] Gregory of Tours, *Historiae* V.43; VI.40, ed. Krusch and Levison, pp. 249–50, 310–13.

this present codex at an early stage.[82] In the compilations in the Vatican and The Hague, however, the canon law texts are an integral part of the original manuscript along with the Felician recension. The statement on fol. 4r of the Vatican codex records that from the martyrdom of Pope Marcellinus until the twenty-fifth year of the glorious King Charles's reign is *VIII KL aprl anni XXXXCC et menses III* (that is, 25 March 793). Because the list of popes runs to Paschal I (†824), this may indicate the date of the exemplar rather than that of the Vatican copy.

The Felician epitome could have been a late sixth- rather than an eighth-century Frankish composition as Simperl has suggested. Alternatively, as Verardi has argued, it may be that the text was originally composed in Rome. A process of abridgement can surely involve a number of editorial choices, such as summarizing in different words and paraphrase or the simple cutting of sentences and phrases. Someone abridging a text some time after its original composition might also add information from other sources. Textual differences, therefore, could also be the consequence of a later eighth-century attempt to summarize the material and use knowledge derived from other texts, relating to relevant popes, such as conciliar or canon law material, when devising this distinctive combination of texts. In the Life of Leo I, for example, an explicit reference is made to the *Tome* in association with the Council of Chalcedon, and the Life of Hormisdas supplies fuller detail about discussions in Constantinople and the condemnation of Acacius. A further possibility is that, rather than adapting the text for the purpose of each composite book, the compiler used an already existing abridged version, whether by choice or because it was all that was available.

Whatever the case, the Felician epitome contrives, by omitting most of the building activity of the popes and much of the circumstantial political detail, to highlight the Trinitarian doctrinal disputes with Constantinople, the popes' insistence on orthodoxy, and papal contributions to law, liturgy, and ecclesiastical organization. The texts included with the Felician epitome in these three surviving manuscripts fully reinforce this marked emphasis on defining orthodox faith in the form of exposition and validating historical narrative as well as in conciliar statements. They

---

[82] Kéry 1999, pp. 45–6.

were clearly designed for very specific use. In this respect, the overall codicological context and the selection of information in these epitomes are crucially complementary.

Bern 225 + Bern 233 + Orleans 313 offers yet another variant on codicological context. Its truncated and abbreviated text of the *Liber pontificalis*, with a version of the Lives from Peter to Liberius that has many similarities with the Felician recension, is part of an elaborate set of texts commenting on biblical passages, creeds, and the Lord's Prayer; reference summaries and lists, of Creation events, biblical tithes and characters, clerical vestments and grades, councils, popes, and Church Fathers; and moral, pastoral, and spiritual texts. Anna Dorofeeva has proposed that this codex can be seen as a compilation responding to the early Carolingian reform programme in all its diversity. It accords, for example, with the teaching programme outlined in Hraban Maur's *De institutione clericorum,* and thus it could have been useful for canons, priests, and lay brothers as both a reference work and a teaching manual.[83]

The Epitomes and their Implications 2: the Cononian Epitome

The Cononian epitome of the *Liber pontificalis* survives in two eighth-century Burgundian manuscripts, Paris, BnF lat. 2123 and Verona LII (50). While highlighting the legislative and liturgical activity of the popes, the compiler of Paris, BnF lat. 2123 also shared the doctrinal preoccupations of the codices containing the Felician epitome.[84] Its contents buttressed the *Liber pontificalis* text, headed *Incipit ordo episco-porum Romae,* with extracts from the first Council of Ephesus, the Lateran Council of 649, Gennadius of Marseilles's treatise *De ecclesiasticis dogmatibus,* and a number of commentaries on the Creed, definitions of the canon of Scripture, and the biblical apocrypha. The decree *De libris recipiendis et non recipiendis,*[85] as well as the canon law collection known as the *Herovalliana,* a collection of legal formulae to be used in

---

[83] Dorofeeva 2015, pp. 41–3.

[84] See also above, Chapter 5, pp. 145–51, and Verardi 2016, pp. 60–7.

[85] Ed. von Dobschütz. For discussion see McKitterick 1989, pp. 200–5.

administering a diocese, and the *De viris illustribus* of Jerome–Gennadius were also inserted.[86] The codex efficiently provides an historical and specifically Roman and Western framework for the statements from the Eastern church councils, the definitions of the bishops' diverse responsibilities, and texts to assist a bishop in the discharge of these responsibilities. Such a range of normative texts entirely accords with the interests and preoccupations as well as links with Italy enjoyed at Autun and Flavigny. These are reflected in other manuscripts from Autun and Flavigny of a similar date, especially the Autun recension of the canon law collection known as the *Vetus Gallica*,[87] and a number of important liturgical books of the eighth century, not least the misleadingly named *Missale Gothicum*. It was neither a missal nor Gothic, but a lavish sacramentary designed for use by a bishop in a Frankish and Burgundian urban setting, most probably Autun.[88]

The codicological context of Verona LII (50) is very different from that of BnF lat. 2123, and rather more neutral. The codex now comprises three codicological units bound together, but all three have strong associations with Rome.[89] Its quire signatures suggest that the codex was originally two separate volumes, albeit probably written in the same centre. Quires 2–13 (fols 1–99) contain a homiliary arranged in liturgical order and Quires 14–35 contain the Rule of St Benedict and other monastic texts as well as the Cononian epitome of the *Liber pontificalis*. Script and layout as well as content, however, would suggest that this second set of quires also once comprised two books, with the first (Quires 14–23, fols 100–189v) containing the Rule of St Benedict and other monastic texts.

A second small codex was formed from Quires 24–35 (fols 190r–276v). Thus, the original codicological context for this copy of the Cononian epitome appears to have comprised a possible pilgrim itinerary to the Holy Land, a list of the ecclesiastical provinces of Gaul, and an odd little commentary on the two words *Gloria* and *Alleluia*. There

---

[86] For full discussion see McKitterick 2019. For the *De viris illustribus* paired with the *Liber pontificalis* in Verona, Biblioteca Capitolare XXII (20), see above, p. 184.

[87] See Mordek 1973, and *Vetus Gallica*, ed. Mordek.

[88] *Missale Gothicum*, ed. and trans. Rose. On the manuscript BAV reg. lat. 317 see *CLA* VI, pp. xiv–xv and the exhibition catalogue *Regards* 1995.

[89] For discussion of the Roman links of the texts in Part I and II see Verardi 2016, pp. 57–60.

is no doubt that the manuscript was in Verona by the first quarter of the ninth century, for it includes the distinctive annotations of the Archdeacon Pacificus of Verona. A particular note of interest is on fol. 266v in Life 66 of Gregory I, a life only a little abbreviated in the Cononian version. In the reference to Gregory's writings, Pacificus adds XXXV to indicate the number of books in the *Moralia in Job* and XX for the number of homilies on Ezekiel. Between *Ezekiel* and *pastoralem* he added *dialogorum libri IIII*, which is what the full text supplies. These additions could have been made because of Pacificus's own knowledge of Gregory's works. That Pacificus has referred to a full text of the *Liber pontificalis* seems more probable, however, for the supply of further details is at precisely the correct place in the text. Pacificus's second addition to the Life, where he added that Gregory's second batch of ordinations was in September, also appears to have been derived from the full text. Pacificus's special interest in this life of Gregory may be connected to the rich supply of works by Gregory already in Verona library, and in which more of Pacificus's annotations are to be found.[90]

The Epitomes and their Implications 3: the Shorter Epitomes

The survival of the Felician and Cononian recensions in these Frankish manuscripts suggests the intensely creative reception of older texts from the Merovingian past and from Italy in Francia, and how these were digested and presented in a new context apparently deemed to be the most useful for use within their respective dioceses. In the case of Verona LII (50), moreover, the compendium prepared in Burgundy was apparently readily received in its new context in Verona.

Such an instance of cross-referencing between various accounts of the historical development of the Christian church in its early years becomes an increasingly common phenomenon in the ninth, tenth, and eleventh centuries.[91] The epitome in Leiden, VLQ 12 from ninth-century Tours,

---

[90] Adami and Faccini 2005.

[91] See also Ademar of Chabannes and his summary of the *Liber pontificalis* in Paris, BnF lat. 2400, discussed by Landes 1995, pp. 109–10; Abbo of Fleury, *Liber pontificalis*, ed. Gantier.

for example, may seem to be little more than an extended list of popes. Yet the compiler of VLQ 12 added material on the Bishop of Tours which seems to incorporate local church history into the history of the papacy. The texts in the Fulda manuscript, Leiden, Universiteitsbibliotheek Scaliger 49, moreover, weave the local ecclesiastical history of Mainz and Fulda into that of the history of the popes.[92] The *Liber pontificalis* epitome in that codex is rather fuller than that in VLQ 12. It mirrors, in the formulaic reiteration of the ordination of bishops, priests, and deacons, what I have characterized as the 'cultural memory of episcopal succession', which incorporated the ritual of the laying on of hands and reflected the action of every subsequent bishop in office, in every diocese, as a successor to St Peter.[93]

The *Liber pontificalis* epitome in Scaliger 49, however, opens up still more instances of the dissemination of *Liber pontificalis* texts and extracts, for this particular abridgement is to be found in a number of Frankish manuscripts ranging in date from the ninth to the early eleventh century. The entries only run as far as Stephen II (Life 94); thereafter, some of the manuscripts include the names only of the next pope Paul I, or from Paul I to Hadrian, suggesting not only that it may have been an abridgement compiled between 773 and 795 and that it was made from the full text that only contained Lives 1–94, but also that this brief version enjoyed considerable popularity. In the first section of a composite four-part manuscript, for example, written by the Regensburg scribe Ellenhart in the time of Bishop Baturich in the second quarter of the ninth century, the earliest extant instance of this *Liber pontificalis* epitome occupies fols 8v–13v. In an obvious association of ideas, Ellenhart placed the epitome after a set of Easter tables starting from 741 and a copy of the pseudo-Clementine letter to James, Bishop of Jerusalem, reporting how Peter had made Clement his successor to the see of Rome.[94] As in Scaliger 49, the epitome runs to Stephen II, but it then has simply the name of Paul with no other details. The same epitome is to be found in a

---

[92] McKitterick 2014, pp. 208–34, at pp. 211–12 for Leiden, VLQ 12 and pp. 213–34 for Scaliger 49; a diplomatic transcription of the text in Scaliger 49 and English translation are on pp. 218–32.

[93] McKitterick 2014, p. 217. [94] Clm 14387, fols 1–13v: Bischoff 1980, p. 123.

Carolingian manuscript, thought to have been written in the Reims region in the later ninth century, and added to an anonymous commentary on the Gospel of Matthew.[95] In this epitome, the names have unused spaces left for details to be added, and continue from Paul I to Hadrian I. The epitome is also to be found in Munich, Clm 6385, a tenth-century Freising collection of short texts relating to explanations of Scripture, where the *Liber pontificalis* epitome ends with the three names Paul I, Stephen, and Hadrian. Further, BAV pal. lat. 39, an eleventh-century Rhineland collection of explanatory texts relating to the Psalms as well as a calendar, full psalter, and canticles with musical settings, includes the very same epitome, though the popes' names continue as far as Paschal I (but omit Stephen III).

Abridgements of the *Liber pontificalis* are so often little more than a record of the length of pontificate and the number of ordinations that the divergence in the Regensburg epitome and its siblings to include more information extracted from the full text is all the more significant. A notable absence from this epitome is the city of Rome itself. Hardly any of the elaborate lists of papal endowments, foundations of churches to honour particular saints, repairs to church buildings, and lavish gifts of gold, silver, and bronze liturgical furniture and vessels are mentioned at all. It is instructive, therefore, to assess what is preserved in this selection of topics, not least in the context of the themes highlighted in the previous chapters in this book.

The selected details relate to doctrine, clerical discipline, ecclesiastical organization, liturgy, and very occasionally to particular writings or dramatic incidents in the Life of a particular pope. The statements or confirmation of particular ecumenical synods about the faith by Silvester I, Leo I, Hilarus, and Martin I are recorded; Hilarus broadcast letters on the catholic faith throughout the whole of the East and confirmed the synods of Nicaea, Ephesus, and Chalcedon.[96] The note for Leo I specifies the 1200 bishops who expounded the catholic faith that 'in one Christ

---

[95] Valenciennes, BM 72 (65).

[96] The Regensburg scribe's attention faltered a little at this point and he wrote *congregavit* instead of *confirmavit.*

there are two natures, God and man'.[97] For particular events associated with the popes, the epitome preserves the notes that Cletus received the request from Peter to govern the Roman church, that Cornelius raised up the bodies of Peter and Paul from the catacombs, that Damasus had been cleared of a charge against him of adultery, that Sixtus III was cleared of a charge brought against him by Bassus, that Theodoric the king gave judgement in the case of the disputed election between Symmachus and Laurentius, that Boniface I defeated his rival Dioscorus, that there was a great flood during the pontificate of Pelagius I, and that John IV redeemed Dalmatian captives.

The Regensburg epitome and its siblings also register the writings and liturgical innovations made by the popes. Among the popes whose writings are mentioned, the epitome notes that Peter wrote two epistles and the Gospel of Mark; Anteros ordered the recording of the *Gesta martyrum;* Gregory I's writings, his contribution to the canon of the Mass, the institution of a Mass at the shrine of St Peter, and his conversion of the English are summarized. For many of the other popes, it is similarly the claims about their contributions to the liturgy that are highlighted. Telesphorus, for example, is again credited with instituting the season of Lent, the Christmas Eve Mass and the singing of the *Gloria* in the Mass; the singing of the *Gloria* on Sundays and saints' days is attributed to Symmachus. Celestine supposedly decreed that an antiphon should be sung before the sacrifice of the Mass. Victor, following Pius, decreed that Easter should be on a Sunday, Damasus promoted the singing of the psalms, Innocent instituted a fast on Saturdays, Sergius introduced the *Agnus Dei* into the Mass as well as litanies on the Marian feasts, and later Pope Gregory II introduced fasting on Thursdays as well (a practice that the full *Liber pontificalis* states had earlier been forbidden by Pope Miltiades).[98]

Clerical organization is another topic summarized in a number of these abridged lives, such as the ecclesiastical grades credited to Hyginus

---

[97] McKitterick 2014, pp. 223 and 231: *hic congregavit episcopos mille ducentos qui exposuerunt fidem catholicam duas naturas uno in Christo deum et hominem.*

[98] The epitome omits the reason given in the full text that this was for fear of emulating 'pagans': *LP* I, Life 33, p. 168, and cf. *LP* I, Life 39, p. 212. For Easter Sunday see Lives 11 and 15, *LP* I, pp. 132 and 137, for Pius and Victor.

and also to Gaius, the creation of parishes and dioceses attributed to Pope Dionysius, the reference to Boniface IV apparently legislating on sanctuary, Julius forbidding clerics to appear in a public law court, and Pope Leo II proscribing simony. Whereas comments are made about the learning or particular skills of a number of popes in the full text, it is only for Gregory II that there is a note of his virtues included in the epitome, namely, that he was learned in both Greek and Latin, knew all the Psalms by heart, and was most 'elegant and subtle' in their interpretation.

Further questions about the form in which knowledge of papal history was disseminated are raised by Luciana Cuppo in her discussion of a twelfth-century copy of a *Chronicon pontificum*.[99] She suggests that the first part of this 'Chronicon' was an independent composition made in the middle of the seventh century, subsequently extended with entries relating to Pippin III, the eighth-century popes, and Leo III, and the continuation of the papal list well into the twelfth century.[100] There is a closer resemblance between this 'Chronicon' and the lists of popes added to canon law manuscripts discussed in the previous chapter than to the epitomes discussed above. The differences in length of reign recorded in the various lists could also be significant in relation to how information about the popes was disseminated and received.[101] The entry for Pope Eusebius seems, for example, to reflect information drawn from a different source concerning baptism. Cuppo also notes that Pope Martin I is described as a martyr rather than as a confessor. This 'Lombard' papal list certainly emphasizes apostolic succession and institutional continuity. It simply records the succession of bishops and rarely incorporates any details at all, apart from noting which of the popes were martyred and under which emperor they were killed. Cuppo observes of this 'papal catalogue' that it appears in consequence to reflect a different attitude towards, and way of thinking of, the *Liber pontificalis* as a memorial to martyrs. Cuppo also stresses that this short papal catalogue, like the Frankish epitome, omits the physical city of Rome that is so prominent a feature of the full text. As she puts it, to compiler and readers alike, 'material culture mattered little'. Her further suggestion that the author

[99] BAV Vat. lat. 1348, fols 182–188v.　　[100] Cuppo 2008, p. 67.
[101] Above, pp. 155–6 and tabulated by Mommsen, *LP*, pp. xxviii–xl.

of this north Italian 'Chronicon' was more interested in the popes as successors of Peter than as bishops of Rome, however, is less applicable to the Frankish epitomes.[102] On the contrary, in the Frankish epitomes, the entries single out the essentially episcopal concerns in doctrinal, liturgical, and ecclesiological matters, as well as the systematic ordination of new clergy.

The circulation of particular abridgements as well as the full text of the *Liber pontificalis* among a number of widely disparate centres emerges as a major element in the dissemination of knowledge of the text and the history of the bishops of Rome it contains. The Frankish origin of most of the manuscript compilations is not in doubt, but it remains uncertain whether the epitomes are indeed Frankish renderings of the Roman history, as distinct from a form of the text, emanating from Rome, in which the papal history circulated north of the Alps.

I have argued in the three preceding sections that the codicological context of these Frankish copies of the epitomes indicates that the compilers of these books used the *Liber pontificalis* text as an essential element of historically ordered dossiers relating to orthodoxy, doctrinal correctness, liturgical observance, and ecclesiastical organization. The epitomes, therefore, appear to serve a variety of functions in the manuscripts in which they were included. The multiplication of particular epitomes across a wide geographical and chronological range is striking, and is paralleled by the far better-known extensive distribution of the full text north of the Alps.[103] What all these epitomes have in common, however, is the absence of most of the information from the full texts about the material history of Rome, papal endowments, and the building of so many basilicas dedicated to Roman saints.

Frankish Interpolations

The creation of the epitomes, together with both the variant versions of particular papal biographies and the manuscript classes identified by Duchesne and later commentators, accords with what Carmela Vircillo

---

[102] Cuppo 2008, p. 65.   [103] Guenée 1980, Map 2, p. 252.

Franklin has described as the 'constantly variable, "living" character of the text … subject to local interpolation and manipulation'.[104] The variant versions of a number of other Lives, notably those of the popes from Gregory II to Stephen II in the first half of the eighth century, are another notorious instance of 'local interpolation and manipulation'. These eighth-century biographies have long since been shown to offer different perspectives on relations between the Lombards, the Franks, and the popes.[105] Apart from the thoroughly studied 'Lombard' version of Life 94 of Pope Stephen II (752–7) referred to above, the incidence of the variant lives in the various classes of *Liber pontificalis* manuscripts identified by Duchesne and Mommsen needs further scrutiny for what this may reveal about the distribution and reception of the whole text as well as of individual Lives. Only a beginning on this large topic can be attempted here.

Duchesne noted, for example, that Life 91 of Gregory II (715–31) appeared to have been produced in an earlier version during his lifetime. It was quoted by Bede in his *De ratione temporum*, and was incorporated into the 'A' and 'C' manuscripts, of which ninth-century examples are extant from Lucca and the Frankish centres St Amand and Weissenburg respectively.[106] What this might imply is that a full text was already in these centres, to which the new Life or small set of Lives, received in the form of a *libellus* or pamphlet, was then added. Certainly, as stated above, analysis of the *Liber pontificalis* text in Lucca, Biblioteca Capitolare Feliniana 490, compiled at Lucca *c*.800, has suggested that it was possibly copied from at least three portions of the *Liber pontificalis* assumed to be already at Lucca before *c*.800 to serve as exemplars: one from the beginning to 715; one with the Lives of Gregory II (715–31), Gregory III (731–41), Zacharias (741–52), and Stephen II (752–7); and a third with the Lives of Paul (757–67), Stephen III (768–72), and Hadrian I (772–95).[107]

---

[104] Franklin 2018, p. 105   [105] See Lo Monaco (ed.) 2013, and Lo Conte 2010.

[106] Lucca, Bibilioteca Capitolare Feliniana 490, Leiden, VLQ 60, and Wolfenbüttel, Herzog August Bibliothek, Cod. Guelf. 10.11 Aug.4°.

[107] Gantner 2013a and above, p. 182.

A later recension of Life 91 of Pope Gregory II, probably devised about twenty years after the first version in the middle of the eighth century, is preserved in the 'B', 'D', and 'E' manuscript classes.[108]

Again, ninth-century Frankish examples of the 'B' and 'D' classes and Italian examples of the 'E' recension are extant. The inclusion of the later mid-eighth century version of the life of Gregory II in the Italian group, of which unfortunately the earliest now extant, but incomplete, copy dates from the eleventh century, might indicate that it was the preferred version disseminated from Rome as a replacement. But the coexistence and continued copying of the earlier version in the 'A' and 'C' classes of manuscript in both Italy and Francia would equally indicate that this preferred later version was not always substituted, even supposing it to have reached all centres.

All the 'B' class of manuscripts are entirely Frankish in origin, but the 'B' recension is also important because it contains the Frankish interpolations made to Lives 92–5, that is, of Popes Gregory III, Zacharias, Stephen II, and Paul I. These interpolations are also to be found in Lives 92–4 of the 'D' recension.[109] In a copy from the early ninth-century monastery of Weissenburg, moreover, the margins of this 'C' class codex are replete with the scribe's attempt to note the Frankish additions from a 'B' text. It is significant that the Abbot of Weissenburg at the time this copy was made was Bernhar, also Bishop of Worms (803–26), a kinsman of Charlemagne and sent by Charlemagne to Rome in 809 to discuss the *filioque* clause in the Creed.[110]

All these Frankish interpolations are significant for providing extra information about Franks and from a Frankish perspective, but especially the Franks' interest in how their own history became intertwined with

---

[108] *LP* I, pp. ccxx–ccxxv, and see also Davis's summary, *Eighth-Century Popes*, pp. 1–2, and see the schematic table above, p. 179.

[109] See *LP* I, pp. cxciii–cxcv, represented by the ninth-century Tours manuscript(s) BnF lat. 5516 (Lives 1–104) and BnF lat. 2769, now containing only Lives 90–6, a well as two later copies from Beauvais.

[110] Wolfenbüttel, Herzog August Bibliothek Cod. Guelf. 10.11 Aug.4°. Like Leiden, VLQ 60, moreover, it also contains the 'Lombard' recension of Life 94; see Gantner 2013a, pp. 78–9. On Bernhar see *Concilium Aquisgranensis* 809, ed. Willjung, pp. 88–9 and 287, and Hummer 2005, pp. 82–3.

that of the popes. Above all, the interpolations give important indications both of the profile of distribution of the manuscripts in which they occur, and the origin of the interpolations themselves. This becomes apparent in Life 92 of Pope Gregory III (731–41). Here, the one major addition found in the Frankish MSS in classes 'B' and 'D' concerns the appeal Pope Gregory made to Charles Martel, carried by his envoys Bishop Anastasius and the priest Sergius 'to his excellency Charles the shrewd man who then ruled the kingdom of the Franks'.[111]

The only other evidence for such an appeal is to be found in another papal source, preserved in the Frankish compilation of papal letters to the Carolingian rulers known as the *Codex epistolaris Carolinus*. It is a carefully constructed collection, presented with explanatory *lemmata* at the head of each letter and in a sequence matching that of the papal senders, namely, Gregory III, Zacharias, Stephen II, Paul I, Stephen III, Hadrian I, and, out of order, Pope Constantine II. It is extant in only one medieval manuscript, now Vienna, ÖNB 449, possibly owned by Archbishop Willibert of Cologne (870–89). Its presence at Cologne has been explained by surmising that an earlier Archbishop of Cologne, Hildebold, who had been archchaplain at court at precisely the time the collection was made, may have returned to his see with a copy.[112]

The interpolation in Life 92 of Gregory III in the *Liber pontificalis* appears to relate to the first two letters in this collection, usually dated late in Gregory's pontificate.[113] Letter 1 also refers to the extra information that will be provided by Charles's envoy Anhat when he brings the pope's letter to Charles. Given that the interpolated entry in Life 92 includes the details, not mentioned in the letters, about Liutprand pitching his tents in the *campus Neronis,* and shaving the Romans in

---

[111] *LP* I, Life 92, c. 14, p. 420: *Carolo sagacissimo viro, qui tunc regnum regebat Francorum;* and compare p. ccxxiii with Duchesne's surmise that this interpolation was added under Pope Stephen II, that is, between 752 and 757.

[112] See Espelo in press. On Hildebold at court see McKitterick 2008, pp. 139–40.

[113] *Codex epistolaris Carolinus* 1 and 2 (Gundlach 2 and 1), ed. Gundlach, pp. 476–9. Gundlach put the letters into what he surmised was the correct chronological order. For a German translation and reprint of Gundlach's edition, reordered to follow the sequence in the manuscript, see Hartmann and Orth-Müller (eds.), pp. 33–8; for an English translation also according to the sequence in the manuscript, see McKitterick, Pollard, Price, and Espelo in press.

Lombard fashion, it might be presumed that these stories were part of Anhat's oral report and remembered with glee in Carolingian court circles. The final entry in the Life of Gregory II, furthermore, concerns the granting of an archiepiscopal pallium to Wilchar of Vienne. Bishop Wilchar is one of the envoys mentioned in many letters in the *Codex epistolaris Carolinus,* and he is given the title archbishop in an early letter from Pope Hadrian.[114]

The Frankish Interpolations and the Frankish Royal Court

This hypothesis about a connection between the Frankish interpolations and the Frankish royal court is reinforced by the additions to Lives 93–5. In Life 93 of Pope Zacharias (741–52), the interpolator inserted a note specifying 'the great silver arch weighing 70 lbs' that Carloman had presented to St Peter before his retreat to the religious life.[115] In Life 94 of Pope Stephen II (752–7), the interpolations offer a number of Frankish perspectives and details. There is the very negative description of Hunald of Aquitaine and how he 'urged the Lombards on in their wickedness';[116] a curious sentence about Stephen's munificence to his clergy, giving them vestments and paying their debts;[117] a description of the pope and King Pippin meeting at the abbey of St John Maurienne and the gifts exchanged;[118] and details about the king's envoys, including his half-brother Jerome, sent to escort the pope back to Rome, where he was greeted by a crowd of priests and the *populus.* The granting of the pallium to Bishop Chrodegang of Metz was also noted.[119]

All these have the character of eyewitness accounts, as if reported by a member of the royal entourage. The added details about the pope's

---

[114] CC 9, 19, 27, 39, and archbishop in Epp. 50, 61, 96, 97 (Gundlach 7, 22, 14, 25, 51, 65, 96, 95), ed. Gundlach, pp. 493, 525, 512, 530, 571, 593, 644, and 637. On Wilchar, see Schilling 2002.

[115] *LP* I, Life 93, c. 21, p. 433; trans. Davis, *Eighth-Century Popes,* p. 47: *arcum argenteum maiorem pens. lib LXX.*

[116] *LP* I, Life, 94, c. 4, p. 441; trans. Davis, *Eighth-Century Popes,* p. 54: *Langobardis exediens, maligna adortans.*

[117] *LP* I, Life 94, c. 12, p. 443.   [118] *LP* I, Life 94, c. 35, p. 450.

[119] *LP* I, Life 94, cc. 38 and 53, pp. 451 and 456.

institution of night office and the arrangements for the services at St Peter's indicate a particular interest in the liturgy and monastic organization on the part of this witness. Similarly, a description is given of the image of Mary given by the pope to the church of Santa Maria Maggiore, and a reference to the tower built at St Peter's and 'the bell to call the clergy and people to divine office'.[120] The final interpolation in this life also concerns additions made to St Peter's, in the atrium, but reports briefly the conversion of the mausoleum (of Honorius) into a basilica honouring St Petronilla. When he had been in Francia, the pope 'had promised that king that he would place St Petronilla's body there'.[121] The story of Petronilla is continued in the Frankish addition in the brief Life 95 of Paul I (757–67), and is entirely concerned with describing the translation of this new saint, supposedly the daughter of St Peter, to her new resting place. A note is added about a few other embellishments made to St Peter's.[122] A final extra note is at the end of this Life's entry, after the formulaic phrase that the see was vacant for one year and one month: the interpolator added that this was the period when the trespasser Constantine was an intruder into the apostolic see.[123] This could be taken as the way the Frankish interpolator was able to take account of the presence of two letters from Pope Constantine II preserved in the *Codex epistolaris Carolinus*.

Such a Frankish court-associated promotion of the history and historical authority of the popes and Rome is too large a topic to be expanded upon here, but it is obviously of crucial importance for our understanding of the Carolingians' relations with Rome and the popes, and Frankish political ideology in relation to Rome, the papacy, the shape and performance of the liturgy, and the authority of canon law in the course of the ninth century. Further support for the creative association between Carolingian court officials and the Frankish editions of the *Liber pontificalis*, moreover, can be derived from a consideration of the ways copies of

---

[120] *LP* I, Life 94, c. 47, p. 454; trans. Davis, *Eighth-Century Popes*, p. 73: *qui clerum et populum ad officium Dei invitarent.*

[121] *LP* I, Life 94, c. 52, p. 455; trans. Davis, *Eighth-Century Popes*, p. 76: *quae praedicto benignissimo Pippino rege in Francia spoponderat ut beatae Petronillae corpus ibidem conlocaret.* On Petronilla see Goodson 2015 and McKitterick 2018a.

[122] *LP* I, Life 95, cc. 3 and 5, p. 464.   [123] *LP* I, Life 95, c. 7, p. 465.

the *Liber pontificalis* may have reached Francia as part of the baggage of any one of the umpteen royal and papal legates crossing the Alps, bearing letters, requests, and gifts,[124] brokering agreements, or attending synods, not least the infamous Synod of Rome in 769 attended by thirteen Frankish bishops.[125] That group comprised Wilchar of Sens, George of Amiens and Ostia, Wulfram of Meaux, Lull of Mainz, Gaugenius of Tours, Ado of Lyon, Hermanarius of Bourges, Daniel of Narbonne, Ermembert of Worms, Erlolf of Langres, Tilpin of Reims, Berowulf of Würzburg, and Gislebert of Noyon, and the list of the episcopal participants is preserved in one ninth-century Frankish copy of the *Liber pontificalis*.[126]

There are, of course, any number of formal and informal means by which the *Liber pontificalis* may have travelled beyond Rome. The narrative and epistolary material, as well as the presence in Francia of many other kinds of book with texts such as liturgical prayers, *ordines*, and canon law apparently of Roman origin, point to sustained exchanges between Italy and the realms beyond the Alps. The royal Frankish annals and other Frankish narratives, the *Liber pontificalis*, and specific references in the *Codex epistolaris Carolinus* offer many precise indications of individuals travelling as royal and papal emissaries between Rome, Ravenna, the northern Lombard kingdom, Spoleto, Benevento, and Byzantium, and many acting as couriers for books and other gifts as well as letters and oral messages. Among the most prominent are Droctegang, Abbot of Jumièges in 753;[127] Chrodegang, Bishop of Metz in 753 (the subject of an interpolation in Life 94);[128] Fulrad, Abbot of St Denis in

---

[124] CC 25 and 82 (Gundlach 24 and 89), pp. 529 and 626. On the books sent by Pope Leo III see Buchner 1926; Bougard 2009, pp. 134–5 thought these books 'très probablement' included the *LP*.

[125] The only other record of these names is the remnant of the *Acta* of the Synod of Rome 769 in Verona LVII (55), fol. 109v. See McKitterick 2008, pp. 299–302, McKitterick 2018b, and McKitterick 2020b.

[126] *LP* I, Life 96, c. 1, p. 468, though the list of names is preserved only in the mid-ninth century copy of the *Liber pontificalis*, probably from Auxerre, Leiden, VLQ 41, fol 103r. On these bishops see McKitterick 2008, pp. 299–305 and McKitterick 2020b, pp. 17–20. Compare Nelson 2016.

[127] *LP* I, Life 97, c. 16, p. 491, and CC 10, 11, 41 (Gundlach 4, 5, 6).

[128] *LP* I, Life 94, c. 18, p. 445.

755–6, 758, and 779;[129] Wilchar, Bishop of Vienne between 755 and the 780s (the subject of the Frankish interpolation in Life 91);[130] Bishop George of Amiens and Ostia on many occasions between 756 and 782, who also attended the Synod of Rome in 769 and travelled to England as royal and papal legate in 786;[131] Wulfard, Abbot of Tours in 758;[132] Hitherius, royal *cancellarius* and *capellanus* to Charlemagne, from 770 to 787;[133] Maginarius, Abbot of St Denis, also *capellanus* and *cancellarius* from 781/2 to 788;[134] and Rado, royal notary and Abbot of St Vaast in 790–1.[135] The Anglo-Saxon Bishop Burchard of Würzburg (742–53) went as emissary on behalf of Archbishop Boniface of Mainz to Pope Zacharias in Rome in 748.[136] As claimed in the Royal Frankish annals, Burchard may have made a second visit to Rome in 750 or 751, though I doubt it; he may nevertheless have served as an emissary to Rome with Fulrad on other occasions for diplomatic purposes.[137] Bishop Bernulf or Berowulf, as already noted, was one of the bishops learned in Scripture and canon law sent by Charlemagne and Carloman to attend the Synod of Rome in 769. Charlemagne himself with his entourage visited Rome in 773–4, 781, and 800. It is hardly to be wondered at that Roman texts reached Francia.

Even to point to formal contacts in this way implies the acquisition of whole books or *libelli* as part of a diplomatic or synodical exchange in some formal way, as if the dissemination of copies were organized. The text of a new Life, as indicated above, could well have been a formal way

---

[129] *LP* I, Life 94, c. 24, p. 447, and CC 7, 8, 9 (Gundlach 6, 11, 7).

[130] See p. 210, note 114, above.

[131] *LP* I, Lives 94, c. 23; 96, c. 17; and 98, c. 26, pp. 446, 473, 494; CC 3, 4, 6, 8, 15, 23, 29, 70 (Gundlach 10, 9, 8, 11, 17, 18, 16, 73). On George of Ostia/Amiens see Story 2003, pp. 55–92, and Cubitt 1995, pp. 154–5.

[132] CC 27, 31, 32, 41 (Gundlach 14, 27, 37, 26)

[133] Hitherius was also Abbot of Tours: CC 41, 68 (Gundlach 56, 71); see also McKitterick 2008, pp. 204–8.

[134] CC 68 (Gundlach 71).

[135] CC 85 (Gundlach 91) and see the full list of Frankish and papal legates in McKitterick, Pollard, Price, and Espelo in press, and compare Hack 2006–7, pp. 486–696.

[136] Zacharias, letter to Boniface 748, preserved in collections of Boniface's letters, *Epistolae*, ed. Rau, Ep. 80, p. 256. On Burchard see Levison 1946, p. 80.

[137] McKitterick 1990. See also McKitterick 2004b, pp. 133–55.

of signalling the election of a new pope,[138] but there was surely a variety of ways in which copies of the *Liber pontificalis* could have been acquired. We may be entitled to assume that the papal officials themselves supervised the making of copies, even if they did not actually orchestrate the dissemination thereof; there is sufficient consistency in the earlier sections of the text up to 715 to suggest that the papal administration itself maintained a degree of control. In a letter from Pope Martin (649–53) to Bishop Amandus of Maastricht, Martin alludes to the failure of someone Amandus had sent to Rome to obtain copies of certain texts, saying 'the codices are now exhausted in our library and we have no supply from which to provide him; he was not able to transcribe the text since he hastened to depart from this city in a hurry'.[139]

A number of scenarios can perhaps be envisaged. Texts could have been made available to visitors or foreign scribes to copy. The papal administration may have exerted some control over the copying process, sold or given copies to visitors, sent copies as diplomatic presents, or had a system for formal distribution at particular moments. Visitors to Rome and the Lateran palace may have been supplied with authorized copies. Alternatively, they may have made, or been required to make, their own copies from authorized versions available in the papal archive, paying for, or supplying from their own resources, both scribes and writing material. It is impossible to ascertain how much supervision of the copying process may have been exercised by the papal officials, but we may be entitled to imagine envoys arriving with supplies of parchment and a scribe in their entourage whose job it was to make copies, not only of the *Liber pontificalis* but also of texts relating to Roman liturgy, Roman martyrs, papal letters, and conciliar records.

The variety of extant copies in terms of their end dates, the number of Lives included, the mixing of recensions of the eighth-century lives, the range of plausible routes for texts to reach Francia, and the apparent haphazardness of the distribution evident from the manuscripts and

---

[138] Bougard 2009, p. 135 and see above, p. 180.

[139] Price, Booth, and Cubitt 2014, p. 411, and *PL* 87, col. 138: *Nam codices iam exinaniti sunt a nostra bibliotheca, et unde ei dare nullatenus habuimus, transcribere autem non potuit, quoniam festinanter de hac civitate regredi properavit.*

places of production or preservation considered in this chapter do not exclude any of these possible scenarios for acquiring and making copies of the papal history. We are, after all, equally ignorant about how other Roman texts were transmitted from Rome to other centres in Italy, beyond the Alps, or across the Mediterranean, apart from occasional glimpses. The *Codex epistolaris Carolinus* mentions the Roman sacramentary sent by Hadrian on request from Charlemagne, and one early ninth-century copy of this sacramentary refers to it being *ex authenticum*.[140] Similarly, reference is made to the canon law *Collectio Dionysio-Hadriana* received from Rome, Pope Paul sent 'a volume of antiphons and responsories, and also the *Grammar* of Aristotle, the *Geometry* of Dionysius the Areopagite, a book on orthography and one on grammar, all written in Greek, and also a night clock',[141] Pope Constantine II sent Pippin III the text in Latin and Greek of the synodical statement of faith made by Patriarch Theodore of Jerusalem, and Pope Hadrian I sent Charlemagne a copy of Pope Leo I's *Tome*.[142] Some of the specialist liturgical books may have been carried by the cantors who journeyed from Rome to Francia and England to teach chant, such as John the archcantor, and the singers associated with Chrodegang of Metz and the Bishop of Rouen.[143]

The Frankish copies of the *Liber pontificalis* are already at one remove from the acquisition of exemplars by whatever means. Most of them appear to reflect intervention on the part of the Franks themselves as well as Frankish reworking after receiving the text from Rome. Among all the Frankish copies of the papal history extant, this was particularly the case with the 'B' group containing the Frankish interpolations. The Frankish interpolations in the *Liber pontificalis* text, therefore, could have been made within the Carolingian royal writing office, or in a centre closely associated with the court with access to this collection. The

---

[140] CC 82 (Gundlach 89), Sacramentary of Bishop Hildoard of Cambrai: Cambrai, BM, MS 164. See Vogel 1981, pp. 79–85.

[141] CC 25 (Gundlach 24), p. 529: *id est antiphonale et responsale, insimul Artem grammaticam Aristolis, Dionisii Ariopagitis geometricam, orthografiam, grammaticam, omnes Greco eloquio scriptas, nec non et horologium nocturnum.*

[142] CC 76 (Gundlach 70) and CC 99 (Gundlach 99).

[143] CC 43 (Gundlach 41). See Ó Carragáin 2013.

coincidence between the Frankish interpolations in the *Liber pontificalis* and the *Codex epistolaris Carolinus,* moreover, suggests that they may have been complementary parts of a project in the late 780s and the early 790s to promote papal authority, to enhance knowledge of the history of Rome and its bishops, and to consolidate the association between the Franks and Rome.

The Contribution from the Abbey of St Denis?

It may be possible to get even closer to the source of these Frankish interpolations. The place of production of the 'B' copies of the *Liber pontificalis* which contain them is significant, for all the extant 'B' manuscripts can be located to major Carolingian centres: St Denis, Reims, Auxerre, Laon, Cologne, St Amand, and St Bertin. All these centres, especially St Denis and its abbots, had connections with the royal court in the early Carolingian period. The earliest 'B' codex, Paris, BnF lat. 13729, merits special attention in this respect, for it seems to offer the key to the origin of the Frankish interpolations. The codex was probably written at St Denis in the 820s, and contains the *Liber pontificalis* up to Life 97 of Pope Hadrian I. Both the abbey of St Denis and its abbots had close associations with the Frankish royal court and the Carolingian rulers from the middle of the eighth century until the end of the ninth century. The book itself looks as if it was written for someone of high social standing. It is large, exceptionally elegant in its layout, and very well written. It has an elaborate sequence of title pages at the beginning of the book, ornamental use of alternating lines of red and black capital letters, and careful indication of each new biography with a red numeral and the name of each pope in large, graceful uncial letters. The book itself was clearly designed with a prominent EXPLICIT to end with the Life of Hadrian. The marginal notes in a later ninth-century hand than that of the main text are added from fol. 7r onwards. They take particular note of provisions the popes made for clerical organization and liturgical innovation in the form of abbreviated or summary subject indicators in the margin, many of which appear to refer to a copy of the Felician epitome as well. Because it went no further than the Life of Hadrian, Duchesne considered the St Denis codex and its twin, made at

Laon for the Archbishop of Cologne,[144] to have been copied from an exemplar made *c.*792.[145] The surmise was based on the manuscript containing no papal biographies after Pope Hadrian I (†795) but, as we have seen, the number of copies of the later lives that reached Francia is so meagre that it may give us no more than an approximate indication of the date of the exemplar. If Duchesne were correct, this would suggest that the interpolations had been composed by 792. Whatever the case, the St Denis manuscript prompts speculation about who made the Frankish interpolations as well as who ensured their further dissemination.

The date of the codex itself is crucial, for it was produced during the abbacy of no less a personage than Hilduin, Abbot of St Denis (785–855 and abbot from 815), chaplain at the Carolingian court in the early part of the reign of Louis the Pious. Hilduin accompanied the co-Emperor Lothar to Rome in 824 in relation to the election of Pope Eugenius, and he has also been associated with a number of literary projects, especially those concerned with the cult of St Denis or Dionysius.[146] He may even have been responsible for a portion of the *Annales regni Francorum.* Hilduin himself, however, was the successor as abbot of a long line of prominent supporters of the royal house, notably Fulrad (751–84) and Maginarius (784–92), who had served as envoys to Italy and Rome, advisers to Pippin, Charlemagne, and his brother Carloman, and had been active in matters of church reform and discussions of doctrine and liturgy as well as politics. They were succeeded in the abbacy by the Lombard Fardulf (792–806), another loyal political supporter of the Carolingian ruler.[147] Quite apart from the abbots' special connections to the Carolingian rulers, the abbey of St Denis was especially favoured by

---

[144] *LP* I, pp. clxxvi–clxxvii.

[145] On Laon, BM Suzanne Martinet, MS 342 see Contreni 1978, pp. 50–1. The other ninth-century Group 'B' manuscripts are Cologne, Dombibliothek 164, Leiden, VLQ 41, Brussels, Bibliothèque royale MS 8380-9012, Vienna, ÖNB Cod. 473. Group 'D' identified by Duchesne is very close to 'B' and shares the Frankish interpolations. Its ninth-century representatives are Paris, BnF lat. 5516 and BnF lat. 2769, though the latter contains Lives 91–4 only: see Duchesne, *LP* I, pp. cxciii–cxciv, and the comment by Bougard 2009, p. 134.

[146] Brown 1989, Brown 2005, Taylor 2013, and Lapidge 2017.

[147] Stoclet 1993, McKitterick 2008, pp. 43–9, Garipzanov 2008, pp. 301–3.

Charlemagne's father King Pippin III, and it was there that Pippin III was buried in 768. Pippin's successors maintained this close association, and Louis the Pious was of particular importance for his patronage of the abbey, its intellectual pursuits, and the crucial position of the abbey and its saint in Carolingian politics.[148] The Carolingian church of St Denis even emulated St Peter's basilica in Rome and it would be perverse not to entertain the notion that the papal examples of church-building in the *Liber pontificalis* could have served as one inspiration.[149] It is significant that it was also at St Denis that the earliest copy of the *Constitutum Constantini* or 'Donation of Constantine' was preserved, albeit based on a still earlier exemplar. The *Constitutum Constantini,* moreover, was added to the 'St Denis formulary', which includes no fewer than eight papal charters in favour of St Denis and a letter from Pope Hadrian I to Abbot Maginarius.[150] Given the knowledge, interests, and connections of the abbots of St Denis, their court connections, and ultimately the abbey's production of the exceptionally fine copy of the *Liber pontificalis* in Paris, BnF lat. 13729, it may not be too great a conjecture to suppose a St Denis abbot's responsibility for the Frankish interpolations of the 'B' text of the *Liber pontificalis,* or at least the role in their composition of someone at St Denis.

The concentration of the interpolations in the Life of Pope Stephen II, who played such a pivotal role in the legitimization of the Carolingian dynasty, makes the contriving of the interpolations in the time of Fulrad, Maginarius, or Fardulf of St Denis more likely. Hilduin's intervention cannot be excluded, but he can presumably get some credit for the further promotion and dissemination of these Frankish interpolations. The composition of the Frankish interpolations in the last decade of the eighth century or later becomes more probable in relation to Duchesne's 'C' class, that is, the other family of Carolingian copies of the *Liber pontificalis.* They lack the Frankish interpolations.

---

[148] Fully demonstrated by Brown 1989.   [149] Emerick 2011.
[150] Paris, BnF lat. 2777: *Constitutum Constantini,* ed. Fuhrmann, and on Paris, BnF lat. 2777 see McKitterick 2008, pp. 43–9. See the discussion of this manuscript by Große 2018.

Arn of St Amand and Salzburg

The earliest 'C' manuscript extant was produced at the monastery of St Amand in the late eighth century, during the abbacy of Arn, later Bishop of Salzburg. The palaeographical indications make a date of *c.*790 probable, but the script unfortunately cannot be more precisely dated.[151] The text stops with Life 94 of Pope Stephen II. The list of popes at the beginning of the manuscript also only went as far as Stephen II, though the names from Paul I to Stephen V were added by a later hand. The text of Life 94, however, is neither the 'Frankish' nor the 'original', but the 'Lombard' or Lucchese version. This would indicate that the 'Frankish' version was not yet available. By the time another St Amand copy of the *Liber pontificalis* was produced, in connection with the crowning of Charles the Bald at Metz in 869, the Frankish version of Life 94 was substituted.[152] Again it is necessary to speculate from whom or from which centre the St Amand copy might have been procured. The entire text, including the 'Lombard' version of Life 94, could have been acquired when Arn was visiting Italy. Arn himself went to Rome in 787 with Abbot Hunric of Mondsee in relation to the dispute between Charlemagne and Tassilo of Bavaria, in 798 to receive the pallium for Salzburg, and again in 799–800 as part of the commission of enquiry into the circumstances surrounding the election of Pope Leo III.[153] Arn also served in Pippin of Italy's administration at the end of the eighth century.[154] As François Bougard points out, moreover, even after his elevation to the bishopric of Salzburg, Arn continued to visit St Amand. Arn's special interest in Rome had a practical and devotional dimension in addition to his political and diplomatic activities. It can be documented in another late eighth-century book with which he is associated and which he may have commissioned or owned. Among other texts it contains two famous topographical notes with itineraries for a pilgrim visiting the extra- and intramural saints' shrines of Rome.[155] All this

---

[151] Leiden, VLQ 60.   [152] Vienna, ÖNB 473: see above, pp. 194–5.

[153] See Bougard 2009, pp. 141–2.

[154] On Arn's varied career see Niederkorn Bruck and Scharer (eds.) 2004 and Diesenberger 2015.

[155] ÖNB 795: see McKitterick 2006, pp. 45–7.

makes St Amand's production of such a fine copy of the *Liber pontificalis* all the more explicable, but Arn's court connections also make it likely he would have included the Frankish interpolations had they existed when the copy was made.

Conclusion

The manuscripts discussed in this chapter reflect how the *Liber pontificalis* texts offered an historical understanding of the papacy as a fundamental element of the Christian church in all the centres where copies of the text were made, preserved, used, and read. Both Lombards and Franks were fitted into this Christian history by the additions they made to the text, by the codicological context into which the *Liber pontificalis* was inserted, and by the cultural and intellectual contexts in which the book found its place. Meagre though the number of survivors be, the papal administration continued to disseminate this form of representation of the popes well into the ninth century. The unique combination of narrative and definition of doctrinal or other ecclesiological matters, especially in the accounts of councils, was an important vehicle of communication and potentially for consultation. It is conceivable that the text was perceived as presenting the popes as a virtual presence, as well as offering an important source of textual authority and an historical framework within which to understand all the other texts emanating from Rome that were so fundamental to the beliefs and practices of the Christian church.

The *Liber pontificalis* may not have been a text people had to possess in the early middle ages, but nevertheless, as a full, truncated, or abridged text, it can be located to a remarkable number of centres in Italy and Carolingian Francia. As observed above, only a handful of any extant copies of the full text, and none at all of the epitomes, include Lives after Life 94 of Stephen II. Most codices revert to a simple list of names and rarely even details of the length of the pontificate for the popes thereafter. When incomplete copies or abridgements were made of the *Liber pontificalis,* therefore, we need to consider whether this is because that was all that was available or because the copyists and those who commissioned the copies wanted it in this form. Is every text in every manuscript not only a possible consequence of decision and choice but also to fulfil a particular purpose? To what degree does it retain Vircillo Franklin's notion of 'local interpolation and manipulation'?[156] Ultimately, it is on these broader questions that the reception and recopying of the full text of the *Liber pontificalis* in so many different places, the creation of the epitomes, and the composition of local interpolations invite us to reflect.

For later eighth- and ninth-century audiences, especially within the Carolingian realm, the extant manuscripts suggest that the earlier portion of the text, from St Peter to Constantine I, was available as a richly textured historical narrative, full of powerful claims about papal authority and the championing of orthodoxy, the apostolic succession, the papal contributions to the organization of the church and the liturgy, the history of the early church and martyrs of Rome, and of the papacy as an institution.

Still more questions than answers have emerged, most particularly about the functions of the text, or at least portions of it. There are many more things which could and should be said about all these manuscripts, but for my purposes here I wish to emphasize that it looks as if the text of the *Liber pontificalis,* at least to 715, was disseminated as a whole in the early Carolingian period, and it may be that the Naples and Turin fragments indicate that the whole text, as originally conceived in the recension of the mid-sixth century, but possibly in a revised edition made in the seventh century, was also once transmitted in its entirety. As already mentioned, Gregory of Tours knew the text as early as the 590s, and Bede's use of the text when writing both the *De ratione temporum* and the *Historia ecclesiastica* is obvious.[157] Textual comparisons are invaluable for providing information about possible connections between the centres or scribes responsible for producing the different members of a text family, but there is still a great deal of work to be done in this respect.

The arguments about the date of redaction of the first section of *Liber Pontificalis* are still far from settled. The oddities of the manuscript

---

[156] Franklin 2018, p. 105.   [157] Hilliard 2018.

transmission, so fully explored in the past century and a half, are inextricably entwined with questions about the production and distribution of this fascinating text. Variant versions also suggest the lack of control that could be exerted by Rome once the text had reached another destination. In its new homes, the text could fulfil the purpose the authors had intended, but serve other purposes as well. Common sense would suggest that each surviving manuscript witness to the *Liber pontificalis* was designed for a particular context, but the preceding discussion has exposed how difficult it is to be certain or precise about many of these contexts.

From all this evidence of full copies, epitomes, and papal catalogues, the routes and the circumstances by which the *Liber pontificalis,* sections of it, or abridged versions may have reached centres in Italy or north of the Alps can only be a matter of speculation. I have indicated a cluster of indications that the Carolingian court itself was implicated in the dissemination of a special 'Frankish' redaction of the papal history. It will be clear from the foregoing discussion how often it is necessary to fall back upon possible connections or circumstances to explain the physical presence of so many copies of the text. Yet the manuscripts do reflect how the *Liber pontificalis* came to be in a position to shape perceptions of Rome and the history and authority of the popes in the early middle ages. The *Liber pontificalis* did not always retain the character of contemporary polemic and political argument that had been such an important aspect of its initial production and continuation. The epitomes in particular appear to indicate the principal tags for remembrance attached to individual popes, but the full texts also witness to scribes and commissioners of manuscripts wanting all the details, not least the exhaustive lists of donations and buildings. The creative codicological associations of conciliar records, canon law, and papal decretals in many early manuscripts containing copies of the *Liber pontificalis* in one form or another are significant for what they reveal about the dissemination and reception of the text as well as the conceptualization of ecclesiastical authority. The compilers, scribes, commissioners, annotators, and epitomizers of the late eighth- and ninth-century copies of the text that included the history of the popes only up to the second half of the eighth century were apparently more interested in the *Liber pontificalis* for its historical, doctrinal, liturgical, and legal content than for an account of contemporary papal politics. But that same historical and legal framework and the authority of the popes it incorporated was subsequently put to the service of new contemporary arguments.[158]

---

[158] See Harder 2014 and 2015.

Conclusion

The Power of a Text

I HAVE ARGUED IN THIS BOOK THAT THE *LIBER PONTIFICALIS* constructed a distinctive image of the popes and a particular representation of their history, of their role as successors to St Peter, and of the city of Rome itself as a holy city of Christian saints and martyrs. The city of Rome was transformed in the imagination as well as in the text. I have shown how the *Liber pontificalis* acts as a prism through which we can observe the politics and ideology of Rome's transformation from imperial city to Christian capital, the way the Bishop of Rome is represented as establishing a visible display of power within the city, and how the text reiterates the spiritual and ministerial role of the bishop both within Rome and for the wider Christian community.

In making my principal focus the set of papal biographies before the mid-eighth century, and especially the first section of the text produced in sixth-century Rome, I have echoed the concentration of this part of the text in its early manuscript manifestations, even taking into account the way Franks turned their attention in the eighth-century Lives to the integration of the Franks into the history of the popes. That papal history, moreover, was designed to emulate imperial history, in which the history and identity of Rome itself and the perception of the imperial past were gradually transformed, while simultaneously acting as a continuation of the Acts of the Apostles.

I have emphasized that the text of the *Liber pontificalis* has to be considered as a whole, that is, the original sixth-century composition above all, together with its seventh- and eighth-century continuations, and the epitomes. Thus, information about particular events or buildings from individual biographies has to be critically assessed within the context of the overall purpose and content of the text. The *Liber pontificalis* creates an image of a holy city of Christian martyrs alongside and organically developing from the antique and imperial past. The text constantly evokes the city of Rome itself, its imperial past, its people, and its public monuments. Although the *Liber pontificalis* occasionally offers glimpses of other members of Rome's population acting as patrons, it presents an overwhelming impression of a papal monopoly of church building in the city. The textual replacement of emperors with popes as patrons and benefactors in the *Liber pontificalis* has a material counterpart. For those in Rome, the *Liber pontificalis* acted to reinforce the foundations by placing them in an historical context and proposing a chronological sequence for the buildings in the city, many of which had been constructed a good century before the composition of the original sixth-century text. For its readers, therefore, the *Liber pontificalis* could act as a virtual Rome, displaying a Christian city grafted onto its imperial foundations. The city space is effectively mapped in writing in which the bishop and the people are dynamically active players, all set within an historical narrative.

Alongside the succession of popes from St Peter, the *Liber pontificalis* also constructed a new Petrine chronology. Yet the popes are credited with establishing many aspects of the liturgical rhythm of the year as well as the daily religious veneration, articulated in text and chant, and choreographed in ritual performance and procession in the city's churches and streets. In emphasizing the pope's role, the *Liber pontificalis* offered a new and Roman framework in which to understand the Christian liturgical past as well as the regulation of the city's perceptions of time, its space, and its rituals. The *Liber pontificalis* reflects the way the popes developed their power and control within the city in the practical attention to the city's fabric and to the people of Rome. I have also examined the way the text pays special attention to the elaboration of ecclesiastical rules and decisions, and how papal influence and the affirmation of papal responsibility were extended far beyond the city in the context of the dissemination and reception of canon law. These ecclesiological aspects of the text reinforce the understanding that the production of the text within the papal administration was most probably encouraged by the pope, and neither a covert nor a subsidiary venture.

The *Liber pontificalis* might be considered to be unnervingly selective when set in the context of the sophisticated theological, pastoral, and exegetical treatises, letters, and sermons produced by the popes who form the subjects of the *Liber pontificalis*. Yet I have also suggested that it was distinctive in relation to all the other texts produced in Italy when the *Liber pontificalis* was being composed. It was a pioneering historical enterprise, essentially transforming an archive into an historical narrative. No other historical narrative, moreover, gave much more than walk-on parts to the popes, let alone set them centre stage. In proposing that the *Liber pontificalis* in consequence potentially had a key role to play within early medieval Europe in forming perceptions and shaping the memory of the city of Rome and of its bishops, I have highlighted the text's clever emphases in the history of the popes, its distinctive commentary on events, and the prompts to memory it contains. The *Liber pontificalis* can be understood both as a record of memories and as a shaper of memory, and as a textual expression of physical and ideological developments. The ideological agenda developed in the *Liber pontificalis*, moreover, was not static. The initial conception in the middle of the sixth century was taken up and developed further by the subsequent authors. The whole history can be seen to have acquired textual authority in its own right, for it became an instrument for the propagation of the notions of institutional authority and orthodoxy.

Any text has to be read with its potential audience in mind. By audience, I do not mean simply the likely categories, numbers, or geographical distribution of people who may have had access to it, though these are important too. It is also a question in the *Liber pontificalis*'s case of the mental predispositions of its immediate audience. This can only be surmised from the way the text itself was constructed, and the degree to which its structure and content not only fulfilled the expectations of its intended audience in terms of theme, but how the authors relied on the intended audiences' cultural preparedness and existing knowledge, their attitude and sensitivity to genres, their appreciation of the style of presentation of the subject matter, and appetite for certain details. The *Liber pontificalis* was designed to articulate the cultural memory of Christian Rome. It was certainly a precis of a far vaster compendium of information and reports, but it distilled the essential elements that the authors wished to communicate. The papal history emerges therefore as a particular form of communication of a very special history and a statement of the papal position on essential points of doctrine and the history of the church. The *Liber pontificalis* forms an essential complement to the range of other texts emanating from Rome which were the bedrock of the Christian communities of Europe.

The manuscript evidence, moreover, offered the opportunity to investigate further the question of audience and to trace the potential power of the text by investigating its transmission and reception, especially in Italy and Francia in the early middle ages. I have suggested that the text's dissemination, although oddly weighted in favour of Francia and northern Italy, nevertheless indicated a very extensive dissemination and use in many different contexts of this distinctive presentation of papal history and description of the physical city.

For historians, there is a constant tension between representation and reality in interpreting the primary evidence, and a further tension between any self-consciousnesss of a particular historical context on the part of our sources, and our own interpretations thereof. The resources of past texts, historical knowledge and tradition, legal claims, and assertions of authority on which the writers of the *Liber pontificalis* drew were not necessarily objective or neutral in themselves, but designed to shape memory. This book has suggested that the *Liber pontificalis* is one lens through which we as modern historians are directed towards a particular understanding of the history of the popes and of the city of Rome by its sixth-century writers and seventh- and early eighth-century continuators. The *Liber pontificalis*'s narrative, drawing on its own particular resources of the past and cultural memory, therefore, presents a positive and dynamic picture of a new institutional identity, apparently created to persuade posterity that Christian Rome's early history of low social status, poverty, persecution, and vulnerability was a formative strength. It is a text whose composition and purpose as well as its content both documented and induced change. The popes are represented as active agents in the gradual development of the papacy as an institution, and thereby as the core of the Christian church. In the insistence on the apostolic succession, the pope became the logical continuation and institutionalization of the work of Christ and his disciples. As we have seen from the discussion of the text's reception in the eighth and ninth centuries in the final chapter of this book, the *Liber pontificalis* is a remarkable instance of a text with power, compiled in the early middle ages and widely disseminated with a palpable effect. It can be understood as part of an effort to shape the time and context in which it was written by means of a particular representation of the past. The *Liber pontificalis* not only constructed the historical identity of the pope as Bishop of Rome and head of the universal church, and thus *invented* the papacy, but continued the history of Rome itself in a way which definitively and durably augmented and enriched the identity of the city.

Bibliography

Primary Sources

Abbo of Fleury, *Liber pontificalis*, ed. L. M. Gantier, *L'abrégé du* Liber pontificalis *d'Abbon de Fleury (vers 950–1004): une histoire des papes en l'an mil* (Louvain la Neuve, Leuven, and Brussels, 2004).

Agnellus, *Liber pontificalis ecclesiae Ravennatis*, ed. D. M. Deliyannis, CCSL Continuatio Mediacvalis 199 (Turnhout, 2006), and English trans. D. M. Deliyannis, *The Book of Pontiffs of Agnellus of Ravenna* (Washington, DC, 2004).

Amalarius of Metz, *Liber officialis*, ed. J. Hanssens, reprinted with English trans. E. Knibbs, *On the Liturgy: Amalar of Metz* (Washington, DC, 2014).

Anon., *Vita sancti Amandi* I, ed. B. Krusch, MGH SRM 5, pp. 428–49.

Anonymus Valesianus, ed. I. König, *Aus der Zeit Theoderichs des Großen: Einleitung, Text, Übersetzung, Kommentar einer anonymen Quelle* (Darmstadt, 1997); ed. and trans. J. C. Rolfe, in *Ammianus Marcellinus* III (Cambridge, Mass., 1972), pp. 532–69.

Arator, *De actibus apostolorum*, ed. Λ. P. MacKinlay, *Aratoris subdiaconi de actibus apostolorum*, CSEL (Vienna, 1951); ed. A. Orban, *Aratoris subdiaconi Historia apostolica*, CCSL 130, 130Λ (Turnhout, 2006); English trans. R. J. Schrader, J. L. Roberts, and J. F. Makowski, *Arator's On the Acts of the Apostles* (Atlanta, Ga., 1992).

Bede, *De ratione temporum*, ed. C. W. Jones, *Bedae opera didascalica*, CCSL 123A–C (Turnhout, 1975–80), trans. F. Wallis, *Bede: the Reckoning of Time* (Liverpool, 1999).

Bede, *Historia ecclesiastica gentis Anglorum*, ed. B. Colgrave and R. A. B. Mynors, *Bede, The Ecclesiastical History of the English People* (Oxford, 1969).

Benedict of Nursia, *Regula*, ed. A. de Vogüé and J. Neufville, Sources chrétiennes 181–6 (Paris, 1971–2).

Boniface, *Epistolae*, ed. R. Rau, *Bonifatii Epistolae. Willibaldi Vita Bonifatii* (Darmstadt, 1968).

Capitula episcoporum, ed. P. Brommer, MGH Capitula Episcoporum (Hanover, 1974).

Carmen de synodo Ticiensi, ed. L. Bethmann, MGH SRL 1 (Hanover, 1878), pp. 189–91.

Cassiodorus, *Historia ecclesiastica tripartita*, ed. R. Hanslik and W. Jacob, *Cassiodorus–Epiphanius, Historia ecclesiastica tripartita* (Vienna, 1952).

Cassiodorus, *Variae*, ed. T. Mommsen, MGH AA 12 (Berlin, 1894), English trans. (selection) S. J. B. Barnish, *Selected Variae of Magnus Aurelius Cassiodorus Senator* (Liverpool, 1992).

Catalogus episcoporum Neapolitanorum, ed. G. Waitz, MGH SRL 1 (Hanover, 1878), pp. 436–9.

Codex epistolaris Carolinus, ed. W. Gundlach, MGH Epp 5, Merowingici et Karolini aevi III (Berlin, 1957); German trans. F. Hartmann and T. Orth-Müller, *Codex epistolaris Carolinus: frühmittelalterliche Papstbriefe an die Karolingerherrscher* (Darmstadt, 2017); English trans. R. McKitterick, R. Pollard, R. Price, and D. van Espelo, *Codex epistolaris Carolinus*,

Translated Texts for Historians (Liverpool, in press); facsimile ed. F. Unterkircher, *Codex epistolaris Carolinus*, Codices Selecti 3 (Graz, 1962).

Collectio Avellana, ed. O. Guenther, *Epistolae imperatorum pontificum aliorum inde ab a. CCCLXVII usque ad a. DLIII datae Avellana quae dicitur collectio* (Vienna, 1895).

Collectio Dionysiana, ed. A. Strewe, *Die Canonessammlung des Dionysius Exiguus in der erstern Redaktion* (Leipzig, 1931).

Comes Romanus Wirziburgensis, ed. H. Thurn, *Comes Romanus Wirziburgensis: Faksimile Ausgabe des Codex M.P.th.f.62 der Universitätsbibliothek Würzburg* (Graz, 1968).

Concilium Aquisgranensis 809, ed. H. Willjung, *Das Konzil von Aachen 809*, MGH Conc. 2, Suppl. 2 (Hanover, 1998).

Concilium Chalcedonensis 451, ed. E. Schwartz, *Acta conciliorum oecumenicorum* 2.3 (Berlin, 1935); trans. R. Price and M. Gaddis, *The Acts of the Council of Chalcedon*, 3 vols (Liverpool, 2005).

Concilium Constantinopolis 553, ed. E. Schwartz, *Acta conciliorum oecumenicorum* 4.1 (Berlin, 1971); trans. R. Price, *The Acts of the Council of Constantinople of 553; with Related Texts on the Three Chapters Controversy*, 2 vols (Liverpool, 2009).

Concilium Constantinopolitanum a. 691/2 in Trullo habitum (Concilium Quinisextu), ed. H. Ohme, *Acta conciliorum oecumenicorum, Series secunda* 2.4 (Berlin, 2013).

Concilium Lateranense a. 649 celebratum, ed. R. Riedinger, *Acta conciliorum oecumenicorum, Series secunda* 1 (Berlin, 1984); English trans. R. Price, P. Booth, and C. Cubitt, *The Acts of the Lateran Synod of 649* (Liverpool, 2014).

Concilium universale Constantinopolitanum tertium (680/1), ed. R. Riedinger, *Acta conciliorum oecumenicorum, Series secunda* 2.2 (Berlin, 1990–1).

Constitutum Constantini ('Donation of Constantine'), ed. H. Fuhrmann, *Constitutum Constantini*, MGH Fontes Iuris Germanici Antiqui 10 (Hanover, 1968).

Corpus Inscriptionum Latinarum (Berlin, 1863–).

Cyprian, *Epistolae*, ed. G. W. Clarke and G. F. Diercks, *Sancti Cypriani episcopi Opera*, CCSL 3 (Turnhout, 1972).

De libris recipiendis et non recipiendis, ed. E. von Dobschütz, *Das Decretum Gelasianum de libris recipiendis et non recipiendis*, Texte und Untersuchungen zur Geschichte der altchristlichen Literatur 38, Heft 4 (Leipzig, 1912).

Didascaliae apostolorum; canonum ecclesiasticorum; traditionis apostolicae versiones latinae, ed. E. Tidner, Texte und Untersuchungen zur Geschichte der altchristlichen Literatur 75 (Berlin, 1963).

Donation of Constantine, *see Constitutum Constantini*.

Eberhard of Friuli, will, ed. I. de Coussemaker, *Cartulaire de l'abbaye de Cysoing et de ses dépendances* (Lille, 1885), reprinted in P. E. Schramm and F. Mütherich, *Denkmale der deutschen Könige und Kaiser* 1 (Munich, 1981), pp. 93–4.

Einsiedeln Itinerary, ed. G. Walser, *Die Einsiedler Inschriftensammlung und der Pilgerführer durch Rom (Codex Einsidlensis 326): Facsimile, Umschrift, Übersetzung und Kommentar* (Stuttgart, 1987).

Ennodius, *Opera*, ed. F. Vogel, MGH AA 7 (Berlin, 1885).

Epigraphic inscriptions, ed. L. Cardin, *Epigrafia a Roma nel primo medioevo (secoli IV–X): modelli grafici e tipologie d'uso* (Rome, 2008).

Epiphanius of Salamis, *Panarion*, ed. F. Williams, *The Panarion of Epiphanius of Salamis in Cyprus* (Leiden, 2nd ed., 2009).

Eugippius, *Excerpta Augustini*, ed. P. Knoll, CSEL 9.1 (Vienna, 1885).

Eugippius, *Regula* 1, ed. F. Villégas and A. de Vogüé, CSEL 87 (Vienna, 1976).

Eusebius-Jerome, *Chronicon*, ed. R. Helm, *Eusebius Werke* 7: *Eusebii Chronicon: Hieronymi continuatio*, Die griechischen christlichen Schriftsteller der ersten Jahrhunderte 70, 2nd edition (Berlin, 1956); *Eusebii Chronicon Hieronymi continuatio*, ed. B. Jeanjean and B. Lançon, *Saint Jérôme Chronique: continuation de la Chronique d'Eusèbe, années 326–378* (Rennes, 2004).

Eusebius–Rufinus, *Historia ecclesiastica*, ed. T. Mommsen, 'Die lateinische Übersetzung des Rufinus', in E. Schwartz, ed., *Eusebius Werke* 2.1, *Die Kirchengeschichte*, Die griechischen christlichen Schriftsteller der ersten drei Jahrhunderte 14 (Leipzig, 1903); trans. P. R. Amidon, *Rufinus of Aquileia, History of the Church* (Washington, DC, 2016).

Flodoard, *De triumphis Christi*, ed. P. C. Jacobsen, *Flodoard von Reims: sein Leben und seine Dichtung 'De triumphis Christi'*, Mittellateinische Studien und Texte 10 (Leiden, 1978).

Flodoard, *Historia Remensis ecclesiae*, ed. M. Stratmann, *Die Geschichte der Reimser Kirche, Flodoard von Reims*, MGH SS 36 (Hanover, 1998).

Frechulf, *Historiae*, ed. M. Allen, *Frechulfi Lexoviensis episcopi opera omnia*, CCCM 169 (Turnhout, 2002).

Gesta episcoporum Neapolitanorum, ed. G. Waitz, MGH SRL 1 (Hanover, 1878), pp. 398–436.

Gesta sanctorum patrum Fontanellensis coenobii, ed. P. Pradié, *Chronique des Abbés de Fontenelle (Saint-Wandrille)* (Paris, 1999).

Gregory I, pope, *Dialogorum libri IV de miraculis patrum italicorum*, ed. A. de Vogüé, Sources Chrétiennes 251, 260, 265 (Paris, 1978–80).

Gregory I, pope, *Registrum epistolarum*, ed. D. Norberg, CC 140, 140A (Turnhout, 1982); English trans. J. R. C. Martyn, *The Letters of Gregory the Great*, 3 vols (Toronto, 2004).

Gregory I, pope, *Regula pastoralis*, ed. F. Rommel, Sources Chrétiennes 381–2 (Paris, 1992).

Gregory of Tours, *Historiae*, ed. B. Krusch and W. Levison, MGH SRM 1.1 (Hanover, 1951).

Gregory of Tours, *In gloria martyrum*, ed. B. Krusch and W. Levison, MGH SRM 1.2 (Hanover, 1951).

Hilduin of St Denis, *Passio S. Dionysii*, ed. M. Lapidge, *Hilduin of St Denis, The passio S. Dionysii* (Leiden, 2017).

Hincmar of Reims, *Epistulae*, ed. E. Perels, MGH Epp 8 (Berlin, 1939).

History of the Patriarchs of the Coptic Church of Alexandria Attributed to Sāwīrus ibn al-Muqaffaʿ, Bishop of el-Ashmunein, ed. and trans. B. T. A. Evetts, *Patrologia orientalis* 1, fasc. 2 and 4; 5, fasc. 1; 10, fasc. 5 (Paris, 1904–14).

Hraban Maur, *De institutione clericorum*, ed. D. Zempel, *Hrabanus Maurus, De institutione clericorum libri tres*, Freiburger Beiträge zur mittelalterlichen Geschichte 7 (Frankfurt am Main, 1996).

Irenaeus of Lyon, *Contra haereses*, ed. D. Unger and J. Dillon, *Against the Heresies, St Irenaeus of Lyon* (New York, 1992).

Itineraria, ed. R. Valentini and J. Zucchetti, *Itineraria et alia geographica*, CCSL 175 (Turnhout, 1965).

Jerome, *De viris illustribus*, ed. C. A. Bernouilli, *Hieronimus und Gennadius, De viris inlustribus* (Freiburg im Breisgau and Leipzig, 1895), and E. C. Richardson, *Hieronymus de viris inlustribus. Gennadius de viris inlustribus* (Leipzig, 1896).

Jerome, *see also* Eusebius–Jerome.

Jordanes, *Getica*, ed. L. Möller, *Jordanes, Die Gotengeschichte* (Wiesbaden, 2012) and *Romana et Getica*, ed. T. Mommsen, MGH AA 5.1 (Berlin, 1882); English trans. L. Van Hoof and P. Van Nuffelen (Liverpool, 2019).

Justinian, Pragmatic Sanction 554, ed. R. Schöll and G. Kroll, *Corpus iuris civilis* III: *Novellae* (Zurich, 1968), App. VII, pp. 799–802; English trans. D. J. D. Miller and P. Sarris, *The Novels of Justinian: a Complete Annotated English Translation* (Cambridge, 2018) II, pp. 1116–30.

Lateran Council of 649, *see Concilium Lateranense a. 649 celebratum*.

Liber genealogus, ed. T. Mommsen, MGH AA 9, *Chronica minora* 1 (Berlin, 1892), pp. 154–96.

Liber pontificalis, ed. L. Duchesne, *Le Liber pontificalis: texte, introduction et commentaire*, 2 vols (Paris, 1886–92, repr. 1955); English trans. L. R. Loomis, *The Book of the Popes* (Liber pontificalis) (New York, 1916); trans. R. Davis, *The Book of Pontiffs* (Liber pontificalis): *the Ancient Biographies of the First Ninety Roman Bishops to* AD *715*, 3rd ed. (Liverpool, 2010);

BIBLIOGRAPHY

The Lives of the Eighth-Century Popes (Liber pontificalis), 2nd ed. (Liverpool, 2007); *The Lives of the Ninth-Century Popes* (Liber pontificalis): *the Ancient Biographies of Ten Popes from AD 817–891* (Liverpool, 1995); French trans. M. Aubrun, *Le livre des papes:* Liber pontificalis *(492–891)* (Turnhout, 2007).

Liber pontificalis, ed. T. Mommsen, *Liber pontificalis (pars prior)*, MGH Gesta Pontificum Romanorum 1.1 (Berlin, 1898).

Livy, *Ab urbe condita*, ed. B. O. Foster, *Livy in Fourteen Volumes* (Cambridge, Mass., 1967).

Lorsch book list, ed. A. Häse, *Mittelalterliche Bücherverzeichnisse aus Kloster Lorsch: Einleitung, Edition und Kommentar*, Beiträge zum Buch- und Bibliothekswesen 42 (Wiesbaden, 2002).

Martin I, pope, *Epistolae*, *PL* 87, cols 105–212.

Milo, *Vita sancti Amandi episcopi*, ed. B. Krusch, MGH SRM 5, pp. 440–83.

Missale Gothicum, ed. E. Rose, CCSL 159D (Turnhout, 2005); English trans. E. Rose, *The Gothic Missal* (Turnhout, 2017).

Monza relic list, ed. A. Petrucci, T.-O. Tjäder, and G. Cavallo, *Chartae Latinae Antiquiores* XXIX (Italy X) (Dietikon-Zurich, 1993).

Ordines Romani, ed. M. Andrieu, *Les Ordines Romani au haut moyen âge* II: *les Textes (Ordines I–XIII)* (Leuven, 1971); English trans. of *Ordo* I, E. G. C. F. Atchley, *Ordo Romanus Primus* (London, 1905) and J. G. Romano, *Liturgy and Society in Early Medieval Rome* (Farnham, 2014), pp. 219–48.

Papal charters, ed. H. Zimmermann, *Papsturkunden 896–1046*, 2 vols (Vienna, 1988).

Paul the Deacon, *Gesta episcoporum Mettensium*, ed. and English trans. D. Kempf, *Paul the Deacon, Liber de episcopis Mettensibus* (Leuven, 2013).

Pelagius II, pope, *Epistolae* 1, *PL* 72, cols 703–60.

'Pittacia (oleorum modeotiana)', ed. F. Glorie, in *Itineraria et alia geographica*, ed. R. Valentini and J. Zucchetti, CCSL 175 (Turnhout, 1965).

Procopius, *Wars*, ed. and trans H. B. Dewing (Cambridge, Mass., 1962); revised trans. A. Kaldellis, *The Wars of Justinian: Prokopios* (Indianapolis, 2014).

Reichenau book list, ed. P. Lehmann, *Mittelalterliche Bibliothekskataloge Deutschlands und der Schweiz* I: *die Diözesen Konstanz und Chur* (Munich, 1918), pp. 240–52.

St Gallen book list, ed. P. Lehmann, *Mittelalterliche Bibliothekskataloge Deutschlands und der Schweiz* I: *die Diözesen Konstanz und Chur* (Munich, 1918), pp. 66–82.

Strabo, *Geography*, ed. and English trans. H. L. Jones, *The Geography of Strabo* (Cambridge, Mass., 1932).

Theodoric, *Edictum Theoderici regis*, ed. F. Bluhme, MGH Leges nationum germanicarum 5 (Hanover, 1889), pp. 149–70.

Theophanes, *Chronicon*, English trans. C. Mango, R. Scott, and G. Greatrex, *The Chronicle of Theophanes Confessor: Byzantine and Near Eastern History, ad 284–813* (Oxford, 1997).

Vetus Gallica, ed. H. Mordek, *Kirchenrecht und Reform in Frankenreich: die* Collectio Vetus Gallica, *die älteste systematische Kanonessammlung des fränkischen Gallien. Studien und Edition*, Beiträge zur Geschichte und Quellenkunde des Mittelalters 1 (Berlin and New York, 1975).

Vetus Latina online edition of St John's Gospel, ed. P. H. Burton, J. Balserak, H. A. G. Houghton, and D. C. Parker (2007, updated 2015), www.iohannes.com.

Walafrid Strabo, *Libellus de exordiis et incrementis quarundam in observationibus ecclesiasticis rerum*, ed. and English trans. A. L. Harting-Corrêa, *Walahfrid Strabo's Libellus de exordiis et incrementis quarundam in observationibus ecclesiasticis rerum: a Translation and Liturgical Commentary* (Leiden, 1996).

BIBLIOGRAPHY

Secondary Literature

Adami, C. and A. M. Faccini, (2005), 'I manoscritti', in *Gregorio Magno e le radici cristiane dell'Europa* (Verona).

Adams, J. N. (1976), *The Text and Language of a Vulgar Latin Chronicle (Anonymus Valesianus II)* (London).

Adams, J. N. (2003), *Bilingualism and the Latin Language* (Cambridge).

Adams, J. N. (2016), *An Anthology of Informal Latin, 200 BC–AD 900: Fifty Texts with Translation and Linguistic Commentary* (Cambridge).

Adams, J. N. and N. Vincent (eds.) (2016), *Early and Late Latin: Continuity or Change?* (Cambridge).

Adams, J. N., M. Janse, and S. Swain (eds.), (2002), *Bilingualism in Ancient Society: Language Contact and the Written Word* (Cambridge).

Alchermes, J. A. (1995), 'Petrine politics: Pope Symmachus and the rotunda of St Andrew at Old St Peter's', *Catholic Historical Review* 81, pp. 1–40.

Allen, P. and B. Neil (eds.) (2013), *Crisis Management in Late Antiquity (410–590): a Survey of the Evidence from Episcopal Letters* (Leiden).

Allen, P. and B. Neil (eds.) (2015), *The Oxford Handbook of Maximus the Confessor* (Oxford).

Amerise, M. (2005), *Il battesimo di Costantino il Grande: storia di una scomoda eredità*, Hermes Einzelschriften 95 (Munich).

Amory, P. (1997), *People and Identity in Ostrogothic Italy, 489–554* (Cambridge).

Andaloro, M., G. Bordi, and G. Morganti (eds.) (2016), *Santa Maria Antiqua tra Roma e Bisanzio* (Rome).

Arnold, J. J. (2017), 'Theodoric and Rome: conquered but unconquered', *Antiquité tardive* 25, pp. 113–26.

Arnold, J. J., M. S. Bjornlie, and K. Sessa (eds.) (2016), *A Companion to Ostrogothic Italy* (Leiden).

Ashtor, E. (1984), *Histoire des prix et des salaires dans l'Orient médiévale* (Paris).

Assmann, A. (1999/2011), *Erinnerungsräume: Formen und Wandlungen des kulturellen Gedächtnisses* (1999, Munich); English translation: *Cultural Memory and Western Civilization: Functions, Media, Archives* (2011, Cambridge).

Assmann, J. (1999/2011), *Das kulturelle Gedächtnis: Schrift, Erinnerung und politische Identität in frühen Hochkulturen* (1999, Munich); English translation: *Cultural Memory and Early Civilization: Writing, Remembrance, and Political Imagination* (2011, Cambridge).

Aste, A. (2014), *Gli epigrammi di papa Damaso* (Tricase).

Atchley, E. G. C. F. (1905), *Ordo Romanus Primus* (London).

Augenti, A. (1996), *Il Palatino nel medioevo: archeologia e topografia (secoli VI–XIII)* (Rome).

Augenti, A. (2000), 'Continuity and discontinuity of a seat of power: the Palatine Hill from the fifth to the tenth century', in Smith (ed.) 2000, pp. 43–54.

Azzara, C. (1997), *L'ideologia del potere regio nel papato altomedievale (secoli VI–VIII)*, Testi, studi, strumenti 12 (Spoleto).

Babcock, R. (2000), 'A papyrus codex of Gregory the Great's Forty Homilies on the Gospels (London Cotton Titus C XV)', *Scriptorium* 50, pp. 280–9.

Baldovin, J. F. (1987), *The Urban Character of Christian Worship: the Origin, Development and Meaning of Stational Liturgy*, Orientalia Christiana Analecta 228 (Rome).

Baldwin, M. C. (2004), *Whose Acts of Peter? Text and Historical Context of the Actus Vercellensis* (Tübingen).

Ballardini, A. (2014), '"In antiquissimo ac venerabili Lateranensi palatio": la residenza dei pontefici secondo il *Liber Pontificalis*', in *Le corti nell'alto Medioevo*, Settimane 62, pp. 889–928.

Balzaretti, R., J. Barrow, and P. Skinner (eds.) (2018), *Italy and Early Medieval Europe: Papers for Chris Wickham on the Occasion of his 65th Birthday* (Oxford).

Bardill, J. (2012), *Constantine, Divine Emperor of the Christian Golden Age* (Cambridge).

Barnish, S. J. B. (1992), *Selected Variae of Magnus Aurelius Cassiodorus Senator* (Liverpool).

Barnish, S. J. B. (2008), 'Roman Responses to an unstable world: Cassiodorus' *Variae* in context', in S. Barnish, L. Cracco Ruggini, L. Cuppo, R. Marchese, M. Breu, *Vivarium in Context* (Vicenza), pp. 7–22.

Bauer, F. A. (2004), *Das Bild der Stadt Rom im Frühmittelalter: Papststiftungen im Spiegel des Liber pontificalis von Gregory dem Dritten bis zu Leo dem Dritten* (Wiesbaden).

Bauer, S. (2006), *The Censorship and Fortuna of Platina's Lives of the Popes in the Sixteenth Century* (Turnhout).

Bausi, A., C. Brockmann, M. Friedrich, and S. Kienitz (eds.) (2018), *Manuscripts and Archives: Comparative Views on Record Keeping* (Berlin).

Bavant, B. (1979), 'Le duché byzantine de Rome: origine, durée et extension géographique', *MEFRM* 91/1, pp. 41–88.

Behrwald, R. (2016), 'Senatoren als Stifter der Kirche im Spätantiken Rom', in M. Verhoeven, L. Bosman, and H. van Asperen (eds.), *Monuments and Memory: Christian Cult Buildings and Constructions of the Past. Essays in Honour of Sible de Blaauw*, Architectural Crossroads: Studies in the History of Architecture 3 (Turnhout), pp. 162–76.

Behrwald, R. and C. Witschel (eds.) (2012), *Rom in der Spätantike: historische Erinnerung im städtischen Raum* (Stuttgart).

Bevenot, M. (1961), *The Tradition of Manuscripts* (Oxford).

Bianchini, F. (1718), *Vita romanorum pontificum a beato Petro apostolo ad Nicolaum I perductae cura Anastasii s.r.e. bibliothecarii*, reprinted in *PL* 127 and 128 (1852, Paris).

Bischoff, B. (1967), 'Eine Sammelhandschrift Walahfrid Strabos (Cod. Sangall. 878)', *Mittelalterliche Studien* 2 (Stuttgart), pp. 34–51.

Bischoff, B. (1980), *Die sudostdeutsche Schreibschulen und Bibliotheken* 2 (Wiesbaden).

Bischoff, B. (1983), 'Manoscritti nonantolani disperse sull'epoca carolingia', *La Bibliofilia* 85, pp. 99–124.

Bischoff, B. (1998–2017), *Katalog der festländischen Handschriften des neunten Jahrhunderts (mit Ausnahme der wisiogotischen)* I: *Aachen–Lambach*, II: *Laon–Paderborn*; III: *Padua–Zwickau* (Wiesbaden).

Bischoff, B. and V. Brown (1985), 'Addenda to CLA', *Medieval Studies* 47, pp. 318–66.

Biscottini, P. and G. Sena Chiesa (eds.) (2012), *Costantino 313 d.C* (Milan).

Bjornlie, M. S. (2013), *Politics and Tradition between Rome, Ravenna, and Constantinople: a Study of Cassiodorus and the Variae 527–554* (Cambridge).

Blaauw, S. de (1994a), *Cultus et décor: liturgia e architettura nella Roma tardoantica e medievale. Basilica Salvatoris, Sanctae Mariae, Sancti Petri* (Vatican City).

Blaauw, S. de (1994b), 'Das Pantheon als christlicher Tempel', in H. Brandenburg, M. Jordan-Ruwe, and U. Real (eds.), *Bild und Formensprache der spätantiken Kunst: Hugo Brandenburg zum 65. Geburtstag* (Münster), pp. 13–26.

Blaauw, S. de (2016), 'Die Gräber der frühen Päpste', in B. Schneidmüller (ed.), *Die Päpste: Amt und Herrschaft in Antike, Mittelalter und Renaissance* (Regensburg), pp. 77–99.

Blair-Dixon, K. (2007), 'Memory and authority in sixth-century Rome: the *Liber pontificalis* and the *Collectio avellana*', in Cooper and Hillner (eds.) 2007, pp. 59–76.

Blaudeau, P. (2006), *Alexandrie et Constantinople (451–491): de l'histoire à la géo-ecclésiologie*, BEFAR 327 (Rome).

Blaudeau, P. (2012a), 'Between Petrine ideology and Realpolitik: the see of Constantinople in Roman geo-ecclesiology (449–536)', in G. Kelly and L. Grig (eds.), *Two Romes: Rome and Constantinople in Late Antiquity* (Oxford), pp. 364–86.

Blaudeau, P. (2012b), *Le siège de Rome et l'Orient (448–536): étude géo-ecclésiologique*, Collection de l'École française de Rome 460 (Rome).

Blaudeau, P. (2015), 'Narrating papal authority (440–530): the adaptation of *Liber pontificalis* to the apostolic see's developing claims', in Dunn (ed.) 2015, pp. 127–40.

Bobrycki, S. (2018), 'The flailing women of Dijon: crowds in ninth-century Europe', *Past and Present* 240/12, pp. 3–46.

Bolgia, C. (2006), 'The mosaics of Gregory IV at S. Marco, Rome: papal response to Venice, Byzantium, and the Carolingians', *Speculum* 81, pp. 1–34.

Bolgia, C. (2017), *Reclaiming the Roman Capitol: Santa Maria in Aracoeli from the Altar of Augustus to the Franciscans*, c.500–1450 (Abingdon).

Bolgia, C., R. McKitterick, and J. Osborne (eds.) (2011), *Rome Across Time and Space: Cultural Transmission and the Exchange of Ideas*, c.500–1400 (Cambridge).

Bonamente, G., N. Lenski, and R. Lizzi Testa (eds.) (2012), *Costantino prima e dopo Costantino / Constantine Before and After Constantine* (Bari).

Bordi, G. (2011), 'Committenza laica nella chiesa di Sant'Adriano al foro romano nell'alto medioevo', in A. C. Quantavalle (ed.), *Medioevo: i commitenti* (Milan), pp. 421–32.

Bordi, G., J. Osborne, and E. Rubery (eds.) (2020), *Santa Maria Antiqua: the Sistine Chapel of the Early Middle Ages* (Turnhout).

Borgolte, M. (1995), *Petrus Nachfolge und Kaiserimitation: die Grablegen der Päpste, ihre Genese und Traditionsbildung*, Veröffentlichungen des Max-Planck-Instituts für Geschichte 95, 2nd ed. (Göttingen).

Bosman, L, I. Haynes, and P. Liverani (eds.) (2020), *The Lateran Basilica* (Cambridge).

Bougard, F. (2008), 'Anastase le Bibliothécaire ou Jean Diacre? Qui a récrit la Vie de Nicolas Ier et pourquoi', in J.-M. Martin, B. Martin Hisard, A. Paravicini Bagliani (eds.), *Vaticana et medievalia: études en l'honneur de Louis Duval-Arnould* (Florence), pp. 27–40.

Bougard, F., (2009), 'La composition, la réception et la diffusion du *Liber pontificalis* pour les vies des VIIIe–IXe siècles' in Bougard and Sot (eds.) 2009, pp. 127–52.

Bougard, F. and M. Sot (eds.) (2009), *Liber, gesta, histoire: écrire l'histoire des papes et des évêques, de l'Antiquité au XXIe siècle* (Paris).

Bowersock, G. W. (2005), 'Peter and Constantine' in W. Tronzo (ed.), *St Peter's in the Vatican* (Cambridge), pp. 3–15.

Bowman, A. K. and G. Woolf (eds.) (1994), *Literacy and Power in the Ancient World* (Cambridge).

Bowman, A. K. and G. Woolf (1994), 'Literacy and power in the ancient world', in Bowman and Woolf (eds.) 1994, pp. 1–16.

Boy, R. V. (2014), 'History of wars: narratives of crisis in power relations between Constantinople and Italy in the sixth century', in D. Dzino and K. Perry (eds.), *Byzantium, its Neighbours and its Cultures*, Byzantina Australiensia 20, pp. 209–22.

Brandenburg, H. (2004), *Die frühchristlichen Kirchen Roms vom 4. Bis zum 7. Jahrhundert: der Beginn der abendländischen Kirchenbaukunst* (Regensburg).

Brandenburg, H. (2011a), 'Petrus and Paulus in Rom? Die archäologischen Zeugnisse die Basilika S. Paul vor den Mauern und der Kult den Apostelfürsten', in O. Brandt and P. Pergola (eds.), *I Marmoribus vestita: miscellanea in onore de Federico Guidobaldi*, Studi di antichità Cristiana 83 (Vatican City), I, pp. 213–62.

Brandenburg, H. (2011b), 'The use of older elements in the architecture of fourth- and fifth-century Rome: a contribution to the evaluation of spolia' in Brilliant and Kinney (eds.) 2011, pp. 53–74.

Brandt, O. and F. Guidobaldi (2008), 'Il battisterio lateranense: nuove interpretazioni delle fasi strutturali', *Rivista di archeologia Cristiana* 84, pp. 189–282.

Bray, M. and R. Lanza (eds.) (2000), *Enciclopedia dei papi*, 3 vols (Rome).

Bremmer, J. M. (ed.) (1998), *The Apocryphal Acts of Peter: Magic, Miracles and Gnosticism* (Leuven).

Brent, A. (1995), *Hippolytus and the Roman Church in the Third Century: Communities in Tension before the Emergence of a Monarch Bishop*, Vigiliae Christianae Suppl. 31 (Leiden).

Bresslau, H. (1888), 'Papyrus und Pergament in der päpstliche Kanzlei bis zur Mitte des XI. Jahrhundert', *Mitteilungen des Instituts für Österreichische Geschichtsforschung* 9, pp. 1–33.

Brilliant, R. and D. Kinney (eds.) (2011), *Reuse Value: Spolia and Appropriation in Art and Architecture from Constantine to Sherrie Levine* (Farnham).

Brock, S. (1982), *The Liturgical Portions of the Didascalia*, Grove Liturgical Study 29 (Bramcote, Notts.), pp. 1–4.

Brown, E. A. (2005), '*Gloriosae:* Hilduin and the early liturgical celebration of St Denis', in S. A. Hayes-Healy (ed.), *Medieval Paradigms: Essays in Honor of Jeremy Du Quesnay Adams* (New York and London), pp. 39–82.

Brown, G. (1989), 'Politics and Patronage in the Abbey of Saint-Denis 814–898: the Rise of a Royal Patron Saint', unpublished DPhil. thesis, University of Oxford.

Brown, T. S. (1979), 'The Church of Ravenna and the imperial administration in the seventh century', *English Historical Review* 94, pp. 1–28.

Brown, T. S. (1984), *Gentlemen and Officers: Imperial Administration and Aristocratic Power in Byzantine Italy A.D. 554–800* (Rome).

Brown, T. S. (1998), 'Urban violence in early medieval Italy: the cases of Rome and Ravenna', in G. Halsall (ed.), *Violence and Society in the Early Medieval West* (Woodbridge), pp. 76–89.

Brubaker, L. (2010), 'Gifts and prayers: the visualization of gift giving in Byzantium and the mosaics of Hagia Sophia', in Davies and Fouracre (eds.) 2010, pp. 33–61.

Brubaker, L. and J. Haldon (2011), *Byzantium in the Iconoclast Era (c.680–850): a History* (Cambridge).

Buchner, M. (1926), 'Zur Überlieferungsgeschichte des *Liber pontificalis* und zu seiner Verbreitung im Frankenreiche im 9. Jahrhundert: zugleich ein Beitrag zur Geschichte der karolingischen Hofbibliothek und Hofkapelle', *Römische Quartalschrift* 34, pp. 141–65.

Buckton, D. (1988), 'Byzantine enamel and the West', *Byzantinische Forschungen* 13, pp. 235–44.

Burgersdijk, D. W. P. and A. J. Ross, (eds.) (2018), *Imagining Emperors in the Late Roman Empire* (Leiden).

Burgess, R. W. (2012), 'The Chronograph of 354: its manuscripts, content, and history', *Journal of Late Antiquity* 5, pp. 345–96.

Burrus, V. and R. Lehmann (2012), 'Introduction: shifting the focus of history', in Burrus and Lehmann (eds.) 2012, pp. 1–23.

Burrus, V. and R. Lehmann (eds.) (2012), *Late Ancient Christianity*, The People's Christianity 2 (Minneapolis, Minn.).

Burton, P. H., J. Balserak, H. A. G. Houghton, and D. C. Parker (2007, updated 2015), online *Vetus Latina* edition, http://www.iohannes.com.

Caffaro, A. (2003), *Scrivere in oro: ricettari medievali d'arte e artigianato (secoli IX–XI). Codici di Lucca e Ivrea* (Naples).

Cain, S. (2009), *The Letters of Jerome: Asceticism, Biblical Exegesis, and the Construction of Christian Authority in Late Antiquity* (Oxford).

Camerlenghi, N. (2018), *St Paul's Outside the Walls: a Roman Basilica, from Antiquity to the Modern Era* (Cambridge).

Cameron, Alan (2011), *The Last Pagans of Rome* (Oxford).

Cameron, Averil (1985), *Procopius and the Sixth Century* (Berkeley).

Cameron, Averil (1994), 'Texts as weapons: polemic in the Byzantine Dark Ages', in Bowman and Woolf (eds.) 1994, pp. 198–215.

Cameron, Averil (2009), 'Roman studies in sixth-century Constantinople', in P. Rousseau and M. Papoutsakis (eds.), *Transformations of Late Antiquity: Essays for Peter Brown* (Farnham), pp. 16–36.

Cameron, Averil (2015), 'Flights of fancy: some imaginary debates in late antiquity', in G. D. Dunn and W. Mayer (eds.), *Christians Shaping Identity from the Roman Empire to Byzantium: Studies Inspired by Pauline Allen*, Vigiliae Christianae Suppl. 132 (Leiden), pp. 385–406.

Campiani, A. (2018), 'Setting a bishopric/arranging an archive: traces of archival activity in the bishoprics of Alexandria and Antioch', in A. Bausi, C. Brockmann, M. Friedrich, and S. Kienitz (eds.), *Manuscripts and Archives: Comparative Views on Record Keeping* (Berlin) pp. 231–72.

Canella, T. (2006), *Gli Actus Silvestri: genesi di una leggenda su Costantino imperatore* (Spoleto).

Capelle, B. (1949), 'Le texte du *Gloria in excelsis*', *Revue d'histoire ecclésiastique* 44, pp. 439–57.

Capo, L. (2009), *Il* Liber pontificalis, *i Longobardi e la nascità del dominio territoriale della chiesa romana* (Spoleto).

Cardin, L. (2008), *Epigrafia a Roma nel primo medioevo (secoli IV–X): modelli grafici e tipologie d'uso* (Rome).

Carleton-Paget, J. and J. Schaper (eds.) (2013), *The New Cambridge History of the Bible* I: *from the Beginnings to 600* (Cambridge).

Carmassi, P. (2003), 'La prima redazione del *Liber pontificalis* nel quadro delle fonti contemporanee: osservazioni in margine alla vita de Simmaco', in Geertman (ed.) 2003, pp. 235–66.

Carpegna Falconieri, T. di (2002), *Il clero di Roma nel medioevo: istituzioni e politica cittadina (secoli VIII–XIII)* (Rome).

Carpegna Falconieri, T. di (2012), 'La militia a Roma: il formarsi di una nuova aristocrazia (secoli VII–VIII), in J.-M. Martin, A. Peters-Custot, and V. Prigent (eds.), *L'Héritage Byzantine en Italie (VIIᵉ–XIIᵉ siècle)* II: *les cadres juridiques et sociaux et les institutions publiques* (Rome), pp. 559–83.

Cavadini, J. (1995), *The Last Christology of the West: Adoptionism in Spain and Gaul, 785–820* (Philadelphia).

Chadwick, H. (1957), 'St Peter and St Paul in Rome: the problems of the *memoria apostolorum ad catacumbas*', *JTS* n.s. 8 (1957), pp. 31–52.

Chazelle, C. and C. Cubitt (eds.) (2007), *The Crisis of the Oikoumene: the Three Chapters and the Failed Quest for Unity in the Sixth-Century Mediterranean* (Turnhout).

Chiesa, P. (2005), 'Gregorio al lavoro: il processo testuale della "Regula Pastoralis"', in Petrucci (ed.) 2005, pp. 3–99.

Clemente, G. (2017), 'The Roman senate and the politics of religion in the *Collectio Avellana* (IV–VI century AD)', *Scripta classica israelica* 36, pp. 123–39.

Coates-Stephens, R. (1997), 'Dark-Age architecture in Rome', *PBSR* 65, pp. 177–232.

Coates-Stephens, R. (1998), 'The walls and aqueducts of Rome in the early middle ages', *Journal of Roman Studies* 88, pp. 166–78.

Coates-Stephens, R. (1999), 'Le reconstruzioni alto medievali delle mura aureliane e degli aquedotti', *MEFRM* 111/1, pp. 209–25.

Coates-Stephens, R. (2003a), 'Gli impianti ad acqua e le rete idrica urbana' in Geertman (ed.) 2003, pp. 135–54.

Coates-Stephens, R. (2003b), 'The water-supply of Rome from late antiquity to the early middle ages', *Acta ad archaeologiam et artium historiam pertinentia* 17, pp. 65–86.

Coates-Stephens, R. (2006), 'Byzantine building patronage in post-reconquest Rome', in Ghilardi, Goddard, and Porena (eds.) 2006, pp. 149–66.

Coates-Stephens, R. (2012), 'The walls of Aurelian', in Behrwald and Witschel (eds.) 2012, pp. 83–110.

Coates-Stephens, R. (2017), 'The Byzantine sack of Rome', *Antiquité tardive* 25, pp. 191–212.

Cohen, S. (2015), 'Schism and the polemic of heresy: Manichaeism and the representation of papal authority in the *Liber pontificalis*', *Journal of Late Antiquity* 8, pp. 195–230.

Connolly, R. H. (1929), *Didascalia apostolorum: the Syriac Version Translated and Accompanied by the Verona Latin Fragments* (Oxford).

Contreni, J. (1978), *The Cathedral School of Laon from 850 to 930: its Manuscripts and Masters* (Munich).

Cooper, K. (1999), 'The martyr, the *matrona* and the bishop: the matron Lucina and the politics of martyr cult in fifth- and sixth-century Rome', *EME* 8, pp. 297–317.

Cooper, K. (ed.) 2000, *The Roman Martyrs and the Politics of Memory*, *EME* 9.

Cooper, K. and J. Hillner (eds.) (2007), *Religion, Dynasty, and Patronage in Early Christian Rome, 300–900* (Cambridge).

Cooper, K. and C. Leyser (eds.) (2016), *Making Early Medieval Societies: Conflict and Belonging in the Latin West, 300–1200* (Cambridge).

Corradini, R. (2014), 'Pieces of a puzzle: time and history in Walahfrid's *Vademecum*', in McKitterick (ed.) 2014, pp. 476–91.

Costambeys, M. (2000), 'Property, ideology, and the territorial power of the papacy in the early middle ages', *EME* 9, pp. 367–96.

Costambeys, M. (2001) 'Burial topography and the power of the church in fifth- and sixth-century Rome', *PBSR* 69, pp. 169–89.

Costambeys, M. (2002), 'Intra-mural burial in sixth-century Rome', in F. Guidobaldi and A. Guiglia Guidobaldi (eds.), *Ecclesiae urbis: atti del Congresso internazionale di studi sulle Chiese di Roma (IV–X secolo), Roma, 4–10 settembre 2000* I (Vatican City), pp. 721–32.

Costambeys, M., M. Innes, and S. MacLean (2011), *The Carolingian World* (Cambridge).

Costambeys, M. and C. Leyser (2007), 'To be the neighbour of St Stephen: patronage, martyr cult, and Roman monasteries, *c*.600–*c*.900', in Cooper and Hillner (eds.) 2007, pp. 262–87.

Crivello, C., C. Denoel, F. Mütherich, and P. Orth (2011), *Das Godescalc-Evangelistar: eine Prachthandschrift für Karl den Großen* (Munich).

Croke, B. (1983), '476: the manufacturing of a turning point', *Chiron* 13, pp. 81–119.

Croke, B. (2001), *Count Marcellinus and his Chronicle* (Oxford).

Croke, B. (2005), 'Justinian's Constantinople' in M. Maas (ed.), *The Cambridge Companion to the Age of Justinian* (Cambridge), pp. 60–86.

Croke, B. (2007), 'Late-antique historiography, 250–650 CE' in J. Marincola (ed.), *A Companion to Greek and Roman Historiography* (Oxford), 2, pp. 567–81.

Cubitt, C. (1995), *Anglo-Saxon Church Councils, c.650–c.850* (Leicester).

Cubitt., C. (2014) 'The Roman perspective', in Price, Booth, and Cubitt 2014, pp. 40–59.

Cuppo, L. (2008), 'The other Book of Pontiffs: a view from Lombard Italy (MS. BAV, Vat. Lat. 1348)', in S. Barnish, L. Cracco Ruggini, L. Cuppo, R. Marchese, M. Breu, *Vivarium in Context* (Vicenza), pp. 55–76.

Curran, J. (2000), *Pagan City and Christian Capital: Rome in the Fourth Century* (Oxford).

Daileader, P. (1993), 'One will, one voice and equal love: papal elections and the *Liber pontificalis* in the early middle ages', *Archivum Historiae Pontificiae* 31, pp. 11–31.

David, M. (2013), *Eternal Ravenna from the Etruscans to the Venetians* (Turnhout).

Davies, W. and P. Fouracre (eds.) (2010), *The Languages of Gift in the Early Middle Ages* (Cambridge).

Davis-Weyer, C. (1989), 'S. Stefano Rotundo and the oratory of Theodore I', in W. Tronzo (ed.), *Italian Church Decoration of the Middle Ages and Early Renaissance* (Bologna), pp. 61–80.

D'Avray, D. L. (2019), *Papal Jurisprudence c.400: Sources of the Canon Law Tradition* (Cambridge).

Dearn, A. C. M. (2007), 'Persecution and Donatist identity in the *Liber genealogus*', in H. Amirav and B. ter Haar Romeny (eds.), *From Rome to Constantinople: Studies in Honour of Averil Cameron* (Leuven), pp. 127–38.

Declercq, G. (2000), Anno Domini: *the Origins of the Christian Era* (Turnhout).

Deliyannis, D. M. (2010), *Ravenna in Late Antiquity* (Cambridge).

Deliyannis, D. M. (2014), 'The Roman *Liber pontificalis*, papal primacy, and the Acacian schism', *Viator* 45, 1–16.

Delogu, P. (1995), 'Lombard and Carolingian Italy', in McKitterick (ed.) 1995, pp. 290–319.

Delogu, P. (2000), 'The papacy, Rome, and the wider world in the seventh and eighth centuries', in Smith (ed.) 2000, pp. 197–220.

Delogu, P. (2001), Il passaggio dall'antichità al medioevo', in A. Vauchez (ed.), *Storia di Roma dal'antichità a oggi* 2: *Roma medievale* (Rome), pp. 3–40.

Delogu, P., M. S. Arena, L. Paroli, M. Ricci, L. Sagu, and L. Venditelli (eds.) (2001), *Roma dall'antichità al medioevo: archeologia e storia* (Milan).

Delogu, P. and L. Paroli (eds.) (1993), *La storia economica di Roma nell'alto medioevo alla luce dei recenti scavi archeologici* (Florence).

Demacopoulos, G. M. (2013), *The Invention of Peter: Apostolic Discourse and Papal Authority in Late Antiquity* (Philadelphia).

Denzey Lewis, N. (2018), 'Damasus and the derelict relics', *EME* 26, pp. 417–39.

Dey, H. (2008), 'Diaconia, xenodochia, *hospitalia* and monasteries: "social security" and the meaning of monasticism in early medieval Rome', *EME* 16, pp. 398–422.

Dey, H. (2011), *The Aurelian Wall and the Refashioning of Imperial Rome, AD 271–855* (Cambridge).

Dey, H. (2015), *The Afterlife of the Roman City: Architecture and Ceremony in Late Antiquity and the Early Middle Ages* (Cambridge).

Dey, H. (2019), 'Politics, patronage and the transmission of construction techniques in early medieval Rome *c.*650–750', *PBSR* 87, pp. 177–206.

Dickey, E. (2016), *Learning Latin the Ancient Way: Latin Textbooks from the Ancient World* (Cambridge).

Diesenberger, M. (2015), *Predigt und Politik im frühmittelalterlichen Bayern: Arn von Salzburg, Karl der Große und die Salzburger Sermones-Sammlung* (Berlin).

Divjak, J. and W. Wischmeyer (2014), *Das Kalenderhandbuch von 354: der Chronograph des Filocalus* (Vienna).

Döhler, M. (2017), *Acta Petri: Übersetzung und Kommentar zu den Actus Vercellensis* (Berlin).

Dorofeeva, A. (2015), 'The Reception and Manuscript Context of the Early Medieval Latin Pre-bestiary Physiologus', unpublished PhD dissertation, University of Cambridge.

Duchesne, L. (1877), *Étude sur le Liber pontificalis* (Paris).

Duffy, E. (1997), *Saints and Sinners: a History of the Popes* (New Haven).

Dufourcq, A. (1900–7), *Étude sur les Gesta martyrum romains*, 5 vols (Paris).

Dunn, G. D. (2015a), '*Collectio Corbeiensis, Collectio Pithouensis* and the earliest collection of papal letters', in Neil and Allen (eds.) 2015, pp. 175–205.

Dunn, G. D. (2015b), 'The emergence of papal decretals: the evidence of Zosimus of Rome', in Greatrex, Elton, and McMahon (eds.) 2015, pp. 81–92.

Dunn, G. D. (ed.) (2015), *The Bishop of Rome in Late Antiquity* (Farnham).

Dyer, J. (1995), 'Prolegomena to a history of music and liturgy at Rome in the middle ages', in G. M. Boone (ed.), *Essays on Medieval Music in Honour of David C. Hughes* (Cambridge, Mass. 1995), pp. 86–107.

Eastman, D. (2015), *The Ancient Martyrdom Accounts of Peter and Paul* (Atlanta).

Edwards, C. (1996), *Writing Rome: Textual Approaches to the City* (Cambridge).

Edwards, C. and G. Woolf (2003), 'Cosmopolis: Rome as world city', in Edwards and Woolf (eds.) 2003, pp. 1–20.

Edwards, C. and G. Woolf (eds.) (2003), *Rome the Cosmopolis* (Cambridge).

Ekonomou, A. J. (2007), *Byzantine Rome and the Greek Popes: Eastern Influences on Rome and the Papacy from Gregory the Great to Zacharias, A.D. 590–752* (Lanham, Md.).

Elsner, J. (1995), *Art and the Roman Viewer* (Cambridge).

Elsner, J. (1998), *Imperial Rome and Christian Triumph* (Oxford).

Elsner, J. (2003), 'Inventing Christian Rome: the role of early Christian art', in Edwards and Woolf (eds.) 2003, pp. 70–99.

Emerick, J. (2011), 'Building *more Romano* in Francia during the third quarter of the eighth century: the abbey church of Saint-Denis and its model', in Bolgia, McKitterick, and Osborne (eds.) 2011, pp. 127–50.

Esch, A. (2011) 'On the reuse of antiquity: the perspectives of the archaeologist and the historian', in Brilliant and Kinney (eds.) 2011, pp. 13–32.

Esders, S. (2019), '"Great security prevailed in both East and West": the Merovingian kingdom and the sixth ecumenical council (680/1)', in Esders, Fox, Hen, and Sarty (eds.) 2019, pp. 247–65.

Esders, S., Y. Fox, Y. Hen, and L. Sarty (eds.) 2019, *East and West in the Early Middle Ages: the Merovingian Kingdoms in Mediterranean Perspective* (Cambridge).

Espelo, D. van (in press), 'The *Codex epistolaris Carolinus:* compilation and contexts', in McKitterick, Pollard, Price, and Van Espelo in press.

Evers, A. (2013), 'East and West, emperor and bishop: Hormisdas and the authority of the see of Rome', in Fear (ed.) 2013, pp. 167–88.

Evers, A. (2019), 'The *Collectio Avellana* – collecting letters with a reason', in Lizzi Testa and Marconi (eds.) 2019, pp. 13–28.

Ewald, B. C. and C. F. Noreña (eds.) (2015), *The Emperor and Rome: Space, Representation and Ritual* (Cambridge).

Faro, D. (1996), *The Urban Image of Augustan Rome* (Cambridge).

Fear, A. (ed.) (2013), *The Role of the Bishop in Late Antiquity: Conflict and Compromise* (London).

Ferrari, G. (1957), *Early Roman Monasteries: Notes for the History of the Monasteries and Convents at Rome from the V through the X Century* (Vatican City).

Ferreiro, A. (2005), *Simon Magus in Patristic, Medieval and Early Modern Traditions* (Leiden).

Finney, P. C. (1994), *The Invisible God* (Oxford).

Foot, S. (2019), 'Mental maps: sense of place in medieval British historical writing', in Jahner, Steiner, and Tyler (eds.) 2019, pp. 139–58.

Fornasari, M. (1966), 'Collectio canonum Mutinensis', *Studia Gratiana* 9, pp. 247–356.

Fouracre, P. (ed.) (2005), *The New Cambridge Medieval History* I, *500–700* (Cambridge).

Fowden, G. (1993), *From Empire to Commonwealth* (Princeton).

Fowden, G. (1994), 'The last days of Constantine: oppositional versions and their influence', *Journal of Roman Studies* 84, pp. 146–70.

Francesco, D. de (2017) *Il papato e l'approvvigionamento idrico e alimentare de Roma tra la tarda antichità e l'alto medioevo* (Rome).

Franklin, C. Vircillo (2017), 'Reading the popes: the *Liber Pontificalis* and its editors', *Speculum* 92, pp. 607–29.

Franklin, C. Vircillo (2018), 'Theodor Mommsen, Louis Duchesne, and the *Liber pontificalis:* classical philology and medieval Latin texts', in M. Formisano and C. Shuttleworth Kraus (eds.), *Marginality, Canonicity, Passion* (Oxford), pp. 99–138.

Franses, R. (2018), *Donor Portraits in Byzantine Art: the Vicissitudes of Contact Between Human and Divine* (Cambridge).

Frere, W. H. (1930–5), *Studies in Early Roman Liturgy*, 3 vols (Oxford).

Fuhrmann, H. (1959), 'Konstantinische Schenkung und Silvesterlegende in neuer Sicht', *Deutsches Archiv für Erforschung des Mittelalters* 15, pp. 523–40.

Gamble, H. Y. (1995), *Books and Readers in the Early Church: a History of Early Christian Texts* (New Haven).

Gantner, C., (2013a), 'The Lombard recension of the Roman *Liber pontificalis*', *Rivista di storia del cristianesimo* 10, pp. 65–114.

Gantner, C. (2013b), 'The label "Greeks" in the papal diplomatic repertoire in the eighth century', in W. Pohl and G. Heydemann (eds.), *Strategies of Identification: Ethnicity and Religion in Early Medieval Europe* (Turnhout), pp. 303–49.

Gantner, C. (2014), *Freunde Roms und Völker der Finsternis: die päpstliche Konstruktion von Anderen im 8. und 9. Jahrhundert* (Vienna).

Gantner, C. (2015), 'The eighth-century papacy as cultural broker', in Gantner, McKitterick, and Meeder (eds.) 2015, pp. 245–61.

Gantner, C., R. McKitterick, and S. Meeder (eds.) (2015), *The Resources of the Past in Early Medieval Europe* (Cambridge).

Ganz, D. (2002), 'Roman manuscripts in Francia and Anglo-Saxon England', in *Roma fra oriente e occidente, Settimane* 49/1 (Spoleto), pp. 607–47.

Ganz, D. (2010), 'Giving to God in the Mass: the experience of the offertory', in Davies and Fouracre (eds.) 2010, pp. 18–32.

Garipzanov, I. (2008), *The Symbolic Language of Authority in the Carolingian World (c. 751–877)* (Leiden).

Gasbarri, G. (2015), *Riscoprire Bisanzio: lo studio dell'arte bizantina a Roma e in Italia tra ottocento e novecento* (Rome).

Gautier Dalché, P. (1997), *Géographie et culture: la représentation de l'espace du VIe au XIIe siècle* (Aldershot).

Geertman, H. (1975), *More veterum: il* Liber pontificalis *e gli edifici ecclesiastici di Roma nella tarda antichità e nell'alto medioevo* (Groningen).

Geertman, H. (2003a), 'Documenti, redattori e la formazione del testo del *Liber pontificalis*', in Geertman (ed.) 2003, pp. 267–84.

Geertman, H. (2003b) 'Le biografie del *Liber pontificalis* dal 311 al 535: testo e commentario', in Geertman (ed.) 2003, pp. 285–355.

Geertman, H. (2004), Hic fecit basilicam: *studi sul* Liber pontificalis *e gli edifici ecclesiastici di Roma da Silvestro a Silverio* (Leuven).

Geertman, H. (2009), 'La Genesi del *Liber pontificalis* romano: un processo di organizzazione della memoria', in Bougard and Sot (eds.) 2009, pp. 37–107.

Geertman, H. (ed.) (2003), *Atti del Colloquio internazionale Il Liber Pontificalis e la storia materiale Roma, 21–22 febbraio 2002,* Mededelingen van het Nederlands Instituut te Rome 60/1 (*Antiquity* 2001/2) (Assen).

Gem, R. (2013), 'The chronology of Saint Peter's basilica', in McKitterick, Osborne, Richardson, and Story (eds.) 2013, pp. 35–64.

Getzeny, H. (1922), *Stil und Form der älteste Papstbrief bis auf Leo d. Gr. Ein Beitrag zur Geschichte des römischen Primats* (Gunzburg).

Ghilardi, M., C. J. Goddard, and G. P. Porena (eds.) (2006), *Les cités d'Italie tardo-antique (IVe–VIe siècle): institution, économie, société, culture et religion,* Collection de l'École française de Rome 369 (Rome).

Gillett, A. (2012), 'Advise the emperor beneficially: lateral communication in diplomatic embassies between the post-imperial West and Byzantium', in A. Becker and N. Drocourt (eds.), *Ambassadeurs et ambassades au coeur des relations diplomatiques, Rome-Occident médiévale-Byzance (VIIIe s. avant J.-C. – XIIe s. après J.-C.)* (Metz), pp. 257–85.

Gioanni, S. (2010), 'Vies', in Philippart (ed.) 2010, pp. 371–445.

Giry, A. (1925), *Manuel de Diplomatique* (Paris).

Goddard, C. J. (2006), 'The evolution of pagan sanctuaries in late antique Italy (fourth–sixth centuries A.D.: a new administrative and legal framework. A paradox', in Ghilardi, Goddard, and Porena (eds.) 2006, pp. 281–308.

Goodson, C. (2007), 'Building for bodies: the architecture of saint veneration in early medieval Rome', in Ó Carragáin and Neuman de Vegvar (eds.) 2007, pp. 51–80.

Goodson, C. (2010), *The Rome of Paschal I: Papal Power, Urban Renovation, Church Rebuilding and Relic Translation, 817–824* (Cambridge).

Goodson, C. (2015), 'To be the daughter of Saint Peter: S. Petronilla and forging the Franco-Papal Alliance,' in V. West-Harling (ed.), *Three Empires, Three Cities: Identity, Material Culture and Legitimacy in Venice, Ravenna and Rome, 750–1000* (Turnhout), pp. 159–82.

Gorman, M. (1982), 'The manuscript tradition of Eugippius' *Excerpta ex operibus sancti Augustini*', *Revue Bénédictine* 92, pp. 7–32 and 229–65.

Grafton, A. (1990), *Forgers and Critics: Creativity and Duplicity in Western Scholarship* (Princeton).

Granier, T. (2002), 'Les échanges culturels dans l'Italie méridionale du haut Moyen Âge: Naples, Bénévant et Mont-Cassin aux VIII^c–XII^c siècles', in R. Le Jan (ed.), *Les Échanges Culturels au Moyen Âge* (Paris), pp. 89–106.

Graumann, T. (2018), 'Documents, acts and archival habits in early Christian church councils: a case study', in A. Bausi, C. Brockmann, M. Friedrich, and S. Kienitz (eds.), *Manuscripts and Archives: Comparative Views on Record Keeping* (Berlin), pp. 273–94.

Gray, N. (1956), 'The Filocalan letter', *PBSR* 24, pp. 5–13.

Gray, P. T. (2005), 'The legacy of Chalcedon: Christological problems and their significance', in Maas (ed.) 2005, pp. 215–38.

Greatrex, G., H. Elton, and L. McMahon (eds.) (2015), *Shifting Genres in Late Antiquity* (Farnham).

Green, R. P. H. (2006), *Latin Epics of the New Testament: Juvencus, Sedulius, Arator* (Oxford).

Griffin, S. (2019), *The Liturgical Past in Byzantium and Early Rus* (Cambridge).

Grig, L. (2004), *Making Martyrs in Late Antiquity* (London).

Grig, L. (2005), 'The paradoxical body of Saint Agnes', in A. Hopkins and M. Wyke (eds.), *Roman Bodies: Antiquity to the Eighteenth Century* (London), pp. 111–22.

Grig, L. and G. Kelly (eds.) (2012), *Two Romes: from Rome to Constantinople* (Oxford).

Grimaldi, G. (1972), *Descrizione della basilica antica di S. Pietro in Vaticano: il codice Barberini 2733, Biblioteca apostolica vaticana*, ed. R. Niggl (Vatican City).

Große, R. (2018), 'La collection de formules de Saint-Denis (Bibl.Nat.Fr., lat. 2777): un dossier controversé', *Bibliothèque de l'École des chartes* 172 for 2014, pp. 185–97.

Große, R. and M. Sot (eds.) (2018), *Charlemagne: les temps, les espaces, les hommes. Construction et déconstruction* (Turnhout).

Guenée, B. (1980), *Histoire et culture historique dans l'occident médiévale* (Paris).

Guidobaldi, F. (1992), *San Clemente: gli edifici romani, la basilica paleocristiana e le fasi alto-medievali* (Rome).

Guidobaldi, F. (2000), 'L'organizzazione dei titulo nello spazio urbano', in Pani Ermini (ed.) 2000, I, pp. 123–9.

Guidobaldi, F. and A. Guiglia Guidobaldi (eds.) (2002), *Ecclesiae urbis: atti del Congresso internazionale di studi sulle Chiese di Roma (IV–X secolo), Roma, 4–10 settembre 2000* (Vatican City).

Guillou, A. (1971), 'Inscriptions du duché de Rome', *MEFRM* 83/2, pp. 149–58.

Gülzow, H. (1975), *Cyprian und Novatian: der Briefwechsel zwischen den Gemeinden in Rom und Karthago zur Zeit der Verfolgung des Kaisers Decius* (Tübingen).

Hack, A. T. (2006–7), *Codex Carolinus: päpstliche Epistolographie im 8. Jahrhundert*, Päpste und Papsttum 35, 2 vols (Stuttgart).

Haldon, J. (1990), *Byzantium in the Seventh Century: the Transformation of a Culture* (Cambridge).

Halporn, J. W. and M. Vessey (2004), *Cassiodorus: Institutions of Divine and Secular Learning. On the Soul* (Liverpool).

Halsall, G. (2005), *Barbarian Migration and the Roman West, 376–578* (Cambridge).

Hansen, M. Fabricius (2003), *The Eloquence of Appropriation: Prolegomena to an Understanding of Spolia in Early Christian Rome* (Rome).

Harder, C. (2014), *Pseudoisidor und das Papsttum: Funktion und Bedeutung des apostolischen Stuhls in den pseudoisidorischen Fälschungen* (Cologne).

Harder, C. (2015), 'Der Papst als Mittel zum Zweck? Zur Bedeutung des römischen Bischof bei Pseudoisidor', in K. Ubl and D. Ziemann (eds.), *Fälschung als Mittel der Politik: Pseudoisidor im Licht der neuen Forschung. Gedenkschrift für Klaus Zechiel-Eckes*, MGH Studien und Texte 57 (Wiesbaden), pp. 187–206.

Harris, W. (ed.) (1999), *The Transformations of Urbs Roma in Late Antiquity, Journal of Roman Archaeology* Suppl. 334 (Portsmouth, RI).

Hartmann, F. (2006), *Hadrian I. (772–795)* (Stuttgart).

Häse, A. (2002), *Mittelalterliche Bücherverzeichnisse aus Kloster Lorsch: Einleitung, Edition und Kommentar*, Beiträge zum Buch- und Bibliothekswesen 42 (Wiesbaden).

Hathaway, N. (1978), 'Compilatio: from plagiarism to compiling', *Viator* 20, pp. 19–44.

Hen, Y. (2011), 'The Romanization of the Frankish liturgy: ideal, reality, and the rhetoric of reform', in Bolgia, McKitterick, and Osborne (eds.) 2011, pp. 111–23.

Herbers, K. (1996), *Leo IV. und das Papsttum in der Mitte des 9. Jahrhunderts* (Stuttgart).

Herbers, K. (2009), 'Agir et écrire: les actes des papes du IXe siècle et le *Liber pontificalis*' in Bougard and Sot (eds.) 2009, pp. 127–52.

Herbers, K., S. Heide, and M. Simperl (eds.) (2020), *Das Buch der Päpste: der Liber pontificalis – ein Schlüsseldokument europäische Geschichte, Römische Quartalschrift* 115.

Hess, H. (2002), *The Early Development of Canon Law and the Council of Sardica* (Oxford).

Hiatt, A. (2004), *The Making of Medieval Forgeries: False Documents in Fifteenth-Century England* (London and Toronto).

Hilhorst, A. (1998), 'The text of the Actus Vercellenses', in Bremmer (ed.) 1998, pp. 148–60.

Hilliard, P. (2018), 'Bede and the changing image of Rome and the Romans', in E. Screen and C. West (eds.), *Writing the Early Medieval West* (Cambridge), pp. 33–46.

Hillier, R. (1993), *Arator on the Acts of the Apostles: a Baptismal Commentary* (Oxford).

Hillner, J. (2006), 'Clerics, property, and patronage: the case of the Roman titular churches', *Antiquité tardive* 14, pp. 59–68.

Hillner, J. (2007), 'Families, patronage, and the titular churches of Rome, *c*.300–*c*.600', in Cooper and Hillner (eds.) 2007, pp. 225–61.

Holford-Stevens, L. (2011), 'Church politics and the computus: from Milan to the ends of the earth', in I. Warntjes and D. Ó Cróinín (eds.), *The Easter Controversy of Late Antiquity and the Early Middle Ages: its Manuscripts, Texts, and Tables* (Turnhout), pp. 1–20.

Holloway, R. H. (2004), *Constantine and Rome* (New Haven).

Hoskins, M. (2015), 'Prolegomena to a Critical Edition of the Letters of Pope Leo the Great: a Study of the Manuscripts', unpublished PhD dissertation, University of Edinburgh.

Houghton, H. A. G. (2016), *The Latin New Testament: a Guide to its Early History, Texts and Manuscripts* (Oxford).

Hummer, H. J. (2005), *Politics and Power in Early Medieval Europe: Alsace and the Frankish Realm, 600–1000* (Cambridge).

Humphries, M. (2007), 'From emperor to pope? Ceremonial, space, and authority at Rome from Constantine to Gregory the Great', in Cooper and Hillner (eds.) 2007, pp. 21–58.

Hunsacker, R. G. R. and E. J. J. Roels (2016), 'Eine vergessene Erinnerung an das byzantinische Rom. Neudeutung und Rezeptionsgeschichte einer Grabinschrift aus dem 7. Jht. in der S. Cecilia in Trastevere', in M. Verhoeven, L. Bosman, and H. van Asperen (eds.), *Monuments and Memory: Christian Cult Buildings and Constructions of the Past. Essays in Honour of Sible de Blaauw*, Architectural Crossroads: Studies in the History of Architecture 3 (Turnhout), pp. 31–42.

Hurtado, L. W. and C. Keith (2013), 'Writing and book production in the Hellenistic and Roman periods', in Carleton-Paget and Schaper (eds.) 2013, pp. 63–80.

Inglebert, H. (1996), *Les Romains chrétiens face à l'histoire de Rome: histoire, christianisme et romanités en occident dans l'antiquité tardive, IIIe–Ve siècles* (Paris).

Jahner, J., E. Steiner, and E. Tyler (eds.) (2019), *Medieval Historical Writing: Britain and Ireland, 500–1500* (Cambridge).

James, L. L. (2017), *Mosaics in the Medieval World: from Late Antiquity to the Fifteenth Century* (Cambridge).

Jasper, D. and H. Fuhrmann (2001), *Papal Letters in the Early Middle Ages* (Washington, DC).

Jeffery, P. (1984), 'The introduction of psalmody into the Roman Mass by Pope Celestine I (422–432): reinterpreting a passage in the *Liber pontificalis*', *Archiv für Liturgiewissenschaft* 26, pp. 147–65.

Jeffery, P. (2013), 'The early liturgy of Saint Peter's and the Roman liturgical year', in McKitterick, Osborne, Richardson, and Story (eds.) 2013, pp. 157–76.

Johnson, M. (1995), 'The fifth-century oratory of the Holy Cross at the Lateran in Rome', *Zeitschrift für Geschichte der Baukunst*, pp. 128–55.

Johnson, S. F. (ed.) (2012), *The Oxford Handbook of Late Antiquity* (Oxford).

Jong, M. de (2009), *The Penitential State: Authority and Atonement in the Age of Louis the Pious, 814–840* (Cambridge).

Jong, M. de (2015), 'Carolingian political discourse and the biblical past: Hraban, Dhuoda, Radbert', in Gantner, McKitterick, and Meeder (eds.) 2015, pp. 87–102.

Jong, M. de (2019), *Epitaph for an Era: Politics and Rhetoric in the Carolingian World* (Cambridge).

Joosten, J. (2013), 'Varieties of Greek in the Septuagint and New Testament', in Carleton-Paget and Schaper (eds.) 2013, pp. 22–45.

Kaczynski, B. M. (1988), *Greek in the Carolingian Age: the St Gall Manuscripts* (Cambridge, Mass.).

Kaldellis, A. (2004), *Procopius of Caesarea: Tyranny, History, and Philosophy at the End of Antiquity* (Philadelphia).

Kamesar, A., (2013), 'Jerome', in Carleton-Paget and Schaper (eds.) 2013, pp. 653–75.

Keefe, S. (2002), *Water and the Word: Baptism and the Education of the Clergy in the Carolingian Empire* (Notre Dame).

Kelly, J. N. D. (1975), *Jerome: His Life, Writings and Controversies* (London).

Kennell, S. A. H. (2000), *Magnus Felix Ennodius: a Gentleman of the Church* (Ann Arbor).

Kéry, L. (1999), *Canonical Collections of the Early Middle Ages (ca. 400–1140): a Bibliographical Guide to the Manuscripts and Literature* (Washington, DC).

Kim, Y. R. (2015), 'The transformation of heresiology in the Panarion of Epiphanius of Cyprus', in Greatrex, Elton, and McMahon (eds.) 2015, pp. 53–68.

Kinney, D. (2011), 'Introduction', in Brilliant and Kinney (eds.) 2011, pp. 1–12.

Kinney, D. (2012), 'Instances of appropriation in late Roman and early Christian Art', *Essays in Medieval Studies* 28, pp. 1–22.

Kirschbaum, E. (1959), *The Tombs of Saint Peter and Saint Paul* (London).

Klauser, T. (1935), *Das römische Capitulare evangeliorum: Texte und Untersuchungen zu s. ältesten Geschichte* (Münster).

Kötte, J.-M. (2013), *Zwischen Kaisern und Aposteln: das Akakianische Schisma (484–519) als kirchlicher Ordnungskonflikt der Spätantike* (Stuttgart).

Krautheimer, R. (1980/2000), *Rome: Profile of a City, 312–1308* (Princeton).

Krautheimer, R., S. Corbett, and V. Frankl (1937–77), *Corpus basilicarum christianarum Romae: le basiliche cristiane antiche di Roma (sec. IV–IX) / The Early Christian Basilicas of Rome (IV–IX cent.)*, 5 vols (Vatican City).

Krautheimer, R., E. Josi, and W. Frankl (1952), 'S. Lorenzo fuori le mura in Rome: excavations and observations', *Proceedings of the American Philosophical Society* 96, pp. 1–26.

Kudock, A. (2007), 'Demetrias ancilla dei: Anicia Demetrias and the problem of the missing patron', in Cooper and Hillner (eds.) 2007, pp. 165–89.

Ladner, G. (1941), *I ritratti dei papi nell'antichità e nel medioevo* (Vatican City).

Lafferty, S. D. W. (2013), *Law and Society in the Age of Theoderic the Great: a Study of the Edictum Theoderici* (Cambridge), pp. 54–100.

Lai, A. (2011), *Il codice laudiano greco 35: l'identità missionaria di un libro nell'Europa altomedievale* (Cargeghe).

Landes, R. (1995), *Relics, Apocalypse, and the Deceits of History: Ademar of Chabannes, 989–1034* (Cambridge, Mass.).

Lanéry, C. (2010), 'Passions' in Philippart (ed.) 2010, pp. 15–369.

Lapidge, M. (2017), *Hilduin of Saint-Denis: the Passio S. Dionysii in Prose and Verse* (Leiden).

Lapidge, M. (2018), *The Roman Martyrs: Introduction, Translation, and Commentary* (Oxford).

La Rocca, C. (2014), '*Mores tuos fabricate loquuntur:* building activity and the rhetoric of power in Ostrogothic Italy', *The Haskins Society Journal* 26, pp. 9–13.

La Rocca, C. (2018), 'An arena of abuses and competing powers: Rome in Cassiodorus's *Variae*', in Balzaretti, Barrow, and Skinner (eds.) 2018, pp. 201–12.

La Rocca, C. (ed.) (2002), *Italy in the Early Middle Ages, 476–1000* (Oxford).

Leal, B. (2016), 'Representations of Architecture in Late Antiquity', unpublished PhD dissertation, University of East Anglia.

Leclercq, H. (1930), '*Liber pontificalis*', in F. Cabrol and H. Leclercq (eds.), *Dictionnaire d'archéologie chrétienne et de liturgie*, 9/1 (Paris), cols. 354–481.

Lehmann, P. (1918), *Mittelalterliche Bibliothekskataloge Deutschlands und der Schweiz I: die Diözesen Konstanz und Chur* (Munich).

Levison, W. (1913), 'Handschriften des Museums Meermanno-Westreenianum in Den Haag', *Neues Archiv* 38, pp. 503–24.

Levison, W. (1924), 'Konstantinische Schenkung und Silvester-Legende', *Miscellanea Francesco Ehrle: scritti di storia e paleografia* 2, Studi e testi 38 (Rome), pp. 159–247.

Levison, W. (1946), *England and the Continent in the Eighth Century* (Oxford).

Leyser, C. (2001), 'Shoring fragments against ruin? Eugippius and the sixth-century culture of the *florilegium*', in Pohl and Diesenberger (eds.) 2001, pp. 65–76.

Leyser, C. (2010), 'Pope Gregory the Great: ego trouble or identity politics', in R. Corradini, M. Gillis, R. McKitterick, and I. van Renswoude (eds.), *Ego Trouble: Authors and Their Identities in the Early Middle Ages*, Forschungen zur Geschichte des Mittelalters 15 (Vienna), pp. 67–77.

Leyser, C. (2016), 'The memory of Gregory the Great and the making of Latin Europe, 600–1000', in Cooper and Leyser (eds.) 2016, pp. 181–201.

Leyser, C. (2019), 'Law, memory, and priestly office in Rome, *c.*500', *EME* 27, pp. 61–84.

Lietzmann, H. J. (1927), *Petrus und Paulus in Rom: liturgische und archäologische Studien* (Berlin).

Linderski, J. (1985), 'The *libri reconditi*', *Harvard Studies in Classical Philology* 89, pp. 207–84.

Lindsay, W. M. (1915), *Notae Latinae: an Account of Abbreviation in Latin MSS. of the Early Minuscule Period (c. 700–850)* (Cambridge).

Lippsmeyer, E. (1981), 'Donor and Church Model in Medieval Art from Early Christian Times', unpublished PhD dissertation, Rutgers University.

Liverani, P. (1988), 'Le proprietà private nell'area Lateranense fino all'età di Costantino', *MEFRA* 100, pp. 1–13.

Liverani, P. (2006), 'L'architettura costantiniana, tra committenza imperiale e contributo delle élites locali', in A. Demandt and J. Engemann (eds.), *Konstantin der Große: Geschichte – Archäologie – Rezeption. Akten des Internationalen Kolloquiums, 10–15. Oktober 2005, Trier* (Trier), pp. 235–44.

Liverani, P. (2008), 'St Peter's, Leo the Great and the leprosy of Constantine', *PBSR* 76, pp. 155–72.

Liverani, P. (2011), 'Reading spolia in late antique and contemporary perception', in Brilliant and Kinney (eds.) 2011, pp. 33–52.

Liverani, P. (2013), 'Saint Peter's and the city of Rome between late antiquity and the early middle ages', in McKitterick, Osborne, Richardson, and Story (eds.) 2013, pp. 21–34.

Liverani, P. (2019), 'Osservazioni sul *Libellus* delle donazioni Costantiniane nel *Liber pontificalis*', *Athenaeum* 107, pp. 169–217.

Liverani, P. and G. Spinola (2010) *The Vatican Necropoles: Rome's City of the Dead* (Turnhout).

Lizzi Testa, R. (2013), 'Rome during the Ostrogoth kingdom: its political meaning as apostolic see', in H. Harich-Schwarzbauer and K. Pollman (eds.), *Der Fall Roms und seine Wiederauferstehungen in Antike und Mittelalter* (Berlin), pp. 131–49.

Lizzi Testa, R. (ed.) (2013), *The Strange Death of Pagan Rome: Reflections on a Historiographical Controversy* (Turnhout).

Lizzi Testa, R. and G. Marconi (eds.) (2019), *The* Collectio Avellana *and its Revivals* (Newcastle).

Llewellyn, P. (1974a), 'The Roman church in the seventh century: the legacy of Gregory the Great', *Journal of Ecclesiastical History* 25, pp. 363–80.

Llewellyn, P. (1974b) *Rome in the Dark Ages*, 2nd ed. 1996 (London).

Llewellyn, P. (1976), 'The Roman church during the Laurentian Schism: priests and senators', *Church History* 45, pp. 417–27.

Lo Conte, F. (2010), 'La "versione Longobarda" del "Liber pontificalis" (Bergamo, 20 novembre 2009)', *Rivista di storia della chiesa in Italia* 64, pp. 583–8.

Lo Monaco, F. (ed.) (2013), *Le* Liber pontificalis, *Rivista du storia cristianesimo* 10.

Loomis, L. R. (1916), *The Book of the Popes (*Liber pontificalis*)* I: *to the Pontificate of Gregory I* (New York).

Loschiavo, L. (2015), 'Was Rome still a centre of legal culture between the 6th and 8th centuries?', *Rechtsgeschichte / Legal History* 23, pp. 83–108.

Lowe, E. A. and V. Brown (1980), *The Beneventan Script: a History of the South Italian Minuscule*, 2 vols (Rome).

Lozovsky, N. (2000), *The World is our Book* (Ann Arbor).

Maas, M. (ed.) (2005), *The Cambridge Companion to the Age of Justinian* (Cambridge).

Maccarrone, M. (ed.) (1991), *Il primato del vescovo di Roma nel primo millennio: ricerche e testimonianze. Atti del Symposium storico-teologico (Roma, 9–13 ottobre, 1989)* (Vatican City).

MacGeorge, P. (2002), *Late Roman Warlords* (Oxford).

Machado, C. (2010), 'Public monuments and ancient life: the end of the statue habit in Italy', in S. Gasparri and P. Delogu (eds.), *Le trasformazione del V secolo: l'Italia, i barbari e l'Occidente romano* (Turnhout), pp. 237–58.

Machado, C. (2017), 'Dedicated to eternity? The reuse of statue bases in late antique Italy', in K. Bolle, C. Machado, and C. Witschel (eds), *The Epigraphic Cultures of Late Antiquity* (Stuttgart), pp. 323–61.

Machado, C. (2019), *Urban Space and Aristocratic Power in Late Antique Rome (AD 270–535)* (Oxford).

Machado, C. and B. Ward-Perkins (2013), '410 and the end of new statuary in Italy', in J. Lipps, C. Machado, and P. von Rummel (eds.), *The Sack of Rome in 410 AD: the Event, its Context and its Impact* (Wiesbaden), pp. 353–64.

Mackie, G. (2003), *Early Christian Chapels in the West: Decoration, Function and Patronage* (Toronto).

MacKinlay, A. P. (1942), *Arator: the Codices* (Cambridge, Mass.).

MacKinnon, J. (2000), *The Advent Project: the Later Seventh-Century Creation of the Roman Mass Proper* (Berkeley).

Maiuro, M. (2007), 'Archivi, amministrazione del Patrimonio e proprietà imperiali nel *Liber pontificalis*', in D. Pupillo (ed.), *Le proprietà imperiali nell'Italia: economia, produzione, amministrazione. Atti del Convegno Ferrara–Voghiera, 3–4 giugno 2005*, Quaderni degli Annali dell'Università di Ferrara, Sezione Storia 6, pp. 235–58.

Marazzi, F. (1995), 'Le proprietà immobiliari della Chiesa romana tra 4 e 8 secolo: reddoto, struttura e gestione', in O. Faron and E. Hibert (eds.), *Le sol et l'immeuble* (Lyon and Rome), pp. 151–68.

Marazzi, F. (1998), *I 'Patrimonia sanctae Romae ecclesiae' nel Lazio (secoli IV–X): struttura amministrativa e prassi gestionali*, Nuovi studi storici 37 (Rome).

Marazzi, F. (2000), 'Rome in transition: economic and political change in the fourth and fifth centuries', in Smith (ed.) 2000, pp. 21–42.

Marcos, M. (2013), 'Papal authority, local autonomy and imperial control: Pope Zosimus and the Western churches (a. 417–418)', in Fear (ed.) 2013, pp. 144–66.

Marder, T. and M. Wilson-Jones (eds.) (2015), *The Pantheon from Antiquity to the Present* (Cambridge).

Markus, R. (1997), *Gregory the Great and His World* (Cambridge).

Markus, R. and C. Sotinel (2007), 'Epilogue', in Chazelle and Cubitt (eds.) 2007, pp. 265–78.

Marrou, H.-I. (1948/1956), *A History of Education in Antiquity* (1956, London, from the original French edition of 1948).

Märtl, C. (2016–18), 'Papstgeschichtsschreibung im Quattrocento: vom *Liber pontificalis* zu Platinas *Liber de vita Christi ac omnium pontificum*', in U. Friedrich, L. Grenzina, and F. Rexroth (eds.), *Geschichtsentwürfe und Identitätsbildung am Übergang zur Neuzeit*, II (Berlin), pp. 242–56.

Maskarinec, M. (2015), 'The Carolingian afterlife of the Damasan inscriptions', *EME* 23, pp. 129–60.

Maskarinec, M. (2018), *City of Saints: Rebuilding Rome in the Early Middle Ages* (Philadelphia).

Mathews, T. (1993), *The Clash of Gods* (Princeton).

McClure, J. (1979), 'Handbooks against heresy in the West from the late fourth to the late sixth centuries', *JTS* 30, pp. 186–97.

McCormick, M. (2011), *Charlemagne's Survey of the Holy Land: Wealth, Personnel, and Buildings of a Mediterranean Church Between Antiquity and the Middle Ages* (Dumbarton Oaks).

McEvoy, M. (2013), 'The mausoleum of Honorius: late Roman imperial Christianity and the city of Rome in the fifth century', in McKitterick, Osborne, Richardson, and Story (eds.) 2013, pp. 119–36.

McKitterick, R. (1981), "The scriptoria of Merovingian Gaul: a survey of the evidence' in H. Clarke and M. Brennan (eds.), *Columbanus and Merovingian Monasticism*, British Archaeological Reports, International Series 113 (Oxford), pp. 173–207, reprinted in McKitterick 1994, Chapter 1.

McKitterick, R. (1985), 'Knowledge of canon law in the Frankish kingdoms before 789: the manuscript evidence', *JTS* n. s. 36, pp. 97–117, reprinted in McKitterick 1994, Chapter 2.

McKitterick, R. (1989), *The Carolingians and the Written Word* (Cambridge).

McKitterick, R. (1990), 'Frankish uncial in the eighth century: a new context for the work of the Echternach scriptorium', in P. Bange and A. Weiler (eds.), *Willibrord, zijn wereld en zijn werk* (Nijmegen), pp. 350–64, reprinted in McKitterick 1994, Chapter 5.

McKitterick, R. (1994), *Books, Scribes and Learning in the Frankish Kingdoms, Sixth to Ninth Centuries* (Aldershot).

McKitterick, R. (1998), 'L'idéologie politique dans l'historiographie Carolingienne', in R. Le Jan, S. Lebecq, and B. Judic (eds.), *La royauté et les élites laïques et ecclésiastiques dans l'Europe Carolingienne (du début du IXe siècle aux environs de 920* (Lille), pp. 59–70.

McKitterick, R. (2000), 'The illusion of royal power in the Carolingian annals', *English Historical Review* 115, pp. 1–20.

McKitterick, R. (2004a), 'Takamiya MS 58 and the transmission of Jerome's Epistle 106 in the early middle ages', in T. Matsuda and R. Linenthal (eds.), *The Medieval Book and a Modern Collector: Essays in Honour of Toshiyuki Takamiya* (Woodbridge), pp. 3–18.

McKitterick, R. (2004b), *History and Memory in the Carolingian World* (Cambridge).

McKitterick, R. (2005), 'History, law and communication with the past in the Carolingian period', in *Comunicare e significare nell'alto medioevo*, Settimane 52 (Spoleto), pp. 941–80.

McKitterick, R. (2006), *Perceptions of the Past in the Early Middle Ages* (Notre Dame).

McKitterick, R. (2008), *Charlemagne: the Formation of a European Identity* (Cambridge).

McKitterick, R. (2009), 'La place du *Liber Pontificalis* dans les genres historiographiques du haut moyen âge', in Bougard and Sot (eds.) 2009, pp. 23–36.

McKitterick, R. (2011), 'Roman texts and Roman history in the early middle ages', in Bolgia, McKitterick, and Osborne (eds.) 2011, pp. 19–34.

McKitterick, R. (2012), 'The scripts of the Prague Sacramentary, Archivo O 83', *EME* 20, 407–27.

McKitterick, R. (2013a), 'Narrative strategies in the *Liber Pontificalis:* the case of St Paul, *doctor mundi, doctor gentium,* and San Paolo fuori le mura', *Rivista di storia cristianesimo* 10, pp. 115–30.

McKitterick, R. (2013b), 'The representation of Old Saint Peter's basilica in the *Liber Pontificalis*', in McKitterick, Osborne, Richardson, and Story (eds.) 2013, pp. 95–118.

McKitterick, R. (2014), 'Rome and the popes in the construction of institutional history and identity in the early middle ages: the case of Leiden Universiteitsbibliotheek Scaliger MS 49', in O. Phelan and V. Carver (eds.), *Rome and Religion in the Medieval World: Studies in Honor of Thomas F. X. Noble* (Aldershot), pp. 207–34.

McKitterick, R. (2015), 'Transformations of the Roman past and Roman identity in the early middle ages', in Gantner, McKitterick, and Meeder (eds.) 2015, pp. 225–44.

McKitterick, R. (2016a), 'The papacy and Byzantium in the seventh- and early eighth-century sections of the *Liber pontificalis*', *PBSR* 84, pp. 241–73.

McKitterick, R. (2016b), 'The work of the scribes in the Prague Sacramentary', in M. Diesenberger, R. Meens, and H. G. E. Rose (eds.), *The Prague Sacramentary: Culture, Religion, and Politics in Late Eighth-Century Bavaria*, Cultural Encounters in Late Antiquity and the Middle Ages (CELAMA) 21 (Turnhout), pp. 13–42.

McKitterick, R. (2017), 'Liturgy and history in the early middle ages', in K. A.-M. Bugyis, A. B. Kraebel, and M. E. Fassler (eds.), *Medieval Cantors and Their Craft: Music, Liturgy and the Shaping of History, 800–1500* (York), pp. 23–40.

McKitterick, R. (2018a), 'Charlemagne, Rome and the management of sacred space', in Große and Sot (eds.) 2018, pp. 165–79.

McKitterick, R. (2018b), 'The *damnatio memoriae* of Pope Constantine II (767–768)', in Balzaretti, Barrow, and Skinner (eds.) 2018, pp. 231–48.

McKitterick, R. (2018c), 'The popes as rulers of Rome in the aftermath of empire, 476–769', in S. J. Brown, C. Methuen, and A. Spicer (eds.), *The Church and Empire*, Studies in Church History 54, pp. 71–95.

McKitterick, R. (2018d) 'Romanness and Rome in the early middle ages', in W. Pohl, C. Gantner, C. Grifoni, and M. Pollheimer-Mohaupt (eds.), *Transformations of Romanness in the Early Middle Ages: Regions and Identities*, Millennium Studien / Millennium Studies 71 (Berlin), pp. 143–56.

McKitterick, R. (2019), 'Perceptions of Rome and the papacy in Late Merovingian Francia: the Cononian recension', in Esders, Fox, Hen, and Sarty (eds.) 2019, pp. 165–86.

McKitterick, R. (2020a), 'Reflections on the manuscript transmission of the *Historia ecclesiastica* of Eusebius–Rufinus in the early middle ages', in K. Yavuz and R. Broome (eds.), *Transforming the Early Medieval World: Essays in Honour of Ian Wood.*

McKitterick, R. (2020b), 'The church and the law in the early middle ages', in R. McKitterick, C. Methuen, and A. Spicer (eds.), *The Church and the Law*, Studies in Church History 56, pp. 1–29.

McKitterick, R. (2020c), 'The Constantinian basilica in the early medieval *Liber pontificalis*', in L. Bosman, I. Haynes, and P. Liverani (eds.), *The Lateran Basilica* (Cambridge).

McKitterick, R. (in press a), 'Anglo-Saxon links with Rome and the Franks in the light of the Würzburg book-list', in C. Breay and J. Story with E. Jackson (eds.), *Manuscripts in the Anglo-Saxon Kingdoms: Cultures and Connections* (Dublin).

McKitterick, R. (in press b), 'The *Liber pontificalis* and the transformation of Rome from pagan to Christian city in the early middle ages', in J. Stenger et al. (eds.), *Being Pagan, Being Christian in Late Antiquity and the Early Middle Ages* (London).

McKitterick, R. (ed.) (1990), *The Uses of Literacy in Early Mediaeval Europe* (Cambridge).

McKitterick, R. (ed.) (1995), *The New Cambridge Medieval History* II: c. 700–c. 900 (Cambridge).

McKitterick, R. (ed.) (2014), *Being Roman after Rome, EME* 22.

McKitterick, R., J. Osborne, C. Richardson, and J. Story (eds.) (2013), *Old Saint Peter's, Rome* (Cambridge).

McKitterick, R., R. Pollard, R. Price, and D. van Espelo (in press), *Codex epistolaris Carolinus* (Liverpool).

McLynn, N. (1994), *Ambrose of Milan: Church and Court in a Christian Capital* (Los Angeles and London).

Meneghini, R. (2000), 'Intra-mural burials at Rome between the fifth and seventh centuries', in J. Pearce, M. Millett, and M. Struck (eds.), *Burial, Society and Context in the Roman World* (Oxford), pp. 263–9.

Meneghini, R. and R. Santangeli Valenzani (2004), *Roma nell'alto medioevo: topografia e urbanistica della città dal V al X secolo* (Rome).

Merrills, A. (2005), *History and Geography in Late Antiquity* (Cambridge).

Miles, M. R. E. (1993), 'Santa Maria Maggiore's fifth-century mosaic: triumphal Christianity and the Jews', *Harvard Theological Review* 86, pp. 155–72.

Mommsen, T. (1898), 'Prolegomena', in MGH Gesta pontificum Romanorum 1.1: *Liber pontificalis (pars prior)* (Berlin), pp. vii–cxxix.

Montinaro, F. (2015) 'Les fausses donations de Constantin dans le *Liber pontificalis*', *Millennium* 12, pp. 23–9.

Moore, R. I. (2016), 'The weight of opinion: religion and the people of Europe from the tenth to the twelfth century', in Cooper and Leyser (eds.) 2016, pp. 202–19.

Moorhead, J. (1978), 'The Laurentian schism: East and West in the Roman church', *Church History* 47, pp. 125–36.

Moorhead, J. (2015), *The Popes and the Church of Rome in Late Antiquity* (New York).

Moralee, J. (2018) *Rome's Holy Mountain: the Capitoline Hill in Late Antiquity* (Oxford).

Mordek, H. (1973), 'Die *Collectio vetus gallica*, die älteste systematische Kanonessammlung des fränkischen Gallien', *Francia* 1, pp. 45–61.

Mordek, H. (1991), 'Der römische Primat in den Kirchenrechtssamlungen des Westen von IV. bis VIII. Jahrhundert', in Maccarrone (ed.) 1991, pp. 523–55.

Moreau, D. (2010), '*Non impar conciliorum, extat auctoritas*: l'origine de l'introduction des lettres pontificales dans le droit canonique', in J. Desmulliez, C. Hoet van Cauwenberghe, and J.-C. Jolivet (eds.), *L'étude des correspondances dans le monde romain de l'antiquité classique à l'Antiquité tardive: permanence et mutations* (Lille), pp. 487–506.

Moreau, D. (2015), '*Ipsis diebus Bonifacius, zelo et dolo ductus:* the root causes of the double papal election of 22 September 530', in Dunn (ed.) 2015, pp. 177–95.

Moreau, D. (2019), 'The compilation process of Italian canonical collections during late antiquity', in Lizzi Testa and Marconi (eds.) 2019, pp. 336–69.

Morison, S. (1972), *Politics and Script: Aspects of Authority and Freedom in the Development of Graeco-Latin Script from the Sixth Century B.C. to the Twentieth Century A.D. The Lyell Lectures 1957*, ed. and completed by N. Barker (Oxford).

Morisson, C and J. C. Cheynet (2002), 'Prices and wages in the Byzantine world', in A. E. Laiou (ed.), *The Economic History of Byzantium from the Seventh Through the Fifteenth Century* (Washington, DC), pp. 815–78.

Mulryan, M. (2014), *Spatial 'Christianisation' in Context: Strategic Intramural Building in Rome from the 4th–7th c. AD* (Oxford).

Neil, B. (2006), *Seventh-Century Popes and Martyrs: the Political Hagiography of Anastasius Bibliothecarius* (Turnhout).

Neil, B. (2011), 'Imperial benefactions to the fifth-century church', in G. Nathan and L. Garland (eds.), *Basileia: Essays in Honour of E. M. and M. J. Jeffries*, Byzantina Australiensia 20 (Brisbane), pp. 55–66.

Neil, B. (2012), 'Crisis and wealth in Byzantine Italy: the *Libri Pontificales* of Rome and Ravenna', *Byzantion* 82, pp. 279–303.

Neil, B. (2015), '*De profundis:* the letters and archives of Pelagius I of Rome (556–561)' in Neil and Allen (eds.) 2015, pp. 206–20.

Neil, B. (2017), 'Papal letters and letter collections', in Sogno, Storin, and Watts (eds.) 2017, pp. 449–66.

Neil, B. and P. Allen (2014), *The Letters of Gelasius I (492–496), Pastor and Micro Manager of the Church of Rome* (Turnhout).

Neil, B. and P. Allen (eds.) (2015), *Collecting Early Christian Letters from the Apostle Paul to Late Antiquity* (Cambridge).

Neil, B. and M. Dal Santo (eds.) (2013), *The Companion to Gregory the Great* (Leiden).

Nelson, J. L., (2016), 'Charlemagne and the bishops', in R. Meens, D. van Espelo, B. van den Hoven van Genderen, J. Raaijmakers, I. van Renswoude, and C. van Rhijn (eds.), *Religious Franks: Religion and Power in the Frankish Kingdoms: Studies in Honour of Mayke de Jong* (Manchester), pp. 350–69.

Ng, D. and M. Swetnam-Burland (eds.) (2018), *Reuse and Renovation in Roman Material Culture* (Cambridge).

Nicolet, C. (1991), *Space, Geography and Politics in the Early Roman Empire* (Ann Arbor).

Niederkorn Bruck, M. and A. Scharer (eds.) (2004), *Erzbischof Arn von Salzburg* (Vienna).

Noble, T. F. X. (1984), *The Republic of St Peter: the Birth of the Papal State, 680–825* (Philadelphia).

Noble, T. F. X. (1985), 'A new look at the *Liber pontificalis*', *Archivium Historiae Pontificiae* 23, pp. 347–58.

Noble, T. F. X. (1990), 'Literacy and the papal government in late antiquity and the early middle ages', in McKitterick (ed.) 1990, pp. 82–108.

Noble, T. F. X. (1995), 'Morbidity and vitality in the history of the early medieval papacy', *The Catholic Historical Review* 81, pp. 505–40.

Noble, T. F. X. (2009), *Images, Iconoclasm and the Carolingians* (Philadelphia).

Noble, T. F. X. (2014), 'Greek popes: yes or no, and did it matter?', in A. Fischer and I. Wood (eds.), *Western Perspectives on the Mediterranean: Cultural Transfer in Late Antiquity and the Early Middle Ages, 400–800 AD* (London), pp. 77–87.

Nora, P. (1984–92), *Les lieux de mémoire*, 3 vols (Paris).

Ó Carragáin, E. (2013), 'Interactions between liturgy and politics in Old Saint Peter's, 670–741: John the archchantor, Sergius I and Gregory III', in McKitterick, Osborne, Richardson, and Story (eds.) 2013, pp. 177–89.

Ó Carragáin, E. and C. Neuman de Vegvar (eds.) (2007), *Roma felix: Formations and Reflections of Medieval Rome* (Aldershot).

Orlin, E. M. (1997), *Temples, Religion and Politics in the Roman Republic* (Leiden).

Osborne, J. (1990), 'Use of painted initials by Greek and Latin scriptoria in Carolingian Rome', *Gesta* 29, pp. 76–85.

Osborne, J. (2008), 'The cult of Maria Regina in early medieval Rome', *PBSR* 21, pp. 95–106.

Osborne, J. (2020), *Rome in the Eighth Century: a History in Art* (Cambridge).

Page, C. (2010), *The Christian West and its Singers: the First Thousand Years* (New Haven).

Pani Ermini, L. (ed.) (2000), *Christiana loca: lo spazio Cristiano nella Roma del primo millennio*, 2 vols (Rome).

Papandrea, J. (2008), *The Trinitarian Theology of Novatian of Rome: a Study in Third-Century Orthodoxy* (Lewiston).

Parker, D. (2013), 'The New Testament: text and versions', in Carleton-Paget and Schaper (eds.) 2013, pp. 412–44.

Parker Johnson, R. (1939), *Compositiones Variae from Codex 490, Biblioteca Capitolare, Lucca, Italy: an Introductory Study, Illinois Studies in Language and Literature* 23/3 (Urbana).

Pazdernik, C. (2015), 'Belisarius' second occupation of Rome and Pericles' last speech', in Greatrex, Elton, and McMahon (eds.) 2015, pp. 191–206.

Perry, E. (2005), *The Aesthetics of Emulation in the Visual Arts of Ancient Rome* (Cambridge).

BIBLIOGRAPHY

Petrucci, A. (1971), 'L'onciale Romana: origini, sviluppo e diffusione di una stilizzazione grafica altomedievale (sec. VI–IX)', *Studi medievali* ser. 3, 12, pp. 75–134.

Petrucci, A. (1992), 'Il codice e i documenti: scrivere a Lucca fra VIII e IX secolo', in A. Petrucci and C. Romeo (eds.), *Scriptores in urbibus: alfabetismo e cultura scritta nell'Italia altomedievale* (Bologna), pp. 77–108.

Petrucci, A. (2005), 'Il codici e le sue scritture', in Petrucci (ed.) 2005, pp. 21–9.

Petrucci, A. (ed.) (2005) *Codex Trecensis. La Regola Pastorale di Gregorio Magno I: un codice del VI–VII secolo. Troyes Médiathèque de l'agglomération troyenne, 504,2: studi critici* (Florence).

Philippart, G. (ed.) (2010), *Hagiographies* 5 (Turnhout).

Picard, J.-C. (1969), 'Étude sur l'emplacement des tombes des papes du IIIe au Xe siècle', *MEFRA* 81, pp. 725–82.

Pietri, C. (1976), *Roma Christiana: recherches sur l'Église de Rome, son organisation, sa politique, son idéologie de Miltiade à Sixte III (311–440)*, BEFAR 224 (Rome).

Pietri, C. (1981), 'Aristocratie et société clericale dans l'Italie chrétienne au temps d'Odacre et de Théodoric', *MEFRA* 93, pp. 417–67.

Pietri, L. (ed.) (1999), *Prosopographie du bas empire* II: *prosopographie de l'Italie chrétienne (313–604)* (Rome).

Pilsworth, C. (2000), 'Dating the *Gesta martyrum:* a manuscript-based approach', in Cooper (ed.) 2000, pp. 271–324.

Pitz, E. (1990), *Papstreskripte im frühen Mittelalter: diplomatische und rechtsgeschichtliche Studien zum Brief-Corpus Gregors des Großen* (Sigmaringen).

Pizarro, J. M. (1998), 'Crowds and power in the *Liber pontificalis ecclesiae Ravennatis*', in J. Hill and M. Swan (eds.), *The Community, the Family, and the Saint: Patterns of Power in Early Medieval Europe* (Turnhout).

Pohl, W. (2015), 'Creating cultural resources for Carolingian rule: historians of the Carolingian empire', in Gantner, McKitterick, and Meeder (eds.) 2015, pp. 15–33.

Pohl, W. and M. Diesenberger (eds.) (2001), *Eugippius und Severin: der Autor, der Text und der Heilige*, Forschungen zur Geschichte des Mittelalters 2 (Vienna).

Pohlkamp, W. (1984), 'Kaiser Konstantin, der heidnische und der christliche Kult in den *Actus Silvestri*', *Frühmittelalterliche Studien* 18, 357–400.

Pollard, R. M. (2009) 'The decline of the cursus in the papal chancery', *Studi Medievali* 50, pp. 1–40.

Pollard, R. M. (2013), 'A cooperative correspondence: the letters of Gregory the Great', in Neil and Dal Santo (eds.) 2013, pp. 291–312.

Pollard, R. M. (in press) 'A point of style: rhythm, or its absence, in the *Codex epistolaris Carolinus*', in McKitterick, Pollard, Price, and Espelo in press.

Pomaro, G. (2015), *I manoscritti della Biblioteca Capitolare Feliniana di Lucca* (Florence).

Poole, R. (1873), *Greek Coins in the British Museum* (London).

Pössel, C. (2018), '"Appropriate to the religion of their time": Walahfrid's historicization of the liturgy', in E. Screen and C. West (eds.), *Writing the Early Medieval West* (Cambridge), pp. 80–97.

Price, R. (2005), 'Composition and transmission of the Acts', in Price and Gaddis 2005, I, pp. 75–85.

Price, R. (2014) 'The theological issues', in Price, Booth, and Cubitt 2014, pp. 87–102.

Price, R., P. Booth, and C. Cubitt (2014), *The Acts of the Lateran Synod of 649* (Liverpool).

Price, R. and M. Gaddis (2005), *The Acts of the Council of Chalcedon*, 3 vols (Liverpool).

Price, R. (ed.) (2009), *The Acts of the Council of Constantinople of 553, with Related Texts on the Three Chapters Controversy*, 2 vols (Liverpool).

Purcell, N. (1992), 'The City of Rome', in R. Jenkyns (ed.), *The Legacy of Rome: a New Appraisal* (Oxford), pp. 421–55.

Radiciotti, P. (2002), 'La scrittura del *Liber pontificalis*', in G. Abbamonte, L. Gualdo Rosa, L. Munzi (eds.), *Parrhasiana II: atti del II Seminario di studi su manoscritti medievali e umanistici della Biblioteca nazionale di Napoli. Napoli, 20–21 ottobre 2000* (Naples), pp. 79–101.

Rankin, S. (2011), '*Terribilis est locus iste:* the Pantheon in 609', in M. Carruthers (ed.), *Rhetoric Beyond Words: Delight and Persuasion in the Arts of the Middle Ages* (Cambridge), pp. 281–310.

Rapp, C. and H. A. Drake (eds.) (2014), *The City in the Classical and Post-Classical World* (Cambridge).

Rebillard, E. (1994/2009), *The Care of the Dead in Late Antiquity* (2009, Ithaca, NY), revised version in English of French original, *In hora mortis: évolution de la pastorale chrétienne de la mort aux IVe et Ve siècles dans l'occident latin*, BEFAR 283 (1994, Rome).

Regards (1995), *Regards sur les manuscrits d'Autun, VIe–XVIIIe siècle, catalogue d'exposition* (Autun).

Reimitz, H. (1999), *Der Codex Vindobonensis lat. 473: ein karolingisches Geschichtsbuch aus St-Amand* (Vienna).

Richards, J. (1976), *The Popes and the Papacy in the Early Middle Ages* (London).

Riché, P. (1962/1976), *Education and Culture in the Barbarian West, Sixth to Eighth Centuries* (1976, Columbia, SC); trans. J. J. Contreni from the original French edition of 1962.

Rio, A. (2017), *Slavery after Rome, 500–1100* (Oxford).

Roberts, C. H. and T. C. Skeat (1983), *The Birth of the Codex* (Oxford).

Roberts, E. (2019), *Flodoard of Rheims and the Writing of History in the Tenth Century* (Cambridge).

Roma fra oriente e occidente (2002), Settimane 49 (Spoleto).

Roma nell'alto medioevo (2001), Settimane 48 (Spoleto).

Romano, J. G. (2014), *Liturgy and Society in Early Medieval Rome* (Farnham).

Rossi, G. B. de (1864–77), *La Roma sotterranea Cristiana*, 3 vols (Rome).

Rothschild, C. (2004), *Luke – Acts and the Rhetoric of History: an Investigation of Early Christian Historiography* (Tübingen).

Rubeis, F. de (2001), 'Epigrafi a Roma dall'età classica nell'alto medioevo', in P. Delogu, M.S. Arena, L. Paroli, M. Ricci, L. Sagu, and L. Venditelli (eds.), *Roma dall'antichità al medioevo: archeologia e storia* (Milan), pp. 104–21.

Rupke, J. and A. Glock (2008), *Fasti sacerdotum: a Prosopography of Pagan, Jewish, and Christian Religious Officials in the City of Rome, 300 BC to AD 499* (Oxford).

Rutgers, L. (1995), *The Jews in Late Ancient Rome: Evidence of Cultural Interaction in the Roman Diaspora* (Leiden).

Rutgers, L. (2000), *Subterranean Rome: in Search of the Roots of Christianity in the Catacombs of the Eternal City* (Leuven).

Rutgers, L. (2009), *Making Myths: Jews in Early Christian Identity Formation* (Leuven).

Sághy, M. (2000), '*Scinditur in partes populus:* Pope Damasus and the martyrs of Rome', in Cooper (ed.) 2000, pp. 273–87.

Sághy, M. (2015), 'The Bishop of Rome and the martyrs', in Dunn (ed.) 2015, pp. 37–56.

Salzman, M. (1990), *On Roman Time: the Codex Calendar of 354 and the Rhythm of Urban Life in Late Antiquity* (Berkeley).

Salzman, M. R. (2013), 'Leo's liturgical topography: contestation for space in fifth-century Rome', *Journal of Roman Studies* 103, pp. 208–32.

Salzman, M. R. (2014), 'Leo the Great: responses to crisis and the shaping of a Christian cosmopolis', in Rapp and Drake (eds.) 2014, pp. 183–201.

Salzman, M. R. (2017), 'Emperors and élites in Rome after the Vandal sack of 455', *Antiquité tardive* 25, pp. 243–62.

Salzman, M. R. (2019), 'The religious economics of crisis: the papal use of liturgical vessels as symbolic capital in late antiquity', *Religion in the Roman Empire* 5, pp. 125–41.

Salzman, M. R., M. Sághy, and R. Lizzi Testa (eds.) (2015), *Pagans and Christians in Late Antique Rome: Conflict, Competition and Coexistence in the Fourth Century* (Cambridge).

BIBLIOGRAPHY

Santangeli Valenzani, R. (2014), 'Hosting foreigners in early medieval Rome: from *xenodochia* to *scholae peregrinorum*', in Tinti (ed.) 2014, pp. 69–88.

Sansterre, J.-M. (1983), *Les moines grecs et orientaux à Rome aux époques byzantine et carolingienne (milieu du VIe siècle – fin du IXe siècle)*, 2 vols (Brussels).

Schelstrate, E. (1692), *Antiquitas ecclesiae dissertationibus monumentis ac notis* (Rome).

Schiaparelli, L. (1924), *Il codice 490 della Biblioteca Capitolare di Lucca e la scuola scrittoria Lucchese, sec. VIII–IX* (Vatican City).

Schilling, B. (2002), 'Wilchar von Vienne und das Pallium', in H. Kranz and L. Falkenstein (eds.), Inquirens subtilia diversa: *Dietrich Lohrmann zum 65. Geburtstag* (Aachen), pp. 23–36.

Schoenert-Geiss, E. (1965), *Griechisches Münzwerk: die Münzprägung von Perinthos* (Berlin).

Scholten, D. (2015), 'Cassiodorus' *Historia tripartita* before the earlier extant manuscripts', in Gantner, McKitterick, and Meeder (eds.) 2015, pp. 34–50.

Scholz, S. (2006), *Politik – Selbstverständis – Selbsdarstellung: die Päpste in karolingischer und ottonischer Zeit*, Historische Forschungen 26 (Stuttgart).

Schramm, P. E. and F. Mütherich (1981), *Denkmale der deutschen Könige und Kaiser* I (Munich).

Schultz, S. and J. Zahle (1981–2), *Sylloge nummorum Graecorum* (Copenhagen).

Serfass, A. (2006), 'Slavery and Pope Gregory the Great', *Journal of Early Christian Studies* 14, pp. 77–103.

Sessa, K. (2012) *The Formation of Papal Authority in Late Antique Italy: Roman Bishops and the Domestic Sphere* (Cambridge).

Sessa, K. (2016), 'The Roman church and its bishops', in Arnold, Bjornlie, and Sessa (eds.) 2016, pp. 425–50.

Ševčenko, N. (1994), 'Close encounters: contact between holy figures and the faithful as represented in Byzantine works of art' in A. Guillou and J. Drand (eds.), *Byzance et les images* (Paris), pp. 257–85.

Shaker, C. (2016), 'The "Lamb of God" Title in John's Gospel: Background, Exegesis, and Major Themes', unpublished MA dissertation in Theology, Seton Hall University, http://scholarship.shu.edu/dissertations/2220.

Shuffleton, G. (2019), 'London histories', in Jahner, Steiner, and Tyler (eds.) 2019, pp. 244–57.

Simperl, M. (2016), 'Ein gallischer *Liber Pontificalis*? Bemerkungen zur Text- und Überlieferungsgeschichte des sogenannten Catalogus Felicianus', *Römische Quartalschrift* 111, pp. 272–87.

Smith, J. M. H. (ed.) (2000), *Early Medieval Rome and the Christian West: Essays in Honour of Donald A. Bullough* (Leiden).

Sogno, C., B. K. Storin, and E. J. Watts (eds.) (2017), *Late Antique Letter Collections: Critical Introduction and Reference Guide* (Berkeley).

Somerville, R. and B. C. Brasington (1998), *Prefaces to Canon Law Books in Latin Christianity: Selected Translations, 500–1245* (New Haven).

Sot, M. (1981), *Gesta Episcoporum, gesta abbatum*, Typologie des sources du moyen âge 37 (Turnhout).

Sotinel, C. (1989), 'Arator, un poète au service de la politique du Pape Vigile', *MEFRA* 101–2, pp. 805–20.

Sotinel, C. (2005), 'Emperors and popes in the sixth century: the Western view', in Maas (ed.) 2005, pp. 267–90.

Sotinel, C. (2010), *Church and Society in Late Antique Italy and Beyond* (Farnham).

Stenger, J. (ed.) (in press), *Being Pagan, Being Christian in Late Antiquity and the Early Middle Ages* (London).

Stoclet, A. (1993), *Autour de Fulrad de Saint-Denis (v. 710–784)* (Geneva).

Stoffella, M. (2018), 'In a periphery of the empire: Tuscany between the Lombards and the Carolingians', in Große and Sot (eds.) 2018, pp. 319–36.

Story, J. (2003), *Carolingian Connections: Anglo-Saxon England and Carolingian Francia, c. 750–870* (Aldershot).

Straw, C. (1996), *Gregory the Great* (Aldershot).

Tatum, W. J. (1993), 'The *Lex Papiria de dedicationibus*', *Classical Philology* 88, pp. 319–28.

Taylor, A. (2013), 'Books, bodies and bones: Hilduin of St Denis and the relics of St Dionysius', in J. Ross and S. Conklin Akbari (eds.), *The Ends of the Body: Identity and Community in Medieval Culture* (Toronto), pp. 25–60.

Thacker, A. (1998), 'Memorializing Gregory the Great: the origin and transmission of a papal cult in the seventh and eighth centuries', *EME* 7, pp. 59–84.

Thacker, A. (2007a) 'Martyr cult within the walls: saints and relics in the Roman *tituli* of the fourth to seventh centuries', in A. Minnis and J. Roberts (eds.), *Text, Image, Interpretation: Studies in Anglo-Saxon Literature and its Insular Context in Honour of Eamonn Ó Carragáin* (Turnhout), pp. 31–70.

Thacker, A. (2007b), 'Rome of the martyrs: saints, cults and relics, fourth to seventh centuries', in Ó Carragáin and Neuman de Vegvar (eds.) 2007, pp. 13–15.

Thacker, A. (2013), 'Popes, emperors and clergy at Old Saint Peter's from the fourth to the eighth century', in McKitterick, Osborne, Richardson, and Story (eds.) 2013, pp. 137–56.

Thacker, A. (2014), 'Rome: the pilgrims' city in the seventh century', in Tinti (ed.) 2014, pp. 89–140.

Thompson, G. L. (2015a), *The Correspondence of Pope Julius I* (Washington, DC).

Thompson, G. L. (2015b), 'The *Pax Constantiniana* and the Roman episcopate', in Dunn (ed.) 2015, pp. 17–36.

Thunø, E. (2015), 'The Pantheon in the middle ages', in Marder and Wilson-Jones 2015, pp. 231–54.

Thurn, H. (ed.) (1968), *Comes Romanus Wirziburgensis: Faksimile Ausgabe des Codex M.P.th.f.62 der Universitätsbibliothek Würzburg* (Graz).

Tinti, F. (ed.) (2014), *England and Rome in the Early Middle Ages* (Turnhout).

Toynbee, J. and J. B. Ward-Perkins (1956), *The Shrine of St Peter and the Vatican Excavations* (London).

Tronzo, W. (1986), *The Via Latina Catacomb: Imitation and Discontinuity in Fourth-Century Roman Painting* (University Park, Penn.).

Tronzo, W. (ed.) (2005), *St Peter's in the Vatican* (Cambridge).

Trout, D. (2003), 'Damasus and the invention of early Christian Rome', *Journal of Medieval and Early Modern Studies* 33, pp. 517–36.

Trout, D. (2015), *Damasus of Rome: the Epigraphic Poetry. Introduction, Texts, Translations, and Commentary* (Oxford).

Turner, C. H. (1916), 'Arles and Rome: the first developments of canon law in Gaul', *JTS* 17, pp. 236–47.

Turner, C. H. (1931), 'The Latin Acts of Peter', *JTS* 32, pp. 119–33.

Ubl, K. and D. Ziemann (eds.) (2015), *Fälschung als Mittel der Politik: Pseudoisidor im Licht der neuen Forschung. Gedenkschrift für Klaus Zechiel-Eckes*, MGH Studien und Texte 57 (Wiesbaden).

Unfer-Verre, G. E. (2013), 'Ancora sul manoscritto 490: precisazioni e problemi aperti', *Rivista di Storia del Cristianesimo* 10, pp. 49–64.

Unger, D. and J. Dillon (1992), *Against the Heresies: St Irenaeus of Lyon* (New York).

Van Hoof, L. and P. Van Nuffelen (2017), 'The historiography of crisis: Jordanes, Cassiodorus and Justinian in mid-sixth century Constantinople', *Journal of Roman Studies* 107, pp. 275–300.

Varbanov, I. (2005–7), *Greek Imperial Coins and Their Values: the Local Coins of the Roman Empire* (Bourgas).

Verardi, A. A. (2013), 'La genesi del *Liber Pontificalis* alla luce delle vicende della città di Roma tra la fine del V e gli inizi del VI secolo: una proposta', *Rivista di Storia del Cristianesimo* 10, pp. 7–28.

Verardi, A. A. (2016), *La memoria legittimante: il* Liber pontificalis *e la chiesa di Roma del secolo VI* (Rome).

Verardi, A. A. (2019), 'Between law and literature: the *Liber pontificalis* and canonical collections in late antiquity and the early middle ages', in Lizzi Testa and Marconi (eds.) 2019, pp. 370–87.

Vezin, J. and H. Atsma (eds.) (1986), *Chartae Latinae antiquiores* XVI: *France* IV (Dietikon-Zurich).

Viezure, D. I. (2015), '*Collectio Avellana* and the unspoken Ostrogoths: historical reconstruction in the sixth century', in Greatrex, Elton, and McMahon (eds.) 2015, pp. 93–104.

Vignoli, G. (1724–55), *Liber pontificalis seu De gestis Romanorum pontificum quem cum codd. MSS Vaticanis aliisque summo studio et labore conlatum emendavit*, 3 vols (Rome).

Vinzent, M. (2014), 'Rome', in M. M. Mitchell and F. Young (eds.), *The Cambridge History of Christianity* I: *Origins to Constantine* (Cambridge), pp. 397–413.

Voelkl, L. (1964), *Die Kirchenstiftungen des Kaisers Konstantin im Lichte des römischen Sakralrechten* (Cologne and Opladen).

Vogel, C. (1981/1986), *Medieval Liturgy: an Introduction to the Sources*, trans. and rev. by W. Storey and N. Rasmussen (1986, Washington, DC), from original French edition of 1981.

Vout, C. (2009), 'Representing the emperor', in A. Feldherr (ed.), *The Cambridge Companion to the Roman Historians* (Cambridge), pp. 261–75.

Wallis, F. (1999), *Bede: the Reckoning of Time* (Liverpool).

Walser, G. (1987), *Die Einsiedler Inschriftensammlung und der Pilgerführer durch Rom (Codex Einsidlensis 326): Facsimile, Umschrift, Übersetzung und Kommentar* (Stuttgart).

Ward, G. (in press), *Scripture and Authority in the Carolingian Empire: Frechulf of Lisieux* (Oxford).

Ward Perkins, B. (2014) 'A most unusual empire: Rome in the fourth century', in Rapp and Drake (eds.) 2014, pp. 109–29.

Warland, R. (2003), 'The concept of Rome in Late Antiquity reflected in the mosaics of the triumphal arch of S. Maria Maggiore in Rome', *Acta ad archaeologiam et artium historiam pertinentia* 17, pp. 127–41.

Warntjes, I. and D. Ó Cróinín (eds.) (2017), *Late Antique Calendrical Thought and its Reception in the Early Middle Ages* (Turnhout).

Webb, M. (2001), *The Churches and Catacombs of Early Christian Rome: a Comprehensive Guide* (Brighton).

Wessel, S. (2012), 'Theological argumentation: the case of forgery', in S. F. Johnson (ed.), *The Oxford Handbook of Late Antiquity* (Oxford), pp. 916–34.

West-Harling, V. (ed.) (2015), *Three Empires, Three Cities: Identity, Material Culture and Legitimacy in Venice, Ravenna and Rome, 750–1000* (Turnhout).

Westwell, A. (2017), 'The Dissemination and Reception of the *Ordines Romani* in the Carolingian Church, *c.*750–900', unpublished PhD dissertation, University of Cambridge.

Westwell, A. (2019), 'The *ordines* of Vat. lat. 7701 and the liturgical culture of Carolingian Chieti', *PBSR* 86, pp. 127–52.

Whelan, R. (2018), *Being Christian in Vandal Africa: the Politics of Orthodoxy in the Post-Imperial West* (Oakland, Calif.).

Whiting, C. (2015), 'Jerome's *De viris illustribus* and new genres for Christian disputation in late antiquity', in Greatrex, Elton, and McMahon (eds.) 2015, pp. 41–52.

Wickham, C. J. (2005), *Framing the Middle Ages* (Oxford).

Wienand, J. (ed.) (2015), *Contested Monarchy: Integrating the Roman Empire in the Fourth Century AD* (Oxford).

Williams, F. (2009), *The Panarion of Epiphanius of Salamis in Cyprus* (Leiden).

Winterhager, P. (2016), 'Rome in the seventh-century Byzantine Empire: a migrant's network perspective from the circle of Maximos the Confessor', in N. S. M. Matheou, T. Kampianti, and L. M. Bondioli (eds.), *From Constantinople to the Frontier: the City and the Cities* (Leiden), pp. 191–206.

Wirbelauer, E. (1993), *Zwei Päpste in Rom: der Konflikt zwischen Laurentius und Symmachus (498–514). Studien und Texte*, Quellen und Forschungen zur antiken Welt 16 (München).

Wirbelauer, E. (2014), 'Agnès et les évêques de Rome jusqu'au VII^c siècle: un plaidoyer pour une rélecture historico-critique du *Liber pontificalis*', *MEFRM* 1/126 (2014), pp. 125–35.

Wirbelauer, E. (2015), 'La riche mémoire d'un évêque de Rome méconnu, Silvestre', in P. Blaudeau and P. Van Nuffelen (eds.), *L'historiographie tardo-antique et la transmission des savoirs*, Millennium Studies 55 (Berlin), pp. 319–32.

Wolfram, H. (1988) *History of the Goths*, revised English edition (Berkeley), from first German edition (1979, Munich).

Woolf, G. (2003), 'The city of letters', in Edwards and Woolf (eds.) 2003, pp. 203–21.

Zechiel-Eckes, K. (2013), *Die erste Dekretale: der Brief Papst Siricius' an Bischof Himerius von Tarragona vom Jahr 385 (JK 255). Aus dem Nachlass mit Ergänzungen von Detlev Jasper*, MGH Studien und Texte 55 (Hanover).

Zelzer, K. (1994), 'Benedikt von Nursia als Bewahrer und Erneurer der monastischen Tradition der suburbicaria', *Regulae Benedicti Studia* 18, pp. 203–19.

Zelzer, M. (1994), 'Gregors Benediktvita und die Bibel', *Regulae Benedicti Studia* 18, pp. 221–33.

Zironi, A. (2004), *Il monastero longobardo di Bobbio: crocevia di uomini, manoscritti e culture* (Spoleto).

INDEX OF MANUSCRIPTS

GENERAL INDEX

GENERAL INDEX

Printed in the United States
by Baker & Taylor Publisher Services